Mountaineering in Scotland

The Early Years

Ken Crocket

SCOTTISH MOUNTAINEERING TRUST

Published in Great Britain by the Scottish Mountaineering Trust, 2015

First published 2015

ISBN 978-1-907233-20-3
A catalogue record for this book is available from the British Library

This book is published by the Scottish Mountaineering Trust, a charitable trust. Revenue from all books published by the Trust is used for the continuation of its publishing programme and for charitable purposes associated with Scottish mountains and mountaineering. For more information see <www.smc.org.uk/trust/trust.htm>

Illustrations
Front cover: WA Morrison belayed by FS Goggs on the crux of Crowberry Ridge Direct, Buachaille Etive Mor, Glen Coe, July 1905. (AE Robertson © SMC)

Production: Scottish Mountaineering Trust (Publications) Ltd
Design: Ken Crocket & Tom Prentice
Typesetting: Ken Crocket
Set in Adobe Caslon Pro 11 on 13

Printed & bound in Spain by Novoprint S.A., Barcelona, Spain

Distributed by Cordee Ltd
Tel: +44 (0) 1455 611185 • Fax: +44 (0) 1455 635687 (w) www.cordee.co.uk

Contents

Introduction

This book describes and analyses the rise of mountaineering in Scotland during its formative years. In doing so, it focuses primarily on those who were in the main explorers, who sought to find and climb the hills and mountains by following natural features such as snow and ice gullies, rocky ridges and buttresses, in summer and in winter. They used the same equipment and techniques as in the Alps, and essentially were seeking out new ways.

As will quickly become evident, the prime source of this new game in Scotland, the driver of its vibrant energy in this early period, and by far the major source of its literature, was the Scottish Mountaineering Club (SMC). Founded in Glasgow in 1889, its Journal has been published continually since 1890, and, like the Club, quickly became the leading fount of knowledge. At the same time, its members made up the vast majority of those climbing in Scotland.

It soon became obvious that so rich was the early history, that to cover it in a meaningful way would demand its own volume. Over the last four years of research and writing, my estimation and respect for the early mountaineers has followed a steadily rising curve. They were exploring and climbing new ground at almost every outing, in all weathers, and often in winter.

Through their efforts they laid the groundwork for what is now recognised as the unique Scottish approach to winter climbing in particular, a style which attempts to climb a route cleanly and leave it as it was found, so that those next to attempt it can enjoy the same exploratory delight as the first. That they continued to do this, despite a virtual lack of any protection while climbing, and with no fatalities until well after the First World War, is an outstanding record.

The start of the Great War, in July 1914, was a logical point to end this volume. The demographic changes which the war, in part, amplified or began, would inevitably influence mountaineering in general. However, the period before then is a fairly discrete part of the sport's history which lends itself to a single volume. Where possible, brief biographical details of many of the activists lend interesting background to their mountain deeds.

I have learned much during its writing, and I trust that some of what has given me a deeper feeling for and better knowledge of the pioneers, including a continuing respect for their routes, will have the same effect on the reader.

Ken Crocket, 2015, Menstrie

Acknowledgments

I thank the Scottish Mountaineering Trust, who accepted the commitment of publishing this book. In turn, knowing that any profit will be returned to the Scottish mountains helped sustain my resolve in its research and production. No amount of resolve however would be enough were it not for the assistance received from various experts. Robin Campbell not only provided a Foreword, his knowledge of the early mountaineers in particular is second to none, and his patience in answering my many queries lightened my workload considerably.

Bob Aitken was a similar spirit, and generously gave his time in reading the manuscript and making available his impressive database of early SMC members. Mike Cocker was another reader who made helpful contributions to the project, while Susan Jensen proofed a late version and helped moderate my ever-evolving styles.

My understanding of mountaineering events in the Cuillin of Skye was considerably helped and enriched by the generosity of Stuart Pedlar, who made freely available his unpublished MS '*Across Unmeasured Space - A History of Climbing in the Cuillin*'. The amount and depth of his research on this subject is truly staggering.

The various major clubs in the UK and their respective journal editors have all been helpful with permission to quote from their archives. This of course includes the Scottish Mountaineering Club, whose Journal has been published continuously since 1890, and without which mountaineering in Scotland would now have a very different picture. I thank Noel Williams, Editor of the SMCJ (2008-2014), for various permissions to quote from the SMCJ; Mike Dent, Rucksack Club Archivist, for material from an article by EW Steeple; Alister Macdonald, Editor Cairngorm Club Journal, for three quotations; Andrew Paul, Joint Journal Editor of the Fell & Rock Climbers Club for four quotations; John Yates, Editor Climbers Club Journal, for permission to use material by EW Steeple and LG Shadbolt in two articles on Skye; Fiona Hutchinson, Honorary Secretary of the LSCC, for permission to use material from Helen Stevens' book '*Rising to the Challenge, 100 Years of the Ladies Scottish Climbing Club*' (2010, SMT); The Alpine Club has generously allowed permission for material from their journal, in addition to the use of the photograph taken on Beinn an Dothaidh in March 1909. Apologies to anyone overlooked.

It has been impossible to seek out some publishers of books consulted, and though I have made much effort here a few may have been missed for which I apologise in advance. Those I have connected with have been generous with their help and I thank them here: Palgrave Macmillan, for permission to use material from Marjorie Morgan's book '*National Identities and Travel in Victorian Britain*'; A.M. Heath & Co Ltd, for permission to use material from '*The Last Enemy*' by Richard Hillary (Copyright © Richard Hillary, 1943). Reprinted by permission of A.M. Heath & Co Ltd; Luath Press Ltd, for permission to quote from Ian R. Mitchell's books '*Prelude to Everest: Alexander Kellas, Himalayan Mountaineer*' (2011, Luath Press, Edinburgh), and '*Scotland's Mountains before the Mountaineers*', (2004, Luath Press, Edinburgh.); Ashgate Publishing Limited (Aldershot) for permission to use material from Katherine Haldane Grenier's book '*Tourism and Identity in Scotland, 1770-1914 - Creating Caledonia*' (2005); Robin Campbell, for material from his essay on Green Gully in '*Cold Climbs*' (London, 1983, Diadem Books.); John Barton of Bâton Wicks for material from the Showell Styles essay on Gashed Crag etc in '*Classic Rock*' (Bâton Wicks, 2nd edn., 2007.); Roy Humble, for material from Ben Humble's classic '*Cuillin of Skye;* Chatto & Windus, for an excerpt from *Climbing Days* by Dorothy Pilley, reproduced by permission of The Random House Group Ltd.'

I thank The Royal Forth Yacht Club for help regarding the Raeburn Trophy, The University of St Andrews, for permission to reproduce the drawing by James David Forbes showing his route on Ben Nevis. (Image courtesy of the University of St Andrews Library Special Collections. Reference: *msdep7 Incoming letters 1848, no. 30.*) The Sligachan Hotel, for permission to reproduce two illustrations, Sue Steinberg, for permission to use images from the abrahamphotographic collection, Simon Richardson for a photograph, Colin Wells for his comments on Collie's winter ascent of Steep Gill, Brian Davison for weather data.

David Stone, SMC Custodian of the Image Archive (2006 to present) must be singled out for his unstinting help and expert knowledge of images old and new. A superb photographer himself, his work is pixel perfect. Tom Prentice, SMT Publications Manager, was invaluable for technical advice & other help.

Routes in the early years were not graded, other than the occasional 'a.p.', meaning absolutely perpendicular and therefore presumed hard. I have therefore used grades and metric route lengths as given in the current guide for each area in use in 2014. Thanks to the various authors of these guides, details of which will be found with other books at <http://www.smc.org.uk/publications/>. The reader will spot some place and mountain names with different spellings; rather than laboriously change these as the years advanced, some earlier spellings have been kept as written. The hills remain however and there should be no confusion.

It only remains to accord special thanks and deep gratitude to my wife Aysel, who made all this, and more, possible.

Foreword

A foreword to a History should begin with some history. The history of Scottish mountaineering has been previously delineated in two excellent books: Ronald Clark & Ted Pyatt's *Mountaineering in Britain* (1957) and Ian R. Mitchell's *Scotland's Mountains before the Mountaineers* (1998). The former book is necessarily very selective in its coverage, while the latter comes to a stop when the mountaineers emerge in the 1880s. In addition, we have had four thorough histories of particular mountain groups: Greg Strange's *The Cairngorms* (2010), Ken Crocket's *Ben Nevis* (1986) – enlarged and embellished in a second edition by Crocket & Simon Richardson (2009), Ben Humble's *Cuillin of Skye* (1952), and an unpublished but well-known new history of Skye climbing – Stuart Pedlar's *Across Unmeasured Space* (circulated by email since 2007, a model work which combines infectious enthusiasm for its topic with exemplary scholarship).

Crocket's new History is a comprehensive review of activity up to the outbreak of war in 1914, and thus includes the period of general exploration from 1880 to 1914 that constitutes our 'Golden Age'. Ken is ideally qualified to write such a history. Besides his authorship of the ground-breaking Ben Nevis, he has written several guidebooks, and was Editor of the Scottish Mountaineering Club Journal from 1986 until 2000.

His history may be thought of as an atlas, many of whose pages are described by the six books mentioned above, but it is more than that. It deals with the mountain groups omitted in previous works – Arran, Glen Coe, the Central, Northern, and Southern Highlands, and with the nature and spirit of the groups of climbers who first explored our mountains with rope and axe. Our pioneers were at one time commonly regarded as wealthy middle-aged fuddy-duddies, limited in fitness, enterprise, and boldness. Crocket's history firmly disposes of such mistaken notions. Behind the beards and Norfolk jackets were enthusiastic young men, as fit as boxers, and ready for any and every challenge. Their achievements on rock and ice were not equalled until more than thirty years had passed by, when the marginally superior equipment developed during WWII began to have a helpful effect.

Between the Wars, powerful climbers such as James Bell, Bill Mackenzie, and Bill Murray repeated the more difficult climbs of the pioneers, but in doing so they often believed that they were making new discoveries. To mention just one example, the Mackenzie-Murray rope enjoyed a famous defeat at the last hurdle on what was then known as Garrick's Shelf on Buachaille in December 1936. But when they planned that venture, and when Murray subsequently described it, they had no knowledge of a previous attempt, resulting in defeat at precisely the same final step, by Harry MacRobert and Arnold Brown in March 1910. The climbers of the 30s may perhaps be forgiven for these errors, since no convenient history of our Golden Age was available to them. This excellent history will ensure that today's climbers have no such excuse.

Robin N. Campbell

1

Beginnings (1571-1859)

There is, in a very general sense, a long history of climbing in Scotland; there were strongholds to be overcome, whether by frontal assault or by some more devious route. Dumbarton Rock Castle had been stormed after a daring night climb in 1571. Edinburgh Castle had been taken in a similar fashion in 1314, the year of Bannockburn. Both included sections of free climbing up difficult ground.

Those who had livestock might be called upon to rescue their animals, especially crag fast sheep. Doubtless many untold epic rescues took place, involving hair-raising traverses across steep faces. Shepherds and a few other adventurous souls may have gained the odd summit whilst checking their animals. In summer, shielings, basic shelters of stone and turf, were occupied by younger villagers, tasked with looking after livestock moved to higher grazing.

Perhaps most spectacularly, there were birds and their eggs by the thousand, found on steep sea cliffs, particularly on the western seaboard and islands. These were added to a family's larder by bare-footed natives who surely knew how to climb difficult, mixed ground, and were often lowered from above by horsehair rope or jumped from a small boat onto steep, slimy rock, timing their leap to the vast Atlantic swell. It is doubtful whether any of the above led to any recreational pursuit, in a country dominated by more pressing needs.

Documented accounts are available of the bird fowlers who had to access steep rocks for food, one outstanding population being those hardy souls who scraped a living on the windswept archipelago of St Kilda, 64km west-northwest of North Uist, and the most westerly of the Outer Hebrides.

The island of Hirta, the largest of the archipelago, had been populated since prehistoric days and has Viking graves. One of the historical sources is by Martin Martin (?–1719), a Scottish writer best known for his work *A*

Description of the Western Isles of Scotland (1703).[1] He describes the activities of the islanders, including their harvesting of seabird colonies, mainly gannets and puffins, of which they took scores of thousands every year for oil, feathers, food and fertiliser, and for payment of rent to the island's laird.

A more recent book is that by Richard Kearton.[2] He was a naturalist and photographer, being especially interested in birds, who toured Scotland, and stayed on St Kilda for nine days in June, 1896. He made many friends there, and experienced at first hand some of the local work and traditions.

> The St Kildans are wonderful fellows on the crags, and most of the performances we saw them go through were done without the aid of a rope; but, of course, their bare feet, thoroughly hardened and inured to the touch of the sharp rocks, give them a great advantage over men who wear boots and socks every day of their lives.

Of the ropes used by the St Kildans, Kearton wrote –

> The fowling-ropes now in use are made of Manilla hemp, but formerly they were of horse-hair, which in Martin's time was protected by a coat of cowhide. I was fortunate enough to secure the last old rope on the island for half-a-crown, and upon inquiry discovered that the hair of which it was composed had cost five shillings per pound, and that the last man in St Kilda who knew how to make one was long since dead.

When bird fowling, birds could either be approached from above, by being lowered on a rope, or often from the sea below, jumping onto the rock with a rope round their waist.

There is an interesting account of a climb described by Harold Raeburn some six years before he joined the SMC. The climb was not original, as it was a long-established way of ascending a sea-stack off Papa Stour in the Shetland Islands. It confirms that Raeburn was more than competent at climbing rocks well before he took up mountaineering, and that it formed a necessary part of his deep interest in ornithology. It also gives a good picture of how these bird fowlers worked.

On Friday, 13th June 1890, Raeburn crossed from the island of Papa Stour to reach Foula in a sixern, a boat used in the Shetlands for fishing and powered by six oarmen, one oar each, plus a square sail when the wind was right. A clinker built wooden boat of 20-25 feet in length, it was used as far out as 40 miles from land, and given the speed and ferocity of gales in the area, even in summer, there was heavy loss of boats and lives. After a brief exploration on Foula, the boat next pulled over to the almost inaccessible Lyra Skerry. As Raeburn remarks in his article, the term skerry was incorrect here, a skerry being a low, wave-washed rock. Lyra Skerry was instead a huge stack of porphyrytic rock, 180 feet high and about a quarter of a mile in circumference. The stack was perpendicular on all sides except one small portion at the SE edge, just to the right of the magnificent sea-floored cavern that passes right through the island. *'This was pointed out to me as the "road up"'.*

Raeburn wrote that in the past the men of Papa had a reputation as climbers little inferior to those of Unst or Foula, but that for many years climbing had been almost entirely given up. Only two men on the island were now able to make the ascent of the Lyra Skerry, and Raeburn was fortunate on this occasion, his second visit, to have secured the services of the best, a six-foot three-inch man rejoicing in the name of Long Peter. (Raeburn's first visit had been in June 1887.) Peter wore a pair of rivlins, raw cowhide shoes worn by the Shetlanders, and during the course of the day Raeburn had a good illustration of how useful Peter's enormous reach was in cliff climbing.

> Peter now took a coil of codline in his hand, and, watching his opportunity as the light boat rose on the swell, jumped clear of the water on to a dry ledge. Though I did not relish the look of the said "road up," there was no other way of getting to the top; so I followed him. Peter now explained to me that there were only two "bad bits" - one about half-way up, and the other just at the very top. The first of these is where the rock projects so far as to overhang the sea below, and from where - the men were careful to inform me - a climber had fallen some years before, but, striking the water, was picked up by his comrades in the boat, escaping with a broken arm and a severe shock from a fall of 90 feet. They added, perhaps unnecessarily, that he did not again attempt the ascent.

Peter informed Raeburn that the final 15 feet was the only really difficult section, and Raeburn found that the first 90 feet was fairly easy as the rock, though almost vertical, was sound. He did however remove his india rubber shoes after climbing some 50 feet, as he found, like Peter, that climbing in his stockings provided much greater freedom for his toes. All went well until the crux section was reached, just below the top.

> Here, within fifteen feet of the summit, we brought up against what appeared to me a totally unscaleable piece. We were clinging in a sort of shallow niche of the cliff, which above our heads narrowed to a crack about eight inches wide. If it had been a foot wider the ascent would have been comparatively easy by bracing the body against the sides, but its narrowness precluded this. I now watched Long Peter's movements with interest, and here was the point where his great height and long arms stood him in good stead, for, stretching himself up the left-hand edge of the crack, he seized a small ledge nearly eight feet above the niche we stood in, and slowly and carefully he drew himself up, finding a crevice for his toes, and, getting another grip higher up, he was at the summit in a few seconds. He then passed the doubled codline* down to me, which I fastened under my arms, and, Peter putting a 50 lb. strain on it, I swarmed up the edge of the crack, and stood beside him on the top.

[*Codline was an 18-thread hemp or cotton line used for cod fishing and light rope work on boats. It could be tarred, or left untarred.]

Raeburn found the top of the stack to be about three acres of luxuriant tussocky grass, ungrazed by sheep. He was particularly interested in finding Manx Shearwaters, but was disappointed. According to Raeburn – '…*that accurate and most painstaking naturalist and microscopist, the Rev. Geo. Low, visited Papa Stour (1770) on his Shetland tour, and says of the Lyra Skerry, it is "inhabited by vast numbers of Shearwaters — lyries."*' There was, however, a fine colony of L. marinus, the Great Black-Backed Gull. Once Raeburn's exploration of the summit was complete, there remained the question of returning to the boat.

> But Peter was back with his jersey crammed with eggs, and it was time we were off: to carry anything down the way we came up would be an utter impossibility ; but here the codline came into play, for Peter, walking to the extreme edge of the cliff just over the archway through the island, signalled to the boat to be ready, and lowered his harvest swiftly and steadily straight into the boat, — doing the same with the fishing-basket containing my more modest, if safer, selection.
>
> My enjoyment of the scene upon the summit had been somewhat dashed by thoughts of the descent; but, with the aid of Peter's codline for the top piece, it was soon accomplished, and I was exceedingly glad to again jump on board our boat.

(From *The Zoologist*, 1891, pp. 126-135)

The St Kildans lived there until at their own request they were evacuated en masse to the Scottish mainland in 1930. Their lifestyle had changed very little over the centuries.

❄ ❄ ❄

There are isolated early accounts of Scottish summits being gained by various individuals, but although of interest, these were not done by mountaineering as we regard it, involving of necessity the use of all four limbs to climb steep and difficult ground and all for personal pleasure. Some of these early walkers will be mentioned below, as a way of illustrating the state of Scotland and its geography before mountaineering as understood here began.

The Scottish risings of 1715 and 1745 marked the beginning of the end of the clan system, and ultimately led to sweeping changes throughout the country. Before these momentous events occurred, Scotland was effectively two states; the Lowlands and the Highlands. The topography and poor roads made travel in the Highlands awkward, while most highland Scots spoke Gaelic only, a language all but unknown to those in the Lowlands. Travel by boat was common, especially for the western seaboard and islands.

In 1654 was published the Scottish edition of maps by Johann Blaue of Amsterdam, a result of the survey on foot by Timothy Pont beginning about 1585. The edition by Blaeu led to one later geographer, Dr Stone, declaring that with the appearance of Blaeu's atlas, *'Scotland became one of the best mapped countries in the world.'*[3] Ian R Mitchell, in his book, *Scotland's Mountains before the Mountaineers,* posits that Pont did not speak Gaelic and must have had a Gaelic guide and translator with him, but information is frustratingly poor.[4]

Pont's sketches from the Central Highlands include outline sketches of several prominent mountains, including Ben Lawers, Beinn Vorlich and Stuic a' Chroin, and Ben Nevis. The sketch of the last is particularly interesting, showing the summit plateau, the lower Carn Dearg summit, and what is possibly Coire Eoghain lying between the two. From its appearance, it could have been drawn from a position somewhere on the Sgurr a' Mhaim ridge above Glen Nevis. (See also Project Pont, based in the National Library of Scotland.[5]) These mountain sketches would have been among the very earliest.

In July 1724, George I sent General Wade to Scotland. In the paranoia following the 1689, 1715 and 1719 Jacobite uprisings, he was asked '*to inspect the present situation of the Highlanders* and to *make strict inquiry into the last law for disarming the Highlanders.*' He recommended the construction of barracks, bridges and roads to help control the Highlands. George I immediately appointed Wade as Chief of His Majesty's forces, castles, forts and barracks in North Britain, with the remit to put his own recommendations into practice.

Between 1725 and 1737 Wade directed the construction of some 250mls (400km) of road, plus 40 bridges (including the Tay Bridge at Aberfeldy). The roads linked the garrisons at Ruthven, Fort George, Fort Augustus, and Fort William. His network of roads, primarily built to support the military, would help open up the Highlands to visitors, allowing access to trade, seekers after minerals, botanists, geologists, artists, poets and, gingerly at first then with rapidly increasing frequency, tourists in search of adventure in their own back yard.

Major General William Roy (1726–1790) was born in Carluke, Lanarkshire. In 1747, he joined a team led by Lieutenant Colonel David Watson, then the Deputy Quartermaster General for North Britain, encamped at Fort Augustus, midway between Inverness and Fort William. Their objective was to survey and map the Scottish Highlands, so permitting a series of camps to be developed at salient points, with a network of connecting roads and tracks. Their original maps, drawn in the field, were at a scale of about two inches to one mile. Their work would lead ultimately to the formation of the Ordnance Survey in 1791. As Mitchell notes – '*though they were still quite primitive, Roy's maps were an improvement on what had gone before.'*[6] In short, his use of the latest scientific advances and accurate mathematics led to the start of modern mapping.

❄ ❄ ❄

There now existed not only a subdued native population in the Highlands, but also a network of roads and a military presence. The early tourists to Scotland utilised the roads built by the military, but in discovering and exploring Scotland they remained on the whole unimpressed by the country's beauty, rather emphasising the stark, rugged landscape. Their descriptions would change gradually to a more positive air, but in the interim, some of those living in Scotland had already realised that they were in a country which possessed a beautiful scenery.

As one example, this awareness of Highland landscape beauty was earlier raised by the Rev Doctor James Robertson. In 1791, being minister of Callander Parish at the time, he was required to write a description of the parish for the First Statistical Account of Scotland. He also wrote what was to be one of Scotland's first tourist guides: *A Pamphlet Descriptive of the Neighbourhood of Callander*. Robertson's descriptions of the scenery in the Trossachs area, published in the Statistical Account, predated Scott's in *The Lady of the Lake,* and indeed Scott might even be accused of plagiarism by some in his descriptions of that area.

One early traveller was John MacCulloch, MD, FRS etc (1773–1835), by profession a physician, but by preference a geologist.[7] He made several annual journeys through Scotland between 1811 and 1821, recorded in four volumes and prefaced by letters describing his trips to his life-long friend Walter Scott (later Sir Walter). These accounts undoubtedly influenced Scott, whose own writings, particularly *The Lady of the Lake*, published in 1810, increased the growing enthusiasm for Highland landscapes.[8]

MacCulloch's book of his travels (in four volumes), and his letters to Walter Scott, prompted that author to begin his series of romantic writings which aided the rise in tourism. In particular, the poem *The Lady of the Lake*, which celebrated its 200th anniversary in 2010, is often singled out for being the catalyst for literary tourism in Scotland, though as indicated above, it was not the first. Scott and his family visited the Trossachs in 1809, and his poem uses its scenic beauty as its setting. The poem propelled the area into an enduring favourite spot for tourism.

MacCulloch soon began to rue this effect, especially as to its effect on the Trossachs area, where Loch Katrine was the inspiration for its setting where Ben Venue. –

> ...forms a magnificent termination to a picture which fills the eye by its parts and its ornament;' but Macculloch wishes Sir Walter 'had laid the venue of his

> poem anywhere else than at Ben Venu,' because of the stupid "clanjamfray" of tourists the "Lady of the Lake" had let loose about the place.[9]

In 1814 MacCulloch was appointed geologist to the Trigonometrical Survey which was then preparing a one-inch topographical map of Scotland. In 1826, after a spell as physician to Prince Leopold of Saxe-Coburg he transferred to the Geological Survey when his application to complete the geological map of Scotland was approved. He completed this map in six years. It was the first official geological map of any country in the world, and was finally published (posthumously) in 1840.

A more basic map showing the geology of Scotland was presented to the Geological Society by a student from Geneva in 1808. The student was Louis Albert Necker de Saussure (1786–1861). Necker was born in Geneva in 1786 to a famous family: his grandfather (the great HB Saussure) was a naturalist who helped make possible the first ascent of Mont Blanc while himself making the third. While still a schoolboy, Necker proved to have a talent for science, and went on to college to study zoology and geology. To avoid conscription, his parents sent him to Britain in 1806.

At Edinburgh University Necker attended classes by Robert Jameson, Professor of Mineralogy and himself an important geological pioneer. Over the next three years he made several tours in Scotland, including a trip to Arran and Skye in May 1807. These tours culminated in what would be the earliest known map showing the geology of Scotland. It was hand-coloured by Necker and was presented to the newly formed Geological Society of London on 4th November 1808. His map was never published, and though more basic than MacCulloch's, predates it by some 32 years.

In 1809 Necker was in Geneva, where he became Professor of Natural History. He returned to Scotland in 1831, settling in Portobello near Edinburgh, and in 1832 accompanied David Forbes on his first alpine tour, the two becoming firm friends. Necker never married, and after his mother's death in April 1841 he moved to Portree on Skye, dying there in 1861. He was buried in the old graveyard in Portree. As will be seen later, Necker was to play a small but important part in determining the heights of some of the Cuillin peaks.

In November 1812, a Colonel Peter Hawker (1786–1853) made a trip to Scotland. He was a soldier with the 14th Light Dragoons and saw active service under the Duke of Wellington in the Peninsular War, but was obliged to retire after being seriously wounded at the battle of Talavera (Spain) in 1809 where a shot passed through his thigh shattering his femur. He was a rampant fowler of birds, and wrote a standard text on how to shoot them. Hawker is credited with the first record of cutting steps in snow on a Scottish mountain, in this case Ben Lomond.

Leaving the inn at Luss, Hawker crossed the loch by ferry to gain the inn at Rowardennan, on Loch Lomondside, where he spent the night in a *bed-in-a-hole*. The next morning, with his man and a guide, he set out to ascend Ben Lomond. After three hours they had barely gained the shoulder of the mountain, and when they reached the final steepening they found further advance impossible, with the '*last fifty yards a solid sheet of ice.*'

> ...indeed, for more than the last half-mile we travelled in perfect misery and imminent danger; we were literally obliged to take knives to cut footsteps in the frozen snow, and, of course, obliged to crawl all the way on our hands, knees, and toes, all of which were benumbed with cold, and were repeatedly in danger of slipping in places where one false step would have been certain destruction.

> ...The ascent to the summit of this mountain is, even in winter, sometimes very passable; and in summer so much so, that ladies very commonly go up, and sometimes take with them a piper, and other apparatus for dancing. The summer may, perhaps, have a different effect; but, for my own part, I was so exhausted that, being unable to walk home from the inn, I hired a boat and returned by water.[10]

Hawker had just failed to make the summit, but it was a bold outing and seemingly one not just with shooting birds in mind. Soon after leaving the shore, they left their guns and dog by a rock and continued up the hill, bent on an ascent. The party had been sensible enough not to attempt the very last section, which does indeed have a steep drop into the north-east corrie.

Various artists and authors were influential in promoting tourism in Scotland. George Fennell Robson (1788–1833) was a watercolourist. Born in Durham, his niche was mountain scenery, painting mainly in Perthshire and in the Grampians to the north. In 1814 he had published a book of some 40 etchings, *Scenery of the Grampian Mountains*. He visited Skye and around 1826 painted a view of Loch Coruisk. The mountaineer Norman Collie, (of whom more later), admired his work, and picked him out as being one of the first to appreciate the mountain scenery of Scotland. In 1815, Walter Scott wrote *The Lord of the Isles*, a romantic narrative-poem which described the progress of Robert the Bruce in the Scottish Wars of Independence, and included a section on Skye. Scott was knighted in 1820.

While much of the Scottish Highlands remained awkward of access, the west coast and its islands were particularly open to travel by boat. This relatively easy access also helps to understand the rise of the 'Lords of the Isles', as the early Scots wrested control from the Kings of Norway, whose Norse warriors had ruled here until the Treaty of Perth in 1236. Allied with its remarkable scenery, it would inevitably become an area favoured by tourists. The island of Skye in particular, with its Alpine-like Black Cuillin massif, would become a prime target. One of the highlights of a tourist's itinerary would be the view along Loch Coruisk, more easily gained by boat than the wet trudge down Glen Sligachan. While these early tourists basically confined themselves to lower ground, the necessity of mapping Great Britain led to some early exploration of the Black Cuillin.

❄ ❄ ❄

Thomas Frederick Colby was an employee of the Ordnance Survey (OS) for 44 years and its Director General from 1820 until March 1847. In his mapping career the OS six-inch survey was extended into Scotland. A talented man, Colby was a Fellow of the Royal Society and the Geological Society. He was also an original member of the Royal Astronomical Society, and friends with such scientific luminaries as Banks, Faraday, Herschel and Robert Stevenson.[11]

On the 28th July 1819, Colby and his party of surveyors attempted to '*climb the highest peak of the Coolins*', then thought to be Sgurr nan Gillean, the prominent peak at the north end of the Cuillin, and overlooking Sligachan. They failed, being thwarted by a perpendicular column at the extremity of a vertical ridge. Sadly, all but one of Colby's field journals were destroyed during the Second World War, along with much of the Ordnance Survey Library. However, Portlock's *Memoir* on Colby was published complete in 1869, including material gathered by Major Robert K Dawson, who had been commissioned in the Royal Engineers in 1818 before retiring as a lieutenant colonel from the Ordnance Survey.[12] Significantly for us, Dawson had worked with Colby and had been with him in the Western Highlands and on Skye in 1819. Dawson's report stated –

> ...Not being provided with ladders or ropes the perpendicular rock at the summit effectually baffled our efforts for several hours to find a crevice by which to ascend it. We gained, however, a ridge which reaches out from the perpendicular cliff with a superb column at the extremity of it, and so narrow is this ridge that we were obliged to sit astride upon it... After admiring for a while the magnificence of the prospect, and the dreary and all but chaotic scene around us, we returned to our inn [i.e. Sconser], gratified above measure with what we had seen, though disconcerted with our professional failure.

The Ordnance Survey did eventually climb Sgurr nan Gillean, though without the presence of Colby. He instructed his engineers to '*make the peak in question a principal station of the trigonometrical survey.*' This must have been done sometime after the resumption of the Scottish Survey in 1838. The evidence points to Colby's company in 1819 making their way beneath the Bhasteir Face of the Pinnacle Ridge and, after failing to find a practicable chimney (*crevice*) leading to the summit, continued towards the Bealach a' Bhasteir from which point they attempted to reach the summit of Sgurr nan Gillean by the Western Ridge, but although managing to get onto the lower and very narrow part of this crest (where they were '*obliged to sit astride upon it*') the surveyors were suddenly brought up short by the Gendarme which barred their way to the rest of the Ridge and therefore the summit.[13] Even though they failed on this occasion to gain the summit of Sgurr nan Gillean, they were still the first party ever known to set foot on the main Cuillin ridge. Thomas Colby died aged 69 in October 1852 at New Brighton.

The infamous Gendarme was a prominent block sitting very precariously on the Western Ridge of Sgurr nan Gillean. It was a major obstacle to early pioneers, including Colby's party of 1819. In March 1987, severely weakened by frosts, it finally fell into the corrie. The ridge is now considerably easier. For more information on Colby and his mapping, there is a good article by Graham E Little in the 2013 Scottish Mountaineering Club Journal.[14]

The early 19th century saw tourists becoming more prevalent, one of them being the Rev Charles Lesingham Smith, born in Gloucester, Fellow and late Mathematical Lecturer of Christ's College Cambridge. Common to that profession, summers were long and easy, and Smith was already an experienced traveller and walker, having visited Switzerland, Italy, and the Austrian Tyrol. In 1835 he embarked on his first tour of Scotland. From his experiences he wrote a journal for his family's amusement, but when friends expressed interest he had more copies printed, eventually ending up with a journal covering 1835 and 1836.[15]

His tour took him through Inverary to Mull, Staffa and then Fort William, climbing Ben Nevis on the last day of August. Two days later he was on Skye, ending up at Sligachan Inn which was to become a prime centre for exploration of the Cuillin Hills, though the Inn Smith stayed at was a new version, having been built around 1830 a short distance away from the original. It was described in a recently published contemporary guide as '*the uncomfortable inn at the end of the glen*',[16] but Smith found it comfortable enough, especially after his soaking in a bumpy cart. '*The interior, however, is more cheerful, and I am enjoying extremely the humble luxury of a peat fire, while the clean napkin on the table, and the fine coloured tea-things, invite me to a sober meal. I am content.*'

The following morning, September 5th, the weather was unpromising, as Smith began talking with Duncan MacIntyre, a forester (gamekeeper) employed by Lord MacDonald. Smith learned that it would take about five hours to walk to Coruisk via Glen Sligachan, so he decided to have breakfast and see what the weather brought.

> I set out with the forester, who, from having been employed fifteen years in preserving the red deer among these glens, is acquainted with every stone in them. He wore a sailor's jacket, and carried a stout staff in his hand; and a

telescope in a leathern case swinging by a leathern belt round his shoulders, served him to watch for the deer, and also for poachers.

After a brief stop in Harta Corrie, they continued squelching down the boggy glen, eventually rounding the hill and gaining the Coruisk basin, which Smith admired for some time, '*with an appalling thrill for a scene of such sterility.*' The good forester however, had a secret agenda in mind, and accompanied by the forester's two dogs –

> We proceeded along the small slope that intervenes between the precipice and the lake, in order 'just to view the whole thing,' as my guide observed. When we arrived at the end of the water, he turned round and said, 'We have been just two hours and a half in coming this journey, which takes most gentlemen at least five. I never came so quick before. Now we've a long day before us still; and a shepherd told me that it was possible to get up the rocks just above, and that it was much shorter than to go all the way round as we came. I'll just tell you the truth, I've never been over myself, and I've never liked to propose it to any one I've brought here; but you are a light gentleman, and if you like we'll try. We can but turn back, if we can't manage it, and I think we are now sure of fine weather.'

After a lunch including mutton-ham, biscuits and '*a considerable vacuum in my whisky-flask*' Smith agreed to continue. The two found it easy at first, before it steepened. '*I am sure we shall do well, said I. Best not to be too sure, Sir; one step may send us all the way back*' was his guide's reply. Then the two dogs were constantly in Smith's way. The ground became steeper. Sometimes one would push the other, then the other would pull, and Smith's umbrella became a '*sad nuisance*.'

The two eventually gained the top of the slope, where Smith marvelled at the view; the lochs Coruisk and Scavaig, the mountain tops, the islands of Eigg and Rum. Finally, they scampered down Harta Corrie, back up the tedious boggy slog of Glen Sligachan, and, some seven hours after setting out, regained the Inn. The route would have not been far short of some 30km, and Smith was obviously a good walker. MacIntyre was a servant, but an experienced and valued one. The Cuillin area being predominantly rocky with fewer deer than greener, lower land, he probably had little experience of the ridges and summits, though he would certainly know his employer's glens. He was also a professional guide, albeit an informal and occasional one, not the last that Skye would see.

❄ ❄ ❄

Smith was an experienced walker, a hillwalker in fact, but not quite a mountaineer. If the distinction has to be made then it can have no better example than the man who in the following year also paired up with the 'sturdy Forester', a certain James David Forbes (1809–1868). To Forbes we might award that honour, the title of Scotland's first known mountaineer.

Like MacCulloch before him, Forbes was a Scot, born in Edinburgh. The fourth son of Sir William Forbes, 7th baronet of Pitsligo, he spent his youth at Colinton House, at the foot of the Pentlands, and at his father's estate of Pitsligo, in Aberdeenshire. He was educated at home which left him with time to explore and appreciate his surroundings. Other major influences included the writings of Scott, and later, when he entered Edinburgh University in 1825, the lectures of Professor John Wilson in Moral Philosophy. Wilson was friendly with Wordsworth and Coleridge and was, in all probability, the first tourist to make an ascent of Broad Stand on Scafell (pre 1850) .

Forbes gravitated towards physics, and while still a schoolboy began contributing research papers to the *Edinburgh Philosophical Journal* anonymously, using the signature 'Δ', the Greek letter delta, or 'd'. At the age of 19 he became a fellow of the Royal Society of Edinburgh, then in 1832 was elected to the Royal Society of London. The following year he took the chair of Natural Philosophy at Edinburgh, in competition with Sir David Brewster, remaining there until 1860.

His position at Edinburgh University provided him with long summer holidays, and a succession of some 17 were used to the full with travelling, usually in or near mountains. His third holiday, in 1836, was spent in Scotland, beginning in the Leadhills, moving north to the Cairngorms (taking in Ben Macdui), over to the west coast and Skye, back to Inverness via Loch Maree, walking down by the Caledonian Canal, exploring the glens along the way, then Fort William and Ballachulish, with a day exploring Glen Coe. Writing to his sister from Dalmally on the 23rd July, Forbes extolled the virtues of that glen. Throughout his trip, Forbes was travelling mostly alone, and on foot – '*...yesterday I devoted to a leisure survey of Glencoe* (sic) *which extremely delighted me, and is really the best scenery on the whole I have seen in Scotland, and worthy of comparison with any I know.*'[17]

Forbes had arrived in Skye during the first week in July. Staying at Sligachan, he heard that the high summits were inaccessible. This advice he ignored and on the 6th July he fell into a discussion with Duncan MacIntyre about an ascent of Sgurr nan Gillean, the same *sturdy Forester* who the previous year had shepherded Lesingham Smith into and out of the Coruisk basin. Forbes had also engaged MacIntyre for a similar trip, but it may well have been that the guide recognised in Forbes a better sort of client, for he suggested that they try Gillean. MacIntyre had attempted it several times, both on his own, and with different gentlemen, but on this occasion he had his eyes on a different route. On the next day, the 7th –

> ...we succeeded in gaining the top; the extreme roughness of the rocks (all Hypersthene) rendering the ascent safe, where, with any other formation, it might have been considerably perilous. Indeed, I have never seen a rock so

> adapted for clambering. At that time I erected a cairn and temporary flag, which, stood, I was informed, a whole year; but having no barometer I could not ascertain the height, which I estimated at 3,000 ft.[18]

Hypersthene was then used as a name for gabbro in general, it being a hard, crystalline mineral found in that rock type.

Forbes was then 27 years of age; he had first visited the Alps aged 17 and was to go on to make Alpine ascents including the Jungfrau (in 1841, with Louis Agassiz), the first British ascent of a virgin Alpine peak, the Stockhorn (Wandfluhhorn) in 1842, and the first ascent of the Wäsenhorn in 1844. From the start, he was fascinated by glaciers, then the source of much discussion as to their possible role in shaping the landscape. In 1843 he published his monumental *Travels in the Alps*.[19] This book mixed scientific chapters on glaciers and ice action with descriptions of the Alps. Forbes had seen for himself on Skye the same signs of ice activity which had shaped, and was continuing to shape, the Alpine landscape. As for Duncan MacIntyre, he would have been in his mid-40s when climbing with Forbes. He lived to a grand old 87, dying in June 1867, and is buried in the old graveyard in Portree.

With MacIntyre, Forbes also made the first recorded ascent of Bruach na Frithe in May, 1845, carrying a barometer. From the summit of that hill, he proposed that they continue on to Sgurr nan Gillean. Avoiding the Am Basteir obstacle, a formidable-looking cliff, as he thought it impossible, they dropped into Lota Corrie before following a steep scramble up Gillean. In the meantime his barometer had shown a significant and sudden drop during his outing, which made his height calculations very difficult. Luck was at hand however, as Forbes' friend Necker with another barometer had been making observations at Portree. Comparing the instruments and the pressure readings made it possible for an estimation of the height of Sgurr nan Gillean. Forbes' estimation was less than 40ft different from subsequent Ordnance Survey measurements.

In addition to their first ascent of Sgurr nan Gillean in 1836, Forbes and MacIntyre also made the second ascent of that iconic mountain, in May 1845. Forbes made a complete circumnavigation of the Cuillin range, something which he thought had not been done before. He had also transected the range in several places. All of this permitted him to draw a superb 'Bird's-Eye Map' of the Cuillin, which was not to be bettered until the Ordnance Survey published their first map some 40 years later. One area of the Cuillin was to provide crucial evidence to Forbes of the effects of glaciation. This was Coir' a' Ghrunnda, where to his eye there was unmistakable evidence of ice erosion, similar in many ways to those he had seen on the 'living' glaciers of the Alps. All this research would come together in a landmark scientific paper published in 1846.[20]

Forbes was also very interested in the Ben Nevis massif. In May 1848 he attempted an ascent of the mountain. He described the day in a letter to his wife Alicia. Despite continuing poor weather, he set out with his man on the 30th May. Forbes included a sketch in his letter, which was taken from the north-northwest. It shows that they walked up the Allt a' Mhuilinn glen and gained the Carn Mor Dearg arête at the head of the glen. As the mist was covering the summit, they abandoned plans to gain the summit and instead circumnavigated the mountain. On the final slopes to the arête, Forbes astonished his companion with an unusual technique –

> We kept on the rock as long as we could, and at length found that there only intervened between us and the ridge a short steep ascent of drifted snow, most truly Alpine. It was too late to think of receding, and it was not far ; so, assuming my new mahogany tripod as an Alpine stock, I proceeded foremost to make steps in the most approved Swiss fashion, to the no small edification of my companion, who had never seen such an operation before. The upper few yards were so steep that I actually could not get one foot stuck into the snow before the other, and had to get along sideways. We luckily got to the top safe and sound, and found less mist on the opposite side. We came down a most tremendous steep into Glen Nevis, but without any risk, having been eleven hours incessantly on foot...[21]

It is unclear as to his precise line of descent; he may well have contoured briefly to gain the top of the long slope leading down into Glen Nevis adjacent to the Waterslide, which may be the '*most tremendous steep*.' In any case it was quite an adventure. As to the mention of a tripod, these were very early days for photography, though Sir David Brewster, his competitor for the chair in Edinburgh, was a keen practitioner, and indeed was a member of the Edinburgh Calotype Club, the first photographic club in the world. It is quite possible that Forbes had taken along a camera for this trip, though surviving photographs are not known.

Forbes, even while exploring the wilds of Scotland, was prone to bouts of illness, cause unknown, but with symptoms like those of tuberculosis. In the spring of 1867 his health declined. '*His old enemy, the cough, got a firm hold of him, which he could not shake off*.'[22] He died on the last day of the year in 1868, aged 59. Within two years both his daughters also died, the elder having nursed both Forbes and her sibling.

They were buried in the same grave at Dean Cemetery in Edinburgh, at a spot chosen by Forbes himself. His grave was shadowed by the yew tree which overhung his window when his home was in the old house of Dean. In the interim, the Alpine Club had been formed in London in 1857, Forbes becoming its first Honorary Member.

One of the Alpine Club's earliest members was travel writer Charles Richard Weld (1813–1869), the author of a range of guidebooks including several for Europe and North America. In late July 1859, Weld joined a group of friends who were more interested in hunting and fishing, to visit Skye – '*The Cuchullin Hills and their lakes are the great lions of Skye, and it was to see these that I was principally induced to visit the island.*'

Though an experienced member of the Alpine Club Weld got off to a poor start at Sligachan, being rain-bound for several days. Finally, his third morning started well and off he went with his guide and pony to find Coruisk. He gained Camasunary –

> ...a little oasis in the desert, where the storm-stricken traveller will find shelter and a shake-down in a farm-house at the head of a sandy bay. Not far from the farm is an establishment for reclaiming drunkards, where it is to be presumed the total abstinence system can be enforced with complete success.

Leaving his pony and hiring a boat and four men, he was taken into Scavaig where he landed close to the mouth of the river. Much taken with the scenery, and determined to obtain a view, the next day he retraced his route but, still on a pony, turned up the hillside before reaching Camasunary. Leaving his guide at a col, he continued alone to gain the summit of Sgurr na Stri, just over half the height of the main Cuillin hills. This was the first recorded ascent of this hill, but not the earliest, as local clansmen had been there before. It was Weld's highest point on an otherwise strangely lacklustre trip, though he seems to have been personally satisfied with his ascent –

> All my expectations were realised, and I was the more delighted by the success of my enterprise, because the idea of ascending this peak was my own; neither friend nor guide-book having given me a hint respecting its great advantages as an eyrie.[23]

Describing the fine view obtained from Sgurr na Stri, Weld finished with a reference to what would later be called the Inaccessible Pinnacle, the unusual and prominent rock feature forming the highest point of Sgurr Dearg, and exhorted his fellow Alpine Club members to do something about it –

> At a recent meeting of the Club, the president drew the attention of members to certain peaks on Continental mountains deemed inaccessible, but here, according to the Admiralty surveyor, is one in the British Islands, never trodden by the foot of man. Surely some bold member of the club will scale this Skye peak ere long, and tell us that it is but a stroll before breakfast.[23]

It was going to take a few more years than '*ere long*' before this was to happen, but in the interim we need to leave the Isle of Skye for a moment and cast an eye on what was going on elsewhere in Scotland.

References

1. Martin, Martin. *A Description of the Western Isles of Scotland* (1703).
2. Kearton, Richard. *With Nature and a Camera.* (London: Cassell & Co., 1898) Also online at (http://gdl.cdlr.strath.ac.uk/keacam/index.html).
3. Stone, Jeffrey C. *The Pont Manuscript Maps of Scotland: sixteenth century origins of a Blaeu atlas.* (1989, Map Collector Publications Ltd.)
4. Mitchell, Ian R. *Scotland's Mountains before the Mountaineers.* (Edinburgh: Luath Press, 2004. 2nd edn), pp.13-14.
5. http://maps.nls.uk/pont/ Accessed April, 2014.
6. Mitchell, Ian R. *Scotland's Mountains before the Mountaineers.* (Edinburgh: Luath Press, 2004. 2nd edn), p.38.
7. Bruce-Chwatt, L. J. *John MacCulloch, M.D., F.R.S. (1773-1835) The Precursor of the Discipline of Malariology*, Medical History, 1977, 21: 156-165.
8. MacCulloch, John, *The Highlands and Western Isles of Scotland* (London: Longman, Hurst, Rees, Orme, Brown, and Green, 1824).
9. Campbell, Rev Colin. *Rise and Progress of Mountaineering in Scotland. – III.* SMCJ 3, 16, Jan. 1895, p.188. (Referring to MacCulloch Vol.1).
10. *The diary of Colonel Peter Hawker, 1802-1853*, with an introduction by Sir Ralph Payne-Gallwey, bart. (London, New York: Longmans, Green, and Co., 1893) Vol.1, pp.59-60.)
11. Pedlar, Stuart, *Across Unmeasured Space – A History of Climbing in the Cuillin.* Unpublished MS. 2010.
12. Major-General Joseph Ellison Portlock, 1794-1864, *A Memoir of the Life of Major-General Colby*, 1869, pp.144-145.
13. Pedlar, Stuart, *Across Unmeasured Space – A History of Climbing in the Cuillin.* Unpublished MS. 2010.
14. Little, Graham E. *Mountain Camps, Triangulation Stations and Plum Puddings.* SMCJ 42, 204, 2013, 416-427.
15. Smith, Charles Lesingham. (1837.) *Excursions through the Highlands and Isles of Scotland in 1835 and 1836.*
16. George and Peter Anderson. *Guide to The Highlands and Islands of Scotland* (Inverness: 1827/1834).
17. Letter to Miss Forbes, July 23rd 1836. In: *Life and letters of James David Forbes, F.R.S.*, By John Campbell Shairp, Peter Guthrie Tait, and A. Adams-Reilly. (London: Macmillan and Co., 1873), p.125.
18. Forbes, James David, *Notes on the Topography and Geology of the Cuchullin Hills in Skye, and on the traces of Ancient Glaciers which they present.* The Edinburgh New Philosophical Journal, 1846, pp 79-81.
19. Forbes, James David, *Travels Through the Alps*, (Edinburgh: Black, 1843)
20. *Notes on the Topography and Geology of the Cuchullin Hills in Skye, and on the traces of Ancient Glaciers which they Present*, The Edinburgh New Philosophical Journal, Vol. XL, April, 1846.
21. *Life and letters of James David Forbes*, F.R.S. pp.185-187.
22. Ibid. p.437
23. Weld, Charles, *Two Months in the Highlands, Orcadia, and Skye*, (London:1860)

2

Early Clubs (1866-1884)

By the mid-19th century ascents of Scottish peaks were becoming more frequent. Several visitors were producing books of their travels. The Rev. Thomas Grierson was one such author, writing *Autumnal Rambles Among the Scottish Mountains* in 1850.[1] By the third edition of this in 1856, he had amassed an impressive total of summits, some of which he had climbed more than once. In his book *Scotland's Mountains Before the Mountaineers,* Ian R Mitchell lists the following mountains of over 3,000ft as '*fairly definite first (recorded) ascents…*' – Udlamain, Beinn Achaladair, Ben Vorlich (Loch Earn), Beinn a' Chreachain?, and Ben Alder.[2] Mitchell's book takes an entertaining scamper through the history before the arrival of mountaineers proper, and documents much activity during this period. According to his research, he accords some twelve 'Munros' to MacCulloch, and fourteen to Grierson, a Scot from Galloway. These ascents of course would be made of mountains which would not be called Munros for some years to come.

As an example of how deeply walking was embedded in certain circles, Grierson writes of how he was much taken with a walk before breakfast, his idea of this being 15 or 20 miles before 9am. One somewhat longer walk is described in his Preface –

> In the autumn of 1811, the year of the great comet, I left Glasgow early, breakfasted at Dumbarton, went up Loch Lomond side, crossed at Rowardennan, went over the shoulder of Ben Lomond to Blairhulichan, and stayed all night at Ledard, on the north side of Loch Ard. Next morning started at four, crossed the mountains to Loch Katrine, where I was boated over by a shepherd; over the mountains again, through the Forest of Glen Finglas and its deep bogs, to Balquhidder; over the mountains again to Glen Dochart and Killin; and once more across the mountains to Loch Rannoch side, which I

> reached before twelve o'clock at night – as severe a mountain fag as perhaps ever was performed in one day.[3]

Earlier in his Preface, Grierson apologised for his writing, accepting that it had been not a little egotistical, '*but, from the nature of the case, this could not well have been otherwise.*' He also explains that several of his walks while in the prime of life have been given as examples, '*to prove what may be done by patience and perseverance, for I was never a quick walker.*' While without any more details it is impossible to be certain, it would seem that following paths and tracks in a logical direction Grierson could have travelled at least 65km in 20 hours, taking in several mountain passes: that calculation does not allow for the natural deviations from straight lines so could easily be upwards of 90km.

❄ ❄ ❄

Based in Glasgow was a man who played an important role in the development of mountaineering in Scotland: George Gilbert Ramsay (1839–1921). A scion of an old Scottish family, the third son of Sir George Ramsay, 9th Baronet of Bamff in Perthshire, he was educated at Rugby and at Trinity College, Oxford. He was appointed to the Chair of Humanity at Glasgow University in 1863, aged 24, following in the footsteps of Professor William Ramsay, his uncle, for whom he was an assistant. Some detected the scent of nepotism in his appointment as his uncle's successor. In 1874 *The Bailie*, a weekly Glasgow magazine that published short stories, sketches and cartoons, observed – '*…that many students disliked him, accusing him of humiliating them with sarcastic remarks in class and snubbing them in public.*' Undoubtedly his avowed radical Liberal sympathies would not have endeared him to the more Conservative-leaning publication, while others thought him a good teacher. A keen sportsman, Ramsay was a particularly enthusiastic ice skater.

That he was a painstaking and careful researcher in the classics is only too obvious when reading his publications in this field, mainly on very early Roman texts. Even after he retired in 1906 he continued to write, publishing a translation of the *Histories of Tacitus* in 1915. Ramsay was also a friend of the Cunards, of shipping fame; on a display outside the Britannia Restaurant of the Queen Mary 2, he is quoted as having helped Cunard name their early ships after Roman Maritime provinces such as Mauretania, Parthia, Franconia, Lusitania, etc.

Ramsay's part in the formation of the Scottish Mountaineering Club will be outlined in a later chapter, but before going into that, we note here some very interesting comments he made on the early state of mountaineering in Scotland.[4] Writing in 1896, and taking a retrospective look, he wrote –

> ...it is worth noting that Scotland, strange to say, has been behind England in the matter of hill-climbing. I refer not merely to the Alpine Club — not only the earliest but by far the most distinguished mountaineering club in the world — but to the diffusion of hill pedestrianism in England long before it became a general pursuit — indeed it has never yet become a general pursuit — in Scotland. My own taste for hill-climbing, first inspired by the enthusiastic example of my father, was also largely stimulated by the fact that as a schoolboy I spent several summer holidays in English scenery resorts. In those days, as now, the hills of the Lake district of Derbyshire and Wales were full of pedestrians...scouring over the country with knapsacks on their backs...I have never come across anything like this in Scotland. There are various reasons, no doubt, to account for the difference — the greater inaccessibility of Scotland; the absence of good country inns; the greater compactness and general get-about-ability of the southern hill districts; last, and most important, the sporting character of Highland properties.

This last point regarding hunting, fishing, and shooting on Highland estates was indeed important, and will be expanded later. The comments on the state of hillwalking in Scotland should be taken with a dose of scepticism. The Scottish Rights of Way & Access Society, one of the oldest, (if not the oldest), recreation lobby group in the world, was established in 1845,with the intention of defending rights of way in the Pentland Hills and around Edinburgh. Landowners in the mid-18th century were becoming increasingly irritated with walkers on their land, and we must assume that the Pentlands were then, as now, a popular area for walking. Ramsay must have been aware of this, but as a landowner himself, he presumably remained in that camp. Ramsay continued –

> ...the fact remains that hitherto hill-climbing has been comparatively little practiced in Scotland. No special facilities have existed for it. It has been confined to a certain number of stock mountains, lying on the main routes, ascended and re-ascended by well-worn paths, frequented principally by tourists, and that only in the zenith of the tourist season... Added to this, the glory of climbing hills in the winter was unknown.

A comparison of Alpine and Scottish snows followed, arriving at the summary that in Scotland the snow, particularly towards the approach of spring, was a help rather than a hindrance in overcoming steep routes – the reverse, he said, of the Alpine situation – *'Steep gullies, almost precipitous, are often plastered right over with a splendid coating of firm frozen snow, hard to cut, but which afford splendid foothold under a well-wielded axe.'*

The only real danger Ramsay had come across in Scotland was in *'that most delightful of all luxuries - a glissade.'* He described a personal experience on Ben Achaladair at Easter 1894, when he slipped and, heading towards jagged rocks about 400 or 500ft below, just managed to come to a halt 50ft above them by spreading his arms out in the snow. Continuing to look back to earlier days, and knowing that a club was about to be formed in Scotland, Ramsay stated that –

> I had often longed for the existence of such a club…I had been for years and years expatiating, in season and out of season, on the delights of hill-climbing, but I had found my enthusiasm invariably met by nothing better than an amused incredulity. With the notable exception [of his friend Professor Veitch] … I had never, outside the limits of my own family, met with a single Scotsman who cared seriously to practice the art of mountaineering.

Indeed, Ramsay's elder brother was Sir James Henry Ramsay, the eldest of three brothers and the 10th Baronet (1832–1925). He had climbed in the Alps and had made an ascent of Mont Blanc.[5] However, one has to wonder just how isolated Ramsay was as a senior academic. Besides the above quote, there is no known evidence indicating Ramsay's frustration at not meeting another Scottish mountaineer. If he had been that keen on finding a Scottish club, there was little to prevent him from writing a letter to the Glasgow Herald suggesting the formation of one, as done by Naismith – but more of that later. By the 1850s then, Scotland was on the tourist trail; many hills had been walked up, a few scrambling routes had been pioneered in Skye. It was a beginning, if a tentative one.

❄ ❄ ❄

The Alpine Club of London (AC) was founded in 1857, but there were also several early clubs in Scotland. Two were in reality social clubs, founded by men of similar backgrounds for the purpose of having a good time round a dinner table, occasionally with an outdoor theme. The earliest known was the Highland Mountain Club of Lochgoilhead. This held an annual meeting on Midsummer Day and had been founded in 1815. They met on a local hill and enjoyed food and presumably the national drink. It would be stretching any definition to regard it as a mountaineering club.

The Gaiter Club was a similar, strongly socially based club, founded in 1849 by John Burns, 1st Baron Inverclyde. Lord Inverclyde went on to become a founder of the shipping company G & J Burns and a partner in the Cunard Steamship Company. He was an avid sportsman with perhaps yachting as his primary interest. Friends in this club included Sir Archibald Campbell, Lord Palmerston, Dr Norman Macleod (chaplain to Queen Victoria) and others. Burns was the founder, indeed deviser, its first and continual President, its life and soul. The Club's motto was *Flumina amo silvasque*, basically, 'love the stream and wood'. One of their rules was that *'There shall be no upright speaking in the Club.'* Its mere existence prevented any formality. The banning of speeches set free every tongue to wag in a spirit of fearless conviviality, undismayed by the horror of having to concoct a speech, or the still worse horror of having to listen to speech-makers. But this was not quite a mountaineering club.

In 1866, some nine years following the formation of the Alpine Club, we see the formation of the Cobbler Club in Glasgow. In January 1895, Professor Ramsay wrote the obituary for his friend Professor Veitch, who had died the previous September.[6] John Veitch (1829–1894), was a native of Peebles and Professor of Logic at St Andrews University. The obituary also told of the formation of the Cobbler Club –

> It was the love of the hills that first brought him and me together; and it was in the Old College in the High Street [Glasgow], about the year 1866, that was formed the first Mountaineering Club in Scotland - undoubted progenitor (though I have hitherto scrupulously concealed the fact from our Secretary) of the Scottish Mountaineering Club. The Club consisted of three members - Professor Veitch, Mr Campbell Colquhoun of Clathick, and myself; its name was the Cobbler Club; and its object was to promote the climbing of every hill-top that could be climbed from Glasgow in winter-time within the limits of a Saturday excursion.

Glasgow was the largest conurbation in Scotland, it had a thriving University, and most of all it had wonderful mountain scenery within a reasonably close distance. The club was named after the hill informally adopted by generations of Glasgow climbers, The Cobbler, above Arrochar. We have to burst Ramsay's bubble of self-promotion here however, and downplay his promotion of the Cobbler Club as the '*…undoubted progenitor*' of the Scottish Mountaineering Club (SMC). Note that the object of the club specifically mentioned winter-time; no easy, long summer rambles for this club, but the short days of winter. As academics and landowners, Veitch, Colquhoun and Ramsay would have shot off to their respective estates for their long summer holidays. Ramsay continued –

> In this way, many a good height was discovered and scoured over, from Tinto to Ben Lomond, from Dunmyot to Dungoyne, from Earl's Seat to Neilson Pad, in weather of every kind; many were the cracks we had with country folks by the way, many the snug old farm-houses penetrated for shelter or information.

The second half of the 19th century in Scotland saw the formation of natural history societies; these overlapped civic interests in the country, and were to some extent a reaction to the negative effects of urbanisation, the rise of industrial commerce, urban poverty in Scotland and latterly an underlying anxiety about the empire. Research into these societies, of which there were over 40, showed that some two-thirds were founded after 1870. They promoted a healthy civil society, with natural history fieldwork, public museums, and other urban improvements.

The Aberdeen schoolmaster William Alexander Ewen had an interest in early Scottish Mountain Clubs, and in a survey of Scottish Climbing Clubs in 1946 he mentions several such, including the Innerleithen Alpine Club, founded April 1889 and seemingly lasting five years.[7] They published an illustrated book of their walks, and according to this, the club was formed to study the botany, natural history, and archaeology of the district, which lies south of Edinburgh in the Scottish Borders.

The heart of Scotland produced a club in 1875, with the formation of the Perthshire Mountain Club (PMC). This was a section of the Perthshire Society of Natural Science, itself founded in 1867. Qualification for membership was the ascent of a Perthshire mountain of over 3,000ft. There was a Cairnmaster as Chief Officer who, seated on the cairn, initiated new members, a Quaighbearer being in attendance. Such outings were for participants both social and scientific, reflecting an interest in both the moral values of outdoor recreation, and a developing environmental awareness. This is exemplified by one description of a summer meet of the PMC, in July 1885, when they ascended the Perthshire Stuc a' Chroin and gained its summit.[8]

> Here, amidst the driving mist and pelting rain, a meeting of the Mountain Club was held, at the exact hour for which summonses had been issued. In the absence of the Cairnmaster, the cairn was occupied by the Scribe and Annalist, and the Geometer having declared the altitude of the hill to be 3189 feet above sea-level, a number of new members were initiated, the Quaighbearer being in attendance with the Quaigh. After the toasts peculiar to the Club had been duly celebrated, and other business transacted, the members proceeded to investigate the botany of the peak so far as the mists permitted.

Perhaps the most interesting member of the PMC was Mr Francis Buchanan White (1842–1894), who was Scribe and Annalist and eventually became Cairnmaster. A Scottish doctor and naturalist from Perth, he was a keen botanist and entomologist, concentrating on the Hemiptera (the 'true bugs', including aphids and shield bugs); he also published articles on British Willows. His *Flora of Perthshire* was posthumously published in 1898. A pioneer in biogeography, his later hill explorations were restricted by rheumatism and heart problems. He may be regarded as a major influence in founding the PMC, which may in turn be considered as one of the very first mountain clubs, though there is no evidence of mountaineering *per se*.

There is a reference in the SMC Journal of January 1891 to another walking club – The Sandah Club – (*S*pring *and A*utumn *H*oliday Club). In his article,[9] John M Macharg, an original member (OM) of the SMC, described the club as being a '*little mountaineering fraternity, and consists of about half-a-dozen members. It was in existence some years before the Scottish Mountaineering Club, and has done good work...*' Their good work seems to have been confined to hillwalks. Another and probably similar club was the 'Edinburgh Tramps.' At least half-a-dozen OMs of the SMC confessed to being members, including TFS Campbell, FJ Dewar, WR Lester, RA

Robertson, and JG Stott. We have no date for the formation of either the Sandah Club or the Edinburgh Tramps, but most of their members became OMs of the SMC, and were aged under 30 in 1889. The Dundee Rambling Club, founded in 1886, contributed a couple of OMs and some eight other members to the SMC prior to the Great War. As we will see in a later chapter, it was the coalescence of Alpine experience and ambition from individuals around Scotland which was to lead to the formation of the first genuine mountaineering club.

❄ ❄ ❄

In a book examining the rise of tourism in Scotland,[10] Katherine Grenier discusses the Victorian views of the Scottish scenery. Prevalent in early travellers was the commonly voiced opinions as to the sterility, bleakness, awfulness, emptiness and so on of the landscape. As an example, even while literally walking over grass or standing by a tree in the Loch Coruisk basin, these travellers would state that no vegetation was visible, no life seen. Grenier voices the opinion that the source of the terror associated with visits to lochs such as Coruisk was the '*complete lack of human associations…The Cuillins often seemed to be not only untouched by humanity, but untouchable.*'[11] For this negativity, particularly in the descriptions of the Loch Coruisk basin, we also have to accuse Walter Scott for his statement in the *Lord of the Isles* that Coruisk was devoid of vegetation. Visitors for the most part were echoing parrot fashion what they had read, even as they were standing on vegetation, without recognising that what they had read was patently inaccurate.

According to another historian, Marjorie Morgan, such wild scenery embodied everything which made the English tourist uncomfortable while outdoors in Scotland. The mountains were on a vast scale compared to the more gentle landscapes they were used to, and they felt '*ill at ease*', and '*confined and oppressed.*'[12] This feeling, while repelling some, attracted others. The Scottish mountains for some were a horror show, from which they could emerge frightened but unhurt and thrilled. Even visually, by way of watercolours and oil paintings, these feelings were shown, with glens lined with overhanging rocks, exaggerated angles echoing the feelings of any visitor bold enough to brave the rough way through.

❄ ❄ ❄

There were by now a number of experienced mountaineers in Scotland, many of whom climbed in the Alps during the summer, slowly beginning to realise that Scotland, too, could have something to offer. Their numbers were low, with probably fewer than 25 active alpinists in Scotland up to 1900. This number is based on the number of Alpine Club members who joined the SMC from 1889 up until 1900 and were based in Scotland.[13]

Though few in number, they were committed and enthusiastic, and, as we will see in Chapter 4, they would transform mountaineering in Scotland. Before that, however, we return to the Isle of Skye where, after a seeming lull in the action, a new character appears.

Alexander Nicolson was born at Husabost in Skye, on the 27th September 1827. His father, Malcolm Nicolson, was a tacksman under Macleod of Macleod. (A tacksman — Scottish Gaelic: *Fear-Taic*, meaning *supporting man* — was a land-holder of intermediate legal and social status in Scottish Highland society. He could sub-let the land.) John Veitch described meeting the 18-year old student for the first time, following a college exam in Glasgow -

> ...he was standing with his back against a railing in George Street, pondering perhaps over the kind of answers he had made to the questions, and his chance of success. A tall, slim, fair lad, he was dressed in a long brown greatcoat; something in the look of the grey blue eyes, and the gentle, but somewhat languid expressions of the face, attracted me. We had some brief talk. Thence there sprang up a friendship and affection which was never broken, which for many years – all during our college days – was of the frankest, intensest kind. We met nearly every day or evening, for winter after winter. He was one of the most lovable men I have known, – simple, guileless, unworldly, and in all things true, – with a humour peculiarly his own, and a feeling for poetry, especially Gaelic song, evidently born with him, and due to his Celtic and Scandinavian heredity.[14]

Nicolson quickly became a very good Latin and Greek scholar, but initially aimed for the Church as a career. This he abandoned, finding that, partly through the writings of Tennyson and Carlyle, he became disenchanted about Church confessions and creeds. He then fell back on using literature as a living, in newspapers, and as a sub-editor on the eighth edition of the Encyclopaedia Britannica. He moved on to Law and was called to the Scottish Bar in 1860. This was not particularly successful, though there may have been mitigating circumstances as Veitch explained –

> This has been by some, I think unduly, attributed to indolence or lethargy on his part. The truth in the main is, that he was not fortunate enough to have cases offered to him, and had no chance of showing either energy or the opposite of it. The man and his environments did not apparently suit each other. He would have found his true sphere in a chair of Gaelic Literature.

Nicolson was in fact offered the chair, but reluctantly turned it down, a decision he would come to regret. There is another description of his character, by Walter Smith, which is found in a Memoir published in a book of verses by Nicolson after his death.[15]

> ALEXANDER NICOLSON was perhaps as true a type of the Scottish Celt as this age has seen. Not that he was a pure Celt either, for there was a strain of Norse blood in him, as there is in many of the men of Skye and the Lews. But it

> had been so diluted in the course of time as to leave him practically as thorough a Highlander as ever rejoiced to speak the Gaelic tongue. Somehow the pure Celt is not a success in this life; not for want of abilities, not because he has not force, both mental and bodily, to hold his own with the best. But he is apt to be dreamy, to work by fits and starts, to fail in that persistency which alone secures its end… Nicolson, with all his brilliant faculties "and I have known few men more richly gifted" was certainly not successful, except in winning many warm friends, and never alienating any of them.

Appointed Sheriff-substitute or Stewart of the Stewarty of Kirkcudbright in 1872, he remained there until transferred to Greenock in 1885. He retired in 1889 due to ill-health. Nicolson, '*…a big-boned Celt, with a look of strength and kindliness in his large and strongly marked features,*'[16] was perhaps the most popular man of his time in Edinburgh. He must have been a natural mountaineer, for he took to it easily on his return to Skye, on holiday in 1865. There were at that time few visitors, according to Nicolson, but with the opening of the railway to Strome in 1870 and a series of articles in the magazine *Good Words* in 1875, numbers increased rapidly. *Good Words* was edited by Dr Norman MacLeod, had a national distribution, and was widely read. The Dingwall-Strome rail connection, opened in August 1870, meant it was possible for travellers and mail to reach Portree from Edinburgh in 15 hours. (The Dingwall and Skye Railway was opened in 1870 but only went as far as Strome Ferry on Loch Carron. It would be another 27 years before the railway reached the terminus at Kyle of Lochalsh.) Nicolson wrote in *Good Words* –

> When I knew Skye first, the tourist was among its rarer Fauna. It was known to exist, and the fact that Dr. Johnson and Sir Walter [Scott] had taken the trouble of visiting it was in its favour. But few strangers, except yachtsmen, bagmen, and a stray geologist now and then, ever invaded it. The facilities for getting to it were limited, and such a phenomenon as a male waiter in a white neckcloth was as unknown to the humble inns of the period (they were not called hotels then) as an electric telegraph or a needle-gun. Things are different now. There can be no doubt, whether one likes the fact or not, that Skye actually has become fashionable.[17]

Nicolson's first route was in 1865, guided by the son of Duncan MacIntyre, the gamekeeper at Sligachan. They followed the Forbes / MacIntyre route up Sgurr nan Gillean. This was the fifth ascent. In descent, Nicolson wished for something more sporting, as he always liked to do, and suggested the north-west ridge, going down Coire a' Bhasteir. His guide was quite willing, though he said it had never been done before. Nicolson took the lead, described in an article written during his retirement –

> We proceeded very carefully down that pinnacled ridge till we came to a cleft which seemed to be the only possible way of getting to the bottom, and down which the only mode of progression was crawling on our backs. During the last

few yards of our vermicular descent we could not see where we were to stop, and great was my satisfaction when I found my heels resting at the foot of the precipice among a heap of débris, and nothing formidable between us and the depths of Coir-a-Bhàsadair. Having plenty of time before us, and our appetite for climbing only increased by what we had done, we went round the corrie at the foot of the rocks, and up to the top of Bruthach-na-frithe, from which we had a glorious view to the west and north of the parts.

[vermicular - Like a worm in form or movement]

Where the sun sinks beyond Hunish Head,
Swimming in glory,
As he goes down to his ocean bed,
Studded with islands.'[18]

Nicolson's writings, both in *The Scotsman* in 1872, and in *Good Words* magazine in 1875 certainly helped to popularise the island. In a series of articles he described the scenery and various walks and hills. Here he describes a party setting out from Sligachan Inn to visit Coruisk; five ladies and four gentlemen, some on horses –

...one lady's equipment would have gladdened the heart of Sir Walter Scott, her skirt being a plaid of her own clan tartan, as well became the daughter of a chief. This is one of the many uses to which a plaid can be turned, of which no other garment is susceptible. With the help of a belt, it can, in a few minutes, be made into a full dress for a man; it is the best and lightest of wraps by day, and serves for bed-clothes at night; it can be used as a bag; it will serve as a sail for a boat; it is valuable as a rope in rock-scrambling; it can be turned into a curtain, an awning, a carpet, a cushion, a hammock. Its uses, in fact, are endless, and as a garment it has this superiority over every other, that *there's room in't for twa!*[19]

Nicolson described the Inaccessible Pinnacle in passing –

There is only one peak of all these which is really inaccessible, and that is the summit of Scur Dearg. It consists of a pillar of rock, about fifty feet above the rest of the ridge, and nearly perpendicular. It might be possible, with ropes and grappling irons, to overcome it; but the achievement seems hardly worth the trouble. That pillar, as seen from a distance, has a very peculiar and puzzling appearance; from some points it looks like a chimney can, from others like a wild beast's horn.[20]

Nicolson would in all probability have been more than able to climb the Inaccessible Pinnacle, had he so decided; it would be climbed for the first time by the Pilkington brothers in 1880. In February 1872 he made an ascent of Gillean, perhaps the first time the mountain had been climbed during the winter months, with conditions being mentioned as cold and dull. In 1873 Nicolson made the first recorded ascents of Sgurr na Banachdich and Sgurr Alasdair, the highest summit on Skye. On the latter ascent he was in the company of a local shepherd.

> I had been told at Glen Breatal that another peak, a very beautiful one, which forms a prominent object from the house there, had never been ascended, and had foiled the Ordnance men. This naturally stirred my desire to attempt it, which I did, accompanied by a shepherd, A. [Angus] Macrae, well acquainted with all the hills and passes, and a first-rate climber. He had a peculiar style of walk, a sort of amble, and seemed to glide up the hillside like a cloud. He, too, had never been up, and had never heard of any body having done it.

They firstly climbed Sgurr na Banachdich, moved on to below the Inaccessible Pinnacle, found their way barred so descended into Coire Lagain –

> ...a deep stony corrie, with a small dark loch at its lower end, from which on the previous day I had obtained, out of the midst of driving mist, a single glimpse of this same peak, one of the wildest objects I ever saw...

This peak, for which the shepherd knew no name, Nicolson proposed to name Scur-a-Laghain. They continued up the Great Stone Shoot –

> The climb up on the other side of the corrie was stiff and warm, and some judgment was required to find a way, and still more when it came to circumventing the peak. We did it, however, without much difficulty: one or two places were somewhat trying, requiring good grip of hands and feet; but on the whole I have seen worse places. Whether this peak was really ascended for the first time that day, I cannot say, but it seemed very like it. There was, at any rate, no sign on the top of any one having ever been on it before, and, of course, we thought it our duty to make up for that by erecting a cairn, and adding a few feet to the height of the peak.[21]

The peak was later named Sgurr Alasdair, in honour of Sheriff Nicolson. He returned to make another first ascent of a mountain which gave him and his unnamed companion a stirring adventure. The pair had been visiting an artist at Loch Coruisk. It was September, in the middle of the afternoon, and no time for a long expedition, let alone one which had not before been done.

Nicolson made the first ascent of Sgurr Dubh Mor on Saturday 6th September, 1873. Through some assiduous detective work by Pedlar, the date has been firmly fixed, making it a few days after his ascent of Sgurr Alasdair. His companion for Sgurr Dubh Mor was almost certainly a geologist, one of two staying at Sligachan, along with the wife of one, and Professor Veitch. Nicolson knew there would be insufficient light left but he also knew there would be a moon, and checking his pocket barometer, he was confident that the weather would hold. So off they set. In actual fact, the full moon was that very night, which was probably no coincidence.

The pair scrambled up the rocks above Loch Scavaig, adjacent to the Mad Burn, climbing into An Garbh-Choire, one of the roughest corries on Skye, a jumbled obstacle course of rough and razor-edged boulders. At half-height they sheltered from a rain shower, before continuing. Nicolson's barometer proved itself as the clouds cleared and they gained the summit at 7pm. They now had to descend Coire an Lochain to reach the Coruisk basin, hopefully before it became too dark. About half-way down they came upon a steep wall, whereupon Nicolson employed his woollen plaid rug, of the type he describes above. Using this, his friend would anchor his heels in the ground, allowing Nicolson to descend using the plaid for security. His friend would then slide down the wall to land on Nicolson's shoulders. This they had to repeat several times during the descent, before gaining safe ground above Loch Coruisk –

> I certainly never in the same space of time went through so much severe bodily exercise as in that descent from Scùr-Dubh to Coiruisg. My very finger-tops were skinned from contact with the coarse-grained rock. But the difficulties of the descent were compensated for when we got, with thankful hearts, into the full flood of the moonlight on the last floor of the valley above Coiruisg.[22]

Nicolson's plan was not only to ascend Sgurr Dubh Mor, it was also to see Coruisk in the moonlight. This they certainly did, and his description is full of the joy of that sight. Onwards they had to go however, and initially they attempted the Lesingham Smith / MacIntyre route over Druim nam Ramh to Harta Coire. They were defeated by steep rock and reluctantly descended to follow the west bank of Loch Coruisk, up and over Druim Hain and so regained Glen Sligachan and the Sligachan Inn at 3am. As it was a Sunday morning, they did not wish to make more noise than necessary but a session of bell ringing eventually opened the door for them, with their host as genial as ever, despite the hour. They ate, '*laid us gingerly down on our abraded joints*', and slept till noon.

The Highland Clearances had more or less run its course between 1785 and 1850, with its autocratic and often brutal removal of tens of thousands of clansmen, making way for large-scale sheep farming. A less violent period of discontent took place from 1883-88, with the so-called Highland Land War, or Crofters' War. This was a response to crofter and cottar agitation with excessively high rents, lack of security of tenure, and deprivation of de facto rights of access to land. In 1883 the Napier Commission was set up, as a royal commission and public enquiry into the condition of crofters and cottars. The chairman was Francis Napier, who was the 10th Lord Napier, and the government of the time was William Gladstone's Liberal government.

There were five other members of the commission, and Alexander Nicolson was one of them. The commission's report in 1886 has been described as the most voluminous, authoritative and damning ever compiled on the inequities and hardships experienced by the Gaelic tenantry during the 19th century. As a Skye man, Nicolson would have been instrumental in ensuring that the commission be presented with clear evidence. The report went some way towards calming the agitation, and led to the Crofters' Holdings (Scotland) Act of 1886, though this would be short-lived.

Nicolson ceased climbing in 1886, after making his personal second ascent of Ben Nevis. In 1892 the SMC honoured Nicolson with the office of Vice-Presidency. In his Obituary Notice, his friend John Veitch wrote of the shock of his unexpected death the following year. '*...he was known to almost all the members, and we shall not readily forget his genial face and cheery presence at the Annual Dinner* [of the SMC] *in the Waterloo Hotel.*' John Veitch was the incoming President, and gave the speech *Our Bens and Glens*. In reply to this, Alexander Nicolson replied with his new song, *The Isle of Skye*. This was on Tuesday 13th December. In September of that year, he had contributed an article to the SMC Journal. It was a version of his articles previously published in *Good Words*. In his memoir preface in a book of verse by Nicolson, Walter Smith recalled the final period in his life –

> Possibly the memory of such old friends somewhat saddened his latter days. Still more likely, that weak action of the heart to which I have already alluded, had its depressing influence. He knew of it; but he never spoke of it, and none of us suspected it till the sad end came. The night before he had passed at one of those big tea-meetings where Highlanders congregate annually, and sing Gaelic songs, and listen to English speeches. Next morning, the 13th of January 1893, sitting chatting over his coffee with one of his nieces, suddenly "his countenance changed," and he passed into the great unknown.

Ben Humble summed up Nicolson and his place in mountaineering thus –

> Science came first with Forbes and guides went with him. Nicolson opened the door wide; he was the first real mountaineer and explorer among the Cuillins. His descent of the Coruisk face of Sgur Dubh in darkness was the finest thing done in climbing in Britain up till that time...[23]

Forbes certainly arrived on Skye with scientific research in mind, but his curiosity took him beyond this to the summit of Sgurr nan Gillcan; the hard evidence for glaciation was not to be found on the peaks but in the corries below. Nicolson's mind set was purely one of pleasure in the outdoor environment, best found for him in the mountains and corries of his true home, the Isle of Skye.

In September 1870 Sgurr nan Gillean was the scene of a fatal accident to a tourist, probably the first to occur to a visitor to the Scottish mountains. John Thom from Liverpool and a friend set off for the hill and Thom continued alone when his friend decided not to continue. Reaching the summit alone, Thom left his name in a bottle, but was killed on the descent.

The next mountaineer to arrive on the Island was the Rev William Angus Knight. By the time of his arrival in Skye in 1873 he had two Alpine seasons to his credit, including an ascent of the Matterhorn. On August 12th, with the guide Angus MacPherson he climbed Sgurr nan Gillean by the 'Tourist Route'. Then, after Knight had financially persuaded his reluctant guide to accompany him, the pair scrambled down the north ridge of the mountain to the gap between the fourth pinnacle and Gillean and made the first ascent of the fourth pinnacle, which up till then had been known either as 'The Needle' or the 'Little Horn'; it is now known as Knight's Peak.

Amusingly, the height of Knight's Peak has, with various heightings, oscillated several times around 914m (approximately 3000ft), above which it would be a Munro Top. Recent data held by the Ordnance Survey, following a re-survey, confirmed in August 2006 a height of 914.95m, making it over the 'magic' height of 3,000ft and therefore a Munro Top.[24] In September 2013 the peak was surveyed again, by a commercial company under the aegis of the Munro Society and the SMC. Knight's Peak was found to be 16.5cm too low to qualify as a Top. Presumably, if we wait long enough, isostatic rebound, with Scotland slowly recovering height following the last of the ice ages, will reduce this shortage, and the peak will resume its former position in the list. On the other hand, rising sea levels due to climatic change could negate this. Such diversions are meat for some, but the mountains remain.

❄ ❄ ❄

George Gilbert Ramsay, whom we met at the start of this section, was influential in several respects; one chance event was to show him as an inspiration for one young mind in particular. William Wilson Naismith (1856–1935) was born in Hamilton, just south-east of Glasgow. His father William practised as a physician for two decades in Hamilton, living in the family home Auchincampbell. He had married Mary Anne Murray, of farming stock, and they had two children, Annie and William. Both parents were fond of walking the hills, and Willie Naismith, as he became known, started when he was six or seven, climbing Ben Lomond when about nine. When aged 12, he and an 18-year old female friend made a wintry ascent of Beinn Bhreac (454m) above Tighnabruaich, initially following a frozen burn then kicking steps in snow. Naismith was educated at Gilbertfield House School, Hamilton.

In 1872, at Glasgow University, Professor Ramsay gave his Junior Latin Class a lecture on Alpine Climbing. Naismith was especially fascinated when Ramsay demonstrated the use of his ice axe. To add to this diet, a copy of Edward Whymper's *Scrambles* was '*…devoured with the most intense delight.*' This classic book of early explorations in the Alps had been published the year before, and Naismith thought it was a book that every boy should possess.[25]

Naismith graduated in accountancy from Glasgow University, a profession which we presume suited his careful, considered approach to life, though it was not always so. As his obituary in the Hamilton Advertiser put it, '*Hamilton contemporaries may remember him, to put it mildly, as a rather careless, pleasure-loving young man; and such indeed he would have owned himself to be.*'[26] However, he took up Christianity, reformed his character, and would eventually do much unpaid work for the Church in a financial position. In due course he ceased to climb on Sundays.

In April 1880, the 24-year old Naismith and two friends walked the 30 miles from Stenscholl, in Staffin, to Sligachan. Friday the 23rd of April was a day of east winds. The next day they strolled up Glen Sligachan in rain and fog, thinking an ascent of Sgurr nan Gillean was out of the question. It cleared for a while however, and they decided to attempt the south-east ridge. The fickle and fast-changing Skye weather closed down on them again and they adopted the plan of leaving stones on prominent rocks, the long axes of the stones indicating the course. As the accountancy-trained Naismith described – '*These "stations" were usually within sight of one another, and were carefully numbered and entered in a notebook, compass bearings being also occasionally jotted down.*'[27]

Once on the summit, they entered their names in a paper deposited in a bottle. From this they learned that the previous ascent had been in September of the previous year. Using their stone indicators, they carefully made their descent, finishing, as planned, at Camasunary, having brought with them a letter of introduction for the farmer there. The following morning they made an ascent of Bla Bheinn.

The next day, Monday 26th April, Naismith and his companions made what they thought was the first ascent of the North Top of Sgurr a' Mhadaidh. The Ordnance Survey (OS) had surveyed the Cuillin in 1877 but only published the six-inch map showing the main section in 1879. The one-inch map, scaled down from the six-inch, was not published until 1885, and then contained several confusing errors. It was only after referring to this 1885 one-inch map for his 1890 article that Naismith realised that they had actually made the first ascent of the North Peak of Bidein Druim nan Ramh.

On Sgurr nan Gillean the summit rocks had some fresh snow, while on the Monday the weather deteriorated somewhat, leading to sleet and snow. Partly due to the confusion installed by the OS., and partly due to Naismith's narrative, it is difficult to pin down their route precisely, but Pedlar has made a best case scenario.[28] The party climbed up into Coir' a' Tairneilear and gained the Main Ridge at the low point between An

Caisteal (at the time unnamed) and the north peak of Bidein Druim nan Ramh, Bealach Harta. They attempted to gain the North Peak by a ledge but this tapered away to nothing and they returned to the bealach to try the peak from the Harta Corrie side. However, because Naismith thought they were climbing the northern peak of Sgurr a' Mhadaidh, he presumed they were on the 'Coruisk side' of the mountain. After some difficulty with outward-sloping holds and crossing a six-foot wide gap, they finally reached the summit where they found no trace of previous ascents and built a cairn.

Their target was now Bruach na Frithe, but the intervening ridge '*...was sharp and serrated, and would in any case have occupied much time.*' Instead they descended the large couloir (presumably the one they had gained Harta Bealach by) and made a long detour which involved '*...scaling a smooth unbroken slope of wet grass nearly 1,000 feet in height.*' The upper part of this, Naismith wrote, was terribly steep, even steeper he thought than the slope adjacent to the Gray Mare's Tail (a 60m waterfall near Moffat). An ice axe, he thought, to serve as an anchor and also to cut the occasional step, would have been of use on a slope such as this.

A week later he would make an ascent of Ben Nevis, with the same two unnamed clerical companions. This ascent, on the 2nd May, was written up by a local newspaper man as being the first without guides. The party had tried to find a guide, but failing that set off with a compass and an 'indifferent' map. With walking sticks, they soon gained the slopes above Lochan Meall an t-Suidhe, where the snow began. In mist, they decided to wait for a clearing, spending two hours learning how to glissade. This almost ended disastrously when one of the party began to glissade down a couloir, picking up speed on its hard snow and only halting when he met a projecting rock. The remainder of the ascent went without major incident, gaining the summit cairn in ever deepening soft snow. In a footnote to his article on the Cuillin, and referring to the Ben Nevis ascent, Naismith remarked that they had found eight to ten feet of snow at the summit.[29]

We recall that as a schoolboy, Naismith had been fascinated by Professor Ramsay's demonstration of an ice axe. However, Naismith was not to visit the Alps until 1883. In 1882, his mother and sister came back from Switzerland and urged him to make a visit – at least his sister Annie did, as his mother did not want him to '*go into dangerous places.*' He had no Alpinist friends but worked very hard at his holiday and made just under 100,000ft of ascent in a month , though only of minor snow climbs. Someone lent him an axe for two climbs, but otherwise he used an alpenstock.

In recalling these early ascents in the Alps, Naismith does not say whether or not he employed a guide.[30] Indeed, to anyone wishing to learn more of Naismith, he is particularly frustrating, leaving behind almost nothing personal about his mountaineering. His tiny notebook in the NLS has little more than a date and hill name for each entry.

The following year, in March 1884, he had an educating experience on a very icy Ben More, again carrying an alpenstock. This day was his epiphany, realising that Scotland in winter should be treated as seriously as the Alps – with ropes and axes. Setting off alone, and with the long alpenstock, he at first attempted the north-east ridge, but found the slope too formidable. He then rounded the mountain into its eastern corrie, Coire Chaorach, climbing up an easy snow slope to gain the col between Ben More and Stob Binnein. Careful moves up the south ridge of Ben More, using rocks jutting out of the ice and choosing the easiest routes, allowed him to gain the summit. A careful descent, a brief attempt on the ridge leading up to Stob Binnein, and the realisation followed that it was far too icy to be tackled without better equipment. He then descended into the glen leading to Loch Doine to the south and eventually his planned stop at Strathyre –

> The experience of that day proved to me that in winter and spring the higher Scottish mountains ought to be treated as seriously as Alpine peaks—with the same equipment of axes and a rope…the trouble was that I did not at that early period know of a single friend who would care to join me at such an absurd game.[31]

As a pointer to Naismith's fitness, his route would have been in the order of 38km, with no mention of having used any means of transport. In 1879 at the age of 23 he walked from his Hamilton home to the summit of Tinto and back, a distance of 90km.

As Naismith wished to return to the Alps and build on his experiences of 1883, he sent away to London for an ice axe, built after Whymper's design. He found it badly balanced when compared with the '*modern Swiss axes*', but it gave its owner good use, including an ascent of the Matterhorn, until it came to a bad end, being dropped into a crevasse in the Gabelhorn Glacier. This was probably in 1887, on his second visit to the Alps. He also made a solo ascent of the Eiger, date unknown. With what must have caused some frustration, Naismith appears to have done no more winter climbs in Scotland until 1890. This situation, he wrote, was due to a lack of encouragement for people to '*…use their axes near home.*'[32]

Before looking at what changed this state however, we must return to Skye, where rock climbing was about to burst into bloom.

References

1. Grierson, Rev. Thomas. *Autumnal Rambles Among the Scottish Mountains*, (Edinburgh: James Hogg, 1850.1st Edn.)
2. Mitchell, Ian R. *Scotland's Mountains Before the Mountaineers*, (Edinburgh: Luath Press, 2004, 2nd Edn.)
3. Grierson, 13-14.

4. Ramsay, Professor GG. *The Formation of the Scottish Mountaineering Club*, SMCJ 4, 20, May 1896, 73-91.
5. Ramsay, Paul. *Personal correspondence* (Nov. 2010).
6. Ramsay, George, *In Memorium – Professor John Veitch*, SMCJ 3, 16, January 1895, 175-182.
7. Bell, *J.H.B. Scottish Climbing Clubs: A Survey. II.* SMCJ 23, 137, April 1946, 308.
8. *Proceedings of the Perthshire Society of Natural Science Session 1881-82, 1885-86* (Perth, 1886), July 18, 1885, p.271.
9. Macharg, John M. *Ben Ghlas and Ben Lawers*. SMCJ 1, 4, January 1891, 158-160.
10. Grenier, Katherine Haldane. *Tourism and Identity in Scotland, 1770-1914 - Creating Caledonia*, (Aldershot: Ashgate Publishing Limited, 2005. p.100.)
11. Ibid., p.100.
12. Morgan, Marjorie. *National Identities and Travel in Victorian Britain*, (Basingstoke & New York: Palgrave Macmillan, 2001.)
13. Aitken, Bob. *Personal communication*. February 2014.
14. Veitch, Professor John. *In Memorium. The Late Sheriff Nicolson*. SMCJ 2, May 1893, 254-258.
15. Nicolson, Alexander. *Verses*. (Edinburgh: David Douglas, 1893).
16. Nicolson, Alexander. [no relation] , *History of Skye*, (Alex. Maclaren & Sons: Glasgow, 1930, p. 423.)
17. Nicolson, Alexander. *Good Words*, from Part I of an article on Skye. 1875.
18. Nicolson, Alexander. LL.D., Advocate. *Skye and Sgùr-nan-Gillean in 1865*, SMCJ, 2, 3, September 1892, 99-108.
19. Nicolson, Alexander. *Good Words*, from Part 2 of an article on Skye. 1875.
20-22 Nicolson, Alexander. *Good Words*, from Part 3 of an article on Skye. 1875.
23. Humble, Ben H. *The Cuillin of Skye*, (London: Robert Hale, 1952, p.33.)
24. Ordnance Survey. *Personal Correspondence*, August, 2006.
25. Naismith, William. *Early Winter Climbing*. SMCJ 17, 99, April 1925, 124-132.
26. *Late Mr W. W. Naismith – Member of an old Hamilton family*. Hamilton Advertiser, 5th October, 1935.
27. Naismith, W.W. *Three Days Among the Cuchullins*, SMCJ 1, 2, May 1890, 56-62.
28. Pedlar, Stuart. Across Unmeasured Space – A History of Climbing in the Cuillin. Unpublished MS. 2010.
29. Naismith, W.W. *Three Days Among the Cuchullins*, SMCJ 1, 2, May 1890, 57.
30-32. Naismith, W.W. *Early Winter Climbing*, SMCJ 17, 99, April 1925, pp.124-132.

3

Collie and Company (1880-86)

Alfred (1838–1895), Charles (1850–1918) and Lawrence Pilkington (1855–1941) were brothers from a Lancashire family whose hard work in industry would lead eventually to the glass-making company Pilkington at St Helens. They had begun to visit Skye in 1870, for shooting and fishing holidays, but it was not until 1880 that they began climbing there.

In the summer of that year the brothers, finding no grouse to shoot, decided to visit Sligachan and climb Sgurr nan Gillean. Charles and Lawrence were both members of the Alpine Club and had major alpine ascents under their belts, while the eldest, Alfred, was not an alpinist. On the 15th August, with what turned out to be misplaced confidence, they went straight at the north-west face. The mountain rebuffed them. They took this defeat with good grace however –

> After failing to get up we saw that the W. ridge was easy enough, but as it was getting late we postponed our ascent for the following day. I must say that we felt rather small, as an elder brother, who was not an Alpine Climber, was one of the party. We certainly returned with a much greater respect for the mountain than we had when we started in the morning…[1]

They succeeded on the west ridge the following day, and made an ascent of Blaven on the 17th by its west face. Finally, on the 18th, they succeeded in making the first ascent of the *Inaccessible Pinnacle*. This rocky summit feature of Sgurr Dearg was first named the Inaccessible Peak on the Admiralty Chart of Skye, 1858, and is one of the handful of summits in Scotland which require rock climbing; it is therefore the one which strikes fear in the heart of many a hillwalker intent on climbing all the Munros, and one which provides steady employment for the coterie of professional guides who usher their sometimes trembling clients up and down its very exposed flanks.

As the Pilkingtons had no reliable maps and it was misty, they hired a guide to show them the way to the foot of the Pinnacle. His name was John Mackenzie, and he would in time become one of the best known Scottish guides. He was born in 1856 on a croft in Sconser, about 5km from Sligachan. At the age of ten he had climbed Sgurr nan Gillean. According to Ashley Abraham, he made the first ascent of Sgurr a' Ghreadaidh with William N Tribe in 1870.[2] He was then aged 14, one year younger than Tribe, who would become a very competent alpinist. However, Stuart Pedlar believes this ascent is unlikely, arguing against the chance of two such youngsters meeting and being allowed to embark on such an expedition into the unknown. Also Mackenzie would have known very little English at this age (he was a native Gaelic speaker).[3]

What is known is that when the Pilkingtons reached the foot of the unclimbed pinnacle they offered to take him up and let him down, but he refused, presumably being unhappy with his current personal ability.[4] If so, he must have rapidly improved in skill and confidence, for it seems that the following year he soloed the pinnacle[5] –

> The following year a shepherd got up, after having first taken off his shoes. It was then unclimbed till Walker, Hulton, and my brother made the third ascent in 1883, since which date it has been ascended several times.[6]

On the 19th August 1886, the Reverend AH Stocker and AG Parker, two well-known English climbers, ascended the pinnacle by its short, steep, west side, and by descending via the easier east ridge thus made the first traverse of the Pinnacle. The west side is almost vertical and is usually abseiled in descent by parties who have gone up by the easy east ridge. It is currently graded Very Difficult. Keen to repeat the new route, the Pilkingtons returned in 1887. On June 2nd 1887, Charles Pilkington, Horace Walker, James Heelis, and John Mackenzie recorded the second traverse of the pinnacle, climbing its west side then descending by the east ridge –

> Desirous of following their example, and having reached this end of the rock, we asked Mackenzie, who had come with us, to carry the camera, if he would like to go with us. He had done it from the other side before. 'Oh, yes' was his ready reply. Off went his boots and we tied him on to the rope. I believe his great anxiety for some time had been that we might send him round with the luggage to the other side and not give him a chance of the climb.[7]

Also in 1887, and in different combinations, the same four made first ascents of two Cuillin summits; Sgurr Thearlaich and Sgurr Mhic Coinnich. Heading into Coire Lagan, they scrutinised Sgurr Alasdair, which then had an unclimbed top to the north-east. Charles led the way up the face at the head of the corrie, possibly climbing with Walker as Heelis was photographing, and in all probability would have remained in the corrie with

Mackenzie, helping to carry the heavy equipment. It was decided later, possibly by Collie or Naismith,[8] that this top should be named after Pilkington, as Sgurr Thearlaich, (Charles' Peak). That day the Pilkingtons had also spotted a nameless peak at the back of the corrie.

They returned the next day, 2nd June, and after making the second ascent of the Inaccessible Pinnacle's west ridge (mentioned above) they continued on to climb the peak from the col between it and Sgurr Dearg. As Mackenzie was on this ascent, the three alpinists made a humorous reference to calling it Pic Mackenzie, and so with time it has been known after their guide, Sgurr Mhic Coinnich (Mackenzie's Peak).

❄ ❄ ❄

Mackenzie is inextricably linked to another great name in Scottish mountaineering, John Norman Collie (1859–1942). The Collie family, originally Irish, emigrated to Aberdeenshire in the latter half of the 17th century, a period when Oliver Cromwell was rampaging across that country. *There is*, wrote William Garden, his obituarist in the SMCJ, '*every right to claim that he was a Scot, for his grandfather, George Collie, was a tenant of Wantonwells, Insch, an Aberdeenshire farm.*' [9] In his biography of Collie,[10] William Taylor considers that Collie's ancestry helps explain the man's characteristics –

> From the Collies he inherited the inbred caution of the Scot, the apparently ascetic nature, the dry sense of humour, the quaint old-fashioned mysticism and the wandering instincts…From the Winkworths [on his mother's side] he inherited a love of beauty, a natural skill in writing, an artistic taste exemplified in his collection of beautiful works of art, and from Stephen Winkworth [an uncle] he must surely have learned of the challenge of the mountains.

Stephen Winkworth became a member of the Alpine Club in 1861, some seven years after its founding. He and Collie had a good, close relationship, with Winkworth providing financial support during the early years of Collie's education and career. Winkworth made ascents of several major peaks in the Alps, including Mont Blanc and the Jungfrau. In these he was accompanied by his wife, an unusual occurrence for the times.

Norman Collie, as he became so addressed, was born on 10th September 1859, at Ferns Cottage, Alderley Edge, some 19km south of Manchester. He was the second son of John and Selina Collie. His mother, Selina, was a daughter of Henry Winkworth, owner of mills in Manchester producing silk. She had four sisters, in a family well known for their liberal minds and lack of stuffiness. '*They were able to comment, with intelligence and humour, on the issues of their time without lapsing into moral outrage or narrow-mindedness. It is not difficult to see where much of Norman Collie's character came from.*' [11] When he was six, his father retired to Glassel estate on lower Deeside, about

27km to the west of Aberdeen. Collie believed he first acquired his deep love for the hills from there, with the foothills of the Grampians around Banchory. The Hill of Fare (433m) was about 3km to the north-northeast, and there he spent many days exploring its slopes. Collie enjoyed five happy years there, before the family moved south to Bristol.

After a difficult school period, not helped by the family cotton business crashing during the American Civil War, Collie finally found his academic interest when he began to study science at University College in Bristol. He studied chemistry, completing a doctorate at Würzburg University, Germany (on the action of ammonia on ethyl acetoacetate). Returning home, he suffered two years as a science lecturer at Cheltenham Ladies' College, before moving to London in 1887 to take up a position as a demonstrator at University College, in the chemistry laboratory of Sir William Ramsay.

Collie suffered at Cheltenham as he had no real interest in female companionship; indeed, as Taylor remarks, '*like quite a few scientists, Collie was less interested in human beings than in ideas, objects or colour.*' He was a confirmed bachelor. In London he eventually shared a house at 20 Gower Street with a solicitor, Robert S Cox. Here he held many dinners, attended by mountaineers he came to know, the painter Colin Phillip, the medieval scholar WP Ker, and others.

The house was overlooked by the University of London and was minutes from the Chemistry Department. It is hard to escape from the perception of Collie as living the life he wanted to live; a bit of scientific research here, a deep interest in oriental ceramics, ivories and jade there, a collection of rare books, good wines and cigars, dinners with mountaineers and other friends which gained a reputation for the culinary delights. His house companion Cox supplied the silverware and furniture, Collie the rest, including vintage clarets.

He was fascinated by colours. This interest took him into early colour photography, research into the glazes of his ceramic collection, precious stones and minerals. Collie's biographer Taylor describes how his artistic leanings were intertwined with his scientific work –

> During his investigations into the effects of high energy electric discharges on gases at low temperatures, a colleague said to him, 'Collie, I truly believe that you are far more interested in the colours of the discharges than in the striking phenomena you are recording.' [12]

The colleague in question was his friend, Sir Herbert Jackson. During the latter years of the 19th century, organic chemistry was making rapid advances, particularly important for a highly industrialised nation such as Britain. Collie was a good experimenter, blowing his own glass components for analytical apparatus. Much of his interest lay in the structure, properties and synthesis of a group of organic compounds known as the tetramethyl-phosphonium salts. From this work also came the isolation of methyl fluoride which in the far off scientific future would be used in the manufacture of semiconductor and electronic products. He proposed a dynamic structure for benzene.

His insight that compounds with multiple ketomethylene groups played a role in the biosynthesis of various natural products was only vindicated in 1955. In doing so he invented the term polyketide to describe these compounds; they are now extensively used in the fields of secondary metabolism and biotechnology.[13] It was a fruitful period to be in research, as so much was as yet to be discovered about the basic properties of compounds, let alone new elements waiting to be found.

Perhaps of more interest to the layperson however would be the work in the discoveries of the elemental rare gases. Working at University College, London, as Professor William Ramsay's assistant, Collie's work was of sufficient quality for him to be promoted to Assistant Professor. He was then aged 31. The first of the inert, or 'noble' gases isolated there would be argon. This would be followed by helium.

His scientific career was not without some controversy, principally regarding the discovery of the inert gas neon. His biographer Taylor is of the opinion that Collie should be credited with its discovery in 1898, and not Ramsay, whose laboratory Collie was working in for some time.[14] What Collie himself was adamant about was his invention of the first neon light.

He was also, he claimed, the first to use X-rays for a medical purpose. In 1896, a woman who was suspected of having part of a needle embedded in her thumb had an X-ray taken, which proved that there was indeed a foreign object.[15] This had followed on from Collie suggesting at a lecture that such a photograph be taken of his own hand, where he thought there might be a piece of lead embedded, following a childhood accident when a toy pistol had exploded. He was correct.

Such interests and behaviour could indicate an inward-looking personality, and certainly Collie, other than a few long-standing friends, had little time for other people in his life. In later life he became more and more reclusive. One reason for this, as Pedlar suggests, was increasing deafness. In his book *Eye to the Hills* published in 2001, SMC member Campbell Steven recalls meeting the great man at Sligachan –

> Unfortunately, owing to his deafness, we had no great conversation with him; it would have been good indeed to hear at first hand perhaps of how he had "discovered" the Cioch back in 1906 ... As it was, we found it sad to observe him sitting all evening by himself, not easily approached, seemingly very much alone with his thoughts.[16]

It is well known that deafness can have a very inhibitory effect on a sufferer's social instincts. In addition to his climbing, other outdoor pursuits included fishing and golf.

❄ ❄ ❄

Collie first set foot on Skye in August 1886, arriving at Sligachan on the 14th with his two younger brothers Arthur and Alexander. Collie had three brothers: the eldest, George Henry, born on 13th June 1858, and known as 'Harry', emigrated to Australia and then New Zealand where he ran his own farm. They were on Skye for the fishing, but perhaps we have to thank a spell of good, dry weather for starting Collie in what would be his life-long interest in mountains. The water was low and the fishing poor, so Norman and George decided to explore the mountains. They scrambled into Coire a ' Bhasteir and, looking up, spotted two rock climbers on the face of Sgurr nan Gillean –

> I saw two mountaineers, AH Stocker and a friend, climbing on the rock face of one of the pinnacles. Hundreds of feet above me, on what appeared to me to be rock as steep as the walls of a house, they moved slowly backwards and forwards, but always getting higher till they finally reached the summit.[17]

The climbers were AH Stocker, an English parson and Alpine Club member, and AG Parker, making a possible first ascent on Knight's Peak. Collie must have been mesmerised watching the two experienced climbers, for that evening in the hotel he questioned them at length. Being told that he needed a rope, he ordered one from Buckingham by telegraph. (Before long distance telephone services were readily available or affordable, telegram services were very popular and the only way to convey information speedily over very long distances.) As for the rope ordered by telegraph, it was manufactured by John Buckingham of Shaftsbury Avenue in London. It is worth taking a look at the climbing rope then used, to highlight just how potentially hazardous climbing was, and why, for many decades, the prime rule was that '*the leader must not fall.*'

The best rope, recommended by experts, was that made by John Buckingham, to the specifications of the Alpine Club. It was made of pure manila hemp, one and a quarter-inch in circumference and available in lengths of 40, 60, 80 or 100ft. In modern usage, this equates to about 10.2mm diameter. (Manila is still used in gyms, as a suspended rope for climbing, to strengthen the upper body.) This rope weighed 6.4 lbs per 100ft (2.88kg per 30m), more so when wet, but then there was no other climbing gear to be carried at this time. As for its strength, a report in the first volume of the Alpine Club in 1864 came up with results indicating that it could withstand a fall by a 168lb (75kg) climber of 10ft (3m).

Another report came out in the SMCJ for September 1897. One of the club's best climbers was the 27-year old John Hart Bell (1870–1937), no relation to the later James HB Bell, with whom he has often been confused in history. He was a marine engineer by profession, and obviously no one's fool. With his friend EW Green he tested some old, and some new, Buckingham Alpine Club ropes. Bell and Green first tested the dead weight which the rope would lift, finding that using bowline knots, the strongest of ordinary knots, the rope broke with a load of 1,456 lbs (660kg). (A knot would be the weakest link in such a setup, with the bowline providing just over 70% of the strength of an unknotted rope.) They then tested the rope using falling weights with loops of rope about nine inches long (23cm) and 4.5ft (1.37m) of rope between the loops.

They obviously had a shock on finding that using a falling weight of 85 lbs (39kg) the rope stood a fall of 6.5ft (1.98m). This was equivalent to a fall of only 3.5ft (1.07m) with a weight of 11 stone (154 lbs or 70kg.) Bell continued by admitting that when first doing these experiments, they did not realise the great difference which the length of a rope makes in its power to stop a falling body. To explain, a longer rope will have more stretch and will have more holding power as it can absorb more force.

They then tested various lengths of cord to illustrate this point, and calculated that if they increased the length of rope between the knots to 20ft (6m), it should hold 11 stone (70kg) falling about 9ft (2.75m). As Bell commented – '*Probably many of us have had delusions as to the value of a rope hitched 20 or 30 feet below the leader on steep rocks.*' As he somewhat sardonically noted in his article, using an unreferenced quote from the Alpine Journal – '*It was an awkward moment, for the other man was not well situated for supporting a jerk at the end of 30 feet of rope, which would mean a fall of about 50 feet.*'

Bell also criticised the Alpine Club report of 1864, stating that as there were no details as to whether or not knots were used, the length of rope, and the weight used, it was impossible to estimate the value of the tests. Very obviously, to Bell and Green, a leader should try to minimise the length of fall. His final comment was that before the rope would break, a pressure of 13 cwt (660kg) would come on the ribs of a falling man. '*Whether a man has any chance of standing such a jerk without serious injury is a question for the doctors.*'[18] As we will see in a later chapter, this was a prescient observation.

There were no slings in use then, either as runners, or belays. A belayer used a 'hitch', trying to run the rope over some spike of rock. The belayer also tried to find a position where his body could be braced against a possible fall. This explains fatal accidents to roped parties, where even given that the belayer held the fall, the rope had snapped. There would be little in the way of substantial safety improvements, until nylon ropes appeared during the Second World War. (For an excellent summary of climbing ropes and techniques see the article by RA Smith.[19])

To add to this grim fact, a wet rope, unless carefully dried, was prone to rot. In his book *Mountaineering Art*, first published in 1920, Harold Raeburn gives a personal account regarding a wet rope. His rucsac, containing his boots and a very wet rope, was accidentally taken away by another climber, and was not returned for ten days or so. The rope seemed dry and to all appearances was normal. Some two months later Raeburn began to help a friend seek out some birds' eggs on a cliff. He put a walking stick into the turf, looped a rope over it, and prepared to descend.

> In fixing the rope I bent it sharply, when it at once broke half-way through. It proved to be thoroughly rotten, and unable to bear a strain of more than 50 pounds.[20]

On Skye, when Collie's new rope arrived a few days following his order, Norman and one of his brothers (unnamed) set out for Gillean but failed on the ridge. They failed the next day as well, only succeeding on a third attempt after having consulted with the guide John Mackenzie as to details of the route. The fishing enthusiast Collie had been well and truly caught by the mountains, hook, line and sinker! Indeed, Collie continued his account of this beginning by stating that – *'The temptation was too great, and for the next twenty-five years, mountain climbing became more important to me than fishing...'* Not only had Collie caught the climbing bug, he had met up with Mackenzie, in what would become one of the most famous climbing partnerships in mountaineering history.

❄ ❄ ❄

John Morton Mackenzie (1856–1934) began work at Sligachan as a pony-boy, herding tourists to and back from Loch Coruisk, squelching down boggy Glen Sligachan. There is a brief mention of him by author Robert Buchanan who in the autumn of either 1869 or 1870 walked to Loch Coruisk from Sligachan. '*The guide (a gloomy Gael of thirteen, as sturdy as a whin-bush, and about as communicative) led the way, uttering ever and anon an eldritch whistle much like the doleful scream of the curlew.*'[21] One could add the comment that for many a parent this sounds like a fairly typical thirteen-year old boy!

Mackenzie however rapidly gained experience and was soon guiding clients up the peaks. Sheriff Valentine described him in an SMCJ article on early days at Sligachan –

> His independence he always retained: he had his croft, and could live without the tourist. In latter life, when most of us remember him, he went only occasionally on the mountains, but gave most of the summer to his old and constant ally, Collie. His was a green and sturdy eld. His stride was long and his eyes

> keen. When his companions, wearied by a hard day, had sat themselves down with relief, they would see him set forth in the dusk for the three miles trudge to his cottage, as fresh as a youth in his prime, and that when he was already far on in the sixties. The stalker's cap, the loose jacket and knickerbockers which he wore, suited the man; they seemed to grow out of him.
>
> He had the characteristics of the Highlander; the courtesy joined to self-respect that are the heritage of the clans. His accent to the end smacked something of the Gaelic speaker, and the turns of his phrases showed in what language his thoughts had been moulded. His features were strong and embrowned by weather. He wore in the old style a short beard, whiskers and moustache. Always alert, always cheerful, he was a perfect companion, but it was when the mist came swirling down on the wet rocks, that his worth was known. Scottish cragsmen may be content and proud to have him as a leader and a memory.[22]

Valentine also notes Mackenzie as having climbed the Inaccessible Pinnacle alone, which would have been the second ascent. Like Collie, Mackenzie never married, eventually living at Sconser with two spinster sisters, a nephew and a niece in his croft. This was built in 1912, using his income as a guide, though several commentators later wrote that he was not drawn to his profession by the money alone; rather it allowed him access to the hills.

In the Introduction to his book on Skye [23], Ben Humble relates how he first met Mackenzie, albeit serendipitously. Late in the afternoon, on the second day of a walk round Skye, Humble and his company ran out of energy and enthusiasm on reaching the community of Sconser, three miles short of their target, Sligachan. On enquiring after a lodging they were pointed to Mackenzie's cottage, a but and ben, with a room and kitchen on the ground floor, and a ladder leading to a loft.

Humble noticed a stack of Alpine Club Journals in a corner, a puzzle in such a cottage. Later, after high tea, they were sitting outside, when an old man came up the road. He walked easily, in a suit of plus fours, and carried some trout. His grand white beard would have stood out in any company, Humble remarked. Sitting by the fire in the kitchen, they told him of their intention of climbing one of the peaks later that week, and were then informed that the highest peak, Sgurr Alasdair, was '*just a walk, just a walk.*' More information was forthcoming, with many old climbing photographs, some of them stereoscopic views. He obviously had a mass of information about the Cuillin.

Some more conversation revealed that their host was a guide, and that he had spent the day fishing in Loch Fada with a Professor Collie. At this stage in Humble's climbing career, neither name had any special significance, and it was only later, researching in a library in Glasgow, that Humble realised that they had stepped into the unknown croft in Skye and met, as he put it, '*the only mountain guide of Swiss calibre Britain had ever produced.*' As for the mysterious presence of the AC journals, it seems that the AC had made Mackenzie some sort of associate or honorary member, and duly placed him on their subscription list in appreciation of his services to mountaineering.

In July 1887, a 6ft,1in Irish powerhouse named Henry Chichester Hart employed Mackenzie. Disdaining the use of ropes, this eccentric and athletic botanist along with the 21-year old guide traversed most of the Cuillin Ridge over two separate days of hard scrambling. Hart (1847–1908) was born in Raheny, County Dublin, and obtained his BA (Hons) at Trinity College, Dublin. An expert botanist, he discovered the rare alpine *Arabis alpina* (Alpine rock-cress) high in Coire na Criche. In Britain the Cuillins is the only known site.

Through the research by Stuart Pedlar we know that Mackenzie and Hart can lay claim to the first recorded ascent of Am Basteir, and the first traverse of the exposed traverse ledge across the Coire Lagan face of Sgurr Mhic Choinnich. Mackenzie and Collie made the same traverse the following year, which lent the name Collie's Ledge to the traverse. There is therefore a good argument that it should be more appropriately named Hart's Ledge.

Perhaps one of the reasons Mackenzie and Collie so successfully became a climbing partnership was that neither man was much interested in making money; Collie could have generated an income from patents, following some of his scientific discoveries, but seems not to have done so. Additionally, he spent much of his income building up fine collections of Chinese jade, rare books, precious stones and minerals. This he did not to amass monetary assets, but for personal love of the items he came across. One of his former pupils, James Orme Masson (1887–1962), later to become knighted, recalled in a note to a climbing academic that –

> He collected as he pursued chemical experiments, and as he sought the uncontaminated hills not from pride of capture but simply because to do so enabled him better to admire, to study and learn from things of beauty and to store them in his marvellous visual memory.[24]

Physically, Collie was tall with long limbs, allowing for a good reach to a high rock hold. He seemingly had a liking for wall climbs, which would have suited his build. Valentine writes: '*He also had a faculty, on which he rather prided himself, of insinuating his lengthy frame into crevices, and of making a serpent-like passage along tenuous ledges.*'[25] In their climbing partnership, Collie had the eye for a line and was a strategist, while Mackenzie was a strong leader with an unparalleled knowledge of every nook and cranny of the Cuillin. '…*Collie appears to have been the innovator, the man who saw the possibilities, while on more than one occasion Mackenzie was the actual leader on the climb.'*[26] Collie joined the SMC in 1891.

The pair was not solely involved with putting up new routes; Collie, with a scientist's curiosity, and finding himself in the centre of a major map muddle, worked hard at deciphering the topography of the Cuillin. To put it mildly, the one-inch OS Skye map of 1885 was a shambles, with most of the summits without a published height and, even worse, some guesswork as to topography which led to more confusion. In 1880, as described in Chapter 2, Naismith and his companions had made what they thought was the first ascent of Sgurr a' Mhadaidh but turned out to be the first ascent of the North Peak of Bidein Druim nan Ramh. He only realised this error when he examined the one-inch map of 1885.

Other climbers, too, were finding that the mapping of the Cuillin left much to be desired. One of these was Charles Pilkington, who in 1891 had published his own updated version of the Cuillin, basing it on the OS map but making corrections and additions where necessary. It was advertised in the first volume of the SMC thus –

> Mr C. Pilkington's corrected map of the Coolins
>
> This map has now been reproduced by Messrs J. Heywood & Co., Deansgate, Manchester, who will supply it post free at 6d. a copy. Mr Pilkington says of it that 'it is very rough, but may help others to correct still further.' Be this as it may, it is probably the most correct map of these mountains obtainable.[27]

Collie's approach to the mapping of the Cuillin concentrated on obtaining as accurately as possible the heights of the main summits and bealachs. In order to do this he used an aneroid barometer on the hill, a portable device designed by French inventor Lucien Vidie in 1843. This worked by containing a small, sealed vacuum chamber. Changing air pressures moved a series of connecting levers which in turn were connected to a needle rotating round a scale. The whole design was not that far removed from a quality watch mechanism. Previous to this large, awkward, mercury barometers were used. These were easily broken on a trip, releasing mercury which is a poison (though it was some time before this particular danger became known). The mercury barometer however, had two superior points; it was more accurate, and it 'recovered' more quickly following a change in pressure. Collie's personal aneroid barometer is now in private hands.

Collie, always the scientist, became aware of some mismatched readings of some heights, on one occasion finding a reading at the end of a day which indicated that the Sligachan Inn was below sea level. Air pressure at sea level could change in the course of a day of course, while the aneroid could have a delay before a reading settled. He minimised errors by the stratagem of starting from a peak which had been heighted by the OS, then moving speedily to the next peak which had not and taking a height, before moving on to another peak which had been heighted by the OS. If the first and last readings, as an example, were close to what the OS had recorded, then he felt confident that the interim reading would be a reasonably good one, and so over the space of some six years he carefully recorded the heights of some 60 spots in the Cuillin; summits, pinnacles, bealachs and dips between summits. Of these 60, only eight had been previously measured by the OS.

His findings were published in 1893, in an article in the SMCJ.[28] In addition to using the aneroid barometer, Collie also employed a clinometer, which allowed him to determine whether a distant peak was higher or lower than the one he was standing on. With this, a reading taken from the summit of the Inaccessible Peak (as the Pinnacle was then known) indicated that Sgurr Alasdair appeared to be some 20ft higher. His aneroid readings confirmed this, with a height given for the Inaccessible of 3,255ft, and Sgurr Alasdair 3,275ft. The latter was then confirmed as being the highest summit in the Cuillin. To be fair to the OS, the limitations of their technology made readings all but impossible in anything but the best of weather, and Skye, as is well known, is renowned for its fast changing weather moods. The terrain was another obstacle in their path, and they could be forgiven for not taking their equipment up the Inaccessible Pinnacle.

Collie was a regular visitor to Skye from 1886 to 1891, taking his annual summer holidays on the island. By 1888 he had climbed all the main Cuillin peaks. From 1891 to 1904 he was branching out to other parts, not only on the British mainland, but also, with increasing experience and climbing ability, to other countries; these included Ireland, Norway, the Himalaya, and the Canadian Rockies. On Skye, some first ascents that stand out include the Bhasteir Tooth in 1887, with William Wickham King, gaining the summit after a descent from Am Basteir during a traverse of the Main Ridge from Sgurr nan Gillean to Bruach na Frithe. The following year, Collie with Mackenzie climbed the Tooth from the south. In August 1889, the Alasdair / Thearlaich-Dubh Gap fell to Collie and King.

❄ ❄ ❄

There were a few clues being sprinkled around as to the potential for climbing on the mainland mountains; in 1886, Joe Stott and three friends took the train to Tyndrum and walked the remaining distance to Inveroran Inn on the shore of Loch Tulla. It was May, with the mixed weather conditions that month can produce, as the next day they walked the rough road to Glen Coe over the old moor way. Their target was the Buachaille Etive Mor. They knew no one who had climbed it, and as they surveyed its east face from the Kingshouse they decided to move down Glen Etive a distance until easier ground could be taken. The blizzard hit them not far below the ridge, where they sheltered under a blanket for some time. Finally one of the party ventured out for a look and discovered they were only a few hundred yards from the summit cairn. They staggered up and gained the cairn.

> Usually one feels inclined to yell and dance after conquering a good hill; but it was not so to-day. Hastily gloves were torn off and cards got out; hastily the latter were crammed into a bottle and buried in the snow of the cairn; and then hastily we plunged through the storm back along the ridge to the neighbourhood of the spot whence we had made our rush...We were plastered with snow from head to foot; it filled our ears, our hair, our pockets; it had penetrated everywhere; our eye-brows and moustaches were icicles; we were living statues of winter.[29]

Stott finished his retrospective article by commenting that – '*the Buchaille is a mountain well able to offer hard work on some of its faces to any cragsman who cares to attempt them.*'

This narrative is approaching a point in time in the mid 1880s, an important cusp, where momentous events were about to transform mountaineering in Scotland: the frustrations of indigenous climbers would motivate a few key players to promote the formation of two major clubs; the railways in Scotland would soon complete a major connection, allowing easier access to a prime climbing area, while continuing advances in technology would, for a privileged minority, give them the internal combustion engine and the first mass-produced film camera. Before that cusp however, we must first follow the achievements on Skye of that fascinating team of Collie and Mackenzie, particularly of Collie, as he branched out into the wider world.

❄ ❄ ❄

Collie had been bitten by the bug of climbing in 1886, and for the next four summers fed his new addiction in Skye. At the end of 1891 he returned to an area where he had enjoyed walking and exploring the countryside as a young boy, the Lake District. Up to this time he had been ignorant of the rock climbing developments taking place there, but an article in the magazine *The Pall Mall Budget* for 5th June 1890, carried an illustrated article, describing an ascent of Napes Needle by Haskett Smith. The article was unsigned, but a copy pasted into the Wasdale Climbing Book has a handwritten note attached which states that the article was written by Walter Brunskill. The article galvanized Collie into arranging a trip to Wasdale at the end of 1891.

Haskett Smith had been exploring the Lake District crags for decades, and in 1886 had made a solo first ascent of Napes Needle, a rock pinnacle overlooking Wasdale on Great Gable. In England, this ascent, among others, has been called the birth of rock climbing. The Inn at Wasdale (at the time it was called the Wastwater Hotel) was the Lakes' equivalent of Sligachan Inn, a base for the climbing activists of that period. Collie started off his first visit, in December 1891, by climbing Napes Needle. According to his biographer Christine Mill, Collie climbed it ropeless and in unnailed boots, being grateful for a hand from his companions on the last tricky move. The climb is an exposed route, vastly different from the psychologically safe confines of the gully climbs which were then popular in the Lake District.

It was on Christmas Day, however, that he produced a truly remarkable first winter ascent. Collie set out with two companions, Wilfred L Brodie and EW Marshall. Their target was Steep Gill on Scafell. This is a 210m gully, with its major difficulties high up. Some 35 years or so later, Collie admitted in an article that '*my recollection of it in snow and ice is that it is one of the most dangerous climbs I have ever made.*'[30] Current winter grading for this route is V,4.[31] Colin Wells has climbed this route in winter, using modern equipment and techniques, and makes the following comments –

> When I climbed the route and got a handle on its character and ambience, I formed the strong impression that Collie, still in the first cocky flushes of his ability but not yet really that experienced, was probably lured into the climb by the superficially inviting looking initial chimney which is eminently back-and-footable, but that when he reached the upper scoop he passed a point of no return. Up there is nothing but sloping ice-covered rock, which steepens into a compact chute the higher you go and with no chance of a retreat or escape. I think they simply had to climb for their lives and felt lucky to get away with it. I'm certain this is why Collie kept schtum for nearly 30 years before venturing into print about his experiences and then saying it was unjustifiable.[32]

This outstanding ascent was only recognised lately by Al Phizacklea, and parallels the realisation by Robin Campbell of the significance of Raeburn's ascent of Green Gully in 1906.[33] The latter route is a pure snow and ice route, whereas Steep Gill in winter is a mixed route, with stretches of snow and ice alternating with snow covered rock. It is now regarded as being the first Grade V in climbing history, at least in the UK, and perhaps worldwide. Brian Davison, author of *Lake District Winter Climbs*,[34] and researcher at Lancaster University's Environment Centre has researched into the weather from that period, finding that there was in fact a prolonged and very cold spell, lasting some three weeks.[35]

Collie had only been baptised into rock climbing some five years earlier, now he had well and truly dived into the deep end of winter climbing, an experience which would prove its worth a few years later. He made his first visit to the Alps in 1888. This is recorded in his application for Alpine Club membership but not mentioned in either of his biographies. This is possibly the only experience he had of snow and ice climbing prior to the ascent of Steep Gill. It is perhaps worth a mention that in the history of winter climbing, and especially in the early years, before good protection was devised, some pitches were finished not as a matter of choice, but because, as described by Colin Wells, retreat was not possible. It was, in some cases, literally a case of 'do or die'.

Collie and Mackenzie certainly amassed an unbeatable knowledge of the Cuillin, and made first ascents not only of routes, but of summits. Mackenzie, in his capacity as a guide, must have ushered upwards of thousands of clients in his 50 years' of guiding, with not one recorded incident of an accident. Yet the guide books do not muster a long list of routes, considering the time they spent together on the rocks. Many days, particularly as the years went by, were spent fishing, Collie's first love, and due to his habit of providing only the briefest of notes on an ascent, and not all ascents at that, there were ascents either not recorded, or ascribed to others. He was more than modestly reticent, he was generally tight-lipped, especially when it came to his climbs.

He made ascents on the mainland as will be seen later, and went on to make many expeditions in the higher ranges: the Alps in 1892-94, when he made the first traverse of the Aiguille de Grépon with Hastings, Pasteur and Mummery (1893), first ascents of the Dent du Requin with Mummery, Slingsby and Hastings (1894), and the first guideless ascent of Mont Blanc by the Brenva Spur with Mummery and Hastings (1894) to name a few. In the Himalaya, Collie, Mummery and Hastings launched an audacious attempt on Nanga Parbat. Collie, Mummery and two Gurkhas climbed Diamirai Peak (19,000ft). Tragically, Mummery and a Gurkha, Lhor Khan, disappeared on a further exploration. (In September 2010, an auction at Christie's of a photograph album of Collie's from this expedition, containing 40 photographs, was sold for £7,500.) Collie never returned to the Himalaya, but he did embark on a series of six expeditions to the Canadian Rockies, and three to the Lofoten, all between 1897 and 1911, the Canadian expeditions resulting in first ascents of 21 peaks.

❄ ❄ ❄

In 1899, Collie made what is certainly his best discovery on Skye, the unique rocky feature on the face of Sron na Ciche known to climbers as The Cioch (Gaelic for pap, or breast). Army officer Charlie Bruce, who had joined the expedition to Nanga Parbat for a month, was on Skye with a Gurkha, Harkabir Thapa, as a companion. With Collie, they had spent a day on Sgurr Alasdair. Being delayed by rescuing some sheep, they descended into Coire Lagan in the late afternoon light (it was on the 9th September), with the sun slanting across the huge face of Sron na Ciche. This light threw various features into relief, and in particular produced a huge shadow on the face which, Collie realised, could only be caused by some large, projecting rock feature. He took a photograph, but it would be seven years before he could return and determine its cause. (Collie's original slide showing the shadow is held in the Alpine Club Archives.)

In 1906, the western face of Sron na Ciche remained unclimbed, which surprised Collie. As he wrote in a later article in the Alpine Journal –

> It is curious that this magnificent face of precipices in the lower corrie never seems to have attracted the attention of climbers. For in 1906 it was entirely untouched, though since then dozens of climbs up and down and over it have been made and described in mountaineering journals.
>
> This great wall of rock is almost two-thirds of a mile long and about 1000 feet high. It is built on a very large scale. The great slabs of rock are less cracked and as a rule bigger than elsewhere in the Coolin. From a climbing point of view it is certainly the most remarkable and interesting rock face in the whole range.[36]

That summer of 1906, probably in early July, he returned to Skye to stay at Glen Brittle Lodge with his friend, the painter Colin Phillip. The next day he went alone to investigate the face. He climbed up to below the Chioch (as he spelled the Gaelic), and firstly tried the great slab to its left before retreating. He then tried the gullies on either side, deciding that the gully to the east showed promise. As he was alone, he decided to wait for Mackenzie and try it the following day. His findings that day, and its ascent the next with Mackenzie, prompted Collie to write a full description of his discovery –

> As it turned out, it was a climb full of excitement, for one never knew what was round the next corner. We traversed slabs, we worked up cracks, and went right away from the Chioch into the gully on the E. side, losing sight of the Chioch altogether. Then we fortunately found a queer traverse unlike any traverse I have ever seen, that led out of the gully across the perpendicular face of the cliff, and back in the direction of the Chioch. But the Chioch itself we could not see, until having got round several corners, suddenly it came into view and we found ourselves on the end of the knife-edge. We sat down on that knife-edge, and slowly made our way to the great rock tower at its end, up this we climbed, and John and I were mightily pleased with our climb. After that everyone at Glen Brittle had to climb it and I believe that during that July and August John and I made the first ten ascents of the Chioch.
>
> ...Since then many other ways have been discovered for getting to the top, but I still have a great liking for the original route, for there are so many surprises in it, and one has the opportunity of seeing the Chioch from so many points of view during the ascent.'[37]

Collie, unusually for him, had been so delighted with their find that he found himself recommending its ascent to a host of climbers. They even accompanied climbers to the pinnacle, as indicated both by the above quotation and a letter Collie wrote to GW Young on 2nd May 1942, describing the first ascent. [38]

One of these early ascents led to a variation of *Collie's Climb*, the route taken on the first ascent, which had included a partial ascent of Eastern Gully. The variation avoided this detour and was climbed in late August or early September 1906 by Collie, Slingsby, Colin Phillip, Geoffrey Young and Mackenzie. Cecil Slingsby had come up to Skye that summer, with his son Lawrence, and after a gap of some 15 years. They spent some days as guests of Colin Phillip at Glen Brittle Lodge, before moving to Sligachan. Winthrop Young described his stay in his book *Mountains With a Difference* –

> ...staying at Glen Brittle with the dark bearded painter, Colin Phillip, a man subtle in wit and argument, who devoted his life and art to the hills. They were fishing and stalking deer and climbing in leisurely fashion. John Mackenzie, the handsome islander whom Collie had trained as the first, and for many decades the only real mountain guide our islands knew, was usually of the company. Collie led us up on some solemn pilgrimage to his famous Cioch pinnacle which he had just then discovered. He assured me we were taking a new variation route, up the glorious gabbro of the gigantic Cioch slab.[39]

That same year Collie, probably alone, discovered *Window Buttress* on Sgurr Dearg. A remarkable hole through a pinnacle provides its name, and it gives an entertaining approach to the Inaccessible Pinnacle. The SMC Guide to Skye, published in 1923,[40] stated that although Collie had mentioned climbs on the Bhasteir faces of the Pinnacle Ridge on Sgurr nan Gillean, as he had not submitted descriptions they could not be published, later ascenders having the claim to them instead.

The same guidebook however did credit Collie with five routes on Sron na Ciche, including Amphitheatre Arete, originally known as Collie's Face Climb. This route, with the Cioch and its following descent down Cioch Gully, were the only route descriptions supplied by Collie from this great face.

❄ ❄ ❄

Norman Collie was elected President of the Alpine Club in 1919, and Honorary President of the Cairngorm Club in 1922. Now in his sixties, climbing gradually took second place to fishing, while his summer stays in Skye became longer. In 1929 he retired, his visits to the island lasting from spring through to the autumn. On the 20th July 1933, Collie's friend Mackenzie died, aged 76. Collie wrote his obituary for the SMC Journal –

> As a companion on a long summer day he was perfect. Always cheerful, keenly alive to everything – the wild birds, the fish in the rivers, the deer on the hillside, and all natural things.

> There is no one who can take his place. Those who knew him will remember him as a perfect gentlemen, one who never offended either by word or deed. He has left a gap that cannot be filled. There was only one John, simple-minded, most loveable, and without guile. May he rest quietly in the little graveyard at Struan.[41]

Legend has it – and who are we to doubt it – that Collie climbed Am Basteir one more time on his own, and declared it was his last climb. As to Collie's comment on Mackenzie being simple-minded, we should take that as meaning free of deceit or guile. With the outbreak of war in 1939, Collie locked the door of his house in Gower Street, London, for the last time, and moved to Sligachan. Here he had for company his host and friend, John Campbell, but it was a short-lived reunion, as Campbell died early in 1940. Collie had known Campbell for almost 50 years, and with this death his solitude must have become even more marked. Doubtless his deafness would have contributed to this.

What is probably the last description of Collie, at least in print, is to be found in a book written by Richard Hillary, an RAF fighter pilot. Based in a north-east Scottish coastal village for training in November 1939, and with four days of leave in March 1940, Hillary and a fellow trainee, Noël Agazarian, decided to drive across Scotland to the west coast, where they took the ferry to Skye. A bus advert had a hotel advertisement on its side, which led them to Sligachan –

> The innkeeper welcomed us and showed us our rooms. From every window was the same view, grey mountains rising in austere beauty, their peaks hidden in a white mist, and everywhere a great feeling of stillness. The shadows that lengthened across the valley, the streams that coursed down the rocks, the thin mist turning now into night, all part of that stillness. I shivered. Skye was a world that one would either love or hate; there could be no temporizing.
>
> 'It is very beautiful,' said the landlord.
>
> 'Yes,' I said, 'it's beautiful.'
>
> "But only mountaineers or fools will climb these peaks.'
>
> 'We're both fools,' Noel said shortly.
>
> 'So be it. Dinner is at 8.30.'
>
> We were alone in the inn save for one old man who had returned there to die. His hair was white but his face and bearing were still those of a mountaineer, though he must have been a great age. He never spoke, but appeared regularly at meals to take his place at a table tight-pressed against the window, alone with his wine and his memories. We thought him rather fine.[42]

The next morning, the two climbed Bruach na Frithe, warmed by a rare spring sun which soon dried the dew from the heather. They raced each other to the summit, finishing almost together in the mist. The war was far away and life was good. On the descent, following a burn, they came to a drop of about 20ft. Agazarian stripped off, handed his clothes to Hillary, and dropped into a pool. Trying to follow, Hillary fell in, still dressed and clutching his friend's clothes. By the time they regained the inn, they were both dry.

> Over dinner we told the landlord of our novel descent. His sole comment was 'Humph,' but the old man at the window turned and smiled at us. I think he approved.

Hillary finally flew Spitfires into battle in 1940, and was shot down over the North Sea in September of that year. He was badly burned but was picked up by a lifeboat. Returning to active service, he was killed in an aircrash in January 1943, shortly after writing his book, *The Last Enemy*, about his war service. It has been reprinted many times and remains a war classic. Its title comes from a biblical quote. '*The last enemy that shall be destroyed is death*.'[43] As for Noël Agazarian, who was of Armenian-French parentage, he died in May 1941, when the Hurricane he was flying was shot down over Tobruk, Libya, by a Messerschmitt Bf 109. He is buried in the Knightsbridge War Cemetery, Acroma, Libya. One of the Spitfires he flew during the Battle of Britain, number R6915, still exists, and is preserved in the Imperial War Museum in London.

Collie, too, had a fall, into cold mountain water. In October 1941, on a wet, windy day, he fished in Loch Leathan, below the Storr. He caught 35 trout, but on trying to regain the bank he fell in and was soaked. It was, as it so often is with people of his age, a turning point in his health. Up until recent years he had remained fit and healthy, though latterly he had suffered from neuritis, lumbago and sciatica for which the Portree doctor had prescribed morphia tablets. There would now be no more fishing. Eventually he moved downstairs into a lounge, where a bed had been set up. He lived on for a year, dying on the 1st November 1942, aged 83. A friend for many years was with him at the last, GH Lee. Due to the war, no others could travel to Skye.

Following his wishes, he was buried next to his great friend and climbing comrade John Mackenzie, in the old graveyard at Struan. Breaches in the drystane dyke allow sheep to crop the grass, and the tiny site nestles against a grassy hillock. Two simple, raw stone headstones mark the graves; a basalt rock for Mackenzie, one of gabbro for Collie. The graves lie like ships in line, with Mackenzie leading, much as he had done while together on a climb.

Collie has been given generous space in this chapter; this is due as much to his interesting life and character, as to his actual climbs. On Skye he did much to clarify the topography, in addition to opening up many of the climbing areas. Internationally he is recognised as being one of the great explorers, especially in Canada, where he discovered the Columbia Ice Fields and published *Climbs and Exploration in the* Canadian Rockies.[44] Between 1897 and 1911 he made first ascents of 21 Canadian mountains. One mountain, Mt Collie, 10,312ft (3,143m) in Yoho National Park, British Columbia, though not climbed by Collie (that fell to James Outram and Edward Whymper in 1901) was named after Collie in 1897, by Charles S Thompson. On Skye, Sgurr Thormaid (Norman's Peak) was named after him, just as Sgurr Mhic Choinnich (Mackenzie's Peak) was named after his friend and guide.

While Collie was extremely reticent about providing details of his climbs, when he did lift his pen to paper he was capable of producing excellent prose. We will leave the last words of this chapter to him, with the finishing sentence from his article on the Cuillin, written in May, 1897.[45] In this article he begins with a brief history of those who had visited the island. He then describes the Cuillin, finishing with a wild Atlantic storm gradually diminishing, and leading to a sunset and final quiet night. His writing approaches dangerously close to parody, and at times almost mimics the style which Collie himself denigrated. It is rescued by adding something extra, as below, where visual scenes are melded with sounds. It is prose which demands to be read out to the accompaniment of music, were it not that his words are music enough –

> But the golden glory of the sunset will melt from off the mountains, the light that silvered the great slabs will slowly fail, from out of the corries darkness heralding the black night will creep with stealthy tread hiding all in gloom; and last of all, behind the darkly luminous, jagged, and fantastic outline of the Coolins the glittering stars will flash out from the clear sky, no wind will stir the great quiet, only the far-off sound, born of the rhythmic murmur of the sea waves beating on the rock-bound shore of lonely Scavaig, remains as a memory of the storm.

References

1. Pilkington, Charles, *The Black Coolins*, Alpine Journal, Vol. 13, February 1888, No. 99, pp.434-435.
2. Abraham, Ashley, *Rock-Climbing in Skye* (London: Longmans, 1908), 174.
3. Pedlar, Stuart, *Across Unmeasured Space – History of Climbing in the Cuillin.* Unpublished MS. 2010.
4. Pilkington, Charles, *Letter to W.A.B. Coolidge, Editor Alpine Club Journal, reporting first ascent.*
5. Valentine, G.D. *At Sligachan – The Classic Age*, SMCJ 23, No.136, April 1945, 237.
6. Pilkington, Charles, *Report to the Alpine Club*, December 1887.
7. Ibid.
8. Pedlar, Stuart, *Across Unmeasured Space – A History of Climbing in the Cuillin.* Unpublished MS. 2010.
9. Garden, William. *In Memorium. John Norman Collie. 1859 – 1942.* SMCJ 23, No. 134, April 1943, 95-97.
10. Taylor, William C., *The Snows of Yesteryear* (Toronto & Montreal: Holt, Rinehart and Winston, 1973), 4-5.
11. Mill, Christine, *Norman Collie: A Life in Two Worlds* (Aberdeen: Aberdeen University Press, 1987), 3.
12. Taylor, William. p.8.
13. Bentley, Ronald. *John Norman Collie: Chemist and Mountaineer*, Journal of Chemical Education January 1999, Vol. 76, No.1, p.41
14. Ibid., p.159.
15. Collie, J.N., *Ramsay Papers*, vol. 15, iii. University College London, archives, D.M.S. Watson Library.
16. Steven, Campbell. *Eye to the Hills* (Breedon Books, 2001), 49.
17. Collie, Norman J., *The Island of Skye*, Alpine Journal, Vol. 32, p.164.
18. Bell, J.H. *The Strength of Climbing Rope.* In: Correspondence. SMCJ 4, No.24, September 1897, pp.347-349.
19. Smith, R.A. *Risk Reduction in Rock Climbing*, Sports Engineering, 1, 1998, pp.27-39.
20. Raeburn, Harold. *Mountaineering Art* (London: T. Fisher Unwin, 1920), 172.
21. Buchanan, Robert. *The Hebrid Isles* (1872, 1883 Ed.,), 264.
22. Valentine, G.D. *At Sligachan – The Classic Age*, SMCJ 23, No.136, April 1945, p.237.
23. Humble, B.H. *The Cuillin of Skye.* (London: Robert Hale Limited, 1952.) xiii.
24. Note from J.I.O. Masson to E.C.C. Baly, 22nd November 1942. Donnan Papers 8, University College London archives, DMS Watson Library (quoted in Mill, p.93).
25. Ibid. p.232.
26. Ronald W. Clark and Edward C. Pyatt, *Mountaineering in Britain* (London: Dent – Phoenix House, 1957), 56.
27. *Mr C. Pilkingtons Corrected Map of the Coolins.* Notes and Queries, SMCJ, 1, No.5, May 1891, p.234.

28. Collie, J. Norman. *On the Height of Some of the Black Cuchullins in Skye*, SMCJ 2, No.4, January 1893, pp.168-173.
29. Stott, J.G. *Buchaille Etive*. SMCJ 1, 1. January 1890, pp.25-30.
30. Collie, J.N. *Reminiscences*, F&RCC Journal, 1926, 17,1, 214.
31. Davison, Brian. *Lake District Winter Climbs*. (2006). Fell & Rock Climbing Club. ISBN 1-85284-484-1.
32. Wells, Colin. *Personal Communication*, 2nd February 2011.
33. Campbell, R.N., *The First Scottish Ice Climbers*, SMCJ 30, 1972, pp.48 – 57.
34. Davison, Brian. *Lake District Winter Climbs*. (2006). Fell & Rock Climbing Club. ISBN 1-85284-484-1.
35. Davison, Brian, *Personal Communication*, January 2011.
36. Collie, J.N., *The Island of Skye*. Alpine Journal, Vol. 32, No. 218, September 1918, pp. 167 *et seq*.
37. Ibid.
38. Collie, J.N. In: *Letter to Geoffrey Winthrop Young, 2nd May 1942*. Alpine Club Archives.GWY correspondence C-F B.41.
39. Young, G.W. *Mountains with a Difference* (London: Eyre and Spottiswoode, 1951), 65.)
40. Steeple, E.W., Barlow, G., MacRobert H. *Island of Skye* (Edinburgh: SMC, 1923).
41. Collie, J.N., *John Mackenzie*. In Memorium, SMCJ, 20, No.116, November 1933, pp.124-125.
42. Hillary, Richard. *The Last Enemy* (London: Macmillan, 1943, 1st edition), 40-44.
43. I Corinthians XV. 26. The last enemy that shall be destroyed is death.
44. H.E.M. Stutfield and J.N. Collie, *Climbs and Exploration in the Canadian Rockies* (London: Longman, Green and Co., 1903).
45. Collie, Norman. *A Chuilionn*, SMCJ, 4, No.23, May 1897, p.266.

4

Major Clubs (1847-91)

WITH THE GRADUAL increase in walking in the Highlands, and the continuing clearance of the Highlanders living there, a conflict began to appear between landowners and the new visitors. Estates with huge areas began to appear on the market, purchasers from the south and from other countries claiming the land for their shooting enjoyment. Many were oblivious to the cultural background in Scotland, where there were few obvious boundaries and even fewer fences. The landowners, old and new, began a policy of excluding visitors to their land, to the extent that some ancient rights of way were blocked by gates, or watched over by shotgun wielding employees. Initially this was a Balmoral-led policy, and as hunting, shooting and fishing became more and more popular, the income derived from shooting parties became an irresistible and valued source of income, making it even easier to keep out visitors as the estates spuriously claimed that the mere sighting of a walker would spoil the deer stalking for weeks or more.

The struggle then began in the courts and on the land to regain rights of way and win the argument for better access for walkers and climbers. It would be an occasionally physical and often bad-tempered struggle, but with increasing public awareness and the winning of key arguments in law, landowners were gradually pushed back to a more reasonable position when they realised that they would find it harder and more expensive to mount a blanket resistance to reasonable access.

One famous event which took place in 1847 was the so-called 'Battle of Glen Tilt', the Perthshire confrontation between the irascible Duke of Atholl and John Balfour, who was Professor of Botany at Edinburgh University. The Professor was accompanied by a group of botany students when they met the Duke and ghillies who tried to turn them back because, the Duke claimed, these unwanted hill trampers were disturbing the deer stalking. Spirited discussions took place, changing to anger when the Professor and his party refused to be forced back in the direction of Braemar. They rejected the Duke's claim that he had closed the glen, hopped over a wall and continued down the glen, pursued by the Duke's men.

The skirmish led to legal action against the Duke by the recently formed Scottish Rights of Way Society. They set out to prove that the glen was a through route and a legal corridor, and they eventually won their case. The Scottish Rights of Way & Access Society, as it is now known along with its branding of ScotWays,[1] had been founded in 1845. It was prompted in part by the increasingly aggressive moves of landowners who were becoming more protective of their land. It was originally formed as the Edinburgh Association for the Protection of Public Rights, changed to The Scottish Rights of Way Society, added a temporary 'and Recreation', reverted to the SRWS, and in the 21st century added 'and Access' along with a ScotWays brand name.

The problem of access was prominent in the newspapers of the day. As an example, on the 5th December 1846, *The Scotsman* reported –

> The attempt to shut out the traveller from some of the wildest and most magnificent portions of our Highland scenery, to which we drew attention some months ago, continues to be universally reprobated. So strong and general has been the condemnation pronounced by men of all parties against the proceedings of the Dukes of Athol and Leeds...They should be able to read the meanings of the fact, that throughout the whole press not a pen has been lifted in their defence...

Some 40 years later the Association, by then the Scottish Rights of Way and Recreation Society, became involved in another famous legal battle. A party from the Society led by Walter Smith set out on an expedition through the Mounth and Cairngorm glens to signpost rights of way. In Glen Doll the party was intercepted by the keepers of the landowner, Duncan Macpherson, and the subsequent lawsuit was only finally settled in the House of Lords. The ruling confirmed the status of Jock's Road as a right of way, but it left both the Society and Macpherson bankrupt, such was the cost of litigation.

The continuing problem eventually entered Parliament, with a certain James Bryce attempting to resolve it by the reading of a Bill: his Access to Mountains (Scotland) Bill of 1884. The following is taken from Hansard, wherein is published all debates in both houses, the Commons and the Lords –

> MR. BRYCE (Aberdeen, S.)
>
> I have to move the Second Reading of this Bill, the principle of which has already been affirmed by the House. It is felt in Scotland, and by those who

> visit Scotland, that a great grievance exists in respect of the exclusion of the public from largo [sic] tracts of country containing the finest scenery, and which would be far more accessible to a great number of persons for purposes of health and recreation if the law were amended in the way this Bill proposed.[2]

The paragraph given above is dated 16th May 1900, and is from one of the numerous debates held in Parliament, beginning in 1884 when James Bryce, then the Liberal Member for Tower Hamlets, London, started his campaign to provide in law better access to the Scottish countryside, and in particular its hills and mountains. Bryce's 1884 *Access to Mountains (Scotland) Bill* attracted a leader in the *Times* newspaper. Noting that many tourists went north for the hills, it thundered – '*They are confronted with a fortification of strong fences, locked gates, resolute gamekeepers, men of action and the terrors of the law.*'[3] There were many stories of walkers and climbers being met by – '*tweed-clad thugs with shotguns*,' who brooked no argument.

James Bryce was born in Belfast in 1838, the son of a Glasgow lawyer. Educated at Glasgow High School, Glasgow University, and Oxford, he followed a career in academic law before entering Parliament in 1880 as Member of the Liberal Party for Tower Hamlets in London before becoming Member for Aberdeen South from 1885 to February 1907. His offices in Parliament included President of the Board of Trade 1894-95, and Chief Secretary for Ireland 1905-07; he rounded off his career as a highly successful Ambassador to the United States from 1907 to 1913.

Bryce was an experienced mountaineer, having already climbed in the Alps and other areas. Though never a tiger, he was President of the Alpine Club 1899-1901, and first President of the Cairngorm Club which was formed in 1887. His training as a lawyer gave him a good grounding for the robust verbal fisticuffs occasionally required in the access debates He died on the 22nd January 1922 aged 83, in Sidmouth, Devon. There is a James Bryce Chair of Politics at Glasgow University.

This campaign was interrupted by both World Wars, and was only finished to most people's satisfaction in January 2003, with the passage of the *Land Reform Act (Scotland)*, some 120 years since Bryce first stood up in the House of Commons to argue his case. The Bryce debates are published in Hansard, available on the internet, and makes reading which is at times almost comical, and at other times depressing, as the full weight of landowners, often Tory Members of Parliament, used every trick in their repertoire to block and delay the passage of the Bill.

The *Land Reform Act (Scotland)* produced one of the most progressive access regimes in Europe by granting statutory rights of responsible access to almost all land. Its contents are based on common sense, already present in the Country Code. It helps protect the sensible walker and climber from the few irascible landowners, who are of course still with us. It also helps protect landowners from thoughtless people, who might walk too close to someone's home. Court cases are still with us too, as the Scotways summaries of recent and ongoing cases would confirm.

❄ ❄ ❄

The science of meteorology had for some time been associated with mountains. By 1885, some 51 high level meteorological observatories had been established around the world, some 18 of which were built on mountain peaks. It was thought that in order to better study weather phenomena, a series of stations should be built, as close to each other as possible, but at different altitudes. The highest station then existing in Britain was at Dalnaspidal, at an altitude of 1,414ft (431m). The Scottish Meteorological Society, founded in 1855, took up the challenge, and a design was drawn up by Thomas Stevenson in 1879.

The story of this Observatory, eventually built on the summit of Ben Nevis and opened in 1883, is fully detailed in *Ben Nevis, Britain's Highest Mountain,*[4] but suffice it to say that it was permanently manned from 1883 to its closure in 1904 due to lack of funds. In its time it acted as a magnet for tourists in the summer months, and was occasionally a welcome temporary shelter for climbing parties in winter. It performed observations of various types in parallel with a base station in Fort William. As an indication of how popular Ben Nevis and the Observatory had become, during the summer of 1884 about 4,000 tourists climbed the mountain, about half during the month of August. Tourists, many hoping to view a spectacular dawn from the summit, turned up at all hours of the day in summer, seriously disrupting the work of the observers; this was minimised by the addition of an extra room for shelter. During the winter of 1884-85, not more than a dozen strangers had climbed the mountain.[5]

Queen Victoria's Golden Jubilee took place on 22nd June 1887. The occasion was celebrated throughout the land, including Scotland, and alongside bonfire displays, rockets and other fireworks were to be set off, some on the hills and mountain tops. One such display was lit on the summit of Ben Macdui, the highest mountain in the Cairngorms, by a group of six hillwalkers from Aberdeen. As an aside, at one point this mountain was thought to be the highest in Britain, as a report in *The Scotsman* for 5th September 1832 indicates –

> *The Highest Mountain in Scotland.* Ben Nevis has, till very lately, been considered, the monarch of Scottish mountains, but it now appears, from the trigonometrical survey lately made by order of Government, that he must yield the palm to Ben Macdui, a mountain in Aberdeenshire, who o'ertops him by about twenty feet. The height of Ben Nevis is 4370 feet; of Ben Macdui, 4390

feet. Thus Ben Macdui, is the loftiest mountain, not only in Scotland, but in Great Britain.

The six duly gained the summit just after midnight –

> Around us on all sides, but chiefly towards the north and east, the country was lit up with blazing bonfires. To us, removed from these centres of merriment and revelry, and in utter silence, broken only now and then by the sough of the wind and the occasional muffled sound of falling water borne by the intermittent breeze from the distant corries, the whole had a most mysterious and weird-like effect.[6]

After admiring the panorama (at mid-summer, it would not be completely dark) they set off their cargo of fireworks then descended to Loch Avon where they spent the night under the huge granite block known as the Shelter Stone. This was predictably uncomfortable, and indeed one of the party left the howff to spend what was left of the night by the loch. The next morning they wandered over to the head of the loch, where the Feithe Buidhe entered, at a spot known as Maghan na Banaraich (the Dairymaid's Field). It was here that they decided to form the Cairngorm Club, named after the mountain lying to the north of Loch Avon.

In what might appear to some to be a dilatory approach, the Cairngorm Club was only formally constituted on the 9th January 1889. Amongst its objectives were: to encourage mountaineering, with special reference to the Cairngorm mountains, and to keep under review rights of access to Scottish mountains. James Bryce, its first President, may well have been an influence in the inclusion of the point on access.

The six founders were: William Anderson, Alexander Copland, William A Hawes, Robert Lippe, Alexander Inkson McConnochie (1850–1936), and CC McDonald. McConnochie was perhaps the most prominent, authoring several books including the 1895 book *Ben Muich Dhui and his Neighbours: a guide to the Cairngorm Mountains.* He was appointed Hon Secretary of the Cairngorm Club in 1889, when the constitution was drawn up, and in 1893 became Editor of the club's proposed Journal, remaining in this post until 1910. He served on the Committee of the SMC from 1893-95. He made several contributions to the SMCJ, but it was to the Cairngorms that he devoted most of his energy. Moving to Glasgow in 1910 severed his connections to the North-east club, and finally he retired to London. Bob Aitken suspects that he somewhat re-invented himself, as he may have been born plain Alexander McConnochie.[7]

The first official meet of the Cairngorm Club was held in July 1889, during the holiday weekend of the 9th. The target mountain was Cairngorm and just under 30 people participated. McConnochie was the only founder member present, and lit a fire at the summit, providing the company with hot soup and boiled beef. There then followed a peculiar ceremony known as *douping*. This involved two members pulling an aspirant several times to the top of the cairn, despite his efforts to resist. Some half-a-dozen submitted to the douping on this occasion, and were admitted to membership.

While the Cairngorm Club concentrated on the Cairngorm mountains, and with its members for some decades consisting mainly of hillwalkers, further south, in Scotland's Midland Valley, another club was about to be formed. It was in Glasgow, one of the humming industrial dynamos of Victorian Scotland, that the Scottish Mountaineering Club came about. Its formation would doubtless have been in part due to the growing sense of frustration in the small band of Scottish mountaineers; we have seen the comments by George Ramsay of how, apart from his brother and his friend Professor Veitch, he claimed to know of no other like-minded person. There were some climbers with Alpine experience; indeed, some of them were members of the Alpine Club, which had been founded in 1857. Some of these worked at Glasgow University. The barrier was in social communication – it simply would have been difficult to find each other.

William Wilson Naismith (1856–1935) was to be instrumental in breaking down this barrier. He had been exploring the hills from 1868, and latterly had some Alpine experience. On a solo winter ascent of Ben More in April 1884, equipped with an alpenstock, he encountered hard snow and ice; following this outing he seems to have stayed off the Scottish peaks in winter for some years. A cautious man, an accountant by profession, and with no contacts with whom he could team up and exchange ideas, he probably made a conscious decision to do so, following this experience.

Naismith finally acted in January 1889, writing a letter to *The Glasgow Herald*. In it, he proposed the formation of a *'Scottish Alpine Club'*. The letter was published on Thursday 10th January, one day following the constitution of the Cairngorm Club. One has to wonder whether the dates were coincidental, or whether Naismith had been aware of the Aberdonian activity and had been stung into action. Whatever the reasoning, the letter was answered by another letter in the Herald four days later, on Monday 14th. Naismith's letter began –

> SIR, - Will you kindly allow me to put in a plea in favour of mountain climbing? This glorious exercise is not, perhaps, one that commends itself to the modern 'masher,' who is understood to look upon all hard work as 'bad form'; but for all that it is undoubtedly one of the most manly, as well as healthful and fascinating, forms of exercise, and it is almost a disgrace to any Scotsman whose lungs and heart are in proper order if he is not more or less of a mountaineer, seeing that he belongs to one of the most mountainous countries in the world.

In contemporary slang of the time, a 'masher' was the name usually applied to a flirtatious dandy, or fop. His letter went on to suggest some parameters for membership, such as three 12,000ft peaks in the Alps plus three 10,000ft passes for a Class 1, and in Scotland six mountains of at least 3,500ft for a Class 2. Naismith also mentioned that Baddeley's *Guide* listed some 17 Scottish mountains which attained that height. Mountford John Byrde Baddeley (1843–1906) was a distinguished English guidebook writer of the late 19th and early 20th centuries. His guides appeared in the *Thorough Guide* series, edited by Baddeley and his colleague, Charles Slegg Ward, and included guides to Scotland (parts I to III: The Highlands; Northern Highlands; The Lowlands (all 1894). Orkney & Shetland would follow in 1900.

The answering letter suggested that –

> ...height is no real index to the 'class' of the mountain. For instance, the 3,500 ft. limit would include Lochnagar and Ben Nevis, two very 'cheap' ascents, and would exclude all the peaks of the Coolins, which are the stiffest work in Scotland.

This second letter was signed '*Cairn*'. This turned out to be the pseudonym of two Scots, Gilbert Thomson (1859–1941), a sanitary engineer, and Donald Alexander Archie (1862–1938), a bank clerk, both of whom would become original members of the club that emerged, along with Naismith. They also suggested that –

> Such a club might be of great service, not only as a rallying point for enthusiasts, but in spreading wider the interest which unfortunately is confined to comparatively few, and in giving advice and information to intending climbers.

Naismith replied in a letter published on Friday 18th –

> ... the proposed limit of height to qualify for membership should be lowered so as to include the Cuchullins is a good one. On the other hand, all mountains up which there is a pony track might be excluded. The greatest difficulty, I fear, however, will not be to fix the qualification, but to find a sufficient number of enthusiastic climbers to form a club. Perhaps 'Cairn' will kindly take the matter in hand?

This letter includes another pointer to the fact that Naismith had no contact with like-minded local mountaineers. Fortunately, a fourth reader had been following the correspondence in *The Glasgow Herald*, and followed up Naismith's second letter with one of his own, written on Saturday 19th and published on Monday 21st January. It was from an English climber, then working as a Demonstrator in Medicine at Glasgow University. His name was Alfred Ernest Maylard (1855–1947); he would become the first Secretary; his practical nature and organisational skills were to bear much fruit for the nascent club. He wrote –

> I must say, however, that I should object to the term "Alpine" being applied, especially if such a club were constituted on the lines laid down by Mr Naismith.

> We should suffer like so many other Scotch clubs by the marked inferiority we should bear to the English corresponding club. England in the south is practically destitute of hills, while we have many, and all within comparatively easy reach, there is therefore little reason why we should wish to form an Alpine Club; rather let us have a club which would be peculiarly our own, and one to which many of our southern Alpine climbers would be proud to belong...

Maylard then suggested that the club could be termed a *'Scottish Mountaineering Club'*, and that he would be willing to receive notices of interest from any gentleman (or lady), who was interested, so that he could consider organising a meeting. Some five days later another letter from Maylard indicated a good response, leading to him arranging a public meeting to be held on the 11th of February 1889, in the rooms of the Christian Institute, Bothwell Street, Glasgow, at which Professor George Ramsay, a member of the Alpine Club, was asked to preside. In contrast to the Cairngorm Club, where access to the hills seems to have been inscribed in the constitution, Ramsay went to some pains during his chairing of this meeting to emphasise that he and his friends had no desire to see the proposed club become entangled in any rights of way disputes. As he wrote later –

> We did not desire the Club to become a stravaiging or marauding Club, insisting on going everywhere at every season, with or without leave, and indifferent to the rights and the enjoyments of farmers, proprietors, and sportsmen.

As it happened, the first Honorary Presidents of the SMC were Cameron of Lochiel and the Marquis of Breadalbane. Other landowners were original members.

It was opportune that Maylard was working at Glasgow University, where Ramsay was a professor. Maylard and an unnamed friend, almost certainly Professor Frederick Orpen Bower, had called upon Ramsay at his university office, in the last week of January. Ramsay was delighted by the visit, and presumably Maylard had gone there to ask Ramsay to chair the public meeting. Ramsay was obviously fairly prominent in the university and may well have been known to Maylard through the local grapevine as a mountaineer, as that sport would have been unusual then. Perhaps Naismith, who had attended a lecture on climbing by Ramsay, had pointed Maylard in his direction. In any case, Ramsay was to become the club's first President.

The public meeting duly went ahead, though no ladies seemed to have attended. Naismith was present, but maintained a low profile, though he must have mused on the school lecture he had received in the past from Ramsay. Following this meeting, a series of sub-committee meetings was held before the SMC was formally constituted on Monday, 11th March 1889, some two months after the Cairngorm Club. By then, interest had arrived from all parts of Scotland as well as England, eventually creating a cohort of some 100 original members. Ramsay was the first President, Maylard, later a surgeon based at the Victoria Infirmary, Glasgow, became Secretary, Gilbert Thomson was Librarian, and Charles Gairnder of the Union Bank was appointed Treasurer. In a lengthy article in 1896,[8] Ramsay described the formation of the club, and also provided an interesting geographical breakdown of its initial membership.

Some 39 years later, Maylard had a note in the SMC Journal entitled '*The Foundation of the Club*', in which he went to some pains to correct for the record some of the points made by Ramsay. This article had been prompted by the recent after dinner speech given the previous December by then President Harry MacRobert, who referred to Naismith as the Founder of the Club. Maylard presented several facts pointing out that Naismith was much more of a *Founder*, as Ramsay had it; in fact he should be known as the *Father* of the Club, and so he has to this day. Another interesting point supplied by Maylard was the suggestion that 94 gentlemen were present, all of whom were then designated as 'original members' (OMs). These 94 had gone to the meeting in response to the public appeal set up by Maylard in *The Glasgow Herald*, and as Maylard commented –

> Every "Original" Member, of which there were 94, played some part in encouraging younger men to join the Club, and both by precept and example fostered the pursuit of one of the healthiest and most enjoyable sports in the world... there were not a few in the audience who were not climbers, but who warmly sympathised with the object the promoters had in view. But the proposal that all who were present, whether climbers or not, should constitute the "Original" Members was agreed to.[9]

A further four years on, in the April 1939 SMCJ, Maylard wrote a section of an article entitled '*The Club in Retrospect*'. His section looked at its origin and growth, and here he presented a different set of figures on its formation. He stated that the 'Original Members' totalled some 30 or 40, not the 94 as above, with a subsequent arrangement extending the number to the first 100 of those who joined the Club.[10] This lower figure seems more appropriate, considering the number of Alpinists known to be living in Scotland at this time.

As an indication of the social setup at the inception of the SMC, we know that the 100 OMs included eleven professors, eight knights or baronets, two MPs, four Reverend Doctors, eight other assorted Doctors (LLDs and medics), and two Reverends. Senior legal and financial figures also loom large: in the West, many of them with business addresses in St Vincent Street and the other main commercial streets of Victorian Glasgow; in Edinburgh they often had home addresses in the New Town or in Morningside. As Honorary SMC member Bob Aitken commented, having produced much useful research on the SMC OMs, '*...this was a strongly* *professional coterie from the high-Victorian bourgeoisie of Scotland.'*[11] It would be several decades before changes in society, including more leisure time, better working conditions, higher income levels and so on, were reflected by a wider spectrum of members.

In 1899 the American economist Thorstein Veblen (1857–1929) wrote *The Theory of the Leisure Class: An Economic Study of Institutions.*[12] This was a detailed study of conspicuous consumption. It proposed that the 'lords of the manor' employed themselves in the economically useless practices of conspicuous consumption and conspicuous leisure, while the middle and lower classes were employed in the industrial occupations that supported society as a whole.

Veblen listed several sports which were earnestly pursued by the upper classes. These included yachting, shooting, hunting, golf, tennis, angling, but not included in this list, we note, mountaineering. Some of the characteristics present in the above sports which were necessary for an adherent to be guilty of conspicuous consumption included the need for excess equipment, a *'swaggering gait'*, and certainly for the user to be seen to own a bigger yacht, or to be a consistent winner in competitions. Aggressiveness in the chosen sport, Veblen posited, was a peaceful substitute for violence. Perhaps, we could argue, there were not enough mountaineers around for Veblen to include them in his study. He may even have not spotted them as potential consumers of the useless.

We can find exceptions in his theory, by noting that the likes of Raeburn, a prominent Scottish mountaineer, was a useful contributor to society through his production of beer and as an employer, and was also part-owner of a company. On the other hand, along with his brother, he entered and won competitions as a yacht-racer. But a competitive mountaineer, especially in the late 18th Century, where protection on climbs was practically non-existent, would not have survived for long. A swaggering gait would have gone unnoticed by the masses, given the relatively obscure locations where mountaineering was pursued. And there were, for many decades, no collections of shiny equipment with which to wave in front of any audience or competitor, hoping to impress.

Mountaineering, at least in its early years, had little obvious to add to society, but it was certainly peaceful, where the only excessive consumption was likely to be an extra helping of pudding following a strenuous outing on a mountain. What made it relatively elitist was the need for leisure time and spare cash for travel costs, both of which would be extremely scarce for the lower classes.

Of the original members, 14 were Alpine Club members; some 38 came from Glasgow and the West of Scotland; 17 came from Edinburgh; 13 came from various other towns in eastern Scotland; 12 came from England.

The SMC were out of the starting blocks and hit the mountains running. The first club journal, which was to be so informative and influential for decades, came out in January 1890, under the editorship of Joseph Gibson Stott. Hugh Munro, then plain Mr Munro, joined very early on, sometime between March and December 1889, while Willie Douglas, who would become the second editor from 1892 to 1909, joined in December 1890.

Naismith became familiarly known as the '*father of the club*', but other than starting off the process with his letters, he took little part in setting it up, preferring to remain in the shadows. That honour fell mainly on Maylard's shoulders, who may be regarded as its architect. Indeed, in his article on the formation of the club, Ramsay referred to Maylard as '*a man of action*.' Maylard had a Scottish wife, née Jane Reddie, and, as he wrote in his article on the origins of the Club, his mother had Scottish blood, with ancestors from Scone in Perthshire. As Bob Aitken has theorised –

> Maylard was also a man of sensitivity for Scottish sentiment, perhaps due to his cherished Scottish wife, and modestly promoted the primacy of Naismith to ensure that the SMC had a firmly Scottish frontage.[13]

The first informal climbing meet took place on Friday, 6th April 1889, when Dr Joseph Coats, Prof William Jack, Mark Davidson, Gilbert Thomson, Hugh Munro and George Ramsay spent the night at Lochearnhead, with a plan to cross Ben More to Crianlarich. Saturday was a raw day, with a bitter east wind, mist, sleet and snow. Jack left the group at the base, while the rest navigated up Stob Binnein, down to the col, then over Ben More. The main incidents of the day, Ramsay recalled, were that he had taken leather gloves rather than worsted, and almost suffered frostbite, while another member of the party had a serious slip during descent, which well illustrated the uses of the rope. The party, Ramsay wrote, were also proud of their success with compass and aneroid.

Pleased too was Hugh Munro, as he confessed in an article in the first number of the SMC Journal.[14] Writing of winter ascents, Munro noted that the above day out, traversing Ben More, was '*...one of the most interesting and enjoyable walks I have ever taken.*'

Also in 1889, an SMC expedition to Arrochar well illustrates the difficulties of access at that time, even to a hill so close to Glasgow; the West Highland Railway was still under construction and had not reached Tarbet on the western shore of Loch Lomond. Work started on the railway at Arrochar and Tarbet in 1889 and it opened in 1894. Gilbert Thomson described the trip taken on an autumn holiday in October 1889.[15]

The party made their way to Arrochar the night before, as it would have been impossible to do much from a Glasgow start. Even then, they had to walk the ten miles from Garelochhead, reaching Arrochar at about 9pm.

As they had to reach Glasgow the following night, and the last steamer from Tarbet left at 5pm, they decided on a 5am start.

> As a matter of fact, we got off at 5.15, the delay being due to the necessity of using strong persuasive measures to get some of the party out of bed. We rued that quarter of an hour before the day was done.

They gained the summit of the South Peak of the Cobbler without too much difficulty by 7.20am, but struggled to find a direct continuation to the Centre Peak. They eventually decided that with time and care the direct route would have been quite possible. The Centre Peak was gained by two different routes. '*This peak is much more attractive to one who likes climbing for its own sake than to one who wishes the maximum of view with the minimum of exertion.*' An easy stroll then led to the North Peak, where they made the spine-chilling discovery that a large stone had been removed from its bed and pushed outwards a few feet over the cliff '*...where it seemed to form an admirable trap for anybody of sufficient weight to overbalance it. None of us tried.*'

The day was young, so the party decided that Beinn Ime was the next target. They gained the summit of this just after 9am, unfortunately in the mist. Next, they set a compass course for Ben Vane. The ascent to this summit necessitated a considerable climb, but at least the summit was just about free of mist, with a glimpse of Loch Sloy below. Onwards to Ben Vorlich they continued, gaining Loch Sloy by a steep and rough descent. (This was 50 years before the hydroelectric power schemes were built, and there was of course no dam.) Here they found the solitude to be profound, and they stopped for lunch.

It would be 1.30pm before they finished their climb up the steep grassy west flank of Ben Vorlich, with tiredness understandably settling in. A gaze at the view, which was the best of the day, and they set off down the south ridge to gain the head of Glen Loin. They had to leave Arrochar for Tarbet at 4.30pm, and were promising themselves a mighty dinner before then. They thought an hour to reach Arrochar would suffice, but whether from fatigue or the windings of the path instead of Arrochar at 3.45pm it was seven minutes after the hour at the hotel. That left them exactly 23 minutes for a wash and dinner, half of which had to be regrettably abandoned. They came in sight of Tarbet with the information – '*She's in at the pier.*'

> Our expedition resolved itself into a wild pell-mell rush – "de'il tak' the hindmost" – with a vigorous waving of sticks and other devices to attract the attention of those on board – all of which gave conclusive, but to us most uncomfortable, proof that our energies were not quite exhausted.

That the pioneering members of the SMC were in general prodigious walkers is shown by the outing described by Gilbert Thomson.[16] On Friday,

4th April 1890, Naismith and Thomson took the train from Glasgow to Oban. They then continued on to Ballachulish, presumably by road, as the rail was not to reach Ballachulish until 1903. After a walk up the Pap of Glen Coe they settled into the Clachaig Hotel. The following morning they started at 7.40am and climbed straight up the north-west ridge of Bidean, gaining the summit at 10.20am. Moving along, they next passed the summit of Beinn Fhada and dropped down to the col facing Stob Dubh, the summit of Buachaille Etive Beag. A considerable amount of rock climbing later they were on the peak at 1.50pm.

Next they descended to the highest point of the Lairig Gartain pass, and continued straight up the steep slope aiming for the summit rocks of Stob na Broige, the southerly peak of Buachaille Etive Mor. A long slope of frozen snow made them cut steps up a gully, with a rope for protection. The highest peak, Stob Dearg, was gained at 6.40pm, then a steep shoulder descent lead to Glen Etive and the Kingshouse at 8.50pm. As for the equipment carried by this pair, it included –

> ...a dozen yards of light rope (window sashcord in fact, which was calculated to be sufficiently strong for a party of two), an ice axe carried by Naismith, and an alpenstock carried by the writer. The latter had its spike broken off the day before, and rejoiced now in a large nail with the head filed off.

They had arrived in a famished condition after 13 hours' walking, at the road overlooking the Kingshouse Inn, from where they could see the lights of the hotel. They were so tired they had to rest for some time before making the last few hundred metres. This annoyed the Victorians' tidy minds, so they became determined to test whether it was lack of fitness or food that had made them so tired. At Easter 1892 they took the night train to Dalwhinnie, and at 3.30am they left to walk to Inveroran for a club meet, taking in en route the summit of Ben Alder and the Rannoch Moor. They arrived 16 and a half hours later at Inveroran Inn still going strong, and therefore were satisfied that there was nothing wrong with their stamina, and that as long as they carried sufficient food they could have gone even further. The walk was a distance of 66km (41ml).

Reading the articles and reports from this period we can see that these pioneers were feeling their way about the hills and mountains, testing their clothing and equipment (or the lack thereof), and building partnerships from amongst their new-found fellow club members. Confidence levels were also being strengthened, and their roving eyes began to pick out new challenges. Information gained would quickly be disseminated, both by articles and notes in the journals, and by word of mouth. Club meets were especially useful for passing on such advice.

The first real foray into a route up a Scottish mainland mountain began with an SMC party and the saga of the *Black Shoot* of Beinn Eunaich, a mountain of 989m in Glen Strae, lying just east-northeast of Ben Cruachan. The early history is described in an article by William R Lester.[17] In December 1889, while descending Beinn Eunaich, JR Robertson and WR Lester spotted this deep fissure high up on the rocky eastern shoulder of the mountain. They estimated it as being about 300 or 400ft in length. The rocks were coated in snow and ice and the pair carried walking sticks but no axes. Despite this, they boldly decided to attempt the climb. Robertson entered the gully proper, by which time he had dropped his walking stick. The pair were reduced to finding holds in the rock by picking out or melting snow and ice with their finger tips. After climbing the first 100ft they sensibly beat a retreat.

The second attempt was on April 6th 1890, during an Easter stay at Dalmally. This time the intrepid party of Lester and Thomas Fraser S Campbell had a rope but no axe. The winter's snow had gone, leaving slimy moss and trickling water. '*The shoot was therefore easier, but quite as disagreeable as before.*' On this occasion they managed a further 30ft, finding the rock steepening until all they could see above was an exceedingly steep and smooth chimney, approachable only by wide slabs of rock equally steep and smooth. From where they stood, it was impossible to see whether an exit to the shoot existed above. A strategic withdrawal was made.

The third attempt took place on New Year's Day 1892 with a foursome: John Henry Gibson, Naismith, Thomson and Lester. There was snow and ice, and – '*Our old enemy was found to be in a very bad condition. Such parts of the rock as were not under ice ran with water, or were covered with moss like a wet sponge.*' Lester managed to climb the vertical chimney, which was a waterfall, finally grinding to a halt 30ft higher at a large jammed boulder. It was coated with ice and defeated him. As there was room for one only at this point, and all were wet and miserable, retreat was made. On this attempt, they had come prepared with '*..alpine appliances, including ropes, axes, and even spikes.*' The latter would have been crampons or more likely specialised boot nails, which had so far not been mentioned in relation to Scottish mountaineering.

The fourth, and thankfully successful attempt, was made on the 19th May 1892, when Gibson, Naismith, Lester, and Willie Douglas assembled below the shoot. Gibson was unanimously voted leader, and the party quickly gained the foot of the vertical chimney. As Lester perceptively wrote –

> It has seemed to me remarkable how, on each attempt, we, with perfect ease, reached the highest point previously gained, surmounting without difficulty obstacles which had before taxed us severely. It was only after passing these points that difficulties seemed to begin. The unknown above seemed to magnify the obstacles, as no doubt it does in every first ascent.

The chimney was climbed and it was now up to Gibson to overcome the jammed boulder. The shoot had the last laugh of course, as the boulder was climbed, '*apparently with great ease*', only for the climbing above to present more difficulties. Finally, Gibson succeeded on the third of three possible routes and the team assembled again on the final slopes. The going was now strewn with loose stones, one of which, weighing several pounds, fell 20ft or so onto a shoulder of one of the party, happily resulting in bruising only. After two and a half hours effort, and four attempts, the 300ft of the Black Shoot had finally been overcome.

The successful party agreed that it would never see any of them again. It had given them enough, and more, of its water and mud. '*Should any one foolishly decide to follow in our steps*', concluded Lester, they would be well advised to choose summer and dry weather. It would in fact be a long five years before the second ascent was made, by John Bell and John Napier on 1st January 1897. As Bob Aitken wrote in his biographical sketch –

> Gibson's greatest service to the SMC was perhaps to have finally disposed of this unresolved relic of the classic Gully Era with its mud, slime, and icy water, so that the Club could move on to cleaner and pleasanter climbs.[18]

John Henry Gibson (1862–1898) was one of the most outstanding climbers during the early years of Scottish mountaineering; he joined the SMC in December 1891, along with such luminaries as Norman Collie and Sir Archibald Geikie, the eminent geologist. His life was sadly a short one, and his climbing career even more brief, as he contracted what was probably tuberculosis and died aged 36. He had taken up the family trade as a legal apprentice with the Edinburgh firm of Robert Strathern , and was admitted as a Writer to the Signet in 1888.

When Gibson finally led the successful party up the Black Shoot in May 1892, he had enjoyed five seasons in the Alps and was a member of the AC, having joined early the previous year. It would appear that his Scottish climbing lasted two years only, starting in March 1891 when he attended the SMC Easter meet at Dalmally as '*...an Alpine Club man*', the guest of Robert Augustus Robertson, a fellow Edinburgh solicitor. His last appearance on the records was in March 1893, when he made an audacious attempt on the Lochnagar gully now known as the Douglas–Gibson, but more of this later.

What was now apparent was that climbers in the new clubs, while enthusiastic about winter days in particular, were entering increasingly risky ground. There was no firm adherence as yet to ice axes, with several outings taking alpenstocks on a route while others took an axe, and yet others, neither. Alpenstocks were beginning to be regarded as being good for one thing only, glissading. This dangerous pastime, sliding down a steep snow slope in a semi-upright position, was made easier by the use of an alpenstock, its long wooden shaft trailed behind like the rudder of a small boat. It was not unusual for upwards of five or six hundred feet to be descended in a couple of minutes by this method, but disaster was never really far away. Respect for mountain conditions, gained by many in the Alps, was yet to be fully transferred to the Scottish hills.

As a minor warning, during the Easter 1891 meet at Dalmally, on which John Gibson made his entrance as a guest, John Rennie (1858–1937), an SMC OM, slipped while descending from the summit of Cruachan. Gaining Bealach an Lochain the party had been pleased to find –

> ...grand long snow slopes for glissading right into the big corrie. Rennie, however, slipped, and going head first a good deal faster than he intended, was cleverly brought up by Gibson, who was below, minus a good deal of skin from his hands...[19]

The party was carrying a rope, which some had used as assistance on the final part of the arête leading to the summit, but presumably Gibson had managed to stop Rennie manually, while Rennie suffered burns to his hands while sliding down.

John Rennie, who died a bachelor, seems to have had family money; although listed in the 1891 Census as an electrical engineer, no records of employment have been found. He must have been a competent mountaineer, the slip on Cruachan notwithstanding, as he was with Douglas and King on a traverse of the Meije in 1899, and with Raeburn, Douglas and Ling on their 1901 attempt on Observatory Buttress on Nevis.

His two younger brothers William and James emigrated to California, where Rennie made a visit in July 1913, being a guest of the Sierra Club. James Rennie climbed with the Sierra Club, and Francis P Fraquhar in his *History of the Sierra Nevada* (p229) refers to him as '*the durable Scot*'. The following March, John gave the SMC a slide show presentation, using both his slides and those of AW Russell, a fellow member. It was probable that Rennie met John Muir, the conservationist and mountaineer, while in California, and that he was a party to Muir being made an Honorary Member of the SMC in 1908. Rennie wrote Muir's obituary for the SMCJ in 1915.[20]

❄ ❄ ❄

Early travellers in Scotland, as mentioned in earlier chapters, based much of their transport on sail and steamer. This was due to necessity, as roads were generally very poor and the rail system had not yet been built. Skye, for example, could be gained by regular sailings by 1825. If a trip had to take to the road, it was at first by using horse-drawn transport: a pony and trap, or horse-drawn coach. Push-bikes were in common use by 1900, though in winter these were at the mercy of bad weather and perhaps snow. This explains why Dalmally was a regular venue for early SMC meets; it could be reached by train from Central Scotland. Fort William and Glen Coe were relatively remote and awkward to reach. The prime climbing areas on the west coast, Glen Coe and Ben Nevis, were basically unexplored until opened up by rail.

This state persisted until the opening of Fort William to rail in 1894, when it could be gained from Glasgow in under five hours. The rail reached Ballachulish in 1903. Eventually the rise of motor cars would force road improvements; the 'new' road through Glen Coe for example was built in 1929-30, with its bridges only being rebuilt in very recent years. It replaced in part the old sections which followed either an old drove road dating from 1786, or Telford's roads built in the early 1800s.[21] The ability to hold a club meet in Fort William also allowed for larger parties to gather. In the book by Drummond and Mitchell covering the Rev AE Robertson's outdoor life, Chapter Seven provides interesting details of how he accessed the mountains in order to ascend the Munros.[22]

In the same number of the 1891 SMCJ as the Notes containing Rennie's slip on Cruachan, Joe Stott refers to the second annual report of the Cairngorm Club and noticed with pleasure its *'flourishing condition.'* Stott's reference however was not without a nip at their heels –

> Although the summer excursions of the Club, which partake much of the nature of well-arranged mountain picnics, probably form the extent of the acquaintance of most members with the mountains, much good work has been done on the hills at all seasons of the year by several gentlemen, and some valuable information collected.

The Cairngorm Club certainly enjoyed their outings. In 1890, on the occasion of the Spring Holiday on the 5th May, 162 made it to the summit of Mount Keen. There were 45 ladies, and ages ranged from six to 76. Special train carriages were laid on, marked 'Engaged – The Cairngorm Club'. Despite this, as Sheila Murray's history of the Club recounts –

> The Railway Company were far from kindly in their provision of carriages. Some of the third class carriages belonged to the early period of train-running, and were without cushions. More than three-fourths of the party travelled third class to mark their sense of discourtesy shown by the Railway Company.[23]

Alexander Inkson McConnochie, who we met earlier, was active in both the SMC and the Cairngorm Club. McConnochie seems to have irritated some members of the SMC; perhaps his enthusiasm for the Cairngorms annoyed the wider horizons of the SMC, or it was at a more personal level – there is no direct evidence which suggests a reason – unless we see the start-up of another mountaineering journal as a source. One other possibility was that he probably shared radical views on access with his friend Ernest Baker. At some basic tribal level he could be seen as being disloyal to the SMC. His first number of the Cairngorm Club Journal came out in July 1893, and was reviewed in the SMCJ by Maylard, then SMC Secretary.[24] Maylard began by saying that the publication of a second Journal [in Scotland] would come as no little surprise to some. He then continued by wondering –

> ...why a member of the Scottish Mountaineering Club, a member of the Executive, and a worthy contributor to its Journal, should have thought fit to edit what is practically a facsimile. Under the circumstances, it is right for us to consider what amount of material is likely to exist suitable for publication. Doubtless our field is an extensive one for essentially practical purposes; but whether that field contains a sufficiently inexhaustive stock of material and a sufficient number of those capable of giving suitable expression to it, without sinking to what might be termed twaddle and commonplaces, are questions sufficiently grave to be well pondered over.

Maylard went to some lengths to make it clear that he saw no intent to spoil the way for the SMCJ; he was basically worried that the available information on the Scottish hills might prove unable to sustain two journals. We have to take him at his word. He continued by going back to the actual content of the Cairngorm Club Journal, for which, as he wrote, he found '*nothing but praise.*' (In a footnote to an article containing edited extracts from letters from Stott in New Zealand to Willie Douglas in Scotland, Robin Campbell suggests this is but '*faint praise.*'[25])

Meanwhile, in far away New Zealand, ex-Editor Stott was now working for their National Bank. His successor as SMCJ Editor, Douglas, was sending him copies of the Cairngorm Club Journal. In a letter dated 7th February 1895, Stott wrote to thank Douglas for various favours – '*Next the Cairngorm Club Journal, which always interests me – were it only for their d-----d cheek in imitating us so closely.*'

Further down the same letter, Stott continued –

> I am very much taken with the idea of a 'Climbers Guide to Scotland.' They couldn't find a better man than you for Editor. Put Munro, McConnochie and Collie on the Committee anyway – Hinxman too. The time is premature I think; as there are lots of fine mountains that probably none of you have been on – much less surveyed as you have Cruachan – Laoigh, etc. Still if you don't take it up soon – that man Haskett Smith will cut in, and hash the thing badly.[26]

In the January 1892 number of the SMCJ, Stott reviewed the latest short guide from McConnochie, *Lochnagar*. He wrote a wholly positive review, with no sign of faint praise or indeed any other negative criticism. It would seem that any irritation with McConnochie was indeed caused by the publication of the rival club journal. A simple, human reaction. Stott would of course be receiving copies of the SMCJ. These he would read and reread, before sending a letter to Douglas with an article by article review. Stott had begun to explore New Zealand, being content that his bachelorhood allowed him ample time to do this. He was involved in the formation of the New Zealand Alpine Club, and was a founder Vice-President. On the 7th February 1895 he wrote to Douglas –

> I've been out for 3 years now. Another 2 and I hope to be wi' ye a'. You wish me a happy New Year – thanks – 'and a wife.' No no not the latter. I should give up all my hobbies I fear if I took to such a new hobby as that; and might not even come home. Bide a wee.

This letter turned out to be prescient. On 10th November 1896, he wrote again from Wellington –

> Well, I suppose you've heard the news about me. I have been clean knocked off my perch by a little charmer.
>
> She's all perfection in my eyes – that goes without saying. Some day you'll do the same thing yourself, and then you'll understand. When I come I'll join the old buffers brigade.

Stott's first wife died in 1924. A Bank Inspector, he later moved to Australia, and remarried a banker's widow. He died in Melbourne, on the 7th July 1938, at the age of 77.[27] His obituary in the SMCJ described him as being –

> ...of medium height, stoutly built, a well-made man with prodigious muscular strength and one of the cheeriest companions... Hill-walking was his passion and the longest of days had no terror for him...Perhaps of necessity he had a craze for walking during the night, and he was the ringleader in many mad walks which space forbids me from describing...those who were in touch with him during his long exile can realise that his thoughts and dreams were in the heartbreak words of Robert Louis Stevenson:
>
> 'Blows the wind to-day, and the sun and the rain are flying,
>   Blows the wind on the moor, to-day and now.
> Where about the graves of the martyrs the *whaups are crying,
>   My heart remembers how.'
>
> *whaups – Scots for curlews.

❄ ❄ ❄

It would be a few years before the SMC began their own guidebook publications, but in the interim another type of publication was about to see the light of day with Hugh Munro's Tables of Scottish mountains of 3,000ft or more. Mr Munro (he would not assume his title until the death of his father in 1913) was then 33, with the rheumatism not yet fully holding back his hill days which ceased in 1915. In an astounding burst of work, Munro compiled his list between December 1889 and the summer of 1891. According to RN Campbell, this was at the request of the Club, and probably following the first Committee meeting. We can read into this action an organised approach to documenting the Scottish mountains; first see how many there are and where they are. Next document the common routes of ascent.

Although it can be argued that this aspect of the Scottish mountains – hillwalking – does not quite fall precisely within the mountaineering criterion, nonetheless it is commonly associated with it, and deserves a mention en route. Munro had made a suggestion in December 1889, at the SMC's first Annual General Meeting, that members should mark on a map their routes, and that these maps should then be deposited in the Club Library, available for all to see who had done what routes, in order that information could then be sought more easily.

By January 1891 Munro had progressed sufficiently well enough with his research that he could write a review of the new series of maps published by Bartholomew. These were based on the OS maps and were reduced to a scale of two miles to the inch. They were coloured according to heights and Munro was quite critical of variations within the series. He was also by then a Fellow of the Royal Geographical Society. For his research into the List, Munro used both the One-Inch and the Six-Inch maps. He also relied quite heavily on the knowledge accrued by Norman Collie and Colin Phillip, as well as other club members.

According to Robin Campbell, author of *The Munroist's Companion*,[28] when Munro began his task he had visited only 42 tops. The 3,000ft tops are covered by 30 One-Inch sheets. There was a maximum of 36 Six-Inch sheets per One-Inch sheet, though not all of the larger scale maps would have been required. Still, Campbell estimates that some 600 maps in all might have been needed for consultation.[29]

Initially, it was to have been a 'straightforward' list of the mountains of 3,000ft or more, but looking at the project on the maps and on the ground, Munro decided that what was needed was a listing of separate summits and their tops. He wished to pick out the mountains which were, in his opinion, '*distinct and separate*.' His task was not made easy by the difference between the two series of OS maps; the Six-Inch series contained numerous spot heights and names, but no contours, while the One-Inch series had 250-foot contours but few spot heights or names. He must have become expert at alternating between the two maps covering a hill of interest.

Munro's List appeared in Number six, the last number of the SMCJ Volume One, in September 1891. In his introduction to the Tables, Munro stated that –

> The exact number cannot be determined, owing to the impossibility of deciding what should be considered distinct mountains. For instance, Braeriach and

> Cairn Toul are always counted as separate mountains, and so are the various peaks of the Cuillins, in Skye ; and yet these are no more distinct than are Sron Isean or Stob Daimh from the main two peaks of Ben Cruachan, one and a half and two miles to the west. The names of these peaks, though, are not even given on the Ordnance sheet, but are generally included under the name Ben Cruachan.[30]

In all, Munro listed some 538 tops. There were 283 separate mountains, which are now called 'Munros'. The current print of the SMC guide *The Munros* published in 2013, lists 282 Munros, though this number has varied slightly over the years as surveying technology has become more sophisticated.[31] As detailed in Campbell's book, various mathematical models have been devised in order to attempt a definition of what constitutes a mountain and what constitutes a top. The marvel of it all, however, is how close Munro came to pinning it down for posterity. To date (February 2015), some 5,668 have registered their completion of the Munros with the SMC,[32] with an estimated additional 10% who have remained unregistered. As an aside, Munros Tables proved so popular that issue Number six of the SMCJ in which they were published sold out quickly. Issue Number one had sold out by May 1891. Requests to have it reprinted were however opposed by Munro, presumably because he wished to retain a firm grip on the copyright. As a result, Volume One of the SMCJ is scarce. Munros Tables™ is now a registered trademark, owned by the SMC.

As a footnote to the Tables, the Journal Editor, Stott, acknowledged '*the immense extent of the labour undertaken by Mr Munro.*' In time alone, Stott continued, the work occupied over 300 hours during some five months. Stott admitted that he had been '*somewhat of a task-master in the matter*', but even so, it had been a remarkable piece of orographical research.

Scotland now had organised bands of mountaineers, within which information was flowing freely. There was a catalogue of the mountains, and sets of maps. The railway was rapidly extending its networks and very soon would reach Fort William on the west coast. All that was required now was for the realisation to emerge that Scottish mountains had more to offer than snowy ridges and wintry gullies. A golden age was about to dawn, and 1892 would see significant steps taken in the development of rock climbing.

References

1. Scotways. <http://www.scotways.com/> Accessed September 2013.
2. <http://hansard.millbanksystems.com/commons/1900/may/16/access-to-mountains-scotland-bill>
3. The Times, London. *The Shutting of The Glens*, 5th December, 1846.
4. Ken Crocket and Simon Richardson, *Ben Nevis: Britain's Highest Mountain*

(Scottish Mountaineering Trust, 2009, 2nd edition), 56-83.)
5. An Account of the Foundation & Work at the Ben Nevis Observatory (Edinburgh:1885).
6. Lippe, Robert. Quoted in *The Cairngorm Club – 1887 – 1987*, Sheila Murray (Aberdeen, The Cairngorm Club, 1987), 1.
7. Aitken, Bob. *Personal Communication*. February 2014.
8. Ramsay, Professor George G., *The Formation of the Scottish Mountaineering Club*. SMCJ, 4, 20, May 1896, 73-91.
9. Maylard, Ernest A. *The Foundation of the Club*. In: Notes and Excursions, SMCJ 20, 119, April 1935, 367-369.
10. Maylard, Ernest A. *The Club in Retrospect. I. - Its Origin and Growth*. SMCJ 22, 127, April 1939, 6-13.
11. Aitken, Robert, SMC Original Members : a working biographical list, SMC Archives.
12. Veblen, Thorstein (1953) [1899]. *The Theory of the Leisure Class: An Economic Study of Institutions, the Mentor Edition*. Introduction by C. Wright Mills. (New York: The Macmillan Company, 1899). Also available online at Project Gutenberg: <http://www.gutenberg.org/ebooks/833>
13. Aitken, Bob. *Personal communication*. February 2014.
14. Munro, H.T. Winter Ascents, SMCJ, 1, 1, Jan. 1890, 20-24.
15. Thomson, Gilbert. *The Arrochar Mountains*. SMCJ, 1, 2, May 1890, 63-69.
16. Thomson, Gilbert. *Bidean and the Buchailles*. SMCJ, 1, 3, Sept. 1890, 89-97.
17. Lester, W.R. *The Black Shoot of Stob Maol*. SMCJ, 2, 3, Sept. 1892, 117-120.
18. Aitken, Robert. *John Henry Gibson*. <http://www.smc.org.uk/Gallery/SMC%20Pioneers/JHG.php>
19. Munro, H.T. *Notes and Queries*. SMCJ, 1, 5, May 1891, p.240.
20. Rennie, J. *In Memorium – John Muir*. SMCJ, 13, 76, Feb. 1915, 206-207.
21. Chris's British Road Directory <http://www.cbrd.co.uk/histories/a82/>
22. Peter Drummond and Ian Mitchell, *The First Munroist* (The Ernest Press, 1993).
23. Murray, Sheila. *The Cairngorm Club – 1887 – 1987* (Aberdeen, The Cairngorm Club, 1987), 14.
24. Maylard, Ernest A. *Mountaineering Literature. "The Cairngorm Club Journal"*. SMCJ, 2, 6, Sept.1893, 324-326.
25. Campbell, R.N. *My Dear Douglas*, SMCJ 34, 181, 388-399.
26. Ibid. p.391.
27. Robertson, R.A. *In Memorium – Joseph Gibson Stott*. SMCJ, 21, 126, Nov. 1938, 421-422.
28. Campbell, R.N. *The Munroists Companion* (Scottish Mountaineering Trust , 1999).
29. Campbell, R.N. *Defining and Classifying*. In: The Munroists Companion. (Scottish Mountaineering Trust, 1999), 118.
30. Munro, H.T. *Tables giving all the Scottish Mountains exceeding 3,000 feet in height*. SMCJ, 1, 6, Sept.1891, 276-314.
31. Donald Bennet and Rab Anderson, Eds. *The Munros (*SMT, 2010).
32. <http://www.smc.org.uk/Munros/Munros.php>

5

Rock Climbers (1891-92)

VOLUME 2 of the SMCJ, published in January 1892, opened with a farewell message from Joe Stott; he was off to New Zealand, and although confessedly homesick, would, as far as we know, return only once to Scotland. The new Editor was Willie Douglas, who enjoyed a marathon run of issues from 1892 through to 1909, completing Volume 10 (60 issues), as the Journal was then published three times per year. By all accounts a popular man, and by his own admission not one of the 'tigers' of the club, he nonetheless pops up on many a profitable expedition. With several good Alpine ascents such as the Meije and Assiniboine, he was obviously no mean mountaineer.

The increasing interest in rock climbing was indicated in an article by Gilbert Thomson in the first issue by Douglas, lamenting the fact that it was difficult to find anything new, and that also, with perhaps only half a day to spare in the week, it was next to impossible. Adding to this the fact that without any exercise in the sport, a good day out was easily spoiled by unfitness, Thomson and his climbing friend Naismith discussed the dilemma and concluded that some Saturday afternoons and summer evenings –

> ...might be well spent...in hunting up dainty bits of rock climbing...A precipice 20 feet high does not sound very serious, continued Thomson, but there may be more fun and real climbing in getting up or down such a place than there is in ascending the 4,406 feet of Ben Nevis.[1]

There may have been a touch of tongue in cheek by Thomson with this startling remark, but applying some lateral thinking there is also the possibility that knowing very little of the vast climbing potential waiting to be discovered on the north-east face of Ben Nevis, Thomson was in fact thinking of a pedestrian ascent by the bridle path when he made this remark.

Even Naismith seemed unaware of this potential, since as late as 1889, in his article describing his two early ascents of Nevis, he remarked that –

> ...I may state, on the authority of one of the men at the Observatory, that the great northern precipice is cleft at one place by a gully, by means of which it is possible to scale that side of the mountain.[2]

Whatever the truth, the pair gamely began their explorations for rock in Central Scotland. Cartland Crags near Lanark were examined, with a traverse through the river gorge providing many climbing tests. Edinburgh of course had the Salisbury Crags, even though there would be a semi-permanent state of war between climbers and park attendants. This was usually sorted by climbing before the attendants had risen from their beds. Finally, the intrepid pair homed in on The Whangie, an unusual rock feature found nestling on the north flank of Auchineden Hill, several kilometres west of the Campsie Hills, and relatively close to Blanefield which then was served by train.

At first the pair could find no one who knew where The Whangie was, but they found a description in a book entitled *Rambles Round Glasgow*.[3] Following this, they soon found themselves at the feature, a great slice, or whang of rock, some 90m in length and one to five metres in width. This had parted from the main mass on the hillside, forming a narrow, gloomy passage. The jumbled remains of an earlier landslip lies in front of the existing one. The rock is an olivine basalt, weathering badly on the outer face, and as Thomson and Naismith found, some of it is in a precarious condition.[4]

Having said that, the views are superb, looking over moorland to the Loch Lomond basin, and with care and a top-rope for protection, some good exercise can indeed be gained. After some time spent climbing, they continued their walk over Duncolm Hill, Fynloch Hill and The Slacks, finally catching a train at Kilbowie, whence they arrived at Glasgow's Queen Street station '*...only three-quarters of an hour late.*' Gilbert Thomson, MA FRSE MInstCE, who was a very active member of the SMC and a regular climbing partner of Naismith, was by training a Sanitary Engineer. He was the author of *Modern Sanitary Engineering* (London: Constable, 1912), which ran to more than one edition. Volume 1 concentrated on House Drainage, and we should recall that the population of Glasgow at this time was expanding rapidly, with a commensurate need for housing and particularly better sanitation.

A graduate from Edinburgh, he began to build a practice in Glasgow, meanwhile giving evening lectures at the Anderson College (which would eventually become Strathclyde University). He had replaced Arthur Thomson (no relation) who had resigned to teach in India. Gilbert Thomson's evening lectures in Sanitation started in session 1890-91 and ran for an amazing 48 years. His career was seemingly not without stress, and at one point he resigned from his Civil Engineering position, where he taught during the day, until another lecturer was brought in. Thomson is regarded as having initiated the teaching of both Public Health Engineering and Environmental Health under the aegis of Civil Engineering. He also served continuously on the Board of Studies of the College for at least 43 years. We can assume that his energetic outings in the mountains were a good release of the stress of everyday work.

Thomson almost died using his climbing experience in a professional capacity. He was asked to be an expert witness in a case involving pollution from a Highland factory chimney; the owners of adjacent land used for shooting claimed the factory was affecting the heather. Thomson found a similar chimney in Glasgow and without advice climbed it using steeple-jack's equipment. He stuck his head over the top and almost lost consciousness in the noxious fumes. There is an amusing description of Thomson in an article by Lord Mackay, written in 1950 –

> Physically, he was of a tall, sparse build which somehow always seemed to typify his strong and upright character, with a tall, long neck that carried a small head on top, but that neck was full of character. The eyes in the head had a queer sudden trick of swivelling upon one, with a specially sharp, alert look. When any good point was made the head and neck seemed somehow to me to stretch more and more, up and up as difficulties were involved, so that when he became our first Scots casualty by having a considerable stone come down a gully and fall on his top, I could almost imagine the neck expanding upwards to meet it, as something to be scorned.[5]

Their report of the Whangie outing spread, and a team consisting of Fraser Campbell, Lester and Naismith were soon finding a '*...variety of "sporting variations"*'. A much larger group was hot on their heels, visiting The Whangie on Saturday, 12th December 1891, the day after the third Annual Dinner of the SMC which had been held in the St Enoch Hotel, Glasgow. Thomson reported this outing in a footnote to his article. The party included Horace Walker, then President of the Alpine Club, Professors Ramsay (SMC President) and Veitch, and Maylard, Munro, Naismith, WA Ramsay and Thomson. Despite the icy conditions, with many cracks filled with snow and ice –

> An hour or two...was very enjoyably spent in various pieces of fancy climbing, the concluding part being done to the accompaniment of a fierce snowstorm, which pelted us well as we made our way back over the moor.

The first reported accident on The Whangie occurred on 11th September 1892. Fraser Campbell was climbing with Lester when they began an attempt on 'Thomson's Pinnacle', previously climbed by Thomson. Keeping the rope on, but not actually using it, Campbell gained the summit of the ridge and was about to make the last step, feet firmly planted, and his arms wrapped round a block which formed the apex of the ridge. The entire mass gave way, pushing him out over the cliff face, which here was some 40ft in height. Lester was at this point eight or ten feet lower, and a little distance along the ridge. Seeing Campbell fall, he stepped over the edge to the other side, as far as he could, but unfortunately he was pulled off and fell heavily on to the rocks below. The momentary tug on the rope at least kept Campbell in a heads up position, and he was able to seek assistance at Auchineden House, from a Mr Pollock, on whose property The Whangie was situated. Lester escaped with a compound fracture of a wrist and severe bruising.[6]

❄ ❄ ❄

While the search for climbable rock at low levels was ongoing, at higher altitude the hunt was not quite as successful. Naismith had been to the island of Arran as a youth, in the summers of 1872 and '73. He was then aged 16 or 17, and presumably on family holidays. In 1872 he had walked up 'Malloch Buie' (probably Mullach Buidhe, the 819m top north-east of North Goatfell), while the following year he recorded Goatfell, Cir Mhor, Beinn Tarsuinn, Beinn Nuis, Caisteal Abhail and several others.[7] The memory of the rugged granite slopes of the Arran hills must have remained in his mind, as he set out on a number of exploratory climbs beginning in 1891 with a solo ascent of Summit Chimney on Cir Mhor, a 30m Moderate. He was also prompted into returning to Arran by an earlier visit from Fraser Campbell and Lester who described a circuit of the Glen Sannox hills in an article.[8]

Naismith was back in September 1891, this time accompanied by Gilbert Thomson. Naismith described their ascent of the North-east Face of Cir Mhor in an SMCJ article.[9] There was an inconsistency here between what Naismith described, and what appeared in the Climbers' Guides covering Arran. The correct history was finally printed in the 2014 edition.[10] Until then, SMC guidebooks ascribed ascents of Gully D and Stoneshoot Ridge to Naismith and Thomson, but in his SMCJ article Naismith describes the ascent of one route only, Stoneshoot Ridge. Further, in an article written by Thomson in Volume 3 of the SMCJ, accompanied by a fine drawing of the north face of Cir Mhor, it is quite clear that 1891 saw an ascent of Stoneshoot Ridge only. Gully D, as it is now named, was climbed by Naismith and Douglas in August 1894.[11]

One point is clear; the early climbing on this face was found to be almost universally ghastly, with loose rock, vegetation, slimy gullies, rotten slabs, and all the makings of a climber's nightmare. The mountain might have been better named Janus, given the glorious rock found on the other face, but at least the pioneers were beginning to stretch their horizons, as far as limited time and public transport could allow. We also should bear in mind that glorious rock or not, these pioneers were well aware that to attempt to climb vast, steep expanses of granite slabs or buttresses would be akin to suicide, given the lack of protection. In the dank and often earthy confines of gullies and chimneys they could at least find numerous places to stop and perhaps even throw a rope over a boulder or flake for a belay.

If the Buachaille Etive Mor in Glen Coe epitomises the classic mountain on the mainland of Scotland, then Cir Mhor on Arran could be a suitable island counterpoint. Its North-east face certainly drew the pioneers like moths to a light, with nine routes from the 1890s listed in the current guide. One reason for this was the ease of access to those living in the more densely populated Central Belt (earlier known as the Scottish Midlands) by train and steamer, with weekend climbing easily attainable. Willie Naismith, who with Gilbert Thomson began the campaign in October 1891 with Stoneshoot Ridge, was on at least half of these routes. The routes are not easily disentangled from the early recordings, but fortunately neither are they worth climbing except to those with a love of wet, slimy rock, sandwiched in between grass and scree, and with a leavening of wet cave pitches.

Its true appeal to the modern climber lies mainly in winter conditions, though there are also several newer rock climbs worth climbing. Early explorations are described here as a fine example of Victorian true grit, similar to the various escapades involving the Black Shoot of Beinn Eunaich, but on a much larger scale. Corrie village could be used as a base; the more northerly of Corrie's two harbours is often called Corrie Port and was the stopping off point for the steamers that, from the mid-1800s, linked many of Arran's coastal villages with a wider network of Clyde ports.

On the morning of Thursday, 1st October 1891, Naismith and Thomson roused themselves in their hotel at Corrie and set off at the unlikely hour of 4.45am. They entered Glen Sannox then struck up the north ridge of Cioch na h-Oighe, finally gaining the bealach called The Saddle, east of Cir Mhor's summit. In Naismith's article describing this day,[12] he takes more space describing the awkward approach to the face than he does to their climb, involving, as it did, the crossing of smoothly shelving rocks which dipped the wrong way. Indeed, they roped up for the worst of the traverse.

Finally, the two pilgrims passed a projecting spur and found themselves in the heart of the wild corrie that forms upper Glen Sannox. They picked out three places where they thought an ascent might be possible.

> The first, which was not far away, was where a dyke or rib of rock jutted out between two cracks. We tried the dyke itself, and also climbed to the head of the crack on the right, but soon decided that, if possible at all, an ascent there would have been too tedious for the time at our disposal.

Included in Naismith's article is a hand-drawn sketch of the face. A footnote states that the '*...outline was sketched very rapidly, and afterwards finished from memory, so that it may not be quite accurate in some details.*' Nonetheless, and using the sketch in conjunction with three later drawings, it is possible to be fairly happy with the identity of the major features. Naismith has indicated their entire exploratory wander, from the col, through the traversing approach, the two attempts, and the final ascent, all with a dotted line. It appears that the rib they attempted firstly was probably the 180m Severe line named Ribbish in the 1989 guidebook but now not included in the 2014 edition, which refers to the line as '*appalling*'.

The two '*cracks*' referred to by Naismith are now known as Gullies B1 and B2 – the '*crack on the right*' was probably Gully B2. In summer, B1 was climbed in 1942 and is described as an unpleasant Very Difficult. B2 is also described as an unpleasant Very Difficult, and was first recorded by Raeburn and William Clark in 1897. (As will be seen below, this was probably the second ascent.)

Naismith and Thomson then continued moving rightwards, to find what they thought was the second possible route. This was '*...by a ridge beside a well-marked gully that ran up and across the mountain face, pointing to the left of the summit.*' There were signs of a recent rock fall in this gully, with the slope below strewn with rectangular blocks of yellow granite, '*...some of them as big as an ordinary harmonium.*' This gully would have been Gully D, also known as Trap Dyke Climb. Finally they stood below the third possible route –

> ...seemingly quite manageable,...by means of a great couloir, which, starting only a short distance west of the stone-shoot just mentioned, ascended to the right and struck the ridge between Cir Mhor and Caisteal Abhail four or five hundred feet below the summit of the former.

This was to be named later as the Western Stone Shoot. Returning again to the second possible option –

> After a hurried repast, we again roped, and attacked the ridge beside the stone-shoot. The rocks were steep, and covered with gravel and loose chips with no cohesion. Although the ascent offered no real difficulty, we remarked at the time that descent by this "road" would need a little care...The ridge, which was followed for a considerable way, fell abruptly on our left. On the other side, the shoot became shallower as we rose, so that by way of variety we diverted our course into its channel for a short distance, close to a corner where some large blocks were jammed. We were glad to get out again. Apart from the risk of falling stones, everything was terribly unstable,–our own footing included,–the disintegrated granite that covered the smoothly ground rocks acting much in the same way as "ball-bearings"! At one point the party nearly had an unpremeditated slide down the shoot.

Just below a fresh scar in the rocks, from which they thought the 'harmoniums' had fallen, the gully split into two branches. They chose the left, whence a difficult chimney led to a narrow grass slope. Aiming for a notch above, they were delighted to find that they were only 100ft or so from the summit. The first route up the north-east face of Cir Mhor, *Trap Dyke Climb* (120m Difficult), had been climbed. Sadly, James McGregor Johnstone's 1958 SMC guidebook describes it as a most unpleasant route which should be avoided.[13]

The following year, 1892, two new climbers appeared on Arran: Frank Percy Evers and J Bristow. Evers was a solicitor in Stourbridge, west of Birmingham. Little is known of Bristow. A note of the ascent of their route appeared four years later in the SMCJ, and it belatedly appeared as an ascent of Gully B2 in Johnstone's guidebook.

Naismith and Thomson were back in Arran at the end of September, 1893. On Thursday 28th, another pre-5am start was made from Corrie. On this occasion the rain began as they entered Glen Sannox, and a good drenching was had. They finally succeeded in making the first ascent of the *Western Stone Shoot* (140m Moderate). After this ascent they continued to walk over A' Chir, Beinn Tarsuinn, and Beinn Nuis. About midday the weather cleared, helping in a small degree to dry their saturated clothing. Brodick was reached just in time for the afternoon boat.

By now the word was surely out of a huge mountain face, with easy access from the Central Valley of Scotland, and holding a satisfying number of tempting routes – mostly unclimbed. And so, as Gilbert Thomson wrote, in August 1894, a '*...regular siege of the Arran hills was instituted, and Cir Mhor had its share of attention.*'[14] Willie Douglas, as a sort of commander-in-chief and still a bachelor, booked quarters in Corrie for a month and –

> ...persuaded Naismith (by wheedling, cajoling, and threats of bodily violence) to join him for about half that time; and was aided by flying visits from Boyd, Fraser Campbell, Maclay, Rennie, and myself, among Club members; while assistance was also lent by Dr Douglas, and Messrs Herdman and Sang.

(Willie Douglas had joined the SMC in 1890; we assume that Dr Douglas, a non-member of the SMC, would have been a relative. On Cioch na h-Oighe, a JJ Douglas climbed with Naismith and Thomson on 9th August 1894, and he was very probably the Dr Douglas referred to above, one of Willie Douglas' brothers.)

Thomson's article included an excellent sketch of the face, made from a photograph. Douglas, Naismith and Thomson had taken it in turns to haul a big camera to the top of Ceum-na-Caillich; Willie Douglas took the photograph, and Naismith drew the sketch from it. Yet again, Gully A was attempted, by the trio on a very wet day. They ground to a halt at the first of two steep pitches, with much water coming down. Continuing to prowl further along the foot of the face, Naismith and Dr Douglas found and climbed what had been called Gully D. It was basically a scramble in a groove, over wet and rotten rocks, leading up and leftwards to a grass patch. Gullies B and C also led to this grass from below.

Above the grass they found one of the most interesting bits on the whole face, climbed by what they called the '*cave route.*' Thomson reached Corrie just after the first ascent of Gully D, renamed Trap Dyke Climb. He was invited onto a second ascent, the intention of Naismith and Dr Douglas to '*wander*' him in the cave. They gained the cave by an easier variation to Trap Dyke Climb, scrambling up rock on its right.[15]

> I was invited to go ahead, cheered by the assurance that the thing had been done; but before I could make any attempt at progress, my companions (probably remembering that it was not a comfortable place for a prolonged smoke) changed their minds, and Naismith, with the rope, swarmed up a steep block, and vanished through a black hole in the ceiling.

More wriggling through the depths of the cave and the climbers finally emerged onto a huge pile of blocks in the open air. Apparently Naismith had engaged in much digging and a general clearance of rubbish in order to open up the ways. As Thomson remarked– '*...the route would not be suitable for any one with a "bow window"*', i.e. a sizeable waistline! This gave its name to the climb, as the Bow Window Cave.

A mention should be made about the above reference to smoking. Group photographs from this time increasingly show a number of the pioneers with cigarettes in hand. In 1881 a machine was invented that revolutionised cigarette production. The machine chopped the tobacco, then dropped a certain amount of the tobacco into a long tube of paper, which the machine would then roll and extrude to where it would be sliced by the machine into individual cigarettes. This machine operated at thirteen times the speed of a human cigarette roller. It caused an enormous growth in the tobacco industry until the health consequences of smoking were revealed in the mid-20th century. There is one brief mention in the journals regarding the possible effect of cigarette smoking on hill fitness, but otherwise there appeared to be a sublime ignorance of any possible ill effects.

The next climb found was *Maclay's Chimney* (75m Very Difficult), admirably awarded with the adjective *repulsive* in the current guide. This was another August 1894 climb, and the gladiators on this occasion were Maclay, Douglas and Naismith, with Maclay the leader on the initial difficulties. In Johnstone's 1958 guidebook it is graded as Severe, which would make it the hardest climb on this face to that date.

James Maclay (18??-1925) was a Glasgow solicitor, who gave his name to, amongst other climbs, Maclay's Chimney on the Cobbler. He enjoyed many Alpine seasons, climbing with his sisters and with his brother-in-law,

Godfrey Solly. In his Obituary Notice by Willie Naismith, it was stated that -

> James Maclay feared God, and seemed to know no other fear. One Easter a mountaineering party climbed into Ossian's Cave in Glencoe, under very icy and dangerous conditions. No hitch could be found for the rope, and the position of the last man descending was not an enviable one, but Maclay, who was very muscular, cheerfully undertook that task. [16]

He died while holidaying with his wife and family near Loch Lochay, on the Caledonian Canal, suddenly of a heart failure, on his way to the canal steamer after a day's outing.

Maclay and Naismith were both gluttons for punishment, and were back later in August to climb *Pinnacle Ridge* (140m Difficult). There are four pinnacles to be overcome, with the fourth bypassed on the right as it overhangs. Like most of the early climbs on this side of the mountain, it is far superior in winter conditions, when it gives a III,4. The following month, September, saw John Hart Bell team up with Edward William Green to produce *Bell's Groove* 60m (Very Difficult). Bell, no relation to the later James HB Bell, was one of the early tigers of the SMC. Green, an engineer from Glasgow, was awarded the OBE, (possibly for climbing on this face), and was about to be seconded by Bell for SMC membership. Accordingly, he would probably be on his best behaviour.

In the autumn of 1897, William Clark persuaded Raeburn to show him some climbing on Cir Mhor; their route will be expanded upon below, but they finished by climbing Bell's Groove. The 'boiler plates' of Beinn Nuis, huge rocky slabs akin to those just climbed on Cir Mhor, were indirectly responsible for the huge argument and controversy which arose from comments Raeburn made following their ascent of Bell's Groove. The controversy is outlined later (See Chapter 8), and stemmed from Raeburn stating that he would not trust a climber who had only climbed on Skye.

John Bell and Edward Green returned to Cir Mhor in July 1895, along with Herbert C Boyd and Robert Graham Napier. The latter, a Glasgow Chartered Accountant, joined the SMC in 1896 and was Treasurer from 1901-06, and thereafter Auditor for many years. He was on the first ascent of Church Door Buttress in Glen Coe. He died on Christmas Eve, 1946. Boyd was a lawyer and Writer to the Signet.

The first ascent made by this party, and led by John Bell, was the rocky rib between B and C Gullies, taking in some serious slabs. Firstly, the party tried C Gully. Failing on this, they next attempted a crack to its left, failing again. Finally they attacked the rib of rock, finding initially the rocks broken and fairly easy. Higher up they became smoother, with cracks allowing progress. Higher still, some very stiff slabs were encountered, in places so steep and holdless that Bell required assistance from below.

At this point, 200ft up the face, they entered a steep gully of rotten and treacherous grass, the upper continuation of B Gully, between steep walls. It ended in a jumble of huge blocks where, crawling through a hole, the party entered a small cave about 12ft high. Bell, standing on Green's shoulders, managed to exit via a hole in the roof, then hauled up his companions. Easier ground then led to the top of Stoneshoot Ridge and they finished by Bell's Groove.[17] *B2C Rib* (70m Very Difficult) had been climbed.

William Wickham King added a note to Bell's account, describing that three years earlier, in August 1892, his two friends Evers and Bristow had followed much the same route as Bell, the main difference being that they apparently kept to Gully B2 from the start. They had no rope, and although they '*...encountered some rather difficult pitches, we gather from their description that they had selected a somewhat easier route than Mr Bell's party.*' This letter from King, sent to Willie Douglas as Editor of the SMCJ, ended with King stating that '*Evers if he goes up again would much rather take a rope with him.*'

There remained other variations to be found on this face. On 14th September 1896 Naismith and Haskett Smith traversed the upper part of the face from the head of Stoneshoot Ridge using a prominent grass ledge below the Groove Route and so gained the skyline west of the summit. From the Pinnacle Ridge they found much scrambling in '*...curious places– including a round tunnel worn through the solid rock and a fantastic cleft, where all the skill of the conqueror of the Napes Needle was needed to force a passage.*'[18] This led eventually to the Upper Shelf, which they descended by Gully M, in preference to Maclay's Chimney on its right.[19]

In the autumn of 1897 William Clark and Raeburn climbed the first part of the face by Gully B2. Clark described their day in an article, and although admitting that their route was only partly original, he thought it worth recounting.[20] In particular, their ascent of the Dungeon Bottle Cave is interesting, as it provides yet another fine example of Raeburn at his best. The two climbers moved up Gully B and found themselves seemingly blocked by a huge rock. They noticed a narrow opening at its right end, through which Raeburn managed to scramble. Clark joined him, and they found themselves in a well-formed cave, in the opening of which, about 11ft up from the floor, was an opening, apparently inaccessible to a single-handed climber. It sloped upwards, and at the top was about four feet long by two feet wide. Lower down it widened until it became about four feet across, when it was a full stretch for a climber using shoulders and toes for support. Holds were practically absent and from no walls could a direct climb be made –

> To my surprise the leader, after pacing about for some minutes like a caged lion, declared his intention of going through the hole, and in due course I beheld

him, minus coat and rope, his shoulders pressing one side of the hole, his feet the other side, and so he walked up to the daylight, back downwards and face to the sky. Roped, I endeavoured to follow, but only succeeded in getting one foot and my neck into the hole, which I tenanted for perhaps three minutes, during which time Raeburn gave me excellent advice in a cheering voice. But the laws of gravity and obesity are inexorable, and with a jerk I swung free in the air, and had my revenge as I was lowered over Raeburn's knee, the only available pulley. Ignominiously I beat a retreat through the entrance door, and made a way up the right-hand wall of the gully.

On Sunday, 23rd February 1902, Harry Lawson, Sandy Mackay and Raeburn left their accommodation in Corrie and headed up through the murk to Cir Mhor. They had arrived in Arran the previous day, prompted by a report by Clark of a fine chimney on Beinn a' Chliabheinn. Descending one potential candidate from the ridge, they allowed Mackay to go first, Lawson and Raeburn judging that if Mackay could succeed, they should have no difficulty in following –

[we] paid for our presumption at the second jammed stone pitch by getting fairly hung up for several minutes. Mackay's khaki gabardine suit, though it made him look like a diver without his helmet just ascended from sea bottom, seemed to slither over the rocks, where our tweeds caught.[21]

At the foot of the third pitch, the chimney opened out into a face crack. As everywhere was sheeted with ice and running with water, and with darkness beckoning they decided to turn tail and set off back up the cleft. With no lantern, they took the unheroic plan and retraced their steps back down Glen Rosa, eventually reaching their comfortable headquarters at Corrie, '*…to the accompaniment of the loud squelching of our sodden boots, and the incessant rattle of the rain.*'

Next morning was more promising, though two hours after their start the rain came on; in fact it rained right up until the time of their leaving Arran. They reached the foot of Gully A on the north-east face of Cir Mhor, the lower pitch of which was partially covered by a fine icefall. Unfortunately a river of snow-water was rushing down the gully, and they moved out of it to examine the rocks to one side. Here the rocks were wet and slippery, and with their fingers paralysed with cold, they decided it would make a much more pleasant summer climb. This is now climbed by April Arête (120m Severe in summer, IV,5 in winter). Next they had a peek into B1 and B2 Gullies. Both were filled with solid cataracts of ice which, if possible to climb at all, would have taken many hours' step cutting. They finally decided to follows Bell's route up *B2C Rib* (though Raeburn referred to it in his account as B1C rib.)

It is a capital climb of decidedly over average difficulties. The passage of the cave at the top was now rendered much easier by the large amount of snow which partly filled it up. As no one appeared to long for the "Bell's Groove" finish, we then ascended Cir Mhor by the easy way.

This minimalist account of what must have been a hard winter route may partly explain why it never appeared in a guidebook. Additionally, as Robin Campbell notes –

> The failed attempt on April Arête was attributed to Lawson, Maclay and Raeburn by Johnstone, [author of the 1958 SMC guidebook] and this substitution of Maclay for Mackay was perpetuated by subsequent editors.[22]

Mackay was not finished with Cir Mhor however, though Cir Mhor almost finished Mackay. At the end of 1902, Geoffrey Winthrop Young and Sandy Mackay arrive in Corrie for a New Year holiday. The pair had climbed together in the Alps as regular partners, and Mackay was probably the fellow author of the guide *Roof-Climber's Guide to Trinity.* Robin Campbell takes up the narration –

> Their initial goal was A Gully once again, but just as in February, its left-hand ridge was eventually preferred...Unfortunately, the pair ran out of daylight, food and ideas somewhere on this awkward arête. Doubtful of the descent, they elected to evacuate into A Gully. Mackay lowered Young into the gully (nice of him!), then jumped the 30ft. or so to join Young. Unfortunately, he found a slab extending into the snow-bed and broke a leg. In Young's account of this sorry incident and the subsequent rescue, he suggests that they were on B-C Rib, but examination of letters from Mackay to Young makes the location perfectly clear. Mackay's leg was badly set, and he needed several operations (six casts are mentioned) before the leg could be restored to approximate service.[23] Although Mackay returned to climbing...and to tennis, Young lamented that 'our trusted Alpine partnership was ended, and I never again found his equal as a climbing colleague'.[24]

In Mackay's obituary in The Glasgow Herald,[25] it mentions that the same leg had earlier been badly injured while playing rugby, necessitating 10 weeks in bed. The break was badly set, and had to be rebroken. Mackay was stranded for eight hours on the mountain until help arrived. The same obituary, author unnamed, stated that this accident marked the end of his mountaineering career, but this is erroneous, as he was climbing well at least up to April 1907, when he was on the first ascent of Barrel Buttress on Quinag.

In 1902, on the last day of September, Tuesday 30th, George Bennett Gibbs (1864–1937) was on holiday with his wife in Corrie, when FS Goggs called in to haul him up the hill. Gibbs was a banker's clerk from Sunderland, a strong rock climber with much Lakeland experience, who joined the SMC in 1896. Frank Sidney Goggs (1871–1941), an actuary, was a popular member of the SMC, having joined in 1901. As well as serving as Club

Librarian and Editor of guide books, he edited the SMCJ for a decade, including the Great War years, and was elected President from 1926-28. Though claiming to be a Salvationist (see next Chapter), he was in truth a steady and reliable climber.

What was not as reliable turned out to be their route finding, as they started up a climb they mistakenly thought was Trap Dyke Climb. There was no excuse for this, as Naismith had led Gibbs up that route only two years earlier. In any event, the route they were on became a bit harder than they had expected, and the rope was put on. They eventually entered the clouds and struggled to the top by devious ways.

It only remains to mention one climb and a possible variation on this face. In August 1904, AS Macharg and James Maclay climbed the rib to the left of Maclay's Chimney, the one which had previously been climbed by Maclay's party in 1896, and which appears to have been missed by subsequent guide authors. It is clearly described in the SMCJ and would appear to be both fairly direct and interesting.

Maclay's route above the Upper Shelf, as he mentions, may have been new. In the 1934 Arran Guide, it mentions that it is doubtful if the route can still be followed, as a large fall of rock above the Shelf appears to have rendered it impossible. This route seems to have disappeared entirely from the literature. Although the diagram in the 1934 Guide appears to have a dashed line up the initial rib, only the left- and right-hand gullies are named.

Finally, taking the exploration of this fine vegetable face up to 1912, in September Raeburn, his sister Ruth, MacRobert and James Young climbed from the lower part of Gully B1 into Gully B2, and then about 200ft up traversed to the left onto the rib between these two gullies. This was above the steepest part of the rib, from which a most impressive view was found looking into the great upper chasm of Gully C.

To be fair to the north-east face of the mountain, the distant and technologically bolstered future would see several fine routes here, both summer and winter. Arran is a beautiful and interesting island, not only scenically rich and so close to the centres of population, but geologically of international renown. It has always been a popular holiday centre for families, and the author memorably recalls as a schoolboy soloing up most of one of the Nuis gullies (and obviously surviving). The island even has seven golf courses.[26]

At the end of January 1892, a party of seven attended an SMC Meet to Arran, staying in Brodick. One aim of the meet was to say a final farewell to Stott, though several were unable to attend due to an outbreak of influenza. Stott himself, though present, was just recovering from a recent illness, and had been advised to do nothing strenuous. The others attending were RA

Robertson, Douglas, JH Gibson, Fraser Campbell (all SMC members), and two friends, Dr Leith and Hamilton Fleming. On the Saturday evening, Stott was presented with a travelling clock and dispatch case, the gift of club members. As they sat around the fire that night they could hear the wind and rain outside, but the next morning dawned cold and clear, and an expedition was launched to attempt the A' Chir Ridge, which as far as they were aware had not been traversed in its entirety.

Five of the party attempted the traverse, Stott having gone for a road walk and Douglas continuing up Glen Rosa. The quintet eventually reached the major problem, a huge cleft some 100ft across and about the same depth. Gibson was lowered into this for about 40ft, but they rapidly ran out of rope and he had to abandon the attempt. They retreated some 200ft to gain a narrow crack and decided to descend this on the Glen Rosa side. Here they used a metal piton for protection; driving it into a crack and passing the rope through its ring they dropped down for about 100ft and moved along the base of the precipice to reach the bottom of the great cleft. They could see no way up the face however but on the Rosa side they gained access to the ridge again using a diagonal strip of grass.

By now darkness was looming, but before descending they scaled the rocks on the far side of the cleft where Gibson tied on to a rope and explored the mauvais pas, where a big boulder overhung a particularly unattractive-looking precipice. Gibson succeeded, and following the ridge for a few hundred feet reported that it would go easily. They then descended to the glen and so back to their comfortable hotel. The guide has this as a first ascent.

This brief outing to Arran is interesting for several reasons; it is one of the first, if not the first, report of the use of a piton or peg on Scottish rock, probably one carried up the hill by the then expert alpinist Gibson, and there is the statement in Campbell's article that – *'Whenever there was any work of a particularly breakneck description to be done, Gibson was invariably selected to do it first.'*[27] Gibson was also, of course, the obvious leader on the Black Shoot ascent.

A' Chir was again the setting for another SMC party, when on the 9th of June 1892 Thomson and Naismith arrived in Brodick at about 6pm, and promptly set off up the hill for a planned bivouac on the crest of the ridge, at the great cleft described by Campbell. After a few hours of twilight, they had breakfast at 1.30am, sadly without the use of a stove which had decided to *'...hop, step, and jump into Glen Rosa.'* Having had the prior knowledge from the January attempt they had brought an 80ft rope, which they secured and threw down into the cleft. A lower ledge some 20ft below was gained by climbing down, using the route found by Gibson, from which they then each lowered themselves, hand under hand, down 40ft or so of overhanging rock. A scramble was then taken along the ridge to the Cir Mhor saddle.

On their return to the rope, which they had left dangling down the overhang, and which they had obviously intended to use to regain the ridge, they soon discovered that a thin climbing rope was not well suited to gymnastic exercises, so they made their way to the top by the grass ledge to the left, over the summit of A' Chir, and so descended to the pier just in time to catch the morning boat to Ardrossan.[28]

❄ ❄ ❄

On the mainland, in the Southern Highlands, beginning in 1891 and continuing through 1896 a series of winter routes up the fine north-east corrie of Ben Lui (the name for which is Coire Gaothach, the windy corrie) was recorded. Climbed mostly on snow with some rocky ribs, this face provided much interest to the early pioneers in an alpine atmosphere. Some ascents were made with alpenstocks, while the Central Gully enjoyed its first recorded descent on 13th April 1891, by Fraser Campbell, Naismith and Lester. Two hours of cutting steps in descent culminated in a two-minute glissade of some 600 to 800ft leading to the foot of the corrie.[29] This Central Gully had its first ascent on the 31st December 1892, during an SMC New Year Meet based at Tyndrum. The climbers were AE Maylard, Walter Brunskill, Willie Douglas and James Maclay.

John Gibson followed up his Scottish explorations with an 1892 Easter week spent in the Cuillin of Skye, accompanied by his friends Wicks, Morse and Carr, with whom he had made various ascents in the Chamonix Aiguilles. Their first day on the hill, Tuesday 12th April, was spent climbing the Pinnacle Route on Sgurr nan Gillean. There was a bitter north-east wind. Traversing the western ridge, they next climbed Am Basteir and the Basteir Tooth. Gibson was certainly an accomplished mountaineer, but he also seems to have possessed a sharp tongue judging by some of his comments in print. Here, for example, after climbing the Tooth, he writes that –

> …there is no difficulty in finding the way up this curious rock-tower, though from Mr Maylard's article in the Jan. 1892 number of this Journal it might be gathered that local knowledge was almost needed.[30]

On the Wednesday it snowed hard, and they had a fruitless walk into Coire na Creiche. In Gibson's article he described the topography of this corrie, and uttered another sarcastic comment. He stated that looking at the anomaly whereby there is a peak called Sgurr a' Mhadaidh and a corrie called Coir' a' Mhadaidh, entirely cut off from one another by a high mountain ridge– *'It may be surmised, he wrote, that a possible source of this anomaly exists in that magnificent work of imagination, the old one-inch Ordnance survey of the Cuillins.'* This probably summed up the general view of mountaineers on these early OS maps of the Cuillin, leading to the various attempts by climbers to improve them.

On the Thursday it was the turn of Sgurr Dearg and the *'so-called inaccessible pinnacle.'* They had planned to climb this *'freak of nature'* as he referred to it, by an ascent of the steep western edge, descending by the longer eastern edge, but the wind and snow on the rocks forced an ascent and descent by the eastern edge. Sgurr Mhic Coinnich was the next target. From here they failed twice to traverse to the col between it and Sgurr Alasdair, so as time was passing they retreated back to the col now known as Rotten Gully, and then down into Coire Lagain. Here, the party was most impressed by the all too obvious evidence of glaciation.

Friday saw them back into Coire Lagain again, scrambling up the screes leading to Sgumain's Northern Buttress above the lochan in Coire Lagan. They gained this peak then made their way down to the Alasdair-Mhic Coinnich col. The aim was to *'retrieve our reputation'* for Thursday's failure. After several tries this they did, eventually deciding, following a reading of Norman Collie's route, that they had probably climbed a variation. They then descended a steep snow gully and so gained the head of Loch Coruisk, where following a prior arrangement with the Sligachan Hotel, a Whymper tent and various provisions had been left for them.

> Spare clothes, a warm fire, and a varied meal of Irish stew—cooked in a Silver's self-cooking soup tin—coffee, cold beef, tinned peaches, and whisky, made us feel more at peace with ourselves and the world at large.

As Pedlar states in his MS, with this one-night out under canvas, Gibson's party can lay claim to have carried out the first real mountain-camping at Coruisk.[31] The next morning, having been woken by a curious black-faced sheep, the party packed and leaving their camping gear to be picked up by a ghillie, headed up the hillside for the Bealach Coire na Banachdich. The intention was *'ridge-wandering'*, starting with Banachdich, and ending at Sligachan. On the way they encountered some hard snow, requiring step kicking. Gibson notes that they succeeded in climbing Banachdich, Ghreadaidh and Mhadaidh, after whose four peaks they headed westwards along the Sgurr Thuilm ridge, descending into Tairneilear.

There is, as so often with the Cuillin, an element of confusion here as regards the precise route Gibson's party took. He left a copy of Charles Pilkington's map of the Cuillin, now archived in the Alpine Club Library, marking his routes in various colours. Pedlar has examined this, and has inferred that it is unlikely that all four tops of Mhadaidh were traversed. Nonetheless, given the weather, with a very late winter and fresh snowfall, it was a fine demonstration of near-alpine climbing in Scotland.

Their last day in Skye, based at Sligachan, was an admittedly lazy one by comparison, as five consecutive days on the hill were by now telling on the party's legs. They made an ascent of Bidean Druim nan Ramh via Glen Sligachan and Harta Coire. Gibson concluded his article with some comments on the Cuillin hills as they had encountered them, in an unusually late winter season with masses of snow on the northern and eastern slopes. Combined with a cold wind generally from the north-east, there was a distinctly serious background to their explorations –

> Any one unused to Alpine climbing, or at all events not competent to take the lead in some of the winter sporting variations affected by some of our members, might get into very considerable trouble here.

Alexander Nicolson returned to Skye in September 1892, for what would be his very last visit. He arrived at Sligachan on the 6th and left on the 12th. Some four months later he would die suddenly at home in Edinburgh, of heart failure.

On the 13th September, William Tribe and his wife arrived, in company with two of the Hopkinson brothers and their respective wives. Charles and Edward Hopkinson had visited Sligachan in 1890 when Charles Pilkington had introduced them and several other members of the Alpine Club to the Cuillin. William Wilberforce Tribe (1855–1928) was also a rock climber and in 1887 had descended the upper section of Scafell Pinnacle with the Hopkinsons. Perhaps the weather on Skye was unsuitable for climbing, as no routes were recorded by them, but then Charles and Edward, along with Bertram, a nephew, had other unrecorded routes in Scotland, including, momentously, three on Ben Nevis, climbed only the week before their visit to Skye.

❄ ❄ ❄

The Hopkinsons were the type of family that the Victorian era often seemed to produce; five brothers, all energetic, talented and academic: John, the eldest (1849–1898), an electrical engineer, scientist (a Fellow of the Royal Society) and academic; Sir Alfred (1851–1939), lawyer, politician and academic; Charles (1854–1920), electrical engineer, county councillor; Edward (1859–1921), electrical engineer, politician; Albert (1863–1949), physician, academic. Along with one of John's sons Bertram (1873–1918), an academic and engineer/aviator, all six were prominent in British climbing and alpinism towards the end of the 19th century. There is a useful summary of them by Robin Campbell in the book *Classic Rock.*[32]

The Hopkinsons seemed to specialise in making first descents of some routes, and Ben Nevis was to be no exception. Details of their days on this mountain are minimal, and even then they published nothing until three years later, in August 1895, with a very brief note in the Alpine Journal.[33] On Saturday, 3rd September 1892, John, Edward, and John's son Bertram approached the cliffs from below. According to the log from the summit Observatory, there were showers of snow with squally north and north-east winds.[34] They chose one of the most obvious challenges on the face, the long central ridge which was to be named later as Tower Ridge, due to its prominent feature high on the ridge (later named the Great Tower).

The ridge has an initial feature, large enough to be impressive on any other face, but here its 200m height is dwarfed by its surroundings. This lower pinnacle would be called the Douglas Boulder, a humorous reference to a climber who would be on a first ascent in a few years' time. The Hopkinsons started up the approach gully to the east, leading to a gap separating the 'Boulder' from the remainder of the ridge. This is by inference, as later the brothers returned to make an ascent on the Douglas Boulder, by a route not described.

Their ascent ground to a halt at the Great Tower. They attempted to climb this on the western face, overlooking Coire na Ciste. This is more difficult than the eastern face, which has become the standard way up the Great Tower. They then descended, and given the topography of the ridge, with huge drops on both sides, it would be logical that they would have done so by their ascent route.

Joined by Charles, the quartet rejoined battle on the Sunday, when the temperature had dropped even lower. They took the bridle path to the summit plateau, with mist lingering until around 4pm, and some snow showers in the morning. Descending, they gained the summit of the Great Tower, dropped down the west face, probably using a Very Difficult variation later named Recess Route. This variation received its first summer ascent by Naismith and Thomson on 27th September 1894, when nail marks were noticed, presumably made by the Hopkinsons or by Collie's party the previous winter. They then made an exposed traverse across the western face of the Great Tower and so regained the ridge below the Tower. They continued to descend the ridge, thus completing the first descent of Tower Ridge.

The foursome presumably enjoyed a rest day, returning on the Tuesday. Again, they chose a prominent feature, this time the imposing skyline which is the *North-East Buttress*. The weather had maintained its pattern, with fog or mist early on, clearing later. They must have had a difficult time on Tower Ridge, as they describe their ascent of the North-East Buttress as being interesting, but much easier. Knowing, as we do now, that all lines up this buttress lead to the dreaded obstacle high up the ridge known as the Man-trap, a short but deceptively difficult wall, Robin Campbell has suggested that they overcame this by using a human ladder. As they left no route description we can only guess, though such 'combined tactics' were fairly common in Victorian times.

Two days later, on the Thursday, they were back for one more route, climbing the initial pinnacle of the Tower Ridge by an undescribed route. They descended the pinnacle '*on the north face.*' Several later parties, exploring and climbing the Douglas Boulder, have described descending its north face for some way, then traversing round to gain the north-east ridge and by this gaining easy ground above the entrance to Observatory Gully.[35] It is quite likely that the Hopkinsons would have followed a similar route, as to continue a descent on the Boulder's north face would have quickly led to much more difficult ground.

There remains one mystery connected with Tower Ridge however. SMC Archivist Robin Campbell acquired a postcard which he dates to pre-1885, showing The Great Tower.[36] Plainly visible on its summit is a cairn. The Observatory opened in 1883, with a small team of observers and their cook. There are quite a few stories of their extra-curricular activities, including sledging and skiing, and they had ropes with which in periods of severe weather they roped themselves together to prevent being blown away while making observations. It is not too far-fetched to suggest that in a burst of daring exploration they descended from the plateau with the safety of a rope and built a stone man to make their mark. As this event would have been an extra-curricular outing not in their work description, it would not have been entered in the Observatory Log.

The climbing by the Hopkinson brothers had been a demonstration of their rock climbing abilities and also an example of practised, unguided climbing. In *Classic Rock*, Robin Campbell refers to a passage in *On High Hills* by Geoffrey Winthrop Young, where Young writes that– *'I have heard so often from eye witnesses that the combination of the famous brothers was a model of what team-work might be made.'* They had broken ground on unknown rock, on the huge north-east face of the highest mountain in the British Isles. Their use of descents made much sense when compared with the very palpable dangers facing a leader's fall; even if a descent ended in a cul-de-sac, the climber could be pulled up to try elsewhere. In the current guidebook, Tower Ridge by the easiest route is graded Difficult, with most of the Great Tower variations on the west face being Very Difficult.

That their climbs went unrecorded and unknown for two years led to some irritation by later climbers who thought they were climbing their routes for the first time; it was probably these later ascents which prompted the brief note in the Alpine Club Journal. As exoneration for this behaviour, years later, in an FRCC Journal, Alfred Hopkinson explained that in the early years of Lakes climbing, they had no interest in leaving any detailed notes of their climbs, as they climbed through their enjoyment of the scenery and the challenge of a difficult ascent. As a final, tragic note on the Hopkinson family, in 1898, while climbing the Petite Dent de Veisivi, Dr John, his son John, and two daughters, Alice and Lina had some sort of an accident and, all being roped together, fell to their death.

❄ ❄ ❄

There was another such ascent by a party from England in 1892. In August 1895, Prof George Ramsay and his son Malcolm had an adventurous two days exploring and finally climbing Caisteal Liath (the gray castle), the western peak of Suilven in the north-west highlands. They were convinced they had enjoyed a first ascent of this impressive face and Ramsay had an article published in the SMCJ to that effect.[37] Then a letter was published in the May 1896 issue of the SMCJ, written by Horace Walker and noting an ascent by Walker and Charles Pilkington in August 1892. The letter was a model of diplomacy, and would surely have helped the Ramsays recover from the disappointment at not being the first to ascend the route –

To the Editor of the Scottish Mountaineering Journal.

LIVERPOOL, 7th February 1896.

SIR,

The matter is of little importance, but as Professor Ramsay wishes it, perhaps you will allow me to state that on 26th May 1892 Mr Charles Pilkington and I ascended Suilven by the S.W. angle of the Grey Castle, the route so well described by Professor Ramsay in the Jan. number of the Journal.

We discussed at the time the question of sending a note of our ascent to you, but came to the conclusion that it was hardly likely that this route, the only practicable one which we could discover at or near the west end of the mountain, should have escaped the notice of previous climbers.

I am sure that all readers of the Journal will rejoice with us that we came to that decision, as otherwise they might have missed one of the most charming articles which has graced the pages of the journal.–I am, sir, yours truly

Horace Walker

These ascents, once revealed, would inevitably be a spur to increased activities by Scottish mountaineers, but in the interim they had a world of unexplored mountains and agendas of their own. The Hopkinsons and Walker had very probably made their approaches from the sea; to Fort William in the first case, and Lochinver in the second. The Scots were waiting for the West Highland Line to reach Fort William, which would take place in 1894. Additionally, next to nothing was known of the climbing potential on Ben Nevis. Glen Coe was a similar picture; the rail stopped at Tyndrum and to reach Glen Coe meant a difficult journey by cart over a rough and exposed track.

These factors markedly impeded advances in Scottish mountaineering, compared with climbing in England. The Scots were also tending to concentrate on climbing in winter, given the topography and climate, as well as easier access during the winter months when sporting estates were quiet. The next two years however, would see a sea change in this state, as access, experience, and communication would all improve, allowing for a period of mountaineering in Scotland which would truly deserve the heading of The Golden Age.

References

1. Thomson, Gilbert. *Practice Scrambles.* SMCJ 2, 1, Jan. 1892, 8-12.
2. Naismith, W.W. *Ben Nevis IN 1880 AND 1889.* SMCJ 1, 5, May 1891, 215-221.
3. MacDonald, Hugh. *Rambles Round Glasgow.* (C.L. Wright, Glasgow, 1854). 2nd Edn. Chapter XVII, New Kilpatrick and the Whangie, 314-331.
4. Stark, J. *Origin of Auld Wives' Lifts and The Whangie.* Trans. Geol. Soc. Glas. Vol.16, part iii, Jan., 1920, 329-333.
5. Lord Mackay. *Vignettes of Earlier Climbers.* SMCJ 24, 141, April 1950, 173-174.
6. Campbell, Thos., Fraser S. *Notes and Queries.* SMCJ 2, 3, Jan. 1893, 205-206.
7. Naismith, William. SMC Application Form. SMC Archives.
8. Campbell, Thos., Fraser S. *The Glen Sannox Hills.* SMCJ 1, 1, Jan. 1890, 31-36.
9. Naismith, W.W. *Cir Mhor from Glen Sannox.* SMCJ 2, 1, Jan. 1892, p17-24.
10. Moody, Colin and Little, Graham. *Inner Hebrides & Arran.* SMC Climbers' Guide, 2014.
11. Thomson, Gilbert. *Cir Mhor.* SMCJ 3, 16, Jan. 1895, 212-217.
12. Naismith, W.W. *Cir Mhor from Glen Sannox*, SMCJ 2, Jan. 1892, 1, 17-24.
13. Johnstone, J.M. *Rock Climbs in Arran.* 1958. Edinburgh. Scottish Mountaineering Club, 65.
14. Thomson, Gilbert. *Cir Mhor.* SMCJ 3, 16, Jan. 1895, 212-217.
15. Ibid.
16. W.W.N. [William Naismith]. *In Memorium - James Maclay, LL.B.* SMCJ 17, 100, Nov. 1925, 202-203.
17. *Cir Mhor Face–New Route.* In: Notes and Queries, SMCJ 4, 19, Jan. 1896, 63-64.
18. Naismith, W.W. *Cioch na H'Oighe and Cir Mhor: Variations.* In: Excursions. SMCJ 4, 32, September 1896, 173-174.
19. MacRobert, H. SMC Guide Book - *The Island of Arran.* SMCJ 10, 56, May 1908, 106.
20. Clark, W. Inglis. *A Day on Cir Mhor.* SMCJ 5, 25, Jan. 1895, 29-36.
21. Raeburn, H. *Arran.* In: Excursions. SMCJ 7, 37, Jan. 1902, 113-115.

22. Campbell, Robin. *Incidents on Cir Mhor in 1902.* In: Miscellaneous Notes. SMCJ 38, 193, 2002, 208-209.
23. G.W. Young's account will be found in *Mountains with a Difference* (Eyre & Spottiswoode, 1951), 56-62.
24. The relevant Mackay letters to Young (numbers 988, 989 and 990 in Young's letter-book) are in the Alpine Club Library Archives.
25. *Outstanding Personality of Scottish Courts–Death of Lord Mackay.* Obituary Notice in Glasgow Herald. Thursday, 3rd November, 1955, 9.
26. *Golf on Arran.* <http://www.golfonarran.com/> Accessed June 2014.
27. Campbell, Thos., Fraser S. *The Arran Meet.* Jan. 29th to 31st. SMCJ, Vol.2, 2, May 1892, 75-81.
28. Naismith, W.W. *A Night on A'Cir.* SMCJ 2, 3, September 1892, 138-139.
29. Campbell, T. Fraser S. *Ben Lui.* SMCJ 1, 5, May 1891, 207-214.
30. Gibson, J.H. *Easter in the Cuillins.* SMCJ 2, 5, May 1893, 213-224.
31. Pedlar, Stuart, *Across Unmeasured Space–A History of Climbing in the Cuillin.* Unpublished MS. 2010.
32. Campbell, Robin. *Tower Ridge.* In: Classic Rock, compiled by Ken Wilson. 2nd edition, 2007. ISBN 9781-898573-70-8. 276-281.
33. *Alpine Notes–Ben Nevis.* Alpine Journal, 17, 1895, 520-521.
34. Logbook of Ben Nevis Observatory, Vol.4, 1891-1894. Archives Scottish Meteorological Office, Edinburgh.
35. Clark, W. Inglis, *Stormy June Days in Skye and on Ben Nevis.* SMCJ 6, 6, Sept. 1901, 228.
36. Campbell, Robin. Personal correspondence. 2010.
37. Ramsay, Professor G.G. *Ascent of Suilven by the Grey Castle.* SMCJ 4, 19, Jan. 1896, 23-34.

6

Breakthrough (1892-94)

In the autumn of 1892, the book *Mountaineering* was published, one of a series of books in the Badminton series of Sports and Pastimes, conceived and founded by Henry Somerset, 8th Duke of Beaufort (1824–1899).[1] Thomas Clinton Dent (1850–1912) was the primary author, the Duke of Beaufort the Editor. Dent wrote eight of its 15 chapters, with contributions from his Alpine Club colleagues WM Conway, Douglas W Freshfield, CE Mathews, Charles Pilkington, Sir Frederick Pollock, Henry George Willink, and an Introduction by Mr Justice Wills.

The book must have appeared as the definitive work on the game, with its expertly crafted chapters, and a number of superb illustrations. Other names mentioned as being of assistance included Melchior Anderegg (1828–1912), Professor TG Bonney (1833–1923), and Edward Whymper (1840–1911). Anderegg was an early Alpine guide and one of the foremost, climbing with many AC members.

Bonney was a geologist and theologian, while Willink (1851–1938) was an artist who wrote the chapter on sketching for climbers as well as producing many of the book's crisp and witty illustrations. Born in Liverpool, and settling in Berkshire, he was a member of the Alpine Club, and Vice-President at one time. He climbed in Switzerland in his early years, but his taste was more for walking, in Switzerland, and the English Lakes or North Wales, with his pocket sketch books.

Charles Pilkington, who has already appeared here as an activist on Skye, wrote the chapters on *Climbing Without Guides*, and *Hill Climbing in the British Isles*. In the latter chapter, he begins with general advice on how to approach climbing, then goes into the various areas, finishing with Scotland. Ben Nevis is mentioned in the passing —

His tremendous northern cliffs fall steep and rugged into the depths of the glen below, and few of us could boast of having gained the highest point of our native land, if the only way thereto lay up those beetling crags.[2]

Glen Coe, too, was mentioned ...with its wild corries and bold and seldom explored buttresses.

Dent's *Mountaineering* was well reviewed by Willie Douglas in the SMCJ,[3] the only criticism being that –

We are also sorry that he - although an esteemed member of our Club - is apparently unfamiliar with some of the excellent alpine work that is to be had on the north and north-east faces of many of our Scottish hills in the early months of the year. One of the foremost endeavours of our Club is to show what enjoyable sport exists for climbers at seasons of the year when for several causes it is unobtainable elsewhere, and for this reason we naturally regret that a work which will deservedly become popular, fails to sufficiently recognise the real merits of snow and ice work in our own country.

Whether by coincidence or design, the next issue of the SMCJ carried an article by Naismith on winter climbing in Scotland.[4] The continuing conservative nature of Scottish mountaineers towards rock climbing is indicated by a footnote by Naismith –

If in the Alps the tide of fashion sets towards rock climbing, to the neglect of snowcraft, those of us with conservative instincts will, by encouraging ascents in snow, have the gratification of helping in a small way to stem the prevailing current.

Naismith had been asked by Willie Douglas to write an article on winter climbing in Scotland. Before this was produced, Dent's book was published, in which was a brief reference to snow-climbing in Scotland. Like Douglas, Naismith was openly disappointed by the sketchy coverage of this aspect of mountaineering –

...it may interest any members, he wrote, who as yet know the mountains only in their summer dress, to glance at the subject in somewhat greater detail; at the same time noticing some points of resemblance between winter climbing in Scotland, and summer mountaineering in Switzerland.

As far as Naismith was concerned, and presumably this was also the feeling of a significant number of those climbing in Scotland, the Scottish hills and mountains were a convenient substitute for the Alpine experience. It mattered little that several of the summer months were virtually out of bounds, due to sporting land owners, as for them the winter months supplied the genuine article. Even better, Naismith continued, in Scotland there were no professional guides to lead a party on a winter ascent; the amateur must do all the reconnoitring, the fatiguing step-cutting, and the belaying.

> As yet too there attaches to it something of the zest of novelty which the Alps had for climbers of thirty years ago. There are still any number of "first winter ascents" waiting to be "bagged," as well as endless *variations*.

Naismith continued his article with descriptions of the various types of ice and snow which might be found in a Scottish winter. He even described what sounds remarkably like wind slab, that potentially lethal snow formation which has killed many an unwary climber and walker.

> Now and then snow is covered with a crust of ice, or there may be several layers of crust, with soft snow between. On a level field a thin crust makes walking most fatiguing, but on inclined snow it is sometimes a help to the climber, and enables him to kick a series of "pigeon-holes" with great rapidity.

Glissading also receives a description, writing that it was equally important in Scotland, as in the Alps, that a slope should not end in a precipice. But it was his technique of dealing with a piece of *'unmitigated'* ice which brought him into a confrontation in print with a fellow club member, John Gibson. Naismith believed that –

> ...where it is preferable to prevent a slip, than hope to check it after it has occurred, I believe it is better to hold the axe as if glissading, and dig the spike firmly into the ice about the level of the thigh, before each step, rather than to use the pick as an anchor–the proper method on hard snow, or ice covered with frozen snow.

In the following issue of the SMCJ, John Gibson wrote a long letter in which he strongly disagreed with Naismith on how to use the ice axe in unmitigated ice.[5]

> We are not told whether the climber is supposed to be standing in a step or not–though it may be perhaps assumed that he is–or whether he is ascending, descending, or traversing; but I confess when I read the above-quoted paragraph I felt myself turned into stone...

Gibson was strongly of the opinion that with ice as normally met with in Scotland –

> I take upon myself to assert of my own knowledge that unless ice be of exceptional hardness–ice, in fact, such as I personally have never seen in Scotland, and but seldom in the Alps–a climber is well able, if enough force be used, to get at least a fair hold in ice with the pick, provided always the axe-shaft be kept rigid. Such a hold is quite sufficient to prevent a slip; and even after a slip has occurred, if the pick be driven in promptly the fall can be checked–*crede experto*.

He produced more evidence for his point of view, quoting from Dent's *Mountaineering*. He also referenced one of the illustrations in that book, facing page 52, in which four alpinists can be seen descending a slope and using their picks to either maintain their position or cut steps. Several further arguments followed from Gibson in his letter, quite blunt in manner. He finished –

> ...if I mistake not, his paper was addressed more particularly to beginners, to men some of whom had not handled an ice-axe, and knowing as we all do know that our Treasurer *is* the authority on snowcraft in Scotland which he does not pose to be, they may be very reasonably disposed to take his advice. And this advice, I venture to think, in this case is mistaken. Were Mr Naismith other than he is, I should not have thought it necessary to trouble you with this. But
>
> "Madness in *great* ones must not unwatched go."

The quotation is from Hamlet, where King Claudius is referring to Hamlet. Gibson's letter was followed immediately by a reply from Naismith, in which he stated that the place he had in mind was not a slope of *'excessive steepness.'* There, Naismith continued, holes ought to be cut for the hands. Naismith was referring to very hard ice, in which the pick might fail to grip satisfactorily, in which case the climber might be better using the spike as a prop in order to prevent a slip. Naismith also queried the use of the illustration Gibson mentioned, stating that the axe-heads shown in it appeared to be buried to a depth of several inches – even so he finished, he believed some good Swiss guides would come down even that slope with their axes held like alpenstocks, i.e. with the spikes in the slope.[6] It was an unusual exchange in a time and medium where correspondents normally went out of their way to remain polite.

❄ ❄ ❄

On Christmas Day 1892, Hely Hutchinson Almond (1832–1903) had made an ascent of Beinn a' Ghlo, described by a later writer in a guidebook as *'A beautiful, stony mountain of many remote peaks and corries...the finest mountain in the Mounth between Drumochter and Aberdeen.'* Almond was born in Glasgow, and entered Glasgow University when he was 13. He took the Junior Latin classes held by Professor George Ramsay, as did Naismith, starting sharp at 7.30am. In a biography written two years after Almond's death,[7] it was said that Ramsay was his intellectual foster-father. Further, *'Of the brilliant vivacity and racy humour of Ramsay's style Almond would often speak in his own mature age, and always to contrast it with the lifeless decorum of the Oxford manner.'*

After Glasgow Almond went to Oxford, where he succeeded in a double first, including mathematics. He hated Oxford, but on discovering boating he also found the outdoors and exercise, of which Glasgow was somewhat lacking in facilities in the early days. He came back up to Scotland, falling into teaching, and ending up as the headmaster of Loretto School, on the outskirts of Musselburgh, near Edinburgh. He was able to purchase the failing school in 1862, where he remained as headmaster until his death from lung cancer on the 7th March 1903. He was buried at Inveresk Churchyard. Almond's philosophy of education placed a strong emphasis on 'Muscular Christianity', with robust fresh air games and exercise.

Following his ascent of Beinn a' Ghlo, Almond wrote an article which was published in the SMCJ.[8] The latter half of the article was a supplementary note by HT Munro which, at the request of the Editor, Douglas, described the mountain, The article is singled out, not so much for the ascent or for Munro's dry route description, but for Almond's humorous writing, especially the section where he classified mountaineers into two classes.

> MEMBERS of the Mountaineering Club may be divided into two classes. There are those whose ambition it is to scale the inaccessible side of peaks with unpronounceable names, who look upon a quarry face with fond enthusiasm, as affording chances quite as great, and nearly as glorious, of getting badly hurt, as a genuine mountain does... I admire these people; I like to dine with them, and hear them talk; for the sake of a name, I call them the Ultramontanes. It is delicious and inspiring, in these after-dinner moments, to rise to the faith which is beyond reason, and, like various kinds of spirits, above proof, and to murmur, "*Credo quia impossibile.*" [I believe because it is impossible] But these high thoughts soon pass away.

Almond went on to say that had he known 40 years earlier that Scotland in winter could offer the same as the Alps, it might have been different –

> But let me confess, with all due humility and shame, that I have permanently enlisted in the Salvation Army, which is the name I give to the second class of mountaineers. As our name implies, we like to know that we are safe–absolutely safe. We don't like contusions; we would rather go home to dinner than lie on the ground till people came to set our bones, or carry us off on a stretcher; we have no desire to be the conscious element of an avalanche or a land-slip.

He continued with the admission that –

> ...we like something of the pomp and circumstance of glorious war – an alpenstock, a bit of rope, blue spectacles – a good deal of noise and fuss about it when we come home again. Some of us even like guides. Here I draw the line. With no wish to create divisions–I don't. Now I am going to make a bold assertion – perhaps too bold. I believe the Salvation Army to be in a majority in the Club, and that a vote taken by ballot, and before dinner, would conclusively prove this.

He described how the mountains at Christmas and early winter were so much better than at other times, with cleaner air, less haze, firmer underfoot and so on –

> Even supposing that the weather is unfavourable, surely seven or eight miles in the worst of weather over Highland roads or paths, make any one feel fresher and brighter than a duty trudge along sloppy streets, or suburban roads, in the smooth garments and fine linen demanded by Mrs Grundy, in air never free from fog and smoke, and where, if you try, to warm yourself by a trot, you are stared at by "society," and howled at by the street boy.

Mrs Grundy was a theatrical character, introduced in *Speed the Plough* (1798) by Thomas Morton (1764–1838). Mrs Grundy's character in the play was the personification of the tyranny of conventional propriety. By the 19th century the term Mrs Grundy had become synonymous with the term prude. The reference to being howled at by a street boy may well have paralleled the reaction the early mountaineers raised if spotted carrying axes and ropes.

The terms introduced by Almond in his article were rapidly picked up by Scottish mountaineers, who happily used the terms Ultramontane and Salvationist as convenient labels to explain their respective mountain habits. It may well have been that when Almond wrote his article, the majority of SMC members were Salvationists, but this ratio would eventually reverse, with gradual rises in climbing standards, increasing confidence on rock, and the emergence of a core of mountaineers who would, slowly at first, but with increasing speed, push up technical standards.

This rise in standards would not happen gradually, from within, but as we will soon see, would be the result of a series of bursts of exploratory climbing from a small number of exceptionally talented mountaineers. The Ultramontane would eventually dominate the SMC, though not until after the Great War, when social changes saw an influx of younger climbers, and improved equipment and techniques brought in more realistic protection for climbing. The entry requirements for entry to the SMC would rise commensurately, from the early years when the pedestrian ascent of a few mountains would suffice, to a required minimum standard of technical ability.

❄ ❄ ❄

The SMC New Year Meet of 1892–93 was held at Tyndrum, from where various parties explored the north-east corrie of Ben Lui and made ascents of the Crianlarich hills. Present was Hugh Munro, who had penned a description of the Lochnagar range in the September 1892 issue of the SMCJ.[9] His notes were made following a walk on the 10th July 1892, a cloudy day but one with excellent views. At the New Year Meet were Douglas and Gibson, and it would seem highly likely that Munro would have mentioned his views of the great cliffs of Lochnagar, and their potential for exploration.

Douglas and Gibson, whatever their spur to exploration, decided to have a look at Lochnagar later in 1893. Their problem was, yet again, that of access, but help was at hand as Munro, who lived at the nearby family estate of Lindertis, offered to pick them up at Kirriemuir, to which they had taken the train. He drove them to the inn at Clova, where they spent the night. When we say drove, we really mean by horse-driven means, as the motor car was a rare sight then. Munro does not mention driving a car until about 1912. The next morning, 11th March, they set off for Lochnagar, crossing the Capel Mount to Glen Muick. At this point Munro, who suffered from rheumatism (he was then aged 37), decided to turn back. Gibson and Douglas continued, finally eyeing the north-east cliffs, though a high mist obscured the summits.

Another party was on the hill that day, from Aberdeen, including SMC member William Lamond Howie who was renowned for his photography. The photograph from Lochnagar corrie that day certainly shows mist on the tops. As Douglas wrote in his article, none of the gullies except the easy one known locally as the Black Spout ran in an unbroken line to the top - they all appeared to end in perpendicular cliffs. The pair returned to a cottage in Glen Muick, having arranged a bed for the night there.

The next morning an early start found them at the foot of the cliffs by 9.30am, where they decided to attempt a gully in the *'east corner of the west corrie'*, now known as Douglas-Gibson Gully. If a climb were to be named after some pioneers, and according to their climbing abilities or dominance in leading, it would have been rightly named the Gibson-Douglas Gully, but sadly Gibson died young, and Douglas was highly popular, so there it remains. Perhaps they used the names in alphabetical order. The day was still misty, and the top of the gully unseen. After two and a half hours' climbing, with increasing step cutting required, they arrived at the final stretch of the gully, with an estimated 80-100ft remaining. They were faced however with an impossible vertical wall of smooth black rock. On the left was a slab coated with rotten ice. Faced with a poor belaying situation, having only one man at the bottom to hold a rope, they made a strategic retreat. As Douglas wrote –

> On looking down the gully, which sank in great serpentine waves to some 400 feet below where we stood, I must say I had some misgivings as to how we were to get down, but my confidence was restored by the clear directions and practical assistance given by my companion. I descended first, with my face inwards, and we reached the bottom of the gully in another hour.[10]

They had limited time left now, but were determined to add a stone to the cairn, so they made for the Black Spout, climbing it until it branched about half-way up, where they took the left-hand branch. On top the weather was wild, with a driving mist, hurrying along the top of the cliff and still looking for possible future lines below them. These cliffs alone, Douglas considered, *'would afford excellent sport for several days.'*

Gibson, as we have noted, would soon disappear from the scene, and in these times before antibiotics would die from tuberculosis in April 1898. He had married to a lady from London in February 1894, by the end of which year he seems to have completely withdrawn from both the SMC and the AC. They had no children. There is a tantalising comment, never intended for publication, in a letter Naismith wrote to Douglas upon hearing of Collie's ascent of Tower Ridge in March 1894 –

> ...The Sassenachs have indeed taken the wind out of our sails maist notoriously ... If their bit hillocks could be detected with the naked eye we might still get Gibson to pull himself together and astonish them on their own ground. Couldn't he do the Houses of Parliament by the Clock Tower or a traverse of Beachy Head?...[11]

Gibson, as noted above, showed an aggressive side of his character in addressing an article by Naismith on using an ice axe. Perhaps personal events such as his illness had changed him in some negative way; we shall probably never know the reason. What is evident is that Scottish mountaineering, with the too early demise of Gibson, had suffered a huge loss.

❄ ❄ ❄

The slow but steady march of the West Highland Railway line was approaching Fort William; it would be opened to the public on the 7th August 1894. To a club such as the SMC, with a significant number of members, holding meets without easy transport was still perceived as being awkward, and their New Year Meet of 1893-94 was held in the now familiar hotel at Dalmally, or *'Snug Dalmally'*, as the new club song had it. As the report of the meet wrote *'To many of the older members Dalmally has now become to a great extent an "exhausted centre", all the principal ascents...having been climbed in every weather and at every season...'*[12]

These ascents included the Black Shoot of Beinn Eunaich, described here in Chapter 4, an unappealing dank gully-cum-chimney line. Its confines would only be of interest to club newcomers, those both unaware of its internal horrors, and perhaps wishing to make an impact. Despite a promising New Year's Day, with a sharp frost and brilliant sun, the weather during the meet was mainly poor, and nothing new was done. The weather continued poor, with several dreary months of rain. This situation however, was about to change dramatically for the better, during the next meet, held at Easter 1894 and based at the small inn at Inveroran. As the meet report by TFS Campbell had it –

> And so ended this famous Meet, which will live for ever in the memories of those who were permitted the pleasure of taking their part in it. Never perhaps within the experience of the climbers had the Scottish mountains

> borne an aspect so truly Alpine. Immense quantities of snow filled all the corries, especially to the north. The summit ridges were crowned with huge cornices, overhanging in many places by ten feet or more the grand unbroken slopes below, upon the surface of which were frequently seen the evidences of recent avalanches.[13]

As a testament to the general fitness of these early mountaineers, Naismith and his friend Gilbert Thomson had arrived at the inn at 8.30 the previous evening, having walked some 41mls from Dalwhinnie to Inveroran, taking in Ben Alder en route. They had left Dalwhinnie station at 3.30am, carrying '*...nothing save our axes and a stock of provisions, the latter being calculated on a liberal scale to provide for the not impossible contingency of an enforced bivouac.*'[14] Inveroran, at the west end of Loch Tulla, is situated in one of the outstanding areas of mountain scenery in Scotland, generally called The Blackmount.

The Easter Meet of 1894 took place from Friday, 23rd March to Monday, 26th. Some sixteen members and four guests were present

> The resources of the inn were certainly strained to their utmost, and some of the party sought shelter at Kingshouse, but on Saturday morning no less than seventeen sat down to breakfast at Inveroran.

The guests were Col. Archibald Wavell (Commander of the Black Watch, and later to be an Honorary Member of the SMC), Godfrey Allan Solly, a solicitor from Birkenhead, Joseph Collier, a Manchester surgeon, (the last two being guests of Norman Collie), and Charles Clement Bravo Moss, a wine merchant from London. The last three were AC members.

SMC members were: Professors George Ramsay and Frederick Bower (eventually Regius Professor of Botany at Glasgow University), Dr Coats, Dr Norman Collie, Messrs Lamond Howie, William Lester, William A Ramsay (son of George Ramsay), Willie Naismith, Gilbert Thomson, John Rennie, Willie Douglas, Fraser Campbell, James Maclay, Lionel Hinxman, William Brown, and Herbert C Boyd. Both Solly and Collier were in the Alpine Club; Solly would join the SMC later that year and would be President from 1910-13, while Collier would join two years hence. Also joining in December 1894 would be Wavell and Moss.

As the report of the Inveroran meet mentioned, one of its charms lay in the very fact that it was awkward to get to, with the railway then branching off at Tyndrum. Bridge of Orchy station would be opened the following August cutting the distance from a rail station from 9.5 to 3 miles.

> Inveroran is at present ten miles from anywhere, and a good deal more than that from most places, and the inn thereat is certainly smaller than the Metropole; but a certain amount of roughing it is not ungrateful to the healthy pedestrian, who gaily tramps along the ten miles of road from Tyndrum to Loch Tulla with nothing to carry but an axe, and no care in his mind–beyond

a hope that the cart which follows with his one or two well-packed bags of dry clothes, &c. &c. &c., will be up to time.

There were other accounts of this Meet, including an article in the same issue of the SMCJ by Gilbert Thomson which provides more details of the long weekend.[15] It covers in particular the Monday, when Thomson and five others made for Beinn an Dothaidh. A small error in Thomson's article easily confuses those digging into the history, when Thomson refers to the Monday morning of the meet as being on the 27th March; in fact that Monday fell on the 26th of the month. It is fortunate that other reports of climbing from this meet were published, as Campbell's report in the SMCJ is a masterclass in confusing reportage.

What is clear is that Naismith and Thomson were based at the Kingshouse Inn, while Collie, Collier and Solly stayed one night at Inveroran before moving on to the Kingshouse on Saturday morning. This was almost certainly Collie's plan, as on the Saturday his party set out for the Buachaille Etive Mor, making a new climb up its south-east face now called *Collie's Climb* (300m Moderate). The exact line of this route is unclear, but it probably wound its way up the face between Lady's Gully and Central Buttress and was the first recorded ascent of a climbing route on this iconic mountain. The current guide remarks that it can provide interesting route finding in winter, at a Grade of II/III.

Also climbing on the Buachaille that Saturday and unaware of Collie's party, Naismith, Brown and Thomson made what they thought was the first ascent of Great Gully, the deeply sunk gully leading up from the glen to the final ridge. It must have come as a disappointment to Naismith that evening in the Kingshouse, when he would have presumably met up with Collie and learned that Collie had climbed the gully '*...some years before by the identical route chosen by them.*'[16] The gully received another ascent on the Sunday, by Boyd, Douglas and Rennie.

Stob Ghabhar has an interesting north-east face, its summit buttress pierced on its right by a short gully known as the Upper Couloir. Like the Black Shoot, it saw several attempts over the years before it finally succumbed in its entirety in 1897, led by Ernest Maylard. It was attempted again on the Saturday of the 1894 meet, the party of Ramsay Jnr, Maclay, Boyd, Campbell and Moss deciding it was impracticable due to its icy conditions. What is interesting is that all rocks below the summit buttresses, including what is referred to as the Lower Couloir, were completely obliterated by snow in March 1894, contrasting with the more normal conditions found in April 1892, the latter illustrated by a diagram accompanying the report of the 1892 meet.

Other than hillwalks, first ascents were made on Sunday and Monday of snow gullies on the north-east face of Beinn an Dothaidh. On the

Friday, Naismith, Brown, Thomson and Coats had walked from Bridge of Orchy over Beinn an Dothaidh, Ben Achaladair, Meall Buidhe and Beinn a' Chreachain. Coats had finished the day by walking across the moors and round the west end of Loch Tulla, to rejoin the meet at Inveroran. It is very likely that Coats had described the gullies waiting to be explored there, as on the Sunday both Ramsays, Campbell and Moss made their way there, probably crossing Loch Tulla by boat (as did a party on the Monday) and entering the corrie under the north-east face of Beinn an Dothaidh. The two Ramsays traversed under the face to enter what is now named *West Gully* (300m I). This they cut their way up in two hours.

A glowing report by Ramsay Jnr in the Inveroran Inn easily persuaded another party to set out on the Monday, with Naismith, Thomson, Boyd, Ramsay Jnr and Douglas. They crossed the loch by boat, cutting out some distance to the approach, having already sent on their luggage to Tyndrum, the final destination of the day and of the meet. Once in the corrie, they looked at the gully which split off to the left some distance up West Gully, but seeing its icy condition, they decided that it '*...would probably be too severe a tax upon our time.*' (This quote would be used wittily by the team who recorded what they assumed was the first ascent, naming the gully Taxus in 1969, some 75 years after the Ramsay's visit.) It is now a popular 240m Grade III.

Instead, they continued traversing left, to round the buttress and enter a smaller corrie further up the flank of the hill. Here they split into two teams, with Douglas and Naismith climbing what would later be named *ZigZag Gully*, and the other three climbing *Central Gully*, both 250m Grade I snow ascents. Herbert Boyd took an excellent photograph of Naismith and Douglas climbing up below a huge cornice, on their route ZigZag Gully.[17] Naismith and Douglas found their cornice finish to be about 10ft high, with a considerable overhang in places. The angle of the slope immediately below this final obstacle was measured at 59°.

As time was now pressing, they happily accepted a top-rope from the other three, who had finished their gully and were enjoying seeing other people working hard. The observers had belayed themselves to two ice axes well back from the edge and using a third axe as a runner, laying it down flat near the cornice lip and running the rope over the wooden shaft to reduce friction, they provided some aid to the pair below. Naismith was wearing Mummery spikes*, but for some reason on one boot only. Following lunch on top, they walked over Ben Dorain then descended the east side. They succeeded in glissading for 1,000ft, half of which was one continuous swoop, before walking round to the south face and hence to the road and the walk down to Tyndrum. Next morning most of the party took the first train for town.

*Mummery spikes could be a reference to either nails developed for walking on glaciers or on snow slopes, screwed into a boot, with usually one or two in the heel or to crampons proper, a hinged framework with downward pointing spikes which were fastened to a boot by straps. There is a long history of crampons being used in the Alps, where they probably began as an aid to cutting grass for hay on steep slopes. It is unclear what Naismith was using here. The use of crampons, though used widely in the Tyrol, was regarded as cheating by British mountaineers for many years.

These first ascents, and the second and third ascents of Great Gully had in a sense partly broken new ground. The climbers were beginning to stretch their newly fledged wings, attempting or succeeding on routes which in previous years they might have deemed beyond them. But they were still stuck in a snow climbing frame of mind, continuing their Alpine experiences of climbing snow routes in preference to rock. However, events following immediately after the official Easter Meet at Inveroran would be of even greater significance, as Collie and his two friends continued their explorations in Glen Coe and beyond, on Ben Nevis.

❄ ❄ ❄

After the Kingshouse, they moved on to the Clachaig Inn, from where they enjoyed four days' further exploration. The party made an entry in the Clachaig Visitors' Book, which fortunately has been preserved.[18] Following the original entry, there are several word insertions which help clarify where the climbs were. *Churchdoor* has been added, as has *Coire na Beach* (Coire nam Beithach). It is not known who added these extra words, or indeed when. It is even possible that it was one of Collie's party; personally he was very parsimonious at divulging climbing information.

25-29 March 1894

G A Solly Birkenhead) Climbed Bidein nam Bian. Tried the
J. Collier Manchester) right hand ('Churchdoor') precipice at head of corrie 'Coire na
N. Collie London) Beach' Lochan but were unable to climb it
Went up the big gully between right and left hand buttress. Made a small cairn on top of a
pinnacle in centre of gully. ('Collie's Pinnacle')
Climbed Anoach [sic] Dubh. Came out almost just above Ossians Cave. Tried Gully opposite Inn
on north side of Glen. Got up a little over half way but were then forced out by a waterfall
about 60-80 feet high.
Climbed also into Ossians Cave. N C.
& left a small tin box with our cards on a ledge inside the cave.

If we take the hotel entry as showing the true chronology of events, on the first day they attempted a route up *Church Door Buttress*, under the summit of Bidean nam Bian, but were unsuccessful. It was not climbed until 1898 and is now a Very Difficult. The next climb listed in this hotel book is *Central Gully* (180m I/II), between Diamond and Church Door Buttresses, including an ascent of the pinnacle in the gully, *Collie's Pinnacle* (10m Easy). It would seem logical that it would have been climbed on the same day after their failure to find a route up Church Door Buttress, as it lies immediately to the left.

There is also an intriguing reference to Collie's activities in Glen Coe where in an article on the area, William Brown mentions that Collie had climbed, solo, the north face of Aonach Dubh, taking the '*...craggy face fronting Loch Triochtan.*' Brown describes it as being both interesting and easy. '*The rope is nowhere required, and Dr Collie did it alone, to the no small astonishment and incredulity of certain residents at the foot.*'[19] No date is given for this solo climb, up a face heavily vegetated and no doubt precarious in places.

On day two they climbed the north face of Aonach Dubh by a route lying just left of Ossian's Cave. This may have been the route now named *East Wall Climb* (165m Very Difficult). It was a bold ascent up a face which holds some of the most impressive rock scenery in the glen. On the third day, they tried the gully which slashes down the southern flank of Sgorr nam Fiannaidh, now known as *Clachaig Gully* (520m Severe). This they followed as far as a point '*...which seemed to be impassable.*' succeeding in escaping the gully by a traverse rightwards.

It would be first climbed 44 years later in 1938, by WH Murray and friends. Collie's party had almost certainly been defeated by the first hard pitch in the gully, the Great Cave Pitch, which defeated several attempts following Collie's. Presumably due to snow on the hills and the south-facing aspect, there would have been much water coming down the gully.

Unabashed, on their fourth and last day in Glen Coe, they returned to Aonach Dubh's north face, where they climbed into Ossian's Cave. This is the huge, dark slit high on the face, seemingly first climbed by a local shepherd, Neil Marquis, in 1868. Godfrey Solly wrote an article for the SMCJ giving some history and some of the legend surrounding the cave. Alex Anderson had made an ascent in 1930, by which time at least 48 climbers had braved the horrible approach. A rusty tin containing their names was removed, the same tin which, as Solly recalled, was probably the snow goggles container left by him in 1894.[20]

As to the Neil Marquis, who '*...lived in a cottage on the main road about opposite to Loch Triochtan...*' (presumably the croft Achtriochtan on current maps), Solly's party interviewed him the evening after their climb –

> ...but he seemed very unwilling to talk, and to be very stupid. However, we understood him to say that he had been up and had been helped by a tree, but we could get no description of the tree or of the position in which it had been, nor of the inside of the cave.
>
> Collie was our spokesman, and it seems probable that Marquis had got up, or at least thought he had.

The route is not recommended, having seen several bad accidents over the years, with a loose, steep, vegetatious approach. This leads to disappointment in any case, as the cave has no level floor, sloping down and out at a steep angle. Descendants of Marquis still live in Glencoe village. As for Marquis, he may have given an impression of being stupid through not having any English. (Note that strictly speaking, the glen is Glen Coe, and the village Glencoe.)

❄ ❄ ❄

There are two sources for Collie's activities in Glen Coe and Fort William, three if counting the Observatory Logbook from the Ben Nevis Meteorological Observatory. The first is a report in the SMCJ for September 1894.[21] The report is unsigned, and is the basis for the preceding paragraphs. The second is from the Clachaig Inn Visitors' Book, shown above.

What stands out is the bold approach taken by this team. They were climbing on new territory each time, and attempting lines on steep and imposing ground. It may well be that they failed on Church Door Buttress due to snow and ice; there is no evidence either way though it was a remarkably snowy winter as evidenced earlier on Stob Ghabhar and Beinn an Dothaidh.

What they did bring to this Meet however was their unparalleled experience and standard of climbing; Solly had led Eagle's Nest Direct on High Crag, Buttermere, on a cold day in 1892; the route is currently graded at Mild Very Severe, steep and exposed, and light years ahead of what was being explored in Scotland. Both Collie and Collier had led Severe or harder routes in the Lakes, while Collie had experienced a baptism of ice with the first winter ascent of Steep Gill in 1891, now a Grade V and also in the Lakes. Collie also had Alpine experience, climbing guideless on the Chamonix Aiguilles. Given the opportunity and good conditions, the way was clear for some interesting ascents.

It is certain that on the 29th March they left Glen Coe and travelled up to Fort William. The next day, the 30th, they were on Ben Nevis, making the first ascent of a major route which would shatter the complacency of Scottish mountaineers. The perception of Ben Nevis then prevailing is perhaps best shown by the brief historical quote below from the SMC General Guide of 1902, written by WI Clark. It provides a picture of the state of knowledge and level of ambition then prevalent in 1894.

> From above, the precipices look hopelessly steep and inaccessible, and it is not perhaps to be wondered at that no serious attempts were made to climb them till quite recently. Up till 1892 only one gully, the one marked No. 3 on the map, is believed to have been climbed, and so far as is known, none of the ridges had ever been attempted. So lately as 1894, Mr Whymper, writing to the *Leisure Hour*, spoke of this face thus:- 'This great cliff is one of the finest pieces of crag in our country, and it has never been climbed, though every now and then adventurous ones go and look at it with wistful eyes.' [22]

In March 1894 then, when Collie, Solly and Collier entered the Allt a' Mhuilinn glen and approached the north-east face, climbers were still completely unaware of the explorations of the Hopkinson family two years earlier. As to Collie's friends, Joseph Collier (1855–1905) was born in Hyde, Greater Manchester and was of Scots descent on his mother's side. He was a general surgeon in Manchester, an expert golfer and Captain of the Manchester Golf Club, and as a climber he had an exceptional reach that combined well with his agility. He met his friend Solly through their mutual interest in playing football. His first serious climbing in Scotland was from the 1894 Easter Meet at Inveroran. That same year he climbed in the Caucasus. He joined the SMC in 1896.

Godfrey Allan Solly (1858–1942) was born in Congleton, Cheshire. He had a long and active life, dying in his 84th year, joining the SMC in 1894. Amongst his climbing deeds may be noted 44 alpine seasons, with another two in the Caucasus. He served as Mayor of Birkenhead, was by profession a solicitor, and married the sister of another SMC member, James Maclay. He died in the same year as Norman Collie and was still active on the hill in his mid-70s. He was very proficient in snow and ice and a brilliant rock climber.

Tower Ridge is the longest route on Ben Nevis, with a total length, if one includes the Douglas Boulder at its foot, of 1000m. The Boulder (in fact a sizeable buttress in its own right) is some 200m in length. In winter the Boulder would stand alone as a good route, and parties heading for the ridge usually bypass it on the left. An easy, shallow gully (East Gully) leads to the gap behind the Boulder from which a steep chimney announces the start of the ridge proper. With its length and the shortness of winter days, it is a virtual necessity to solo much of the ridge. Three sections may call for a rope; the initial chimney from the Douglas Boulder Gap, the Little Tower, a steepening about halfway up the ridge, and the Great Tower and Tower Gap beyond. It is also obvious that an early start is useful.

Collie's team started up the ridge just left of East Gully; this is a straightforward slope in good conditions, and can provide a better approach than the gully. Although writing an account of their ascent on Friday, 30th March, Collie couched it in an utterly original and somewhat opaque style of writing.[23] The account begins with the arrival of the three adepts, '*searchers after vast protuberances of the earth, in the land of the Caledones'* where there were many things commending themselves to *'true worshippers of that most mystagorical and delectable pursuit–the oromaniacal Quest into the secret and hidden mysteries of sublime mountains.'* They were in search of a new entrance towards the topmost pinnacle.

Collie, a keen golfer, even inserts the game of golf into his article by stating that there be many who deny that the *'Quintessence of the true enjoyment can so be attained'* (i.e. by mountaineering), arguing that it *'resides in that subtill science, the striking of a ball violently with a stick'*, but, Collie states, *'this is also a mystery.'* (As any golfer would recognise!)

So the three arrive in '*hight Castrum Guillelmi*,' keenly, with great joyousness, and early the next morning '*did they start forth by the straight road'*. They '*bore with them the proper, peculiar, fit, exact, and lawful insignia of the brotherhood, a flaxen rope coiled even as the mystic serpent, likewise staves curiously shapen...for...go we not forth in a savage land, where liveth the green dragon, spoken of by the ingenious J.J. Scheuchzerus, doctor of medicine...'*

Johann Jakob Scheuchzer (1672–1733), was a Swiss scholar born in Zürich. A doctor, scientist and traveller, he wrote papers on the Swiss mountains, meteorology and geology. In 1706, despite himself doubting the existence of dragons, he illustrated reports by men of good faith who had seen dragons in Switzerland by fantastic drawings of dragons. He also published a map of that country which remained the best up until the end of the 18th century.

And so the account continued, on what was a sunny day. Lochan Meall an t-Suidhe they left '...*on the dexter hand'*..., and '*Thus did they fare onward towards the midst of the valley placed between the red Hill and the great Mountain.'* Eventually they saw '*a mighty petrolific ridge, full of points, towers, and pinnacles.'* The ridge they gained by cutting steps...*in a certain mystic manner...'* and '...*First did they traverse a narrow edge of snow fashioned by the wind. ...So did they fare onwards; and by inspection were they aware how others had travelled on the same way, for on the stones and rocks were there certain petrographical scrapings and curious markings deeply graven, and very evident.'*

These markings were evidently nail marks left by the Hopkinsons' explorations of 1892. '*But presently came they to a great rock, a majestic tower; here were they compelled to depart to the right hand, placing themselves in steep and perilous positions on slopes of ice, which downwards seemed to end in the empty air, even in the great void.'* Next, Collie shows his sly sense of humour with a little bit of satire aimed at the Alpine Club, of which all three climbers were members, Collie having joined in January 1893.

> Then were the Three exceeding joyful, for is it not written in the secret books of the Brethren, many operations must they perform amidst the great mountains on the snowy ice, especially, particularly, and metagrabolised*, that

they may be numbered with the True, the Pious, the Elect, even amongst those who are considered worthy of the most mystical and allegorical symbol A.C., by many variously interpreted. For some hold that it signifies "Adepti Cragorum," whilst others "Angelorum Confederatio," for these latter maintain that the Quest can only be rightly pursued, or satisfactorily continued by the aid of wings; but in this matter are they deceived, and argue foolishly after the wisdom of the flesh.

*metagrabolised: totally perplexed and mixed up.

Two years earlier, in 1892, Collie had enjoyed his first season in the Alps, climbing with Albert Frederick Mummery and Geoffrey Hastings. As mentioned earlier, this team made several bold, guideless ascents in the Chamonix Aiguilles, including the first traverse of the Grépon with Pasteur in 1892, and the first ascent of the Requin with Slingsby in 1893. Mummery, despite being one of the foremost climbers of his period, had been refused admittance to the Alpine Club in 1879. His father was part owner of a tannery, and the Alpine Club was, to quote from Christine Mill's biography of Collie '*...an exclusive, often snob-ridden world where a man of low social rank would have no chance at all of entering its portals.*'[24]

Mummery was so upset that it was another eight years before he tried again. Collie, on the other hand, had the '*right family background*', and was admitted after his first Alpine season, in February 1893. One has to conclude that Collie, brought up in a family noted for their lack of stuffiness, and also no lover of fools, was through his article having a really good dig at the practices of the AC.

The trio battled up the west face of the Great Tower, on top of which they found a cairn. Looking down, they saw their footsteps in the snow, '*... looking like scarce seen veins in finest marble. But before them lay the narrow Way, the Ridge, the Cleft, and the white Slope, leading even unto the utmost height...*' They walked carefully along the narrow crest and dropped into Tower Gap '*...symbolical of the precious secret of all philosophies.*' Finally all that remained was the white slope, up which they sought the route. This becomes steeper just before the plateau is gained, and they were almost despairing when '*...lo! from out of the clouds a rope descended, and a voice was heard...*'

The observers at the summit Meteorological station had met them at the top, and led them to their '*heavenly Temple.*' There they were questioned before being admitted, shown the wondrous contents, including '*...mathematical instruments, exquisitely made, for the discovery of small and minute bodies in the air...*'

The three had successfully made the first ascent, and first winter ascent at that, of what would become known as *Tower Ridge* (600m Difficult,

IV,3). Climbing with a short length of hemp rope and long axes, they had climbed the route in five hours, with no prior knowledge or exploration. Their fitness and Alpine experience had demonstrated what could be done with the right attitude.

When winter grading was rationalised many years later, Tower Ridge was given a Grade III rating; more recently, in the first decade of the 21st century, and following pressure from the local mountain rescue team, it was upgraded to IV, in the hope that the significant number of climbing parties running into difficulties through starting too late in the day, or climbing too slowly, or simply underestimating the magnitude of the route, would think twice before attempting the climb. It may be downgraded back to III eventually, but it remains a classic, in summer or winter.

Collie's explorations through Lochaber and Glen Coe were not yet over, however. As an academic, Collie enjoyed a relatively relaxed work atmosphere with generous holidays. As his friends Solly and Collier travelled homewards, Geoffrey Hastings came up to Fort William. Collie was so delighted with his route on Ben Nevis that he and Hastings climbed it on the next day, Saturday 31st March. Collie was again welcomed by the observers at the summit, the second ascent being noted in the Observatory's Log. The following day they walked up Sgurr a' Mhaim, on the south side of Glen Nevis. They then moved south to Glen Coe, staying at the Clachaig Inn again from where they made several ascents, as noted in the Visitors' Book:

April 2nd-4th

G. Hastings) Climbed Aonach Dubh on the left of Ossians cave

N. Collie) Went up into Coir a Lochan Coire na Beach! & climbed the great precipice of

Bidein nam Bian, walked over the top of Bidein nam Bian & Stb Coire Lochan & then came

down through the crags which face the hotel. N C.

It would seem that Collie was content to repeat his climbs with Hastings, though an unsigned note later on in the same journal issue raises a question when it mentions '*...a rock pinnacle which stands out of the great gully which comes down from behind Aonach Dubh and faces the Clachaig Inn.*' This may of course be Collie's Pinnacle, actually climbed before Collie went to Fort William. Collie had been prodded by Douglas to provide a report on his climbs, but as usual he was reluctant to obey, so in all probability Douglas prepared the report which would not have been a perfect account.

The initial effect of Collie's climbing, particularly his spectacular ascent of Tower Ridge in all its winter glory, was one of dismay that he had caught the SMC napping. Naismith knew of the ascent by the 20th April at the latest, as by then Collie had received a congratulatory letter from him. We are very fortunate that Douglas had the foresight to not only retain correspondence; he also bound them into his copies of the SMC Journal. These letters are now safely archived in the National Library of Scotland.[25] Naismith also wrote to Douglas the following undated letter, which, noting the double underlined words, perhaps sums up the Scots' attitude to the ascent –

Hamilton
Saturday night

My Dear Douglas,
Just got yours enclosing Collie's which I return with many thanks. The Sassenachs have indeed taken the wind out of our sails maist notoriously I wull say that. However I suppose we must make a virtue of necessity & try to look pleasant about it. These beggars were more wide-awake than we–in skimming the cream off Glencoe & Ben Nevis the year before the railway opened, while we in our innocence were still planning what we should do after that event.

Collie no doubt is "a pure Scotsman" (tho' perhaps in a Gladstonian sense) but his 3 pals tho' all very nice chaps are undoubted undiluted specimens of the genus pock-pudden. This is truly a sad day for auld Scotland. Let us hope that the hotel keepers at Ft. Wm. took a good few bawbees off the Englishers. Flodden or even Culloden was nothing to this...*

*pock-pudden: a bag pudding, and also then a derogatory name for an Englishman.

Collie wrote to Douglas –

16 Campden Grove
Kensington W.
20.4.94

...I had a letter the other day from Naismith in which he congratulated me in the most delightful manner on my Easter climbs. After I had read your letter I felt as if I had rather been poaching on your ground on Ben Nevis, but I assure you it is many years since I made up my mind that on the first possible opportunity when I could get another man I would rather have a try at the old Ben...

He sent Willie Douglas his article soon thereafter, describing the ascent with a covering letter –

16 Campden Grove
Kensington W.
27th June

...I send an attempt–written largely of experiment–laborious I fear–a pseudo Rabelaisian alchemistic etc attempts–which I commend to your Editorial clemency. Deal gently with it–but don't scruple to say if you don't want it–I go to Switzerland to be dragged over the mountains by Mummery and Hastings in about a month.

Yours in haste

Norman Collie

Joe Stott, in exile in New Zealand, wrote to Douglas on the 22nd October 1894, having received the latest number of the SMCJ (Vol.3, No.15.) In it he commented on Collie's article '*...The "Oromaniacal Quest" is amusing, but so d---nably vague, that but for the notes in "Notes and Queries"–you would not know what they'd been up to on Ben Nevis...*'

It should be added that this route and an ascent of North-East Buttress the following year resulted in one of the few errors to appear in the otherwise well-researched history of Mountaineering in Britain by RW Clark and EC Pyatt. In the chapter outlining mountaineering in Scotland between 1889 and 1914, and describing the general lack of knowledge of the climbing potential on Ben Nevis, the authors wrote –

> This ignorance was encouraged, rather naughtily one may feel, by the Hopkinsons, who failed to record their climbs until, some three years later, they submitted a brief notice of them to The Alpine Journal. News of their climbs had percolated through the mountaineering community, however, and at least a few details appear to have been known to the party, consisting of Norman Collie, Dr Joseph Collier, and G.A. Solly, which attended the S.M.C.'s Easter Meet at Inveroran (Pl. 29) in 1894.[26]

No evidence has been found or provided to back this claim of some prior knowledge, and indeed when the author contacted and spoke with Pyatt in the early 1980s, he admitted that he had no such evidence. Clark and Pyatt also remark that they were unsure of Collie making the second ascent of Tower Ridge, the day following his first; they must have been unaware of the entry in the Observatory Log confirming this fact. These minor points should in no way be regarded as detracting from their history, which

Looking north along Loch Coruisk, Skye. This scene rapidly became popular with early tourists and landscape artists. The figure is his 1st wife, Kate. (AE Robertson © SMC)

Bird Fowling was widely practised in Scotland's western isles for food

Fowler landing on Stac Lii, St Kilda, highly risky due to Atlantic swells

Sgurr nan Gillean on the Cuillin Ridge, Isle of Skye, showing Pinnacle Ridge which attracted many early climbers (© abrahamphotographic)

Alexander Nicolson, poet, writer and early mountaineer

James David Forbes, physicist, geologist, and Alpinist, first ascent of Gillean in 1836

Sligachan Inn, Skye, about 1875, looking towards Glen Sligachan with Marsco on the left and Sgurr nan Gillean on the right. From *'Good Words'* articles on Skye by Alexander Nicolson, which helped to popularise the island for visitors. Artist unknown

The Inaccessible Pinnacle is the rocky feature of the summit of Sgurr Dearg on the Cuillin Ridge, and was first named thus on the Admiralty Chart of Skye in 1858. It was first climbed by the Pilkington brothers from Lancashire on 18th August 1880, and remains the nemesis for many would be Munroists (© abrahamphotographic)

Sketch by James David Forbes of Ben Nevis, sent in a letter to his sister in May 1848. The main features are shown with remarkable accuracy (© St Andrews University)

W Douglas, 2nd Editor, SMC Journal (© SMC)

Professor George Ramsay, 1st Pres. SMC (© SMC)

Ernest Maylard, 1st Secretary SMC (© SMC)

The March 1891 SMC Easter Meet at Dalmally was held in wintry and poor weather. Personnel included: G Ramsay (President, front, 3rd from left), EA Maylard (Secretary, back, 3rd from left); and Rolland, RA Robertson, W Douglas, John Rennie, Gilbert Thomson, Hugh Munro (front, 2nd from left), Campbell, Lester, Joe Stott (1st Editor, front, 1st from left), and John Gibson, front right. Expeditions made included an attempt at the infamous *'Black Shoot'* (© SMC)

May 1891 SMC Meet, Dalwhinnie. Held at the beginning of the month, there was still much snow lying and a heavy snowfall the first night added to the fun for walking. Days of some 25 miles long were the order of the day. Personnel present were L to R: Munro, L. Hinxman, John Gibson, John Rennie & Joe Stott (© SMC)

January 1892, Brodick, Arran. This special meet was attended by RA Robertson, JG Stott, W Douglas, John H Gibson, T Fraser S Campbell (members) and two friends, Dr Leith & Hamilton Fleming. This is a rare photograph of Joe Stott, 1st Editor of the SMC Journal (2nd from left), as he was just about to leave for New Zealand (© SMC)

Approaching Ben Ledi summit from the north. The leading walker is wielding an alpenstock, a long pole with a metal spike. Early mountaineers would plunge the spike into the snow and kick steps. They would also glissade or slide down slopes leaning back on the pole, a risky manoeuvre (WL Howie © SMC)

Tower Ridge Gap, Ben Nevis, a difficult, exposed section high on the climb (JS Napier © SMC)

'Cyclopean Walls on Goatfell', Arran. Willie Naismith belaying. Arran had easy access and soon became popular (W Douglas © SMC)

The NE Face of Stob Ghabhar, from a photograph of 15th April 1892. An attempt at the Upper Couloir led to an ice pitch forcing a move onto the rocks on the right (© SMC)

The SMC Easter Meet of 1894 at Inveroran Inn. From here Collie and friends moved on to Glen Coe and Fort William, with several first ascents including Tower Ridge. Collie is standing, second from right (© SMC)

In addition to Collie's party in March 1894, other climbers were finding new routes. On Monday 26th, Willie Naismith and Willie Douglas climbed ZigZag Gully, Grade I on Beinn an Dothaidh. There was a monster cornice at the top, and they accepted a rope from their friends above for protection. The earlier remains of a collapsed cornice can be seen on the right. The leader is probably using the shaft of a long axe here for upward progress (Herbert Boyd © SMC)

Original artwork for the menu cover of the 1895 (7th) SMC Annual Dinner. The artist, whose signature can be seen top right, was Colin Bent Phillip, AC, RWS, friend of Collie and an excellent watercolourist. The view is looking up Coire na Creiche, Skye, with Sgurr an Fheadain foreground with the line of Waterpipe Gully Bidein Druim nan Ramh seen top right. (Author's Collection)

Coire na Creiche in Skye, with the prominent gash of Waterpipe Gully cutting down Sgurr an Fheadain. Bidein Druim nan Ramh is on the right and An Caisteal just left of centre. The gully was the focus of much attention and a controversial first ascent in 1895 by two unknown climbers from England (AE Robertson © SMC)

This drawing from *'The Graphic'* in 1898 may show Ida Fitzgerald Dalton, who had several climbing trips in the Cuillin with John Mackenzie the guide

In 1897 the enigmatic John Rennie (standing) designed a wooden-framed tent which could withstand the Skye weather. With three of these, four climbers camped at the head of Loch Coruisk (John Rennie © SMC)

The Climbers' Camp at Loch Coruisk, 1897. Four shared two wooden-framed tents, with a third used as a kitchen. The line marked 'B' is the SE Ridge of Sgurr a' Ghreadaidh (Collie & Howell, 1896), while 'CD' is Brown's Climb, Difficult, the first route on this face of Sgurr a' Mhadaidh, climbed by all four (W Douglas © SMC)

August 1898, Sligachan. A large number of climbers descended on Skye. Back: (L to R) W Wickham King, W Douglas, GP Baker. Front: Godfrey Solly, James Maclay, Willie Naismith (GP Baker © Sligachan Hotel)

Appropriately, this image is titled *'A Bad Hitch'*. The second, James Gall Inglis, is striving to maintain the rope over a flake, while the leader, the incomparable Harold Raeburn, works out the next move of this steep route on the basalt of Edinburgh's Salisbury Crag. Inglis was a cousin of William Inglis Clark (© SMC)

William & Jane Inglis Clark, on their Arrol-Johnston *'dog-cart'* S2

William Inglis Clark in 1898, aged 43

An early ascent of the Basteir Tooth, a 45m Severe climb first put up by Willie Naismith and Alexander Mackay on 15th August 1898. The current guide describes this two-star route as *'a good route in an outrageous position.'* Naismith, who was climbing boldly during this period, took the time to explore the route on a rope from above. The recorder of the Meet, George Bennett Gibbs, described the route in his article as *'Though sensational, as any climb on an open face of such steepness is bound to be, the route described is not really difficult.'* (© SMC)

Original artwork for the menu cover of the 1899 (11th) Annual SMC Dinner. Artist unknown, the view is of the summit cliffs of Stob Ghabhar, with the Upper Couloir on the right which received its first ascent in 1897 by Alfred Ernest Maylard. Two other routes were also climbed further left, but never appeared in any guidebook (Author's Collection)

Liathach, April 1900. A constellation of mountaineers, L to R: Raeburn, Ling, Naismith, Mackay & Munro. This SMC Easter Meet saw the first winter ascent of the Northern Pinnacles, by two ropes; Naismith & Mackay, and Raeburn, Ling and Gall Inglis (Inglis © SMC)

'After a Skye blizzard'. SMC Easter Meet April, 1903. A year with *'chaotic and unusual weather'*, rivalling 2012 in that respect. As the President William Smith reported, *'Probably not the oldest member of the Club ever saw the Coolin range under such acute Alpine conditions.'* Such was the amount of ice on the ridges that two experienced parties failed on the Pinnacle Route (John Rennie © SMC)

'On the Castles' of the Cuillin Ridge. The guide looks like John Mackenzie (W Douglas © SMC)

Arthur Walker Russell, Willie Naismith and Gilbert Thomson, Arran, August 1904. *'Lunch below NE Face Cir Mhor'.* This vegetatious face was very popular with the pioneers (W Douglas © SMC)

is a fine milestone in the written history of British mountaineering; it is wide-ranging, authoritative, and patently the product of much research.

In 1894, to celebrate and promote the railway reaching Fort William on the West Highland Railway, *Mountain, Moor, and Loch* was published. This is a delightful book, heavily illustrated with about 230 drawings by Joseph Adam, though the author is not named. There is an essay completing the book by the Rev Norman MacLeod, DD.[27] The illustrations are by pen and pencil, and well show the glory of the Scottish Highlands as seen from the route of the railway. It was reviewed in the SMCJ of September 1894 '... *The fact that the book is not written for mountaineers is sufficiently indicated by the warning given against guideless ascents of Ben Nevis...*'

❄ ❄ ❄

There were other explorations in Scotland in 1894 of course, though not as momentous as Collie's exploits. Colin Bent Phillip (1856–1932) was an excellent water colour artist. He wrote a piece for Notes and Queries in the SMCJ, describing the Dirc Mhor (Great Cut) of Am Faireamh near Dalwhinnie.[28] This feature was almost unknown at the time and is a striking geological feature in the form of a dry ravine, formed by the meltwater channel of a receding glacier and almost 1.5km in length. Its most prominent feature is the 90m Sentinel Rock. There are a number of fine rock climbs in the Dirc Mhor, but these would have to wait a considerable time for standards to rise.

Phillip was not only a superb watercolourist; he had a passionate interest in the topography and nomenclature of the Scottish mountains, and was of considerable assistance to Munro when that man was drawing up his list of 3,000ft mountains. A Gaelic speaker, Phillip would make a point of talking to locals wherever he walked, learning more of the local place-names. He left hundreds of OS maps when he died, heavily annotated with place-name data; sadly these seem to have disappeared.

He would become a friend of Collie in later years, his tenure for some summers of Glen Brittle Cottage aiding in the exploration of the Cuillin. Some of Phillip's paintings may be found in the dining room of the Sligachan Hotel, while others are held by art galleries or are in private hands.

The question of guidebooks began to gain prominence with the publication in 1894 of a guide by WP Haskett Smith to climbing in the British Isles.[29] (The intended Scottish volume never appeared.) Walter Parry Haskett Smith (1859–1946) was born in Kent, and educated at Oxford, studying law. He began rock climbing in 1881 and in 1886 made a solo first ascent of Napes's Needle, thereby promoting rock climbing into the public gaze. The SMC had by now been discussing some sort of formal recording of mountain routes, and had of course already published Munro's listing of mountains.

The book was reviewed in the SMCJ, and not without some justifiable criticism.[30] The review is unsigned. It expresses surprise that '*...a slim booklet of 162 not very closely printed pages can accommodate all that is to be said upon "Climbing in England."*' It then continues to note that the book concentrates on the Lake District, with only a few rock scrambles round the coast and on Dartmoor mentioned elsewhere. The layout of the guide came under especially heavy criticism, being difficult and bewildering, with much page turning required in order to find particular climbs. The illustrations by Ellis Carr were praised.

The review remarked that Scotland would require three or four times the number of pages to cover its riches, in addition to which '*...Scotland, with all its riches, is but a tenth part explored...A single county, such as Ross, Inverness, or Argyle, would supply on a similar scale materials for two such books...*' The Scots were well aware that it was as yet early days in the mountain exploration of their country; it would be very premature, ran the feeling, to rush into a similar publication when many quality routes were still to be found and climbed.

The Scots were also not about to rush up to Fort William until easy access by train was possible. The line to Fort William was publicly opened on 7th August 1894, but that month climbers' attention was firmly focused on the Island of Arran, in the Firth of Clyde. Other than perhaps uncertainty as to exactly when it would be possible to reach Fort William by train, most of the surrounding area would be under stalking, and hence avoided. Additionally, it must be borne in mind that there was still no awareness of the Hopkinson routes in 1892, with Ben Nevis remaining a relatively unknown quality. In any case, there was unfinished business to be attended to on Arran.

❄ ❄ ❄

There were articles by Willie Douglas and Thomson describing their ascents on Arran, and at various times and combinations also by Maclay, Naismith, Rennie, JJ Douglas and others. The Douglas article is especially fine, and provides a good history of explorations on the island.[31] The early exploration of Cir Mhor has been described here in the previous chapter. One area the climbers explored during August of 1894 was the east face of Cioch na h-Oighe. Various roped permutations were involved; principally Douglas and Naismith. Five ledges run up and across this steep face, from lower left to right, and seem to consist mainly of heather and grass. Looking at this cliff it becomes obvious that the pioneers had made a step too far. There are several fine, modern routes in the higher grades, with the ledges being scrappy and best avoided. Naismith and his friends also returned to the north-east face of Cir Mhor, of which Thomson in his article remarked that –

> From a climber's point of view, the strongest feature about Cir Mhor is the variety of work which it affords. There is climbing over firm rocks and over rotten rocks, over screes and along ledges, by gullies and by ridges, and it varies from impossible to easy, not by one big jump, as many hills do, but by innumerable gradations.[32]

To be fair to these early climbers, they found the good rock on Arran next to impossible to climb; nailed boots on smooth granite slabs with a marked dearth of any natural belays or 'hitches' forced them onto the vegetatious gullies and ledges where, despite the insecurity, they could at least make upward progress. Good, climbable rock still beckoned but other than its granite ridges, not profitably on Arran until years in the future.

❄ ❄ ❄

As for advances in Scottish climbing, in addition to the brief spell of Gibson it was Naismith and his climbing partner and friend Thomson who made the next move. On Thursday, 27th September 1894 and enjoying at long last a convenient train journey, they reached Fort William during the Glasgow Autumn Holiday and set out for the north-east face of Ben Nevis. They took what is now the old route up the hill, climbing straight up the western flank of Meall an t-Suidhe where the Aluminium Works are now situated and ascending Coire Dubh. They then descended, crossing just below where the Allt Coire Lochain leaves Lochan Meall an t-Suidhe, dropping slightly into the Allt a' Mhuilinn glen and contouring along its south flank so gained the cliffs.

Perhaps another reason for using this approach which bypassed the bridle path, was the charge now made for using that approach; as the climbers were gaining the Nevis summit by routes up the north-east face, they may have seen little point in paying good money for using a small part of that route. Searching for the route climbed the previous winter by Collie's party, they described both Carn Dearg Buttress and the North-East Buttress.[33]

> Both of these buttresses appear to offer possible routes to the summit for adventurous cragsmen. Between the "Tower Ridge" and the Càrn Dearg buttress several gullies were noticed that are evidently climbable, and one of them has been climbed by Mr Rankin of the Observatory staff.

The climbers gained Tower Ridge by easy rocks on the east side, at a height of '*...about 3,000 feet*'. They had probably scrambled up easy mixed ground on the left of East Gully, entering that loose gully higher up and so gaining the Douglas Boulder Gap. They continued upwards, lunching above the Little Tower (which they did not mention). Next came the Great

Tower, where they followed the pioneers and moved right onto the west face. They saw a recess above, from which they calculated they could gain the top of the Tower. The moves to gain the recess, climbing '*...up eight feet of smooth and almost vertical rock, with not quite satisfactory handholds...*' they found to be '*...the only little bit of the whole day's climb where there was any real difficulty.*'

They gained the '*stone man*' on the summit of the Great Tower and were then faced by the narrow wall with perpendicular sides, leading to a cleft, eight feet deep. About this, the infamous Tower Gap, Naismith repeated a curious anecdote –

> It seems that the builder of the first cairn on the Tower conceived the brilliant idea of making his peak inaccessible; and accordingly, on his way back from the Tower, which he had approached from above, he either manufactured the cleft, or at least deepened it considerably, by throwing down a lot of loose blocks.

As mentioned earlier, a cairn here had existed since before 1885, and may well have been built by the Observers from the summit Meteorological Station. The final rocks were climbed in a few minutes once over the cleft, and Naismith and Thomson, enjoying a day of superb atmospheric clarity, spent two hours on top. They paid a visit to the North-East Buttress and its overhanging precipice, with Naismith obviously scoping it out for a possible ascent.

From the Meteorological Observatory, at 3.30pm Naismith sent a telegraph to Willie Douglas in Edinburgh:-

> *To: William Douglas*
> *Castle St Edr.*
>
> *Precipice Route accomplished not difficult*
> *Splendid panorama.*
>
> *Naismith*

Naismith followed up this telegraph the following day with a letter to Douglas, providing a few details of this third ascent. As in the telegraph, he repeated the news that he found it quite easy, with only two sections demanding care: the introductory chimney section rising up from the Douglas Boulder Gap, and the eight foot wall on the west flank of the Tower. Naismith suggested that a suitable name for the route would be the Tower Ridge, and so it has been known for evermore. But the even more interesting bit in the letter is perhaps the last paragraph:-

> The climb I want to look at when I come back is by the great eastern ridge or buttress due E of the Observatory and next to Collie's ridge on the left as you

> face the Ben. On most views of the hill from Banavie or Corpach this Eastern buttress is seen on the skyline. It is a.p. at the end but might I think be reached higher up.[34]

The reference to a.p. was an abbreviation widely used by climbers at the time meaning 'absolutely perpendicular', and Naismith was referring to what is now named the North-East Buttress. Collie's climbs had galvanised his fellow club members; Naismith was a cautious individual and had been carefully picking his way through this new sport. He had teamed up with a regular climbing partner in Gilbert Thomson; they had found that they needed some form of regular climbing exercise in between their mountain trips, and they were extending the boundaries of what they could safely climb, given the almost total lack of security on either rock or ice.

Naismith had an innate modesty which makes it difficult to determine with any precision just where he should be placed as regards technical ability, but he had already discovered the shortcomings of the alpenstock in winter, and may have experimented with the use of crampons. Luckily we have the article by Lord Mackay, giving vignettes of earlier climbers, including Naismith.[35] Physically of small build and compact, Naismith had small feet which seemed made to go into or on the tiniest hold. He had a neatness and mental sureness, and Mackay never remembers him making a false step.

> He was a human being of the finest steel, modest and self-effacing. Whatever new feat was in "contemplation", whatever party was made up to attack it, Naismith, whose vis vivendi [strength to live] was at its root, would normally hold back from the leadership to which he was so well fitted and go second to some other. He would deprecate his right to lead.'

Naismith had also started events which would culminate in the formation of the SMC, whose influence would dominate Scottish mountaineering for several decades. He was, and remains, despite all his attempts to reside in the shadows, a key figure its development.

The fourth ascent of Tower Ridge was made on the 2nd December, by John Bell, John Napier and John McGregor. (The latter, a good climber, died suddenly in Mexico in 1900.)

❄ ❄ ❄

The SMC held their sixth AGM on Friday 14th December 1894. One of the proposals was for a Climber's Guide to Scotland, proposed by William Brown and seconded by Maylard. Out of this beginning would eventually spring a continuing flow of guidebooks, covering all of Scotland for both walkers and mountaineers, and one of the great strengths of the SMC. Brown had obviously spent some time in thinking through this project, as he detailed what he felt should be included and how the publication should be well illustrated and attractive so as to appeal to the general public.

He also warned of the threat of competition '*The time might not be fully ripe for such a work, but competition was threatened which might encroach upon the information in possession of the Club...*' The motion was unanimously carried, £10 was released from the Club funds for initial outlays, and Willie Douglas was unanimously appointed Editor.[36]

A note in the same Journal section by Hugh Munro commented on the opening of the West Highland Railway, writing that it opened up large tracts of new climbing ground '*...including some of the highest ranges in Scotland, which to the mountaineer whose time is often limited to a Saturday to Monday, or public holiday, has hitherto been almost inaccessible.*' It is too easy to forget that these were the years before easy travel by motor car. Munro continued –

> It is needless to point out that the whole of the Ben Nevis range is now brought within reach of a railway, and it will now be possible to spend a winter's day on the monarch of British mountains and reach Glasgow or Edinburgh the same night.' [37]

The SMC were indeed already planning to utilise the railway, with Tarbet and Fort William arranged for the next New Year and Easter Meets. Munro also looked forward to the completion of a proposed rail extension to Mallaig, in North Morar, which would '*...give access to some of the very wildest mountains in the beautiful West, hitherto only familiar to a few of us.*'

It is fortunate that despite the savaging of the railway system in the UK in the latter part of the 20th century, the Fort William to Mallaig line has been saved and maintained and is now regarded as an international treasure, running the only remaining regular, steam driven train in the country along its 84ml return route. Just as importantly, Scottish mountaineering had developed its own head of steam and the scene was set for great deeds to come.

References

1. Dent. C.T. *Mountaineering*. (London: Longmans, Green & Co., 1892)
2. Pilkington, C. Chapter XI, *Hill Climbing in the British Isles*. In: Mountaineering. London (1892), 342.
3. Douglas, W. *Mountaineering* (review), in: Notes and Queries. SMCJ 2, 3, Sept. 1892, 146-147.
4. Naismith, W.W. *Snowcraft in Scotland*. SMCJ 2, 4, Jan. 1893, 157-167.
5. Gibson, J.H. *Snowcraft in Scotland*. SMCJ 2, 6, Sept. 1893, 322-323.

6. Naismith, W.W. Ibid, 323-324.
7. Mackenzie, Robert Jameson. *Almond of Loretto–Being the Life and a Selection from the Letters of Hely Hutchinson Almond.* (London: Constable, 1905).
8. Almond, Hely. H. *Ben-Y-Gloe on Christmas Day.* SMCJ 2, 5, May 1893. 235-245.
9. Munro, H.T. *The Lochnagar Range.* In Notes and Queries, SMCJ 2, 3, Sept. 1892, 133-134.
10. Douglas, William. *Lochnagar Corrie.* SMCJ 2, 5, May 1893, 246-248.
11. William Douglas Letters. Undated. NLS.
12. *Dalmally Meet.-Jan. 1894.* In: Proceedings of the Club, SMCJ 3, 14, May 1894, 95-97.
13. T. Fraser Campbell. *Inveroran Meet.-Easter, 1894.* In: Proceedings of the Club, SMCJ 3, 14, May 1894, 97-102.
14. Maylard, A. Ernest. *The Club Meets. Inveroran. 14th to the 18th April 1892.* SMCJ 2, 3, Sept. 1892, 121-132.
15. Thomson, Gilbert. *Beinn an Dòthaidh and Beinn Doireann.* SMCJ 3, 14, May 1894, 76-80.
16. Naismith, W.W. *The Shepherd at Home on 24th and 25th* March. In: Notes and Queries–Excursions. SMCJ 3, 14, May 1894, 103-105.
17. SMC Archives.
18. Clachaig Inn Visitors' Book, NLS.
19. Brown, William. *Climbing in Glencoe.* SMCJ 4, 19, Jan. 1896, 48-51.
20. Godfrey A. Solly. *Ossian's Cave.* SMCJ 20, 120, Nov. 1935, 389-393.
21. *Glencoe and Ben Nevis.* In: Notes and Queries–Excursions. SMCJ 3, 15, Sept. 1894, 158-159.
22. Clark, William Inglis. *Ben Nevis Section of the SMC General Guide*, SMCJ 7, 39, Sept. 1902, 144.
23. Orlamon Linecus. *Divine Mysteries of the Oromaniacal Quest.* SMCJ 3, 15, Sept. 1894, 151-157.
24. Mill, Christine. *Norman Collie: A Life in Two Worlds.* (Aberdeen: Aberdeen University Press, 1987), 62.
25. NLS. William Douglas Letters. (See http://www.smc.org.uk/Downloads/Acc11538-11851.pdf).
26. Clark, Ronald W. and Pyatt, Edward C. *Mountaineering in Britain* (London: Phoenix House Ltd, 1957), 109.
27. *Mountain, Moor, and Loch.* (London: Sir Joseph Causton & Sons, 1894).
28. Phillip, Colin. *The Dirc Mhor of Am Faireamh.* In: Notes and Queries, SMCJ 3, 15, Sept. 1894, 161.
29. Haskett Smith, W. *Climbing in the British Isles.* I.-England. (Longman, Green & Co. 1894)
30. Haskett Smith, W. *Climbing in the British Isles, Review.* In: Notes and Queries, Mountaineering Literature. SMCJ 3, 15, Sept. 1894, 170-172.

31. Douglas, W. *The Granite Peaks of Arran*. SMCJ 3, 16, Jan. 1895, 195-211.
32. Thomson, Gilbert. *Cir Mhor*. SMCJ 3, 16, Jan. 1895, 212-217.
33. Naismith, W.W. *Ben Nevis— North Face*, In: Notes And Queries, SMCJ 3, 16, Jan. 1895, 231-233.
34. Naismith, W. *Letter to Willie Douglas* (undated but by inference 27th Sept. 1894). NLS Archives.
35. Lord Mackay. *Vignettes of Earlier Climbers.* SMCJ 24, 141, April 1950, 173-174.
36. Proceedings of the Club. SMCJ 3, 16, Jan. 1895, 229.
37. Munro, H.T. *The West Highland Railway.* In Notes and Queries, SMCJ 3, 16, Jan. 1895, pp238-239.

7

Eldorado (1895-96)

The SMC New Year Meet of 1894-95 was held at Tarbert, Loch Lomond, during which the 'Arrochar Alps' were explored by the usual suspects – including Boyd, Douglas, Maclay, Naismith, Thomson, Maylard, and AE Robertson. As the summing up of the meet report stated, it provided '... *interesting if not on the whole very exciting climbing.*'[1] The Cobbler was traversed by various combinations of routes and parties, with experiments in step-cutting on ice-covered rocks carried out by at least one group, while the surrounding mountains were also traversed.

The main event on the calendar for 1895, however – long put off due to the '*...tardy completion of the West Highland Railway*', was the Easter Meet – held at Fort William. This was from Thursday 11th April through to Tuesday 16th, and was based at the Alexandra Hotel. The report of the meet was compiled by William Brown.[2] So it was that on the Thursday evening some 20 men '*...were ranged round the mahogany at the Alexandra Hotel.*' This vanguard included Collie, who with his colleagues from University College, Alexander Kellas and Morris Travers, had spent the previous fortnight mountaineering round Corpach. With later arrivals, some 27 attended the meet. As is so often the case with Collie, we have no knowledge of his exploits during his fortnight before the official meet. Kellas, a Scot from Aberdeen, joined the SMC in 1898 and would become known for his knowledge of high altitude physiology and his pioneering Himalayan explorations.[3]

> Of the merits of Fort-William as a climbing centre, the Meet was little short of a revelation to those of the members – and they formed the majority – who knew them only by hearsay. A glance at the map is sufficient to show how rich is the field that awaits the climber within easy reach of the hotel door... Small

> wonder, therefore, that some of the more energetic members, finding themselves in such an Eldorado of mountain riches, should have performed feats of "peak bagging" unheard of before at a Club Meet.

So wrote Brown in his Meet Report. He may have been prescient with the use of the word Eldorado, but he was certainly aware, as were his fellow climbers, that suddenly the atmosphere had changed, and that a new and exciting time had arrived. Mountaineering in Scotland was now acquiring a golden hue.

> Nor were the Ultramontanes less active in their attack upon rock faces, couloirs, and arêtes. One of the chief objections these indefatigable persons have to the Ordnance Survey is that it was not specially constructed with a view to exhibiting "sporting" bits that will "go." The Ultramontane, therefore, has to find these out for himself; but on the present occasion this task has been considerably simplified by Dr Collie, who has spent several seasons exploring the ridges and corries of this district.

One route which was not attempted during this meet was Tower Ridge.

> The famous Tower Ridge of Ben Nevis was pronounced impossible, being plastered all over with ice and snow, which hung in great white blossoms from the rocks.

In compensation, however, several new routes were made. On the Friday, a day of thick, gloomy weather, Collie, Naismith, Thomson and Travers made the first ascent of Castle Ridge. It would seem very likely, not least from Brown's comments, that Collie and his two guests had spent some time before the Meet, seeking out possible lines. They could do no further climbing following that, as they were required to be back at the laboratory in London, where they were researching on the newly discovered inert gas Helium.

Castle Ridge (275m, III) is one of four great spurs or ridges which project outwards from the Ben Nevis plateau. It is the rightmost of these ridges and therefore the first to be met from the normal approach up the Allt a' Mhuilinn glen. The other three ridges are, of course, Carn Dearg Buttress, Tower Ridge, and the North-East Buttress. Lionel Hinxman, a keen photographer and SMC member, wrote an article based on Castle Ridge, having made the second ascent on Saturday 13th, the day after the first. Not content with that, two parties made the third and fourth ascents on the Monday: Napier, Bell and party, and Dr Horrocks (guest), Douglas and Maclay.

Following the awkward section below the north face of Castle Ridge, Hinxman and his companions arrived below their target –

> The gully in which we stood ran straight up the face of the precipice, its perpendicular black walls draped here and there with curtains of snow and falls of

> blue ribbed ice. Near the top it forked, enclosing within its branches the great castellated mass of rock which crowns and gives its name to the Castle Ridge.

It was now dawning on the Scots that the 60ft lengths of hemp rope then commonly in use were a grave handicap on long snow and ice routes. With a party of three, this was compounded, so they tied two such ropes together, even then finding it inadequate on some sections of the route. Throughout the day, William Tough was the leader, Brown brought up the rear, and Hinxman was in the middle. As for belaying, there was still no use of separate slings, the best belay being the rope flung over any available rock.

William Tough (1856–1910) was born in Edinburgh; his father was a mason. He may have met Brown at Edinburgh University where both did their degree. He had as qualifications an MA and was also FSA (Fellow of the Society of Antiquaries, Scotland). Tough lived most of his life in Edinburgh, joining the SMC in 1892,and is on the 1901 census as living at 94 Polwarth Terrace, described there as a 'teacher of commercial subjects'.[4] William Tough died in 1910, with cause of death listed as pneumonia. He was the Editor of *The Works and Life of Sir William Mure of Rowallan*, in two volumes.[5] Sir William (d. 1657) was a Scots poet, one of a line of the Mure family who had Rowallan Castle in Ayrshire. As for the name Tough, according to a current SMC member with the same surname, it is generally pronounced '*Tooch*' in the north of Scotland, with this gradually being replaced with '*Tuff*' the further south one goes.[6] This may not help much with the pronunciation of his name though, as while Tough appears to be an Edinburgh man, his father was from further north, from Forfarshire

Tough was very obviously no mean climber, and had partnered with William Brown, another tiger in the SMC. He was about 12 years older than Brown. Together they would help advance standards in Scotland. On Castle Ridge, they followed at first the footsteps of Collie's party from the previous day. Collie, as par for the course, had left no written description, but he was normally generous in passing on information in person to fellow members, and from the previous evening Hinxman was aware of some details of the route. Collie had mentioned a '*...big chimney, ...of whose ascent we had heard graphic accounts the night before.*' However, Tough and his companions somehow departed from Collie's line and ended up with a variation which gave them '*...quite the most difficult and sensational bit of the whole climb.*'

Brown and Hinxman belayed under an overhang, while Tough disappeared round an edge to the right. '*Some time passed ...during which we pictured our leader spread-eagled on the face of the precipice, clinging on with teeth, eyelids, and other adhesive portions of his person...*' About 4ft of nearly vertical rock had been climbed by Tough, with few holds, including an insecure-looking block which had to be trusted with one's whole weight, jutting out over a 'horrid gulf'. The remainder of the route went safely, and they basked in the still air and sunshine above the climb, enjoying a pipe. They met several other parties descending from the summit, aiming for the bridle path. Hinxman mentions how on the previous day, the hot coffee provided by their *'kind friends the observers'* would live in the memory of those who were up in the cold and mist. The three parties who made the ascents following Collie's were unanimous in reporting that *'...although rather short, it afforded about 1,000 feet of excellent sport'*. Best avoided after heavy snowfall, due to avalanche potential, it remains a popular climb.

Good though the climbing on Nevis was, the climb of the Meet was declared to be a route on Aonach Beag, climbed by Naismith, Thomson and Maclay on the Saturday. This route, the *North-East Ridge* (460m III), provided the pioneers with 1,500ft of sustained climbing, and was described in an article by Thomson.[7] Collie's party, as mentioned, had to return to London early, but as Thomson wrote, '*... Collie proved a perfect encyclopaedia of information regarding possible and impossible routes, and even after his reluctant departure he left a valuable legacy behind.*' On Saturday morning the trio accompanied Collie on the train, leaving him to continue homewards and themselves disembarking at Spean Bridge. Collie had spotted a *'beautiful ridge'*, and provided them with full directions as to how to find it. They struck up the valley immediately to the east of the Aonachs, presumably entering An Cul Choire. It was a misty, warm morning, but eventually they spotted a ridge to their right. It looked good, if not quite living up to Collie's description, so they began to climb it.

> ...and for a thousand feet or more made our way patiently up a ridge that was always interesting, but never difficult. In fact, the suspicion of a joke on the part of our informant was not altogether absent, although it seemed incredible that a man like Collie could play off a joke on such a serious subject as a beautiful ridge.

As they neared the top, it became more and more evident that they were on the wrong ridge, confirmed when the mist cleared a bit and looking south they saw the sharp outlines of another ridge, with two or three pitches that were perpendicular in profile. This southerly ridge was presumably the *North-East Ridge of Aonach Beag*, their intended target of the day. They had probably climbed the easy ridge in the north-west corner of An Cul Choire, leading to the ridge west of Stob a' Chul-Choire, and just east of a small col between that top and the main ridge of Aonach Mor.

They were dismayed, but determined to climb their original target. Even then the approach was rough and awkward, with a descent on snow followed by a traverse. Finally they gained a rock arête, at which point some suspicions remained still in their minds that the difficulties were imaginary.

Then a shout from the leader galvanised those behind. Ahead was a level section of the arête, above which rose tier after tier of grand pinnacles. It did not look easy.

Naismith continued to lead up the first of the pinnacles, with Maclay at the end and Thomson in the middle. Pinnacles led to chimneys, ledges, more pinnacles, and then the final pinnacle. This had to be bypassed on the left, by insecure ground, before the angle eased and the last section of snow arête led onto the plateau, about 100ft lower than the summit. As Hinxman had found on Castle Ridge, a 60ft rope was painfully short. The ridge had taken them four hours. For those who can face the three-hour approach march from Glen Nevis, it provides a recommended Grade III route. The happy if tired trio eventually regained Fort William via Glen Nevis just before midnight, in time to disappoint those who were looking forward to the '*...romance of a relief expedition.*'

As an amusing if minor parallel to this account, in 1975 the author went in search of the North-East Ridge, walking in from Glen Nevis. Finding what appeared to be a suitable candidate, and being well ahead of the other four in the party, he decided to solo the route. On gaining the plateau he realised that the true North-East Ridge was a mile further on, and that he had made a first ascent of *The Ramp* (300m II). Modern climbers can also utilise the ski gondola and chairlift on Aonach Mor as an approach strategy. Either way, a remote and peaceful day can be found, eventually. As for the first ascenders of the *true* North-East Ridge, the Meet Report has comments from them such as – '*The best arête in Scotland...beats anything in the Coolins*'. As Brown recorded, these remarks from the first ascent party were sincere. On Monday a second ascent was made by Tough and Brown, who were unable to straighten out the line. The Mamore range and the Grey Corries were also explored on this Meet, by the Salvationists.

> Thus ended a Meet which, whether it be judged by the numbers attending it, by the character of the climbing, or the conditions under which it was undertaken, must be ranked amongst the greatest ever held...We do not wish to compare it with the delightful gathering at Inveroran last Easter, which can never be eclipsed so far as pure enjoyment is concerned. There was a charm indeed about those March days by Loch Tulla which we partly missed at Fort-William. But the latter was altogether on a larger and grander scale. The mountains were higher, the climbs were stiffer, the energy even of the climbers seemed greater.

So did Brown begin his summing up of the 1895 Easter Meet at Fort William. The higher mountains had indeed thrown down a challenge to the mountaineers, and they had responded in kind. From then on, with better means of travel, a heightened awareness of what was possible, and good communication between the activists, the search for good sporting routes was on.

❄ ❄ ❄

In Glen Coe that same April, another classic route received its first recorded ascent, when the *Aonach Eagach* ridge was traversed from west to east by a party of three: Alexander Fraser Jnr., Arthur Walker Russell, and Andrew Robertson Wilson. All three were SMC members, with Fraser and Wilson joining in 1895 and Russell in 1896. Until recently the date of this traverse has been published as being in August, but with the Clachaig Hotel's Visitors' Book being accessible in the National Library of Scotland (NLS), Stuart Pedlar now has it down as being between the 2nd and 15th April.[8] Better still, Arthur Russell's diaries have also been lodged in the NLS.

> …the whole ridge – was traversed from west to east ascending all the pinnacles & was found to give good climbing. It is advisable to have a rope as the ridge is narrow & the rocks are rotten. Care should be taken in ascending & descending from the ridge as some of the gullies are not so simple as they look.[9]

As regards equipment and techniques, not much had progressed since the 1880s, though at least alpenstocks had seen their day and ice axes were now routinely used, summer and winter. In summer, they were used to remove vegetation and unearth holds, and occasionally for the extra hold. Nailed boots were used in all seasons, and there is a brief note in the May 1895 SMCJ providing the information that nails, which had previously had to be imported from Grindewald, Switzerland, could now be ordered from Leeds. It seems that some members of the Yorkshire Ramblers' Club, obviously irritated by the extra cost and delay at using the Swiss source, had persuaded English makers to copy the approved Swiss nails. Readers who are aware of the general financial outlook of natives from that splendid county will nod approvingly. The note was signed by a *G.T.*, probably Gilbert Thomson, who was an engineer by training.[10]

❄ ❄ ❄

Now that Fort William had easy access by train, many eyes were trained on the obvious lines still to be climbed on Ben Nevis. No line attracted more interest than the massive ridge which juts out against the sky high up at the head of the Allt a' Mhuilinn, and now known as the North-East Buttress.

> It was the last Easter Meet that brought this ridge into fame. From being an unnamed and unhonoured incident upon the cliff-face, it became an object of ambition to a large circle of climbers, the chief topic of the smoke room at nights, and the focus of many critical glances during the day. It would also have been climbed had the ice upon the rocks not forbade the attempt…[11]

So wrote William Brown, in a classic article describing an ascent made in May 1895. On the Friday of the Easter Meet of that year, Brown and

Tough were in a party which made an ascent of Carn Mor Dearg, continuing along the arête to the summit of Ben Nevis. Brown had come to the conclusion, from what he saw, that in spite of its formidable appearance in profile, and the presence of a sheer cliff one-third of the way up, it was less inaccessible than its reputation.

A plan was set by Brown and Tough. The date would be the Queen's birthday, Friday, 24th May. The bold pair also thought that on such an auspicious day, the heart of the West Highland Railway might be softened to a cheap fare. In this they were disappointed. '*Cheap fares are only for Glasgow men.*' However, Friday was not feasible. '*It was either Tough or the West Highland Railway that refused to "fit in,"—the point is still in dispute.*' The intrepid pair finally arrived at a plan. They would travel to Kingussie by the night express on Friday, bicycle the remaining 48mls to Fort William, climb their route, then reverse the journey, reaching Edinburgh on Sunday evening.

The account by Brown is entertaining and well worth a read in full; suffice it to say that when they reached Kingussie at 3.50am rain was falling dismally and a dense white mist hung low on the sodden hillsides. They gamely pedalled off, making about 30mls until Brown suffered a puncture. Repairs failed, so Tough continued for three miles to Loch Laggan Hotel hoping for a horse and trap, while Brown pushed his now useless machine along the road.

> Vain expectation! The zoological resources of Loch Laggan Hotel are rich in midges, but include nothing distantly resembling a horse; so we had to face a walk of thirteen miles to Inverlair, under a sun which was now something more than genial.

Onwards they struggled, one man on the bike piled high with equipment, the other trotting or walking alongside, the two taking turns with the bike. They finally gained Inverlair and caught a train for the remaining 18mls or so. A brief lunch at the Alexandra Hotel in Fort William, then up the hill at 1.12pm. The day was now close and sultry. When they finally caught sight of their objective, and closely analysed its difficulties, it seemed steeper and harder, though perhaps, they thought, this was partly due to the sudden approach of bad weather.

> The Red Mountains were still clear and sunny, but round the flanks of Carn Dearg the mist came stealing,—at first in mere wisps of vapour, then in great smoke-like masses, which mounted to the topmost crag, and blotted out nearly the whole mountain. In ten minutes there was scarcely anything to be seen but the scree slope on which we stood, and a black swirling mass straight ahead, where the storm clouds were eddying round the crags of the four great ridges.

They reached the base of the ridge at 5.30pm, where they crouched behind a rock. For ten minutes the rain hammered straight down, their world contracting to a murky circle of 20ft broad. Earlier on, awful penalties had been laid upon the man who should even breath the word *retreat*, but now they shamelessly discussed it. Then the rain suddenly ceased. Not even in Skye had they seen rocks as wet. There was a respectable waterfall coming off the ridge, and many smaller ones. They chose to circumvent the first steep section, now known as the First Platform, on the eastern side, which provided an easy approach to the steep rocks above. Here, at 6.16pm, they roped up. They continued up rocks which they believed were comparatively easy, gaining the Second Platform. The wetness of the rocks and their wearied state made it more difficult of course.

> It was most exasperating to find, whenever a friction grip was necessary, how persistently one's sodden knickers and boots kept slipping on the wet bossy rocks, and how unreliable was the hold thus obtained.
>
> Nowhere was this more apparent than when, having climbed up as we thought to within a few hundred feet of the top, a steep little bastion, with rounded top and smooth unbroken face, loomed up out of the mist. It was crowned by an erection which in the fog, which was again closing thickly round us, *might* have been the Eddystone lighthouse, but which I have reason to believe is a "peeler" of very moderate dimensions. Under ordinary circumstances we would have got up it I think without special difficulty, but a small crack about ten feet up (which is the natural hold) was at that moment extemporised for the descent of a miniature shower-bath. The result was that, perhaps without giving the crack a fair trial, we preferred to try the slabby rocks on the left. 'Twas a most dismal error. These slabby rocks are the man-trap of the ridge. They look quite simple, and are quite the reverse.

Brown and Tough had in fact come up against one of the hard bits of climbing on the buttress, now called the Man-trap after their original description. To be pedantic, they had so named the slabby rocks to the left of the smooth, rounded bulge which climbers now regard as the man-trap, but there is no doubt as to the deceptive wall on its left which is, in any case, contiguous with the bulge.

> Tough, as leader, amused himself among them for nearly three-quarters of an hour. Judging by the movements of the rope, and the vigorous adjectives that reached my ears, the game was more energetic than amusing.

Tough rejoined Brown. It was now 9.45pm and daylight was gone. Brown thought of a bivouac, '*...but the chief guide, while frankly admitting that two inches of nose represented his own limit of vision, drove me at the point of his axe to explore the rocks on the right.*' These went quite easily, and up a short gully the pair raced , to reach the foot of a steep smooth corner about 40ft high, formed by the junction of two rock slabs. '*Here, when I mildly suggested the absence of reliable holds, the inexorable guide gave me the choice* *of going up at the point of his ice-axe, or by pure traction at the end of the rope, along with the luggage. I chose the former.'*

The summit was gained soon after, and the Observatory reached at *10.5*, where they were received with the overflowing hospitality the Club had always received from Mr Rankin and his staff. A brief hour of sleep, between midnight and one, and they descended towards a sea of cloud. The morning sun was shining on the houses of Fort William and the waters of Loch Eil. It was the dawn of another day, the third since leaving Edinburgh. They took the mail-gig for Kingussie at 4am, reaching Speyside five and a half hours later. At 6.15pm, Willie Douglas was greeting them at Edinburgh train station, after some 45 hours of continuing travelling.

Brown added a final note to his article. Following his writing of it, a note had appeared in the Alpine Journal, recording an ascent of the buttress by Messrs J, E and B Hopkinson, on the 6th September, 1892. Brown commented '*...that no suspicion that the ridge was other than a virgin peak ever occurred to us, or any one in the district, or having knowledge of the mountain, with whom we conversed.*' They must inevitably have been personally disappointed, more so considering the heroic effort at reaching and climbing the buttress. We can only guess that the Hopkinsons had finally been shamed into recording their first ascent, given the increased activities by climbers on Nevis.

The third ascent was made only eight days later, by Geoffrey Hastings, Howard Priestman, and Cecil Slingsby, who were also ignorant of the earlier ascents, until they encountered the first cairn which Brown and Tough had left. This third ascent started up the loose gully on the west of the First Platform, *Slingsby's Chimney* (125m Moderate) . A fourth ascent was made on the 8th June, by RG Napier and EW Green, who climbed the rocks on the lower buttress by the independent line of *Green and Napier's Route* (150m Difficult). The following day, both Napier brothers, John and Robert, were joined by Edward W Green for the first ascent of Carn Dearg Buttress, by *Ledge Route* (450m Easy). Their one hour and 20 minutes' ascent was faster than their descent via the North-East Buttress, which on the account of some mist took them just under five hours.

❄ ❄ ❄

The indomitable pair of Brown and Tough were joined by James Rose, an Aberdonian and former school friend of Brown, for the first ascent of North Buttress on the Buachaille in Glen Coe. The 27th July was, as Tough noted – '*...a disgusting morning. The rain was falling dismally, and the whole mountain was concealed in mist...*'[12]. Attempting initially a chimney towards the west flank of the buttress, close to Great Gully, they deemed it a place of last resort, settling instead for an easier line further east. They were happy to climb a series of steep, narrow chimneys, as this partly sheltered them from the bitterly cold wind and rain. They finished close to the cairn overlooking the Rannoch Moor, not that they could see this in the even heavier rain. An awkward descent was made by taking the summit ridge to the second cairn (the actual summit) before turning down and left into Coire Cloiche Finne, descending into Glen Etive and thence back to the Kingshouse Inn. *North Buttress, West Route* (300m Moderate) provides a good introduction to climbing on the Buachaille.

A series of climbs would now be made on this iconic mountain, as along with Ben Nevis it was finally recognised as a veritable rock paradise. John Bell returned to Glen Coe at the end of December, along with John McGregor and the two Napier brothers. On the 29th they went looking for Great Gully. In thick mist they walked past this, climbing up Coire na Tulaich instead. Descending a gully from the summit ridge, they encountered an awkward section and, with little light remaining, they climbed back up again to descend by their initial route. They found later that they had been in Great Gully. Their escapades continued the following day, when again they chose the wrong gully, possibly climbing Narrow Gully. Finally, on New Year's Eve, after a two-day thaw, they returned to a route Bell had failed to complete the previous month, this time succeeding with an ascent of *The Chasm North Wall* (360m Moderate).

During the 19th century, there was one distinct difference between the development of rock climbing in Scotland and England. It was a difference which was, in the main, due to geology. In the Lakes, and other climbing venues in England and Wales, the rocks are generally richer in the number and variety of cracks, spikes, ledges, chimneys, gullies and fissures of all types and sizes. The early climbers there were led naturally into these fissures, as they often provided greater security, with more of the body being used. An open face forces a climber to rely on hand and foot holds, and the psychological pressure provided by the greater exposure and distinct lack of protection is correspondingly greater, whereas in a chimney almost any body part could be employed, perhaps jamming an arm or a leg for a move, or resting with feet on one wall of a chimney or gully, and the back resting against the other. Later on, southern climbers would begin to move out onto more open rock.

In Scotland, such weaknesses in the rock were usually formed by the intrusion of basaltic dykes, a rock which readily erodes, forming loose, dangerous ground. Climbers in Scotland therefore largely missed out the gully and chimney phase as practised in the south, climbing the more open faces almost immediately. Gullies were usually attempted and climbed in winter condition, when loose rock and vegetation were usually covered or anchored by snow and ice. There were, of course, exceptions to this, such as Collie attempting Clachaig Gully in Glen Coe in 1894. Another gully, as prominent on the hillside as that, was on Skye, and in the 1890s this became an obvious focus of attention. Before we turn to Skye however, we return to Lochnagar, where in August 1895 Brown and Tough continued their epic journey through Scotland, with a bold attempt to breach the rock buttresses of that great mountain.

❄ ❄ ❄

Writing in the SMCJ,[13] Tough was surprised that there had been no serious attempt on the cliffs of Lochnagar since Gibson and Douglas had attempted the route now named Douglas-Gibson Gully in March 1893. On 1st August 1895, Tough and Brown entered the corrie and headed for the buttress on the right of that gully. Brown had spent a day the previous month examining the corrie for possible routes from above and below. They knew what they intended to climb, a prominent ridge that was too well-defended at its start. Accordingly, they roped up further left, so as to make a rising traverse across the face to gain their ridge.

From the start they found the climbing difficult, with downward dipping rock, few rocky projections over which the rope could be run for security, and vegetation growing abundantly in every fissure. They succeeded in crossing the first of two shallow gullies, to gain the central of three buttresses. The next aim was to climb up before crossing the second shallow gully, but here they ran into great difficulties on very steep rocks, and had to retreat down a distance to gain a lower traverse line they had seen from below –

> Of course we had seen this route from the first, but as the other appeared more direct and easier we had chosen it, thus falling into the trap which stands ever open for the unfortunate rock-climber and which no amount of experience seems to enable him to avoid.

They finally crossed the second gully and eventually gained a wide grassy ledge which seemed to lead up and right to where they wished to go. This was another trap however, which forced them to make another diversion, this time onto a narrow, rocky ledge with no apparent escape. They took to it nonetheless, and ended up below an overhang. It was either succeeding up that, or retreat. Despite the tiny stance, Tough stood up, first on Brown's knee, then on his shoulder. He was still a couple of feet short of reaching a hold, and almost despairing, when Brown somehow managed to propel him upwards with a powerful jerk. Tough's outstretched fingers managed to catch in a crack, followed in another 40ft by a welcome belay. They were, however, now utterly committed.

The way was now more possible, but never safe. Every ledge was coated in grass or moss, which peeled away underfoot. They found the best way up was to run on all fours, as to stop even for an instant saw them sliding down. '*It... more than once induced in us that feeling of utter helplessness in the face of possible disaster which is surely the high-water mark of mountaineering misery.*' Eventually, after three hours on the rock, they gained the plateau in the mist, with a strong wind. Their ascent, on a route which never became popular in summer, had obviously been an arduous and serious undertaking, with very little protection. What had made it even more dangerous had been people on the plateau trundling rocks down the cliffs, necessitating that the climbers shout out a warning.

One notable feature of their ascent is that they had obviously decided not to take ice axes. Thus far, the pioneering climbers were accustomed to carrying their lengthy axes, summer and winter. In summer they found a use for them in removing vegetation, in addition to using them as aid in overcoming the occasional difficult move. Brown and Tough were confident enough and certainly competent enough to set aside this custom, allowing them to move more freely and quickly. Their time, of three hours, seems to validate this decision, despite the amount of vegetation on the route. *Tough-Brown Traverse* (300m Very Difficult) though now ignored in summer, is a classic IV,3 in winter, with warnings regarding route finding and time constraints. William Inglis Clark, in a later article,[14] quoted the shepherd at Alltnaguibhsaich, who, when Clark intended to climb something on Lochnagar, warned him that – '*...only yin man, ca'ed Broun, ever gaed up thae awfu' rocks, and wha can say if even he did it? Man, I wadna gang yonder for a thousan' pun'. Turn, man, and dinna commit suicide.*'

❄ ❄ ❄

Coire na Creiche is one of the great Cuillin corries, and faces north-west. It is split higher up into two corries by Sgurr an Fheadain, which peak is itself split by a prominent gully. It was Collie who named the peak around 1896, as the Peak of the Chanter, or Water-pipe. [The spelling has slowly evolved to Waterpipe.] The gully is some 400m in length (VS,4b). We know that Collie attempted it due to a retrospective article in the SMCJ by William Wickham King (1862–1959). '*With Collie, ascent of the lower part of Water-pipe Gully. All the time* [1891] *we had fine weather.*'

King joined the SMC in 1891, proposed by Maylard; he was familiar with several of the founders, and indeed climbed in the Alps with Naismith. Trained as a solicitor, he was also a competent amateur geologist. With a penchant for climbing chimneys, he left a trail of *King's Chimneys* scattered through the land. He was a member of the SMC for an impressive 68 years.

The first ascent of *Waterpipe Gully* caused a paper storm. The ascent was by two climbers from England, both virtually unknown in the sport. On the 9th September 1895, Joseph Kelsall, a manufacturer of worsted coating from Bradford and Arthur Hallitt, a consulting chemist from Halifax, climbed the gully. They had been made aware of the route by a Walter Greg, who himself had been the centre of controversy following a slip during a solo outing in September 1893. (He was visiting Camasunary and Loch Coruisk, returned via the main ridge, slipped, causing serious bruising, and, attempting to return, spent two nights out, the first high in Coire a' Mhadaidh, the second lower down in Coire na Creiche.)

Along with Greg on the 4th September, they made an initial investigation of the gully. Following their ascent, Kelsall wrote a good description of the gully in the Sligachan Hotel Climbers' Book. As in most subsequent ascents of the route, they chose to avoid certain direct pitches; they were either too hard, or too dangerously loose. At first they climbed unroped, until a slip resulting in cut hands led them to rope up for the remainder of the climb, with Kelsall leading all the way. Their description ended with the following –

> The gully affords constant, interesting & sometimes difficult climbing. In places great care is needed owing to the looseness of hand & foot hold; there was a certain quantity of water coming down the gully, but in dry weather this would probably be absent.[15]

It seems to have been the above paragraph which incensed two later visiting climbers. On 21st May 1896, Thomas Falcon from Devon and Edward Gray from London, wrote comments in the Climbers' Book. The following excerpts give a flavour:

> As politely as possible (assuming the account to be serious) we desire to protest against the impression left by the description of the gully…It appears to us (and it is putting it mildly) a gross misrepresentation of the actual character of the climbing…it is possible that Messrs Kelsall and Hallit are two of the most eminent and admirable climbers living. We merely record our deliberate opinion of this 'constant, interesting and sometimes difficult' climbing;- and it is based on our fairly intimate knowledge of the Coolins up to and including Dearg…[16]

It is fair to add here that Falcon was on his second visit to Skye, and that he and Gray failed to complete the gully. Sometime later, Kelsall and Hallitt added a brief rejoinder.

> The politeness of the above is certainly beyond question, but the whole of it is a more striking tribute to the abilities of the writers as carpers and sneering sceptics, than as climbers.

Several tigers of the SMC now waded into what was to become, as Stuart Pedlar called it, *'rock-climbing's first slanging match.'* William Brown was first, leading an attempt on the gully with John Bell and the Napier brothers, John and Robert, on the 21st July 1896. Although the party abandoned their attempt after a hard five and a half hours' struggle, having chosen the wrong way at about 850ft up the route, Brown remarked that they found the description of Kelsall and Hallitt accurate in every particular.[17] On the 26th, John Bell and John Napier returned and successfully completed the gully. On the 8th September, more big guns climbed the gully, as Collie, King and William Garden climbed it and also found the original description accurate. More, in their entry into the Climbers' Book, they found the climb '*…an interesting and not specially difficult one to anyone accustomed to gullies.*'[18]

It would take until 1st June 1899 for a direct ascent of the gully to be made, when six members of the Climbers' Club successfully topped out, at 1am. Roger Eykyn Thompson, along with AT Fraser, FM Levi, CA Wordsworth, and CJ and GR Slade made up the party.

In the current guidebook, the text states that the route is '*A huge and serious classic expedition that is too loose to recommend highly.*' In fact, as no stars are given, it could be inferred that it is not recommended at all. Further – '*It has been climbed directly but most parties will choose to avoid many of the main pitches. A time of 10 hours is normal for an ascent*'. It is perhaps best climbed in winter, during a long and hard freeze, when it is graded IV and given one star.[19] In summer it is graded VS,4b. It was, for its ascent in 1895 by two unknown climbers, a remarkable event.

❄ ❄ ❄

By December 1895 the SMC numbered some 141 members, four being Honorary. The Guide Book work was progressing, with Willie Douglas as Editor being assisted by Brown, Hinxman, Jackson, Munro, Phillip, Naismith, Rennie, and Thomson. The meetings of this sub-committee of such luminaries must have been filled with the excitement known only to those privileged to explore and describe unknown lands. In his speech at the Annual Dinner, Munro referred to this guidebook, mentioning the '*…starved information which had so far been published on the subject.*' It was obviously a guidebook eagerly anticipated by the climbers of the day, but the SMC was determined to do a thorough job and not bring out a rushed publication.

The second SMC Easter Meet based at Fort William ran from Thursday 2nd April to Monday 6th April, 1896. As the report went:-'*…Friday set in wet and muggy, and Saturday, Sunday, and Monday went singly and collectively from bad to worse.*'[20] The report was signed *W.B.*, either William Brown, or Walter Brunskill, both of whom were on the meet. The weather may have increased the consumption of Ben Nevis coffee, but it was also a factor in the more serious climbing which took place. '*The sensible view prevailed that you might as well get soaked on the precipice as saturated in Glen Nevis.*' In all, some 32 members and guests were present.

The previous year, Tower Ridge was deemed impossible due to a thick coating of snow and ice; this year it was climbed before the meet began, and by a further four parties during the meet. Two of these four parties even climbed the Great Tower direct, which would surely impress many a modern team. On the Saturday 4th April, instead of continuing round the Tower by the Western Traverse, after turning onto the west face the rocks above were climbed directly by a new route, now named *Cracked Slabs Route.* The only named climber on this route was John McGregor, and the conditions were noted in the Meet report as being wet and glazed, by which we assume iced rocks.

On Friday morning of the meet, another party had forced an ascent of the initial pinnacle of Tower Ridge, now known as the Douglas Boulder. It was named after the ubiquitous and popular Willie Douglas, who was on the first ascent, along with Brown, Hinxman and a guest who would soon be recognised as one of the outstanding Scottish climbers of the period, Harold Raeburn. Brown led the crux of this Very Difficult climb, with showers of hail and a cutting wind. The day being late when they gained the summit of the '*Boulder*', they descended via the easy Douglas Gap West Gully, and were pleased that they did so, on learning that a party on Tower Ridge had taken nine hours.

There is an intriguing note in the Cairngorm Club Journal for July 1896 by William Brown.[21] It seems that he and Raeburn (we assume that he was the 'R' in Brown's note) may have stayed on until the Monday and made an ascent of Tower Ridge. At the Great Tower, they dithered for an hour, unsure whether to follow the Western Traverse, or climb more directly up the west face. Conditions were probably more wintry than during the meet, if Brown's description of Raeburn's lead is anything to go by. The manner in which Brown writes makes it appear that he and 'R' had continued up Tower Ridge immediately following their first ascent of the Douglas Boulder, but we know from the meet report that the Douglas Boulder party had to descend due to lack of daylight hours. There is mention that a ridge on the Douglas Boulder further west, and easier than, the route taken by the Douglas party was climbed on the Monday. This may have been the initial rock pinnacle mentioned by Brown below, in which case he and 'R' made the first ascent of the Douglas Boulder-Tower Ridge intégrale. This easier ridge was perhaps the route named the *South-West Ridge* (180m Moderate), recorded in 1904. Due to the uncertain reporting, this is conjecture.

> Up till Easter of this year the "Tower Ridge" had several times been re-ascended in summer when the rocks were free of snow: but no party had ventured upon it under Alpine conditions. Then, however, the occasion being the Easter meet of the Scottish Mountaineering Club, it was climbed by four parties, of which I had the good fortune to be a member of one. The immediately preceding

> party had encountered very serious difficulties. They got stuck for hours on the ice-glazed rocks of the "Tower", and only reached the top at nightfall after spending nine hours on the rocks. Our party began the climb by scaling a rock pinnacle at the foot of the ridge that had never been ascended from outside before. It proved extremely difficult, and an exciting series of adventures near the top, carried through in a snowstorm, prepared us for the much-advertised perils of the "Tower". In all conscience they were sufficiently alarming. High over head rose a sheer black and white wall of smooth porphyry and smoother ice. From its base a steep snow slope plunged dizzily into the mist. "Royal road" there was none; for plainly the upward journey could only be continued by scaling the wall or trusting our fortunes to some sloping snow-clad ledges that ran brokenly round a projecting corner to unknown dangers beyond. We spent nearly an hour balancing probabilities and making tentative sorties upon the wall and the ledges; then having decided definitely upon the former, never shall I forget the way in which R. led us straight up over ice, rock, and snow to the top. He cut a great part of the way with one hand up an ice-paved gully, the other being occupied in holding on to the microscopical projections by which we resisted successfully the operation of the law of gravity. This was the first time this wall had ever been climbed in winter, for the other parties all pinned their faith to the ledges.

It is uncertain whether the line taken by Raeburn was the *Recess Route*, or *Cracked Slabs Route*. It would also seem that Brown was unaware of the McGregor ascent. *Cracked Slabs Route* is down in the current guide as having been climbed in 1989, with a grade of IV,5. *Recess Route* is recorded as having had a winter ascent in 1937, with a current grade of IV,6. Whichever line Raeburn and Brown climbed, it was yet another piece of climbing by Raeburn ahead of its time.

The principal route of this meet however, was the first winter ascent (FWA) of *North-East Buttress,* climbed on Friday 3rd by a party of five; Naismith, Brunskill, Kennedy, (later Sir Alexander), King and FC Squance. The meet report confined this ascent to one paragraph, and it was not until an astonishing 29 years later, in 1925, that a very brief account would be published in a retrospective article by Naismith. We can only surmise that in the interim, Naismith's innate modesty overruled a clamour for details. What is known is that the rocks were well plastered with snow and ice, forcing several diversions from the summer ascent, including missing out the 40ft chimney, which was lined with blue ice. As Naismith wrote with admirable irony, '*The party was a jolly one, but rather large for speed*'.[22]

Naismith was not content to rest after that, however, and on Monday 6th he made the FWA of *The Castle*, the buttress left of Castle Ridge, and a respectable Grade III. This was in company with Brown, Maclay and Thomson. It seems that this route was a consolation prize, as this party had attempted a route on Carn Dearg Buttress (what would be known as

Waterfall Gully) but had failed. The current guide refers to The Castle as being '*...an advanced route for the time*'.[23] It is a route whose winter conditions must be carefully assessed, with avalanche potential often high.

Also climbed during this meet was *Number Two Gully (*120m II), by an Alpine Club group who were staying in Fort William but at the Chevalier Hotel. There were in total some eight AC members present: Collie, Hastings, Slingsby, Solly, Haskett Smith, Dixon, Collier and HC Bowen. On Good Friday, the 3rd, Slingsby, Hastings and Collier entered the forum. After some indecision, and although at 3.30pm it was late in the day, they decided to attempt a steep and narrow snow gully. They succeeded in this, despite a cornice providing a problematic finish and some frost-bitten fingers and toes in the party. Number Two Gully had been climbed. This left only one of the easier gullies to be climbed, the left-hand branch of Tower Gully, now named Gardyloo Gully.

From the outset, Harold Raeburn (1865–1926) was a pacesetter. An Edinburgh brewer like his father and uncle before him, he was also a keen ornithologist and expert yachtsman.[24] Reading between the lines of various character sketches, it seems he could be assertive in character, possessed with an obsession regarding the time taken to climb a route, and seemingly always confident in his opinions.[25] In 1901, along with William Clark, he climbed *Raeburn's 18-Minute Route* (135m Moderate) on the First Platform on Nevis. In 1903, an aspirant climber William Newbigging, made another ascent on the same buttress, naming it *Newbigging's 80-Minute Route* (200m Very Difficult), a not so subtle dig at Raeburn. From joining the SMC in December 1896 until the Great War all but eclipsed such activities, Raeburn would be instrumental in expanding the known boundaries of Scottish mountaineering, raising the standards in icy gullies, and taking rock standards up to that so far only enjoyed in England and Wales.

❄ ❄ ❄

Seeming to arrive on the climbing scene overnight, Raeburn had learned to be adept on steep ground through his early years of collecting birds' eggs. A collection of his eggs is to this day kept at the Natural History Museum, Edinburgh. He visited the Shetland Islands several times, and wrote a paper on the bird life there, which included, with a local birder, the ascent of a steep rock feature.[26] (See Chapter One.) An interest in hillwalking provided more mountain experience, and he joined the SMC in 1896. His application form begins in 1890 and lists only hills. He was proposed by Willie Douglas and seconded by Naismith.

In April 1896, Douglas, Raeburn and Tough mounted an attack on the snowy cliffs of Creag Meagaidh. Their plan was to climb one of the prominent gullies rising above the small lochan in Corrie Ardair, named locally as 'posts'. One post in particular caught their eye, and this they entered. Though the upper part looked steep, it was filled with snow, and they were confident it could be climbed. The air was warm and muggy, and soon they were knee-deep in snow. Ominously, traces of avalanches were visible on all sides.

Just above half-way up the gully it steepened, becoming more like a chimney. The snow was now like sawdust, and the leader struggled for 15 minutes without advancing a single yard in any direction. Falling snow was also becoming more regular and in heavier amounts, and the party turned back, not a moment too soon as it turned out. The first real avalanche thundered down the gully, and Raeburn was struck on the head by a block of snow. They continued to descend slowly due to poor snow conditions, and were struck by a second avalanche before escaping the gully. They realised how fortunate they had been as the snow was mostly new and consequently lighter.

The following day older snow, mixed with rocks, was thundering down over their old tracks. The party had been lucky to escape, on a mountain which has become infamous for its avalanche prone slopes. As for their target gully, it is now known as the *Centre Post*, Grade III, V if taken direct. But for the poor conditions, the trio would almost certainly have succeeded in following the easiest line. On their return visit the next day they climbed *Easy Gully* (Grade I), dodging falling snow. Tough's article finished with a brief report by Raeburn on the bird species seen by the climbers, including an eagle and snow buntings.[27]

In the same number of the SMCJ was a brief review of a photographic book by George Abraham, the well-known Keswick climber and photographer. With his brother Ashley, he had spent three weeks in May 1896 on Skye, eventually publishing some 50 plus photographs.[28] Briefly reviewed, (presumably by the Editor, William Douglas), all of the photographs were stated as being good. '*Some, however, are rather "theatrical," the figures having been too manifestly posed. They are sold in platinotype, 6x8 inches, at 1s.6d. each.*'[29]

❄ ❄ ❄

On 3rd August 1896, Douglas and Naismith met at Bridge of Orchy. Using the '*popular sporting craze*' of the times, a bicycle, Douglas had cycled from Edinburgh, in two stages each of about 60 miles. Both then cycled on to Glen Coe, a recognised tough section for a bike, walking for less than one mile out of the 13. Their target was no less than Crowberry Ridge, that beautiful if forbidding ridge which from the right point of view seems to lead to the very summit. This far, the only recorded routes on the Buachaille were Great Gully, North Buttress, a vague line by Collie, and Curved Ridge, (240m Moderate) which had been climbed by George Bennett Gibbs the previous month. It's not too fanciful to surmise that Naismith heard from

Gibbs of the steep buttress immediately to the right of Curved Ridge, though of course he would have seen it before then himself.

The time of year was just right for eating crowberries, found in juicy clumps everywhere. Naismith had difficulty in pulling Douglas off them, but it suggested a name for the climb. In his article describing the route, Naismith was in some doubt as to whether a direct ascent of the ridge was possible, considering current climbing standards. Knowing full well the lack of protection, such a climb, Naismith thought, being necessarily a series of boulder problems, would place too great a demand on nerve and muscle. He commented on how valuable the presence of decent rock platforms on a rock climb were, being psychological boosts to an ascent. In this, he was being pragmatic; as accomplished a mountaineer as he was, he was not prepared to take on such a long, steep and serious ascent without some level of safety.[30]

There was an easier way up however, as the pair spotted a line on the right side of the buttress, where the rocks lay back somewhat. This part ran into the steeper buttress like a lean-to shed against a higher building. A shallow groove then continued up the middle of the lower rocks, offering a way up. A loose block was trundled down by Douglas, to protect future climbers, then a few obstacles which led to a slabby section, where the whole 60ft of their rope had to be used before the crest of the ridge was gained. Above they could see a pinnacle, and the route was still not a certainty until they reached a position looking down into the gully on the north (Crowberry Gully). At the top of the pinnacle (Crowberry Tower) they found the cairn left by Collie's party, who had gained it from above Curved Ridge in March 1894. *Naismith's Route* (210m Moderate) on Crowberry Ridge had been climbed. The ridge was eventually given its summer grade of Moderate, with somewhat loose rock in places. It has come into its own in winter, being an interesting IV,5.

The steeper rocks which Naismith determined to be then impossible, were to be climbed some four years later, but yet again he had broken through a psychological barrier with his ascent. The previous April he had made the first winter ascent of North-East Buttress on Nevis, a target for many climbers of the day, now he had plucked another ripe plum with Crowberry Ridge. With these bold ascents, Naismith and his various climbing partners had raised and set standards which would be milestones for decades to come. They were moving inexorably towards the limitations set by existing equipment, but were well aware of these and climbed accordingly. William Brown, another hard man of the times, had referred to the climbing found in the Fort William area as an 'Eldorado of riches.' What the pioneers found themselves in was Eldorado itself. They now possessed the knowledge, fitness, and confidence to attempt outstanding routes: it would be looked back on as Scotland's Golden Age of Mountaineering.

References

1. Proceedings of the Club. SMCJ 3, 17, May 1895, 295-299.
2. Ibid., 300-304.
3. Mitchell, Ian R. *Prelude to Everest: Alexander Kellas, Himalayan Mountaineer.* (Edinburgh: Luath Press, 2011.)
4. Aitken, R. *Personal Communication.*
5. Tough, William. *The Works and Life of Sir William Mure of Rowallan* (London & Edinburgh: Blackwood, 1898.)
6. Tough, Graeme. *Personal Communication*, Sept. 2011.
7. Thomson, Gilbert. *The North-East Ridge of Aonach Beag.* SMCJ 3, 18, Sept. 1895, 332-337.
8. Pedlar, Stuart. *Across Unmeasured Space – A History of Climbing in the Cuillin.* Unpublished MS. 2010, Chapter 7.
9. *Visitors' Book*, Clachaig Hotel, 1890, NLS.
10. G.T. [Gilbert Thomson]. *Nails for Climbing Boots.* In: Notes and Queries, SMCJ 3, 17, May 1895, 307-308.
11. Brown, W. *Ascent of Ben Nevis by the N.E. Buttress.* SMCJ 3, 18, Sept. 1895, 323-331.
12. Tough, W. *Buchaille Etive Mor by the N.E. Face.* In: Notes and Queries. SMCJ, 4, 19, Jan. 1896, 62-63.
13. Tough, William. *Lochnagar by the Cliffs.* SMCJ 4, 19, 35-42, Jan. 1896.
14. Clark, W. Inglis. *Lochnagar and Ben Nevis.* SMCJ 4, 22, 218-223, Jan. 1897.
15. Kelsall, J. and Hallitt, Arthur W. 9th Sept. 1895.Sligachan Climbers' Book, 38-39. NLS.
16. Gray, E. & Falcon, T.A. 21st May 1896. Sligachan Climbers' Book, 45-46. NLS.
17. Brown, W. *The Coolins in '96.* SMCJ, 4, 22, Jan. 1897, 193-213.
18. Sligachan Climbers' Book, Sept. 1896, 57.
19. Lates, Mike. Skye *The Cuillin.* SMC Climbers' Guide, 2011, 85.
20. Proceedings of the Club. SMCJ 4, 20, May 1896, 129-132.
21. Brown, William. *Climbing in Scotland - Ben Nevis.* The Cairngorm Club Journal. Vol 2, 7, July 1896, 5-6.
22. Naismith, W.W. *Early Winter Climbing.* SMCJ 17, 99, April 1925, 124-132.
23. Richardson, Simon. 2002. *Ben Nevis Rock and Ice Climbs.* SMC, 319.
24. K.V. Crocket & J.R.R. Fowler. *Of Beer and Boats.* In: Miscellaneous Notes, SMCJ 36, 1997, 380-383.
25. Lord Mackay. *Vignettes of Earlier Climbers.* SMCJ 24, 1950, 141-180.
26. Raeburn, Harold. *The Birds of Papa Stour, with an account of the Lyra Skerry.* The Zoologist. 1891, 126-135.
27. Tough, William. *Corrie Arder.* SMCJ 4, 21, Sept. 1896, 141-148.
28. Abraham, G., *Skye: A series of Mountain Photographs.*
29. *Mountaineering Literature.* SMCJ 4, 21, Sept. 1896, 190-191.
30. Naismith, W.W. Buchaille Etive Mor – "*The Crowberry Ridge*". SMCJ 4, 21, Sept. 1896, 149-154.

8

Through a microscope (1896-98)

The year 1896 had seen significant ascents on Ben Nevis and in Glen Coe with Willie Naismith being a dominant instigator. Harold Raeburn had climbed as a guest of the SMC and would join that club in December. It was also the year in which the Cuillin of Skye would see an impressive burst of exploration, one which would be well summarised in an article by William Brown.[1]

Such then was the level of climbing taking place at the popular centres in Britain that Brown made the comment that the search for new routes had to be conducted through a microscope. '*The Alps had reached that stage long ago*' he wrote, as had the mountains round Wasdale in the Lake District. He was writing from the perspective that routes could be found only on major features: ridges, arêtes, and so on. Harder, intermediate routes, such as steep face climbs, were as yet beyond their ability.

From June to September, 1896, enjoying a summer of good weather, a host of mountaineers descended on Sligachan. In June, Douglas, William Lamont and James Rennie sailed into Loch Scavaig on the *Ronaval*, and dropped anchor in one of the wildest and most sublime spots in Scotland, where Douglas, beset by his asthma, spent some time reading of early climbs on Sgurr Dubh. These notably included Nicolson's ascent from the Garbh Choire followed by a harrowing and difficult night descent (see Chapter 2). On 11th June the trio scrambled up by the side of the Mad Burn and crossed level ground to the ridge leading to the summit of Sgurr Dubh Beag. This peak had not yet been named, and Douglas referred to it as the East, or lowest peak. The party then continued traversing the ridge westwards.

After lunch, they made the descent of a 20ft *mauvais pas,* the first two protected by a rope, while last man Douglas scrambled down with the rope running over a rock for protection, coming down, '*sailor fashion, with his back to the wall.*' This obstacle is currently graded Severe, with most climbers descending by abseil. More scrambling led eventually over Sgurr Dubh Mor and the west peak. While they were admiring the superb view, two figures appeared on the summit of Sgurr Alasdair; they were Sidney Williams and the guide John Mackenzie.

Also on Skye that June were William Inglis Clark with two friends, who climbed the Pinnacle Ridge, Bla Bheinn and Clach Glas. They too had an interesting ascent of Basteir and the Basteir Tooth, in hail and rain, with difficulties encountered trying to descend from Am Basteir. It was their first visit to Skye, and as Clark confessed, up until then he had been a Salvationist. They had also failed to employ Mackenzie the guide, who by then was proving to be very popular, and were therefore thrown in at the deep end.

In July, the Napier brothers, John Stuart and Robert Graham (they joined the SMC in 1895 and 1896 respectively), along with John Bell and William Brown, spent four days based at Glen Brittle. In addition to several of the classic ridges, they climbed most of Waterpipe Gully, confirming the first ascent details of the mysterious Kelsall and Hallitt. September, however, turned out to contain most of this season's highlights. In contrast to the rest of the country, which suffered continuous rain, the hills were usually clear. The leading party consisted of Collie, Collier, EB Howell (a friend of Collie's), Naismith and Parker, forming various ropes at various times.

On July 1st, Collie and Howell ascended the south-east ridge of Sgurr a' Ghreadaidh from Coruisk. It provided 700m of scrambling on rock. Two days later Collie, Howell and Naismith made the first ascent of the north-west face of Sgurr Alasdair by a route now known as *Collie's Climb* (270m Difficult). The artist Colin Phillip and his wife were also in the corrie, making an ascent by the Great Stone Shoot.

Continuing the explorations of this September, another permutation of 'Collie's Group' climbed the north-west buttress of Mhadaidh from Tairneilear. This route included a '*...very narrow and sensational groove, 60 feet long, across the face of an A.P. cliff*', led by Collie using a stomach traverse. There were other routes, variations, and faces climbed this month, but Brown commented that it was becoming obvious that Sligachan was too remote to be a good base for the western corries. Glen Brittle, he continued, was the best centre, with Glen Brittle House being the ideal base. Unfortunately for those hoping for accommodation it was a private dwelling, with special permission necessary. Camping in Coruisk was another possibility, though there it seemed to rain often. Brown finished his survey by suggesting that an Alpine hut could be built at the head of Coruisk. The land owner was said to be opposed to this however, and it remained a wishful dream.

Two Aberdeen climbers, George Duncan and William Garden, were also on Skye in September 1896; they were to join the SMC in December, in the same intake as Raeburn, Joseph Collier, Cecil Slingsby, and Morris Travers. Garden was an advocate who would be President of the Cairngorm Club in 1925-27, and SMC President in 1934-36. He was a major influence in recruiting Aberdeen climbers into the SMC, and a long-term friend and climbing partner of Willie Douglas in the Alps and Canadian Rockies. They employed the guide John Mackenzie and climbed Pinnacle Ridge. In the same issue of the SMCJ as Brown's article on Skye appeared an Appendix providing the names, heights and positions of the Cuillin summits. It had been prepared by Douglas from several sources, and no doubt helped clear some of the cartographic fog which lay over this complex area.

❄ ❄ ❄

William Inglis Clark had regarded himself as a beginner, and thought that Tower Ridge on Nevis was beyond his capabilities. However, his efforts on Skye without a guide had boosted his confidence, so that along with James Parker he used the Edinburgh autumn holiday on 21st September to attempt an ascent of Tower Ridge. Not prepared for winter conditions, they were surprised on gaining the foot of the cliffs to see that snow plastered the top 600ft. They then gained the summit via Carn Mor Dearg and the arête, and made for the Observatory to borrow an ice axe. A heavy snowstorm had battered them for a couple of hours on the ascent, and three-foot icicles hung from the Observatory door. Some seven inches of snow lay on the summit, as they descended to Fort William, leaving the ice axe at the Half-Way Station.

The next day dawned fine and frosty, and the pair enjoyed the climbing on Tower Ridge. The ice axe lacked a spike and the pick was incomplete, but it finally came into its own on the snow- and ice-encrusted Great Tower, where climbing up its west face they found a difficult 60ft wall which took them one and a half hours. On arriving at the top of the Great Tower they received a standing ovation from a crowd of tourists and others who had been watching their progress lower down the ridge.[2]

On 7th November, Raeburn was on Nevis with William Brown and George Duncan. Their audacious plan, to make a more direct ascent of Carn Dearg Buttress, was defeated by poor conditions, the rocks being coated with a thin, transparent layer of ice, or verglas, as it was called by Swiss mountaineers. The buttress had first been climbed on 9th June 1895 by the brothers John and Robert Napier, and Edward Green, who found an entertaining, zig-zag route up the left flank, using ledges. Now named *Ledge Route* (450m Easy), it is a popular scrambling route.

In an SMCJ note, Raeburn mentions a possible target for the day, a rock gully splitting the buttress. The only real candidate for this line would be

Waterfall Gully on the right flank. His description mentions the summer drainage of the first 30ft now being '*…a mass of huge ribs and stalactites of ice twisted into all kinds of curious forms, but not stable enough to allow of steps being cut in them*'.[3] (A later note in an SMCJ article confirms this line as being the one in Raeburn's mind.) The gully was not climbed until 1959, at Grade IV. Disappointed, the climbers continued up into Coire na Ciste and made an ascent of Number Three Gully, Brown being the leader, with Raeburn, as 'catcher', last man on the rope.

On gaining the Observatory, where they enjoyed hot coffee, they found they were the first visitors since the beginning of October. More usefully, they lowered Brown some 50ft down the finish of the left finishing gully of Observatory Gully, the only easy gully left unclimbed at the end of the 1896 Easter Meet. They decided that it would need much snow to be climbable.

The SMC's New Year Meet for 1897 was held at the Loch Awe Hotel. Sixteen members and two guests assembled there, for a meet which had generally poor conditions. Despite this, on the 1st January, John Bell and John Napier made the second ascent of the ghastly Black Shoot, while on the 2nd, Raeburn and James Maclay made the third ascent. As Raeburn wrote in a later SMCJ article, Maclay was '*…a member well known for his love of steep, slimy, and difficult cracks and chimneys.*'[4]

❄ ❄ ❄

The Salisbury Crags have a secure place in any Edinburgh native's pride, rising in pleated waves above the city. The basalt crags there have also attracted climbers since climbing began. One of these, William Inglis Clark (1856–1932), was to become a prominent member of the Scottish climbing establishment, a noted successful businessman in his specialty, a pioneer in photography, and, to gladden the heart of those who love the internal combustion engine, the first to own a car in his native city of Edinburgh.

Clark was a brilliant student in Chemistry at Edinburgh University, gaining a DSc at 21 (he had to wait a year to be capped, due to regulations). He designed a capsule for containing foul-tasting drugs, along with the necessary machinery for manufacturing the capsules. He would become President of the SMC from 1914-19, following on from a spell as club Secretary, where his organisational prowess ensured that every meet was a success. His wife Jane, and later his son Charles and daughter Mabel were also competent mountaineers who made valuable contributions in different ways to the history of Scottish climbing. We will meet all again in these pages.

On Friday, 22nd January 1897, a strong north-easterly gale scoured Scotland, driving before it dry, powdery snow. Anyone living in Edinburgh with ill-fitting window frames certainly woke up to sparkling crystals of snow on their floors. Walking through Queen's Park by St Leonard's Hill, Clark saw that the Cat Nick, a well-known gully route near the highest point of Salisbury Crags, was almost completely white with snow. He had soloed this route when a boy of 14, and although then of small stature, vividly recalled climbing the overhanging pitch at the top, an event he considered a good claim for manhood. Would it go in the wintry conditions before him?

That morning a friend suggested a glissade at the back of Arthur's Seat – instead they decided to climb the steep slope direct to the Cat Nick. They gained the Radical Road under the route and, despite having neither axe nor climbing gloves, could not resist the challenge. They did have a rope, albeit only one made for packing household goods, and not climbing. Worse still, though they had new gloves with them, they decided not to sacrifice them on a climb, so they started up bare-handed. Their hands and wrists were soon benumbed, as often they had to plunge them elbow deep to find rock holds.

Not far below the top, the second man had to climb with little assistance from the rope, and that under a continuous wave of powder snow. Exposed to this for 10 minutes, he felt a faintness coming on, and had just managed to jam his foot against a rock when he lost consciousness for a few seconds. Clark described well the strange situation they were in; the sound of children tobogganing on St Leonard's Hill with the hum of the city in the background, and yet here they were in a snow-plastered gully with an overhang of seven or eight feet above and grim walls confining them. It was a surreal experience.

Eventually, the leader stood on the second's head and clearing much snow from the rocks succeeded in passing the barrier. It had taken 75 minutes for what was normally a five minute route. Axes, noted Clark, would not have helped that much, as most of the snow was moving and not adhering to the rocks beneath. Their hands took at least 24 hours to recover, and the two resolved never more to climb snow without gloves. Recently joined SMC member Harold Raeburn would publish a guide to the Salisbury Crags, complete with annotated OS Map, in September of that year.[5]

❄ ❄ ❄

Perhaps the outstanding mountaineering event in 1897 was an Easter Yachting Meet, organised by the SMC. Not unnaturally, given the difficulty of travel on the west coast of Scotland before the railway snaked its way northwards, many trips were at least in part made by sea. Also, given the professional cross-section of that club, not a few members enjoyed yachting as a pastime. Raeburn himself was no mean yachtsman, winning trophies with his brother John.[6]

Indeed, both were active members of the Royal Forth Yacht Club, based then, as now, in Granton harbour. The brothers were members from 1900 to 1911, buying the *Teal*, a nine-ton cutter, in 1903. With this, in 1904 they won the RFYC Corinthian Match Challenge Cup. In 1906 John bought the 30-linear rater *Armyne*, which they sailed for the next two years. In this the brothers won the Corinthian Cup in 1906 and '07. As they had now won this three times, they were presented with the cup, which they presented back to the club who named it the Raeburn Trophy, a name under which it was raced for until fairly recently.

The 1897 Yachting Meet used the steam yacht *Erne* (a name for the sea eagle), owned by Captain Turner and jointly skippered with Captain Smith. The *Erne* arrived in Oban on Thursday, April 15th, having rounded the Mull of Kintyre in squally seas. By the end of that evening some 29 members and guests had arrived and found their berths. The weather was poor but at midnight the rattling of the chains told them that the anchor was up and they headed for the Sound of Mull. Even in that sheltered passage rough seas prompted a temporary stop in Tobermory to wait for daylight. Breakfast was served for a hardy few once they gained some shelter by Eigg and Rum, with the more timid sailors retreating once again to their bunks during the rough crossing to Skye, their target destination.

Unfortunately, Loch Scavaig, while a wonderfully scenic anchorage, lies open to a south-west gale, and on this occasion it would not have been prudent to stay; even if a landing had been possible through the horizontal spindrift, a return to the yacht would not. An attempt to anchor in the Sound of Soay was also deemed unsafe, so regretfully they turned tail and sheltered in Rum's Loch Scresort, having lost the morning. In the afternoon Allival and Askival were ascended. Munro had earlier mentioned a steep section on the north arête of Askival, and a party of four consisting of Bell, Brown, Boyd and Raeburn headed for that, successfully soloing up this. The last few hundred feet had accumulated fresh snow, while some ice was encountered .

Friday evening was spent debating a change of plan, with Skye no longer feasible. Eventually, at the suggestion of President Munro, on Saturday morning they made a run for Loch Hourn as the best compromise. They spent two pleasant days there. Almost inevitably, from the anchorage in Loch Hourn, the same foursome as above headed straight for Coire Dhorrcaill to explore its great cliffs. Two attempts on the rocks failed, with a plastering of snow, and eventually Raeburn led the way up the prominent central gully, later inevitably named *Raeburn's Gully* (240m III). A vertical, 100ft pitch of rock was turned on the left. Luinne Bheinn was climbed by another party from the yacht.

There was now only one day left for the official Yachting Meet, and a lively debate again took place on board the *Erne* that Sunday evening. They were determined to try for Scavaig once more, but again the weather was against them, and instead they had Monday breakfast in Loch Nevis. Hillwalking was again the order of the day, with Meall Buidhe and Sgor na Ciche ascended in a day of heavy showers. Cruelly, on their return trip, the weather brightened, so that '*...while we were rounding the dreaded Ardnamurchan all were as festive as possible.*'

A piper was discovered aboard, Munro danced the fling amidst frantic applause and the veteran Captain Smith joined in a foursome reel until exhausted, when the owner's daughter, Miss Turner, took his place. So fast was the return that they entered Oban Bay just after midnight, allowing preparations for the early train on Tuesday morning. Some remained on board for a further two days, sailing firstly for Ballachulich, where a vehicle was hired to take the party to Clachaig and so leading to an ascent of Bidean. On Wednesday, Jura was gained, with an ascent of the Paps.

Throughout the trip, Munro had played his flute and worked hard to secure a successful expedition, as had Turner and his assistants. Prof R Lodge (a guest) concluded in his report of the meet that one memory of the meet which would not fade was the energy and variety of the nightly debates – '*the vigorous assertiveness of Professor Ramsay; the ingenious, if rather noisy, "asides" of Mr Robertson; and the delicate hints conveyed under the guise of studied impartiality by Mr Munro*'.[7] One other comment was regarding the number and variety of cameras on board. Some even developed their films on the boat. Almost every passenger was an amateur photographer, and snapshots were incessant. Despite this, it is sad to find that perhaps only one photograph of the entire meet has survived, luckily that of the group on deck. If ever there was a case for the archiving of such material, it can be found here.

While the nautical meet battled with the wind and waves, a limited Easter Meet for 1897 was held on terra firma, at Tyndrum. On the Saturday, 17th April, Walter Arthur Smith and William Wickham King climbed an easy snow gully on the North Face of Cruach Ardrain, now named Y-Gully, due to the prominent fork the initial gully takes. After the climb, they met Naismith, Thomson and Squance at Crianlarich for afternoon tea. Inglis Clark was also around, seemingly on his own and on a bike. On the Sunday, Smith was the sole remnant of this terrestrial meet. The weather being good, he persuaded three pleasant and active youths from Edinburgh into the north-east corrie of Ben Lui, where a snowy scramble led to the top of Stob Garbh followed by a rising traverse to the west ridge and a glissade into the Eas Daimh glen.

❄ ❄ ❄

A brief note in the May 1897 SMCJ was headed the *Alpine Club in Scotland*, and extolled the fact that Alpine climbers now recognised the value of Scotland at Easter for the practice of snowcraft. This was shown, continued the note, by the unprecedented numbers of AC members who had flocked to Scotland in April 1897, with several on the yachting meet, at least five more at Sligachan, six at Clachaig, and four at Roy Bridge. This was an ironic puff, given how poor the weather had been over the same period, but it was an indication of how popular the Scottish hills had become. It was also, like the skirl of the pipes, a show of pride by the SMC, both of the mountains and of their competence in climbing them, no matter the weather or conditions.

The Alpine Club were partly responsible for a visit to explore Garbh Bheinn of Ardgour by John Bell and William Brown. In April they had hoped to stay at the Clachaig Inn in Glen Coe, but staying there from the 16th to the 22nd was an AC party consisting of Hastings, James Maclay (also in the SMC), Cecil Slingsby (who had joined the SMC the previous year) and Walter Haskett Smith. This mixed party explored Glen Coe, and made an ascent into Ossian's Cave on Aonach Dubh, where they found the tin box left by Collie's party in March 1894.

Brown had heard of Garbh Bheinn from the watercolourist Colin Phillip who recognised the potential to be found there. Brown may well have been hoping to attempt the Church Door Buttress on Bidean, having tried it and failed with his friend Tough in July 1895. His consolation trip to Ardgour turned out to be a happy one, as he and Bell made the first ascent of the Great Ridge (300m Difficult), taking two and a half hours and describing it as one of the most charming and interesting scrambles either had taken part in. Haskett Smith and Hastings were close on their heels, visiting Garbh Bheinn two days later and attempting the gully on the right of the Great Ridge. It was too wet however, and they finished up the ridge on the north side of the gully.

❄ ❄ ❄

Walter Parry Haskett Smith (1859–1946) was a very experienced mountaineer, and had been winter climbing in the Lakes since the 1880s. From Glen Coe Hastings and Haskett Smith moved on to Fort William, where they were presumably joined by ELW Haskett Smith, brother of Walter. This April had been a very wintry one, with the Summit Hotel on Nevis completely buried at the beginning of the month and snow up to the roof of the Observatory. The first three weeks of April remained below freezing on the mountain, with the grip of winter relenting slowly during the last week.

On the Sunday, 25th April 1897, Geoffrey Hastings and the two Haskett Smith brothers succeeded in climbing *Tower Gully* (120m I), the steep right-hand continuation of Observatory Gully which finishes on the east flank of Tower Ridge. Their ascent was witnessed by Observatory staff.[8] There was a huge cornice blocking the exit, overhanging the gully, which took hours to tunnel through. Not content with this, the following day WP Haskett Smith and Hastings returned to make the first ascent of *Gardyloo Gully* (170m II), the left-hand branch continuation of Observatory Gully, and running up under the summit cliffs. On this occasion there was a double cornice. Once again the Scots had been beaten to some prime first ascents. Raeburn and Lawson were to make the second ascent of Gardyloo Gully on 6th April 1901.

Several intriguing ascents were made in the North-West Highlands, early in 1897. Collie and unknown companions climbed the huge western face of Coire MhicFhearchair in Glen Torridon. The ascent was probably in the spring, as they initially cut steps up one of the gullies. It would also be prior to August 1897, as Collie was putting up first ascent of peaks in Canada that month. Perhaps Haskett Smith and Hastings moved on from Fort William towards the end of April but failing further evidence this is only surmise. Collie described the climb in an article (See Chapter 9.)

❄ ❄ ❄

On Stob Ghabhar, *The Upper Couloir* (90m II) had been attempted at least twice by various parties; in 1892 when the climbers were forced out of the gully and onto the rocky rib on the right, and in 1894 when conditions were impossible. Ernest Maylard had been in the first party, and as happens to many a climber with certain routes he became determined to climb it in its entirety. This he finally succeeded in doing on 1st May 1897. The party of four on this first complete ascent consisted of Maylard, Robert Adamson (SMC member and Professor of Logic at Glasgow University), Mrs Adamson, and Miss Weiss, the sister of a member (Frederick Ernest Weiss, Professor of Botany at University of Manchester.)

On entering the couloir, they found that the snow was in excellent condition; more, the rocks on the right-hand rib were glazed with ice and a thin coating of snow. From Maylard's description, it sounds as if they encountered snow-ice, a near-perfect medium in which to cut steps. The party had a 60ft rope, insufficient for all of the party to remain roped at all times, so in leading the crux pitch Maylard brought up Mrs Adamson, while Miss Weiss, who was third, remained unroped at the foot of the pitch. Then Miss Weiss seconded the pitch, and finally Robert Adamson came up. The remainder went easily, though the wind gusted violently just below the cornice. A descent down the easy south ridge led to a meeting with the head keeper at Inveroran Lodge, who was much impressed by the ladies' feat.[9]

This ascent would appear to have seen the occasion of the first ascent of a route in Scotland by the ladies, and not merely a first ascent , but a winter first at that. It was, perhaps, yet another example of Maylard's character, who was not content with organising the birth of the SMC, but happily climbed with a mixed party. Reviewing the newly started New Zealand Alpine Journal, he wrote '*...we note with pleasure that ladies may be enrolled amongst its members.*'[10]

Doubtless, wives and daughters would have been actively hillwalking, but we are unaware of any earlier climbs in Scotland being participated in by women. It would be another decade before the Alpine Ladies Club would be formed, and another year after that, in 1908, before the Scots formed their first Ladies' club. Women had been climbing in the Alps since about the 1850s, and doing so impressively. In 1872, '*A young scotch lady*' made an ascent of Mont Blanc, an event so startling it merited a note in *The Times*.[11] In Britain, mountaineering in general was playing at catch-up, and in an atmosphere more strait-laced than that found on the Continent. The rise of women in mountaineering would be paralleled with suffragette activity, with the Scottish Woman's Suffragette Federation formed in 1906. In Helen Steven's book telling the story of the Ladies Scottish Climbing Club,[12] she mentions rumours that some of the early members were active in the suffragette movement.

❄ ❄ ❄

The May 1897 number of the SMCJ opened with a major article by Norman Collie.[13] It begins with a brief history of the discovery of Scotland's mountain scenery, continues to describe its subtlety as compared with the greater mountain ranges, and moves to the Cuillin of Skye. It finishes with a sunset there (described here at the end of Chapter 3). The article exhibits Collie's full powers of observation and obvious love of the Scottish mountain landscape, in particular that found on Skye.

As mentioned earlier, climbers were beginning to find that Sligachan was a little too distant from the main climbing grounds of the Cuillin. To climb from the Coruisk basin in particular entailed a very long walk in, and hopes of building a climbers' hut there were dashed by the land owner. The energy and ingenuity of the Victorians was not to be so easily thwarted and so arose the Climbers' Camp at Coruisk.[14]

The four mountaineers involved were Willie Douglas, William Brown, John Rennie and Harrison Barrow, a Climbers' Club member from Birmingham. The last named had camped for a week in Glen Brittle in July 1892, climbing with his brother Walter and Howard Priestman, enjoying superb weather and climbing the Inaccessible Pinnacle and other popular climbs. Douglas and Brown we are already familiar with. John Rennie (1858–1937), mentioned in Chapter 4, remains a somewhat enigmatic figure. The brief obituary notice by Maylard describes his naturally reserved disposition. An electrical engineer by training, he never married, seems to have been comfortably well off financially, and '*...devoted his life mostly to the acquisition of knowledge which he only shyly, and with a certain degree of reticence, imparted to those who knew how to extract it*'.[15] Despite his reticence, he served as SMC President from 1904-07 and his singing of the Club Song at the Annual Dinner was appreciated by all. He had climbed Suilven when 16, in 1874, was on Skye in 1881, and made ascents of the popular hills such as Ben Lomond and Goatfell. In 1888 he climbed '*the usual easy points*' in Yosemite. We can deduce that he had a modest hill record, but sharpened his mountaineering through the influence of the SMC.

With the climbers' knowledge of Coruisk weather, they were not going to use standard tents. Instead, they designed wooden huts, still with a regular triangular cross-section, but stoutly made and covered in waterproof felt. The journal article by Douglas included full plans, in addition to a complete listing of supplies taken into the Coruisk basin. Due to the weight of equipment, they hired a boat from John Macrae, a Soay fisherman. This was used to ferry everything to the head of Loch Coruisk where three huts were assembled. Two were used for sleeping, while one, with an extension, was the *Cook-shop*. In his article Douglas supplies a full list of food transported in, though some basic essentials had to be resupplied.

The huts were about eight feet high in the centre, and had space inside for two camp beds with mattresses. A coke-burning stove, a paraffin stove, one folding table and four chairs provided a luxurious camp in a most picturesque position. Seven boat loads in all were necessary up the loch, and they were fortunate indeed that setting up the camp, which of course involved assembling the huts, coincided with three days' perfect weather. They had arrived at Loch Scavaig on 20th July 1897.

Their planned attack on the rocks of the Cuillin had an inauspicious start, as Douglas had an attack of asthma and stayed in camp. The other three had a pleasant if unexciting climb up Bidean Druim nan Ramh. From there Barrow left, with the intention of going to Sligachan for mail, returning at night. The rain began in the afternoon and soon developed into a storm, with Rennie and Brown returning to the camp in a '*drouked* condition.*' Rennie had promised to meet Barrow in the boat at the foot of Loch Coruisk, and set off with a lantern, but returned at midnight without Barrow. The next day, they spotted Barrow limping along the north side of the loch. On his return from Sligachan he had missed his way and had spent the night wandering about in the storm. He was tucked into bed and was well recovered by the next morning.

(*drouked: soaked. The adjective *droukit*, is commonly used in Scotland)

Well recovered was more than could be said for the weather. It turned out to be one of the worst spells of summer weather experienced in Skye, and was so bad two days later that they all slept with their boots on, listening apprehensively to the groaning of the wooden huts. Luckily these had been well built, and well dug in. It rained from the 25th to the 29th, with the latter date providing the heaviest gale so far.

Their boat had been lifted and dumped on the beach, luckily without damage. On the 30th they dried out their belongings, enjoyed some scrambling, and rowed down the loch to meet Macrae in the evening, having spotted his beacon fire. He had brought fresh eggs and a lythe, a fish known elsewhere as a Pollack, one of the cod family.

The 31st turned out to be hot. Too hot for anything energetic, probably due to the humidity. The 1st August was more amenable to climbing but remained misty all day before the now inevitable storm burst upon them in the evening. They had managed to descend into the Alasdair-Dubh gap, one of their targets, but the day was getting on and they left it for the next day. One mistake they made, as they set out after breakfast on the 2nd, was taking too much camera gear, with a whole-plate, half-plate, and quarter-plate. Never again they vowed. They succeeded in climbing up from the gap, with Brown leading.

Barrow had to leave on the 3rd, when they all went down to Scavaig to meet the weekly steamer with its hundreds of tourists. The climbers were after their bread however, which they achieved, as Barrow squelched his way back to Sligachan.

On the 4th August Brown and Rennie climbed the Inaccessible Pinnacle. The 5th saw Rennie and Douglas recover their cameras, which they had stowed away by Coir' an Lochain. A great thunderstorm then burst upon them, forcing them to shelter in a cave. This storm cleared the air, so that on the 6th they felt able to attempt a route they had spied on Sgurr a' Mhadaidh. Heading up into Coire an Uaigneis, they climbed the entire length of the buttress left of South-East Gully, now named *Brown's Climb* (240m Difficult), the first route on the Upper Cliffs of Sgurr a' Mhadaidh.

Over their remaining 17 full days remaining in the camp, eleven were described as having bad weather, two excellent weather, and several others misty. The 23rd was glorious, and they had to spend it packing and transporting equipment. Finally on the 24th they made the last two trips down the loch before catching the steamer out of Scavaig. They had dismantled one of their huts before running out of time, so regretfully had to leave the other two huts, in the hope that the next gale from the south-west would remove all signs of their camp at Coruisk.

Summing up, Douglas remarked that the sultry weather of the first fortnight was even more trying than the storms. It was difficult to summon up enough resolve to do anything. But despite all the discomforts brought by the poor weather, camp life had been thoroughly enjoyed by all. As for the weather, the river at Sligachan one day gained heights which the oldest inhabitant had never seen. Sgurr nan Gillean had been struck by lightning, with the topmost slab split in two, scattering white and charred fragments in all directions. One man had been killed by lightning in the south-west corner of the island during the same storm.

John Rennie appended two short notes to the article by Douglas: the first was of measurements showing the magnetic qualities of Cuillin rocks, with two sets of readings showing as much as 57 degrees difference of bearing of a distant point from stations less than 10 paces apart on the flat. Readings were taken standing up, compass in hand. The second note was of two stonefalls observed. Both took place in the daytime, about noon, and after heavy rainfall. The first came down a gully on the Druim nan Ramh ridge towards Loch Coruisk. As he saw it in profile, and its origin was in the mist, it was impossible to estimate its size.

The second came down Coir' a' Chaoruinn, between Sgurr Dubh Mhor and Sgurr Dubh Bheag. Rennie estimated it had a breadth of 150 to 180yds, and a perpendicular fall of 700 or 800ft. At some points it seemed to sweep the whole of the Sgurr Dubh Mhor side of the corrie. The article by Douglas includes photographs and diagrams showing the design of the huts, including full details which would allow anyone with basic carpentry to emulate the pioneers.

As most mountaineers will be aware, although the gabbro of the Cuillin is superb for climbing on, it often has a blocky disposition. In addition, swarms of basaltic dykes have been intruded through the gabbro at a later date, creating areas of weakness and a rock which is slippery when wet. As the current climbers' guide states – '*Most common [accidents] are those caused by climbers dislodging loose blocks. Extreme weathering, rock type and lack of regular traffic means that blocks of all sizes can move with alarming ease*'.[16]

In 1929, the Ladies Scottish Climbing Club Journal published a retrospective article by Ida Fitzgerald Dalton. The article, '*First Recollections of Skye, 1893*', described a holiday on Skye. Four years later, in 1897, she was back for a family holiday, staying at Sligachan. The Victorian attitude to women climbing was one of suspicion, despite a few adventurous wives and sisters who climbed with husbands or male relatives. Ida's parents seemed relaxed enough to leave Ida to make her own fun, and when she determined to go climbing she engaged John Mackenzie as a guide.

That August she learned to climb with an acknowledged master teacher. On her first outing with Mackenzie she climbed the Tourist Route on Gillean, followed by a descent of the harder Western Ridge, leading over the Gendarme. From the bealach they climbed the Bhasteir Tooth. As Ida had apparently never been on rock before, this was an impressive feat. Fortunately for posterity, Ida was persuaded by the Hotel Manageress, Mrs Sharp, to record her climbs in the Hotel's Climbers' Book, so that we have knowledge not only of her climbing, but also more information on Mackenzie. She praised him both as a guide and as a companion.

Two days later, on 8th August with John and Murdo Mackenzie, she ascended the Inaccessible Pinnacle, up the long side and down the short. The day was warm but the mist and rain made for rocks streaming with water and slippery, especially the basaltic pinnacle. She climbed on several other dates that month, with her final day in Coire na Creiche. Her log entry mentions one or two new climbs with Mackenzie, but sadly these have not been recorded. She was back in September the next year, with several days spent in poor weather, and again in June and July 1889, her last mountaineering holiday on Skye. As Stuart Pedlar remarks in his MS on Skye, information on this remarkable woman climber is minimal; basically the Sligachan log entries, her birth certificate, and two letters she wrote to John Mackenzie some 30 years later in December 1931.

We know she was born in October 1871 at St. Neots, Bedfordshire, her father a retired Army Captain. That would have made her in her late 20s when she took up climbing. Following her three seasons climbing on the Cuillin, she seems to have faded from recorded history much as the sun burns off a morning mist. Pedlar suggests one tantalizing item; on page 50 of Ben Humbles's *The Cuillin of Skye*, there is a reproduction of sketches first published in the *Graphic* of 1898. A tweed-clad woman with a walking stick stands next to a gentleman. The caption reads *Woman Climber in Skye.*[17] Even more interesting is another sketch from the *Graphic*, showing a local guide and a tourist discussing what appears to be the same woman, who this time is some distance away, back to the artist, gazing at the peaks. The caption for this sketch reads –

> *Tourist: "Can she climb, Donald?"*
> *Guide: "Ou aye, she's been all over the inaccessible pinnacles, sir!"*

As Pedlar remarks, the years 1896-98 had been very productive ones on Skye for the SMC, but other than a handful of hardy members, the club seems to have done very little in the years between 1899 and 1903. Other climbers were on the go of course, and in June 1899 six members of the Climbers' Club made their first visit to the misty isle. On 1st June, RE Thompson, CG Slade, AT Fraser, FM Levis CA Wordsworth and TA Falcon made an epic twelve-hour ascent of Waterpipe Gully, making the first direct ascent, with the 80ft pitch, the second, being particularly difficult. They returned to Sligachan just before 5am, where a luxurious supper had been left for them. Mrs Sharp was no stranger to climbers' hours.

❄ ❄ ❄

In 1897, *Rock-Climbing in the English Lake District* by Owen Glynne Jones was published. It was reviewed in the SMCJ, by an unknown writer but possibly Willie Douglas, who prefaced his review by making general comments on climbing in Scotland compared with conditions in England.

> In Scotland the field is wide, exploration is comparatively recent, centres are remote, many of the best things are practically inaccessible save to local enthusiasts, and it must be long, in spite of our efforts, before all is known and recorded. In England, on the other hand, nearly all the best rock-work can be reached in a moderate day from Wastdale.[18]

The review was very generous, recognising both the climbing abilities of Jones, but also his writing. As for the climbing, Jones was obviously in a league of his own. He took standards to higher levels, but perhaps more crucially, he pioneered routes up features which were climbed for their own attractiveness, rather than being major mountain structures such as gullies, ridges and so on, often leading to some summit. So it was that in April 1897 he climbed Kern Knotts Chimney on Wasdale, a 70ft crack on a subsidiary buttress. He had previously top-roped the route, foreseeing a practice some would use for very hard routes in the distant future.

Another comparison of rock climbing in Scotland and England was made by Naismith following his visit to Wasdale Head in May 1896 –

> ...I should say that the English standard of difficulty seems to be a little the higher. Steep passages, which in Scotland would likely have been left alone, have here been reconnoitred, and studied, and worked out, until they were made to go; and now everybody does them, ladies included. Most of the climbs are of course short.[19]

❄ ❄ ❄

On the Edinburgh Autumn holiday of 1897, Raeburn and Clark were on Arran, and spent a day climbing on the vegetatious north-east face of Cir Mhor. The article penned by Clark on their day on the mountain was the cause of some heated correspondence in a later SMCJ, with Clark, Raeburn and William Brown being the players.[20] In Clark's article, he quotes Raeburn as remarking that – '*I would not trust a climber who had only climbed in Skye*'. Clark commented that '*...Such a heretical opinion judged ill for his mental condition.*' Clark provided Raeburn's next statement as saying that – '*...Skye climbing, as far as my experience goes, is ridiculously easy, with the exception of the gap on the Alasdair Dubh ridge and the lower portions of the rocks near Coruisk.*'

Clark, perhaps seeing stormy waters ahead, went off at a slight tangent, and began an analysis of the word *difficult* as referenced in his article, and as applied to climbing. Even with climbers, he wrote, it could be used differently, with the crack [i.e. expert] climbers, for example, refusing to use the word at all. His quoting Raeburn set off William Brown, who strongly disagreed with Raeburn's comments '*...which seem to me to be neither particularly relevant nor well founded*'.[21]

Brown continued to discuss the different rocks and conditions which could easily be met with on Skye, particularly the basalt intrusions which when wet were especially slippery, and the climbing to be found on the steeper and more difficult faces. He was writing from the view of a climber who thought that the Cuillin of Skye provided the finest climbing ground in Scotland, or at least the best that so far had been discovered. Raeburn, it would appear, was writing from the view of a climber who felt on top of his game and was thinking with a wider geographical scope. And Clark was caught in the middle.

Douglas, then Editor of the SMCJ, naturally allowed both Clark and Raeburn to respond to Brown's letter, with all three being published together. Clark was understandably somewhat irritated, and in a very brief response commented that Brown's letter hardly required a serious response from him, especially as he understood that Raeburn was dealing with it. He also criticised Douglas, suggesting that he was short of Journal material.

As for Raeburn, he replied with a pun, and wittily regretted touching the '*...—however abnormally developed—"Skyeatic" nerve of any climber.*' He continued that his comments on Skye were only a minor and subsidiary side issue as he was, with Clark, discussing mainly the rocks of the Southern Tyrol, '*...whose tremendous precipices of almost incredible steepness, yet, in Clark's experience, presented no insuperable difficulties to the enterprising climber.*' Douglas had rightly left out the bits about the Tyrol, as being *foreign*, and possibly Brown would not have known about this editing. Obviously, continued Raeburn, '*...no one would dream of asserting that there are not difficult climbs in Skye. An impossible climb is not a climb at all.*' He finished by stating that the gabbro of Skye is too good, as it makes one discontented with one's power on smoother rocks. '*It is the very [l]uxury of British climbing, and therefore, in my opinion, is not the best place for the training of the novice.*'

This argument, which rumbled on for a few more years, somewhat resembles that of Gibson with Naismith, in discussing the use of an ice axe (see Chapter 5). Fortunately it seems that all three climbers seemed to have simmered down with time. Brown shared another similarity with Gibson in that he died at a tragically young age. He was 33 when he succumbed, after a three-year struggle, to a *wasting disease*. His death certificate records the causes of death as '*Dilatation of stomach, 3 years; phthisis, 6 months.*' He either had a chronic ulcer, or more likely a cancer, while phthisis, which was a polite term for tuberculosis at the time, probably supervened because his system was weakened. Brown had links to the Cairngorm Club; McConnochie was his proposer for the SMC, and his father and brother were both in the Cairngorm Club. He had notes and articles in the journals of both clubs.

The early demise of those two was a major blow to early Scottish mountaineering, but as we will shortly learn, this loss would be compensated in part by Raeburn and others. In his obituary for Brown, Willie Douglas referred to him as '*..that bright and clever spirit.*' In the world of '*what if*', the SMC, with Gibson, Brown *and* Raeburn all alive and bursting with exploratory zeal, would without doubt have made an even bigger contribution to the history of the sport.

❄ ❄ ❄

The SMC New Year Meet of 1898 was held in Fort William. By this time, Scottish climbers were well aware that it was usually a poor time for attempting anything on Nevis; the days were very short, snow and ice conditions often unconsolidated. Nonetheless, William Clark and a new member, Thomas Gibson were in attendance, though with a total of six at the meet it was a poor show. As Clark remarked at the beginning of his SMCJ article – '*To get perfect weather at Fort William is at any season a rarity, but to get it at the New Year time, and under wintry conditions, is a chance that comes but once in a lifetime.*'[22]

Clark and Gibson were at the breakfast table in the Alexandra Hotel just after 6.30am on Monday, January 3rd. It turned out to be the best day of the weekend, with some snow overnight followed by a starry night. Their original intention was an ascent of Observatory Gully, but finding the snow unconsolidated and hoping to catch the afternoon train home, they headed instead for a gully to the left of Number Five Gully. The latter is the broad, easy gully on the left of Carn Dearg, and as Clark remarked, it had been ascended by Collie, and perhaps others. Possibly this ascent took place when Collie and his friends were exploring the area before the previous Easter Meet. An article by Lionel Hinxman in the SMCJ described ascents made during the Easter, 1895 Meet, and, according to Hinxman, only Gullies Number Three and Four had been climbed to that date.[23] Number Five Gully is in the current guidebook as having been climbed by Collie in April 1895; while this likely, for this we have no evidence. No ascent is noted in any edition of the Ben Nevis Guide until 2002, when it was given to Collie as being in April 1895.

Apart from the superb weather, the day was made even better by the glorious sight of a Golden Eagle, lifting off from the Carn Dearg crags and spiralling up in the sunshine – '*...his plumage alternately appeared black or golden as the sun's rays struck on its nearer or further aspect.*'

As they had planned on a short day, they carried light food, including apples, dates, figs, raisins and chocolate. Setting foot on the initial rocks, they were slowed by ice, zig-zagging now and then to avoid the steepest sections. An ice-filled crack required combined tactics, to reach steep snow above. They gained a prominent ledge and finished their sandwiches, filling the centres with snow, as they were not carrying water. On finding it was now 2.30pm, they abandoned any thoughts of the afternoon train, and looked forward in its place to a sunset from the top.

It being Ben Nevis, they had been drawn into a commonplace trap – that of underestimating the size of the cliffs. From below they assumed that the crags above them marked the finish, but imagine their feelings when finishing the last steep pitch they saw above them a cliff of considerable size. The sun had now set, it being about 4.30pm, while the moon shed but a faint light. They soldiered on, trying to find the best line. To the left a great ice-fall barred the way, while the snow slope to the right had stretches of icy rocks. Straight up it would be.

The moon, waxing gibbous, was now producing dazzling snow underfoot, contrasting with the dark sky and sparkling stars above. The wind was increasing however, pushing before it dark masses of cloud, some of which were already obscuring Tower Ridge. There was also a threatening *something* at the skyline, which turned out to be a magnificent cornice, in places some 25 to 30ft in height with, in parts, icicles.

They gained the cornice and found a snow ledge, about 18in wide, below the overhang. As the cornice overhung by about six feet, they were sheltered from the wind, which had at times buffeted them and nearly blown them off their steps. The temperature, Clark noted, was 23°F [-5° Celsius]. The ledge narrowed and eventually, anchoring themselves as best as possible, the other crept along using the ledge as a handhold. Finally they gained a rock rib and moving up the upper part of this on snow they reached the top.

It was now past 8pm and though tempted to make a beeline for the descent, they were low on energy after nine hours of constant step-cutting. They therefore headed for the Observatory, descended its snow staircase, and were welcomed by the inmates. Some suitable refreshment, a telegram to the hotel (just catching preparations for a search party), and they set off down the slopes. All was still clear to the north, with the uplands glistening in the moonlight. They gained the hotel at 11.35pm and sat down to dinner, which even at that late hour, Mrs Doig had prepared for them. A couple of hours later the storm burst, and as they rose for the early train torrents of rain were dashing on the windows.

If it had not been for the moon, the meet report later recorded, they would have had to spend a night on the mountain. Given the break in the weather, events might well have taken a very bad turn. With time, their route was given the appropriate name of *Moonlight Gully* (150m II).

The selection of Fort William for a New Year Meet, with the disadvantages rehearsed above, may have been the cause of a silent revolt within the SMC. Various members went elsewhere, including climbing on Ben A'an in the Trossachs (Douglas, Maclay and Naismith), Spean Bridge (Harry Walker, Harry Giles Walker & Howard Hill), and Inveroran (Scott-Moncrieff Penney, the brothers Harry and Frederick Conradi Squance, Gilbert Thomson and Collie) A complete ascent, the second, of the Upper Couloir of Stob Ghabhar was made, with Collie leading the crux ice pitch.

The Walkers were cousins from Dundee, in a family of jute spinners and manufacturers. Harry (1869–1915) was a member of the Dundee Rambling Club (DRC) and a Vice-President of the SMC which he joined in 1894. As a Lieutenant colonel in the 4th Black Watch, he was one of four DRC members to die in the 4th Black Watch in WW1, three of whom were also SMC members. The Battle of Loos, on 25th September 1915, saw the second highest number of British Army deaths in WW1, the first day of the Somme being the worst.

It was a disastrous day for the 4th and Dundee; out of 20 officers and 420 men who participated in the attack, 19 officers and 230 men were killed or wounded, including Harry, who was Commanding Officer. Harry Giles Walker (1875–1951) and his brother Charles William (1879–1964) were cousins of Harry. Charles climbed the Meije with Raeburn in 1904, his first season in the Alps. He too became a Vice President in the SMC. The Dundee Rambling Club thus made a valuable and energetic contribution to Scottish mountaineering and the SMC.

Raeburn could not manage the New Year, and instead spent Christmas at Wasdale Head. He was very obviously interested in sampling the cream of English rock climbing, and had been in part motivated by a note by Naismith, who with Douglas made a visit there at Whitsuntide, late May, 1896. Raeburn enjoyed two days' sampling Great Gable and Pillar Rock, finding that –

> The rock is usually of first-rate climbing quality, and totally unlike the schist of the central Highlands, or even the granite slabs of Arran. The climbs are usually, as in Skye, easier than they look, owing to the abundance of ledges, chimneys and good hitches.[24]

It would seem that the tigers of the SMC were being assiduous in keeping up with climbing trends; further, with various energetic raiding parties from members of the Alpine Club such as Haskett Smith and Hastings, there was an awareness that any climbing plums found on Scottish mountains would be plucked sooner than later, and preferably by the Scots.

❄ ❄ ❄

The Southern Highlands were not forgotten and Raeburn, with Henry GS Lawson made a raid on the Tarmachans, the craggy group of four peaks above Loch Tay. On Saturday, 19th February, having arrived by train from Edinburgh, Raeburn and Lawson decided to explore Creag na Caillich (Witch's Crag), the closest to Killin. The snow began falling heavily at noon, just as the pair reached photographic distance of the crag. Raeburn estimated the crag as being about 400ft in height at the most. From the south could be seen an overhanging, black crag, with a narrow gully or chimney running up its south side. They followed the chimney which was fairly stiff under the conditions and gained a horizontal ledge which cut across the face for some distance. Above this the face looked impracticable, with fringing icicles. They failed to traverse right but going back left they succeeded in finishing just left of the line of the gully.

For some reason, this route was not recorded. Perhaps Raeburn felt that as a direct continuation of the line could not be climbed that day the route was incomplete. If that day was not a complete success, the following day certainly was, as the two decided to examine the rocks above Lochan na Lairige. This small lochan was then undammed. The highest part of the face included a '*wonderfully straight chimney*', which they immediately christened Arrow Chimney. As they could see an unbroken ribbon of white in the chimney, Raeburn did not foresee any difficulty, but they had not seen the rocky overhangs concealed beneath the snow.

Even the first pitch was deceptive, and beat back the pair three times before being out-manoeuvred by a left flanking move. Further up the chimney it became more difficult, with soft snow needing to be cleared to uncover holds beneath. Twice the climbers had to run out their full rope length of 60 ft before a stance could be gained.

> Progress was only to be made in such places by cutting holds for the left hand and left toe in the somewhat thin and rotten ice on our left wall, and thrusting the right knee into the angle of the chimney, while the right hand wielded the ice-axe with as much vigour as was possible in such a cramped position. Gradually we fought our way up, but gradually the sun sank and the cold increased.[25]

After four and a half hours' almost incessant step cutting, Raeburn developed cramp in his right tricep so that although the next moves were relatively easy, Lawson had to use his shoulder to help Raeburn overcome them. They finally emerged at 6pm into an icy north-west blast and flung themselves into the lee side of the ridge and so descended. Raeburn estimated there must have been some 15° of frost [c. -9°C]. The steel of the ice axes, he wrote, could not be touched with ungloved fingers. *Arrow Chimney* (150m IV) had proved to be, as Raeburn remarked at the end of his article – '*...quite sufficiently exciting.*'

❄ ❄ ❄

The Easter Meet 1898 was held at Ballachulish, from 7th-11th April. Like the Fort William meet described above, the attendance was very poor, and more or less matched by the weather. Hugh Munro provided the meet report, which mentions that '*...On Monday a determined though unsuccessful attack was made on the "Church Door" of Bidean.*' No names were listed for this in the report, but we know from the Visitors' Book of the Clachaig Hotel that the climbers were William Clark, Raeburn, Conradi Squance, and John Bell, a formidable team from the SMC. They descended to within 40 feet of the highest point reached on September 27th 1896. (See Chapter 9 for the story of this much-attempted route.)

The Meet report for Ballachulish by Hugh Munro mentioned that there were climbing parties at Banavie, Fort William, Clachaig, Kingshouse, Inveroran, Kinlochewe etc. Somewhat sniffily, or perhaps because there were no other reports submitted, nothing was recorded in the SMCJ from these alternative venues, with one major exception. Some 13 years later, Raeburn penned an article describing the first three known ascents of Crowberry Gully.[26]

There was no one more qualified, as he had been on all three ascents, the first on 10th April 1898, from the Kingshouse Hotel section of the 1898 Easter Meet. This was probably a 'cave' or unofficial Meet, attended by Bell, Collinson, Glover, Green, Higginbotham, Napier and Raeburn. At the Ballachulish Hotel there were only 10 members present, with Munro in his Meet report commenting that it could hold half the club.[27]

The day before this inspection of Church Door Buttress from above, which was an early example of what would become more commonplace for hard first ascent routes in the future, several Kingshouse teams were making preparations for climbing on the Buachaille. (The spelling of this iconic mountain was for many years Buchaille: there exists a window plaque in the Kingshouse which has this older version.) John Bell had already spent several strenuous days on the mountain, and marshalled the assembled climbers. *'The great gully north of the Crowberry Ridge fell to the share of EB Green and H. Raeburn.'* [28] This *great gully* was, of course, *Crowberry Gully*, as it would be named later.

There is no EB Green listed in the SMC Archives, though there is an Edward William Green who joined in 1895 and was certainly competent enough to have accompanied Raeburn. A Green does appear once more in the SMCJ, on a meet – Easter 1896 Fort William, but no initials given. Also a Green (no initials) was on two FAs on Arran, July 6th and 7th, 1895, Gully 5 and B2C Rib (Very Difficult and bold).Finally, an EW Green appears in the Clachaig Visitors' Book for September 1896, climbing with the Napiers and John Bell.

WH Murray, who wrote the first Rock Climbing Guide to Glencoe and Ardgour in 1949, has it as EW Green. Additional to the routes above, Green was on the first ascents of Green and Napier's Route, and Ledge Route, both on Nevis. We must assume that the SMCJ article contains an erroneous initial, and that Green was the SMC member Edward William.

Murray also writes that the 1898 ascent of Crowberry Gully was done in conditions that were neither summer nor winter – *'...there was much snow, but no snow or ice on the rocks.'*[29] To be pedantic, conditions were wintry, but allowed an easier ascent, with Raeburn's second ascent being more typical of a winter climb. The gully at this time was referred to as 'B Gully', Gully A being Great Gully, and Gully C now being Easy Gully. Only D Gully retains this original nomenclature.

The 1898 season, as Raeburn noted, had been a snowy one and vast quantities of snow lay in the gully. The only real difficulty encountered by Raeburn and Green was where the gully forks, with a short but steep left fork leading to the foot of Crowberry Tower, and the easier right fork continuing upwards to easy ground. Raeburn, naturally, attempted the left fork, climbing by back and foot to beneath a '*far out chockstone*.' Above this the very steep top pitch looked '*horribly uninviting.*' Luckily, at this moment a fierce blatter of hail began, and Raeburn retreated.

Once the hail ceased they resumed the ascent, taking the disagreeably rotten turfy wall in the right fork. Ice and frost held this together, but Raeburn had to run out the full rope length before a reasonable snowy ledge was gained. Green, a much heavier man, required a steady pull on the rope, not that the climbing was too difficult for him, but to ensure that some of the precarious holds did not collapse. The final ice pitch must have been covered by snow, as Raeburn describes only a long, steep snow slope leading up to the rocks of the summit.

Raeburn mentions that the Abraham brothers, in one of their summer visits, had examined the left fork from above - '*Apparently their opinion as regards its feasibility was unfavourable.*'[30] Raeburn's second ascent took place some eleven years later, on Sunday, 11th April 1909. Raeburn was attending the Easter Meet in Fort William, a meet which for the first two days enjoyed splendid conditions. He had arranged however to meet up with four English climbers who were staying at the Clachaig in Glen Coe, and therefore he had a wet and stormy cycle ride from Fort William to the Kingshouse, where they had agreed to rendezvous for climbing on the Buachaille.

Two of the climbers, Haskett Smith and Greenwood, had but recently recovered from influenza, and decided not to face the deluges of rain intermixed with fierce blasts of wind. The other two, WA Brigg and H Scott Tucker, placed themselves in the gentle care of Raeburn. Brigg was then Editor of the Yorkshire Ramblers' Club, while Tucker had climbed in the Alps. The only climb Raeburn could think of suitable for such conditions was Crowberry Gully, given its sheltered position from the elements. What this tiger actually had his eyes on was Crowberry Ridge, but he reported that it was sheathed in ice and hopeless. With a gain in altitude, the rain changed to snow at the foot of Crowberry Ridge. There was less snow in the gully than in 1898, and the first real pitch was only climbed using steps cut in thick ice on the right wall. Most of the other pitches were mostly snowed up, but the junction pitch, where the gully forks, demanded a long traverse out right on ice and new snow. Above, snow made the remaining pitches fairly easy.

Raeburn made some comments on snow conditions during the ascent. In the gully the snow was good, being quite hard, and showing no avalanche tendencies. However, as it had been snowing very heavily, probably since early morning, from Raeburn's description there was an almost continuous stream of new snow or spindrift, coming down the gully. Every now and then a sheet of snow would slip off the rocks and gather into a respectable stream in the gully, cutting a groove in the old hard snow of the gully bed.

> Usually, however, it was easy to avoid the stream. If necessary to cross it, two could easily hitch, while the other waded through. At one pitch, where the gully narrowed, and the only possible route led up the "fall," the party was struck by a larger "rush" of new snow than usual. The leader was buried to the shoulders as he held the second's rope taut round the perfect hitch of his well-buried ice-axe. The second, who at the time was occupying the position of a "chockstone" in the pitch, was completely snowed over, while the third man, at the foot of the pitch, was overwhelmed, and went off down the gully till brought up by the rope. The temperature was too low to permit of ice or old snow coming down with the fresh, otherwise it would have been madness to have persevered with the ascent.

Raeburn's third ascent of Crowberry Gully was in summer conditions, on 18th September 1910. He had long wished to explore Buachaille Etive Beag, the 'wee' Buachaille, and on hearing from Stuart Cumming (1878–1961) that there would be a combined fishing, walking, and climbing meet at Kingshouse, Raeburn squeezed into the hotel. The next day four climbers left the hotel for the hills – Raeburn, Francis Greig (1880–1938), Cumming and Douglas Menzies (1880–1971). Greig and Raeburn, the only two with cycles, went ahead to scout out the wee Buachaille, but were unimpressed with its climbing potential while impressed with the dryness underfoot. Raeburn decided that the time was perfect for an attempt on a summer ascent of Crowberry Gully, and racing back caught the other two just about the usual crossing place of the Coupal River. Reunited, they set off up the Buachaille.

In the gully, a scree slope led to the first pitch, with a cursory glance indicating that it would be impossible without a '*...big "loupin'-on stane" of snow...*' Consequently, the party stopped for lunch, carefully re-packed the sacks, and moved on to the buttress on the right, where the rocks were excellent and allowed the barrier to be bypassed. The general order of climbing was Greig, Raeburn, Menzies and Cumming. Greig had joined the SMC in 1906, Menzies in 1910, Cumming in 1905. Greig gave his name to Greig's Ledge, a short variation on Crowberry Ridge which avoids the Severe crux of the Direct (Difficult, 1907). Cumming, an actuary, served in the Great War as Captain of a mobile Trench Mortar Battery; this sounds like a risky enterprise, and indeed he was awarded the Military Cross.

Several pitches then led to the most remarkable pitch, where a deep cleft led far into the heart of the mountain. Crawling to the end of the cleft, light could be seen coming faintly through a hole in the bed of the gully high above. Far above, and overhanging by many feet, a chockstone was jammed in the jaws of the cleft. The through passage was hopelessly narrow, but the cleft was so narrow that upward progress could be made by inflating the chest to hold firm, and deflating the chest when moving up.

Eventually the chockstone was reached, and although slightly loose, it provided a welcome rest. The leader on this pitch, the '*Thincrack Chimney*', was Francis Greig, of whom it was said in his Obituary Notice that he was so lean his friends joked they could strike matches on his ribs.[31] Once he brought Raeburn up to the chockstone, the lead was exchanged and with a long step out on the wall and an overhanging boulder climbed with a good undergrip, the pitch was completed. In typical winter conditions, this through passage will go unnoticed.

They were now at the Junction, and once again the determined Raeburn headed up the Left Fork with Greig. They climbed the first two pitches, both difficult, but the last pitch, though only 10 or 12 feet, looked exceedingly forbidding. The right-hand wall and the chockstone overhung, while the left wall appeared holdless. Time to retreat again.(The Left Fork was finally climbed on 16th September, 1943, by BN Simmonds and AC Marriott of the Polaris Mountaineering Club, Nottingham.

The chockstone was climbed by back and foot and great was the disappointment when the leader found no finishing hold above, the back and footing having to be continued for some short distance. Simmonds considered the crux to be similar to but harder than that of Walker's Gully on Pillar. Possibly Very Severe, though as in many gully problems this grade is a moveable feast.)

The pair re-joined the other two and the gully was continued, making a right traverse as in the previous winter ascent by Raeburn in 1909. Above, one short if tricky pitch led to easy ground. Cumming and Menzies headed for the summit, while Raeburn and Greig descended to look at the finish of the Left Fork. What they saw convinced them to stay away. As for Crowberry Gully, Greig, who had led most of the climb, considered that it was a finer climb than Slanting Gully on Skye, which he had also led. All agreed that it was a first-rate climb. Modern mountaineers would agree that in winter, Crowberry Gully is indeed a first-rate 300m classic climb at III/IV. Very few will climb the gully in summer, while even fewer will climb the Left Fork, which is given as a IV,5.

References

1. Brown, W. *The Coolins in '96*. SMCJ, 4, 22, Jan. 1897. 193-213.
2. Clark, W. Inglis. *Lochnagar and Ben Nevis*.SMCJ, 4, 22, Jan. 1897, 218-223.
3. Raeburn, Harold, *Ben Nevis in November*. In: Excursions, SMCJ, 4, 22, Jan. 1897, 244-246.
4. Raeburn, Harold. *The Black Shoot – in White*. SMCJ, 6, 35, May 1901, 161-166.
5. Raeburn, Harold. *Arthur's Seat and the Salisbury Crags*. SMCJ, 4, 24, Sept. 1897, 335-341.
6. Crocket, K.V. & Fowler, J.R.R. *Of Beer and Boats*. In: Miscellaneous Notes, SMCJ, 36, 188, 380-383.
7. Lodge, Professor R. *Yachting Meet, Easter 1897*. SMCJ, 4, 23, 288-293.
8. Begg, John S. *Life And Work at Ben Nevis Observatory*. Cairngorm Club Journal 2, 1898, 253-270. Reprinted in SMC Journals for 1984 and 1985.
9. Maylard, A. Ernest. *The "Upper Couloir" of Stob Ghabhar*. SMCJ, 4, 24, Sept. 1897, 307-311.
10. Maylard, A. Ernest. *Notes and Queries*. SMCJ, 2, 4, Jan. 1893, 211-212.
11. '*Mountaineering. Hotel Des Alpes Chamonix*', The Times, August 23, 1872.
12. Steven, Helen. *Rising to the Challenge. 100 Years of the Ladies Scottish Climbing Club*. (Scottish Mountaineering Trust 2010.) 23.
13. Collie, Norman. A Chuilionn. SMCJ, 4, 23, May 1897, pp259-266.
14. Douglas, W. *The Climbers' Camp at Coruisk*. SMCJ 5, 25, Jan. 1898, 1-16.
15. Maylard, A. Ernest. *In Memorium. John Rennie*, 1858-1937. SMCJ, 21, 124, November 1937, 277.
16. Lates, Mike. *Skye The Cuillin*. (SMC Climbers' Guide, 2011.)
17. Humble, B.H. *The Cuillin of Skye*.(London: Robert Hale, 1952), 50.
18. *Rock-Climbing in the English Lake District*, by Owen Glynne Jones: Reviewed in: Mountaineering Literature, SMCJ, 5, 25, Jan. 1898, 42-44.
19. Naismith, W.W. *Wastdale Head*. In: Excursions, SMCJ 4, 21, Sept. 1896, 174-175.
20. Clark, W. Inglis. *A Day on Cir Mhor*. SMCJ 5, 25, Jan. 1898, 29-36.
21. Brown, Clark & Raeburn. *Climbing in Skye*. In: Correspondence, SMCJ 5, 26, May 1898, 82-86.
22. Clark, W. Inglis. *Sixteen Hours on Ben Nevis*, Jan. 1898. SMCJ 5, 26, May 1898, 45-51.
23. Hinxman, Lionel W. *The Castle Ridge of Carn Dearg and the North-Eastern Precipices of Ben Nevis*. SMCJ 3, 18, Sept. 1895, 316-322.
24. Raeburn, H. *Wastdale at Christmas*. In: Excursions. SMCJ 5, 26, May 1898, 86.
25. Raeburn, Harold. *Two Climbs on the Tarmachans*. SMCJ 5, 26, May 1898, 70-76.
26. Raeburn, Harold. *The Crowberry North Gully, Buchaille Etive*. SMCJ 11, 65, June 1911, 255-262.
27. Munro, H.T. *The Easter Meet–Ballachulish*. SMCJ 5, 26, May 1898, 80-81.
28. Raeburn, Harold. *The Crowberry North Gully, Buchaille Etive*. SMCJ 11, 65, June 1911, 255-262.

29. Murray, W.H. *Rock Climbs – Glencoe and Ardgour*. (Edinburgh, SMC, 1949), 147.
30. Raeburn, Harold. *The Crowberry North Gully, Buchaille Etive*. SMCJ 11, 65, June 1911, 257.
31. Cumming, S.F.M. *In Memorium – Francis Greig*. SMCJ 22, 128, November 1939, 141-142.

9

The New Guidebook (1898-1902)

IN SCOTLAND, apart from a few local outcrops such as The Whangie, Loudon Hill and Salisbury Crag, exploratory climbers continued to concentrate on major mountain features. One such feature which had become the target of several parties from both sides of the border was Church Door Buttress, high on Bidean nam Bian in Glen Coe. This had been attempted by such leading lights as Collie, Collier and Solly in March 1894, Brown and Tough in July 1895, Hastings, Haskett Smith and Bowen in early April 1896, the Napier brothers, Green and John Bell in September 1896 and Bell and Raeburn at Easter 1898.

The first ascent of Church Door Buttress is well described in an SMCJ article by John Bell.[1] First named by William Tough, after a fancied resemblance to a church door seen end on, it is the western of two rock buttresses at the head of Coire nam Beith, with the eastern buttress now known as Diamond Buttress. In between is Central Gully, split at its foot by Collie's Pinnacle. This attractive buttress is well seen from the roadside and acted as a magnet to the pioneers. Most early attempts occurred early in the year, often at Easter, when weather and conditions added to the difficulty.

Several investigations by various permutations of climbers gradually added knowledge of the climb. Raeburn was there twice, on the second occasion with Bell when a late start due to poor weather and snow-covered rocks prevented a serious attempt but led to the pair, along with Clark and Conradi Squance, investigating the final section by top rope. The entire route had now been investigated, and the scene was set for a complete ascent.

On Saturday, 16th July 1898, with a poor forecast for the next day, the assault team left the Clachaig Inn. Included were SMC members Herbert Boyd, Willie Douglas, Graham Napier, Raeburn and John Bell. George

Thomson Parker would join the club the following December. The final party was reduced to four, as Parker and Douglas kindly elected to stay as spectators. They had already divided the route into two sections, with a ledge marking the middle followed by a crux section. A toss of the coin meant that Bell would lead the lower section, and Raeburn the upper.

They gained the ledge after about an hour with the weather improving all the while, and Raeburn took the lead, moving forward to climb the chimney. This contained three closely jammed blocks with a fourth jammed block above, behind which is a hole. Raeburn tried the blocks, which push out climbers awkwardly, and came back for a rest. They then tried possible alternatives previously attempted, but were beaten back to the ledge. It was time for another approach.

From their rucksack they pulled out 100ft of string. A stone was tied onto this and an attempt made to throw it over the top jammed block. The first attempt was close, but after failing for the next 30 minutes they abandoned the attempt –

> Raeburn then took off his boots and prepared for another attempt. I went forward to the end of the ledge to try to field him if a slip should occur, while Napier jammed himself in the hole in the ledge, worked Raeburn's rope over the small hitch, and anchored me. This time Raeburn was successful, and wild cheers broke out from us on the ledge, and from Douglas and Parker, who were watching the proceedings from the top of the eastern buttress.

Bell then followed, and then the rucksack, along with an ice axe, was carefully pulled up on the string, Raeburn fretting about the possibility of his boots, contained in the rucksack, taking a tumble should the thin string snap. A 15ft chimney then followed, but Raeburn judged it too risky, and after coming back down he struggled up an adjoining chimney which was just as hard, he thought, but not as exposed. A short traverse led to the top of the corner and the other three climbers followed. Napier had a longer reach, and was able to use a hold which the others could not reach. Thirty feet of easy climbing then led to the top, prompting another burst of cheering. The route had succumbed to Raeburn in his socks. It is now known as *Flake Route* (130m Very Difficult).

On May 26th 1900, the route received an ascent by James W Puttrell from Sheffield and the Abraham brothers from Keswick, George and Ashley. Of their ascent, their entry in the Clachaig Hotel Guest Book states –

> The whole climb is most interesting and to be strongly recommended – the situations and views being quite unique: One short chimney in a very exposed situation is the piece de resistance of the climb, but with a good leader the climb ought to become popular. There was much snow on the lower part of the climb and the exposed chimney, which was very wet and greasy, would probably be found more enjoyable with dry rocks.

George Dixon Abraham (1872–1965) and Ashley Perry Abraham (1876–1951) were two brothers from Keswick in the Lake District. They began climbing in 1890, but their climbing career did not take off until they met Owen Glynne Jones in 1896. They were professional photographers following in the business begun by their father, and they made an arrangement to illustrate Jones' book *Rock Climbing in the English Lake District* , published in 1897, with a right to sell photographs of Jones in action. In the introduction to his book, Jones thanks the brothers for their photographic help. He also added that '*...they are as skilful in tackling severe pitches as they are in taking successful pictures.*'[2] The two brothers will figure prominently later in this chapter.

Several commentators have remarked on the change that had taken place in Scottish mountaineering at about this time. Clark and Pyatt, for example, mention that with the coming of Raeburn, the swing from Salvationist to Ultramontane had gathered impetus.[3] This change was evident in the writing of the day, and older SMC members such as Ernest Maylard noted the stylistic changes taking place. Some 10 years after the founding of the SMC, at the request of Douglas the Editor, Maylard wrote an article reflecting over the events which had happened, and attempted to predict what would take place in the coming decade.[4]

One change which was already happening was a rise in rock climbing activity and standard, epitomised by Church Door Buttress. We have already noted that competition was in the air, with raiders from the south making their appearance in Scotland. Less obviously, there would have been local competition, as Brown and Gibson showed their fellow mountaineers in Scotland what could be achieved. Raeburn must have been inspired to some degree by them, and as we know from Church Door, he had quickly become a dominant force.

In his commentary, Maylard was perceptive and finely balanced; the SMC had begun with hillwalking, and there had been a natural transition to rock climbing. Sport, he wrote – '*...can never be considered a pastime of passive pleasure. Activity is one of its foremost attributes...*' He provided examples of a writing style that echoed what had taken place on the ground, from the early pedestrian notes on nature seen on their walks, to the more recent severe sort as penned by rock climbers. He posed the question – '*Was it that the earlier writers were struck more with what they saw than what they did; while those of the later period are more taken up with what they do than what they see?*' He continued –

> Our worthy President [Robert Augustus Robertson], in his annual post-prandial oration, evidently had overhanging rocks, if not absolutely perpendicular ones, visibly before his mental eye when he said modern mountaineering had no poetry in it. It was refreshing, however, if not encouraging to some of us, to

> hear that doughty old climber, CE Mathews†, refuse to allow that mountaineering possessed no poetry in its pursuit.

[†Mathews was a member of the Alpine Club, and first President of the Climbers' Club, founded in 1898.]

Maylard made the point that it came as no surprise that climbers involved in difficult climbing might fail to notice, as an example, the first primrose of spring peeping through the grass. He might miss such touches in mountaineering writing, he continued, but it did not mean that those writers were destitute of any love of the beautiful or any sentiment of poetry –

> It hardly behoves us to tell the truth, that the keenest rock-climbing is consistent with the deepest love of the beautiful, and that the two positively possess an almost inseparable affinity.

Maylard was well thought of in the SMC, and was also a respected surgeon; as such he would be well versed in keeping up with the latest surgical trends, indeed, he had written a textbook on surgery and had a technique named after him.[5,6] Although never one of the leading climbers, he was more than competent in all seasons, and was President of the SMC from 1899 to 1902. He died at Kingsmuir, Peebles, on 27th June 1947, in his 93rd year.

Another well known mountaineer also made comments concerning the new breed of climber. The previous year Norman Collie had published an article in the September 1898 SMCJ.[7] This was a series of reminisces and comments on past deeds, as told from his after-dinner armchair. The style is almost as though Collie was smoking something more than just tobacco in his pipe, and as he had been out to the Himalaya the previous year this may be more than just a humorous aside. He used the article as a medium in which to briefly present past events, and criticise current trends, rewriting or quoting from other writings such as *The Rubaiyat*, Kipling's *The Three-Decker*, a line from a Tennyson poem, and even a verse from Milton's *Paradise Lost*, in which, paraphrasing, Collie has a golfer see his ball land in a bunker (Collie was a keen golfer).

The meat of his article refers to the letters from Brown and Raeburn where Brown attacks Raeburn for being too critical of Skye climbing. Collie finishes with a mention of a first ascent he made on the Triple Buttresses of Beinn Eighe. In this he succeeds in inserting a sarcastic dig at Brown and Tough's difficult move on Lochnagar using combined tactics, with Brown heaving Tough upwards by sheer muscular strength, allowing a hold to be reached. Collie's party had climbed a snow gully, made an exposed traverse left across the buttress, then found themselves under a sheer, 200ft cliff – *'Only a paltry 200 feet, but they stop, none of the party being sufficiently muscular to propel the leader with a jerk upwards that paltry 200 feet.'* This article contrasts markedly with that by Maylard the following year, and marks Collie down as a steadfast Romantic. Maylard, by contrast, showed a more reasoned approach, and was certainly more receptive of change.

❄ ❄ ❄

As for the route Collie made on Beinn Eighe, he never named his companions on the route. It seems it was made in the spring of 1898, and involved a part ascent of West Central Gully, followed by a traverse left along the prominent ledge marking the boundary between the lower sandstone and upper quartzite rocks of Beinn Eighe. They then descended, but the following day they returned and made a descent from the summit of Central Buttress to reach the cairn marking their high point the previous day. There are doubtless quite a number of Collie's routes scattered across Scotland, particularly on Skye, where some may even have had subsequent ascents by other parties unaware that they had been climbed before.

However, as for more information on the climb, we have a tantalising clue in the form of a photograph bound into a Volume 5 of the SMC Journal, and adjacent to his article.[8] On the photo, which shows the triple buttresses, with snow in the gullies and on ledges, is a marked line, approximating to *Fulmar*, a summer Very Difficult. This may well indicate the route of descent made by Collie and his unnamed companions. There is one other piece of information on this route, as Collie sent a letter to Willie Douglas –

16 Campden Grove
Kensington W.

26th April 1898

My dear Douglas.

We had a great time at Kinlochewe, and I think I have discovered the finest rock climb in the British Isles - on the precipices of Ben Eighe. I enclose two photographs No 1 the precipice itself about 1000 feet of perfect rock and No 2 taken in a gully on the way up. I have sent Naismith details of the climb and photos so get them from him. The last three hundred feet of the climb which we climbed down from the top is at an angle of about 80-85 degrees almost but not quite A.P.

The thing is worthy of a description in the SMCJ I think and if you will promise to give it some good illustrations I will promise to write it.

Yours in haste

J Norman Collie

For some reason a separate description of his climb was never published in the SMCJ, despite Collie's obvious enthusiasm about the climb and his passing on a description to Naismith.

❄ ❄ ❄

The first ascent of Church Door Buttress on the 16th July 1898 was in fact only one day in an energetic week during which upwards of eight climbers made several ascents. The week is described by Willie Douglas,[9] and included the first ascent of *Staircase Climb* (215m Very Difficult) on Ben Nevis by Naismith, Bell and Maclay on Tuesday 12th July. This rarely repeated route takes the buttress on the right of Waterfall Gully, entering that gully near its top. It satisfied an ambition to climb Carn Dearg Buttress. Combined tactics were used several times to overcome short but steep walls, and at one point Naismith found himself lying –

> ...helplessly on his stomach, propped up with one boot against a small projection on the side wall, and possessed with the notion that any attempt to stand upright would result in his sliddering downstairs. The rock he reclined on sloped downwards, and moreover was wet and slimy.

The following day saw a party taking the ferry to Ardgour and cycling to the entrance of Coire an Iubhair, the usual route for Garbh Bheinn. Douglas and Maclay were keen on making a repeat ascent of the Great Ridge but following a suggestion by Bell they attempted an entry from the left and instead were forced to follow a shallow gully to just below the summit. The other three meanwhile, Naismith, Bell and JS Napier, made the first ascent of *Pinnacle Ridge* (180m Moderate) right of Great Gully. All five then had an enjoyable descent of the Great Ridge, protected by the rope.

Thursday 14th was an 'off-day', spent cycling. Friday 15th marked an attempt to climb The Chasm on Buachaille Etive Mor. This is the prominent gully on the south-east flank of the mountain, and the five climbed for six hours before abandoning the route at a height of 1,850ft, where a subsidiary gully branched out to the right and a pitch of some 100ft loomed up above. It would be another 22 years before a complete ascent would be made of this major feature. It is described in *Scottish Rock Climbs* as being the best gully in Scotland.[10] At 450m and Very Severe, it is a classic route providing a fine day's expedition with some impressive rock scenery. (See also *Classic Rock* for this, and other, classic routes.[11])

Saturday was of course the day of Church Door Buttress, described above, while on their last day, the group explored the Aonach Eagach ridge, climbing a ridge on the left of '*...the great gully of Meall Dearg*'. This latter is obviously what is now known as Chancellor Gully. Earlier in the year, at Easter, April 1898, William Clark and his wife Jane had climbed rocks, also on the left of *Chancellor Gully* (525m Severe). This ascent was not recorded but a note was left in the Visitors' Book of Clachaig Inn.[12] Other routes on poor ground were recorded, with Rennie and Raeburn poking away at the Cobbler on 3rd July 1898, making a vegetatious traverse on the South Peak with *Grassy Traverse*, and *Cave Route* on the Central Buttress. Their efforts were not in vain however, as both now provide good winter ascents.

The Cobbler had now seen sufficient activity that in a January 1899 article, Herbert Boyd penned a summary of routes thus far. Complete with a few rudimentary sketches, it would form, along with other articles published at intervals, the skeleton of the club's Climber's Guide to Scotland, which had begun with a motion at the AGM on 14th December 1894. The motion was proposed by William Brown, and seconded by Maylard. This book, Brown explained, might be divided into two parts; the first Introductory, with articles on Snowcraft, Rockwork, Equipment, Mountain Photography and so on, and the second part, a more technical part, containing brief accounts of all the Scottish mountains of a certain height or class, with information as to their physical features, from where to climb them, lines of ascent and so on –

> The book ought to be well illustrated, and should also in its introductory portion be as attractive and interesting as possible. In this way a sale would or might be insured among the general public. The time might not be fully ripe for such a work, but competition was threatened which might encroach upon the information in possession of the Club...[13]

The competition mentioned above was not expanded on, but almost certainly included the Abraham brothers, whose Rock Climbing in the English Lake District had been published in 1887. They were in fact spotted on Skye in early 1896, climbing and photographing, though as events happened it would be some years before either the Abrahams or the SMC published a Skye guide.

❄ ❄ ❄

August 1898 saw good weather on Skye and no less than 11 SMC members enjoying it at various times. George Bennett Gibbs recorded their climbs in the SMCJ.[14] About a dozen new routes and variations were done, including *Naismith's Route* (45m Severe) on the Bhasteir Tooth, a climb which the current guidebook describes as '*...a good route in an outrageous position.*' This comment is due to the steep exposure of the climb, one which can intimidate many a Severe leader.

The adjacent summit of Am Bhasteir is often, probably erroneously, given in English as *The Executioner*. The Rev Ronald Burn, SMC member and second Munro completer, was also a keen collector of local names, helped by his ability to speak Gaelic. His opinion was that it meant deeply split, or cleft. This fits, as there is a deeply cut gully or chimney separating the main Basteir Rock from the Basteir Tooth. Burn was also aware of an Am Basdar in Kintail, down whose split '*...a stone thrown can be heard jingling and rattling as it makes its long descent*'. Finally, there is no word like Basteir in Gaelic dictionaries.[15]

The crucial section of Naismith's Route, climbed on the 15th, includes a crack that was first pointed out by Douglas, who was camped out near the Bealach a' Lieter, and was '*...engaged in demolishing a "jam piece"*'. Naismith was climbing with Alexander Morrice Mackay, (later Lord Mackay, and an Edinburgh Advocate and Court of Session Judge). The pair investigated the upper part of the route from above by rope before committing themselves. Gibbs described the route in his article as – '*Though sensational, as any climb on an open face of such steepness is bound to be, the route described is not really difficult...*' It certainly had a major advantage in saving the long descent by the Lota Corrie screes involved in the old route.

Naismith must have been on form this holiday, and was certainly climbing boldly. On the 16th, along with Gibbs, he attempted Deep Gash Gully, on Sgurr a' Mhadaidh. The current guide likens it to Raven's Gully in Glen Coe. They had to avoid the first pitch by a traverse in from the side, then failed on the second pitch, with Naismith climbing by back and foot and finally being stopped by an overhanging block. The gully was not climbed until 1949, and is graded at Hard Very Severe.

On the 17th, Naismith and Gibbs were joined by W Wickham King, who had almost recovered from an injured thumb. As a distinct contrast to the open exposure of Naismith's Route, they began a subterranean campaign, attempting to climb the deep cleft on the north face that separates the Basteir Tooth from the Rock. This finally saw a first ascent by King, Gibbs and the guide John Mackenzie, on the 25th. Its climbability seems to come and go depending on the whim of moving blocks. It is named *King's Cave Chimney*, is graded at Very Difficult, and in 2009 no sign could be seen of a complete route.

❄ ❄ ❄

On the 10th September 1898, Raeburn met Tom Gibson at Fort William. Their target was The Castle on Ben Nevis, being under the impression that it was unclimbed. They had difficulty following the true line of the ridge, due to sheets of slabby rocks that were just too steep to walk up but poorly furnished with holds. On their return home it was Naismith who pointed out that Brown, Maclay, Naismith and Thomson had climbed the Castle during the Easter Meet of 1896. Raeburn had been a guest on that meet. That ascent under snow was made on the Monday of the meet, and was only briefly mentioned in the report of the meet. Raeburn and Gibson therefore, made the first summer ascent. It was strange that Raeburn had not heard of the ascent during the meet, nor read the meet report.

In August 1896, William Clark and a companion named Shannon attempted a gully on Lochnagar, cursed by thick mist all day. They failed just below the top, at a boulder, and accordingly named the gully Tantalus.[16] Unknowingly, they had in fact tried the gully first attempted in winter conditions by Gibson and Douglas in March 1893, now named Douglas-Gibson Gully.

On 12th November 1898, HGS Lawson, Rennie and Raeburn gained the corrie of Lochnagar after a frustrating journey; train delayed by Queen Victoria decamping from Balmoral, trouble with their bicycles, and of course thick mist all day long. Eventually they found the Black Spout and traversed left to gain the foot of a gully. The corrie was not under snow. They roped up at 3.15pm with failing light, but made good progress until they reached a great overhanging chockstone blocking the width of the gully. The leader, probably Raeburn, advanced as far as he could, but several feet separated him from the upper edge of the boulder. Combined tactics reduced this to two feet short. Raeburn described what followed.[17]

> What was now done was, I fear, unorthodox in the extreme, but Lochnagar appears somehow to lend itself to the unorthodox in climbing, and we can plead the demoralising influence of the heterodoxy of the ridge on our left.
>
> The ice-axe was now employed, first to clear away the earth and stones from the upper edge of the block, then the pick was hung upon the edge, the right hand of the leader found a crevice which admitted of its being inserted and half-clenched, then pushing down with the right arm and pulling hard with the left, the body was raised high enough to allow of the left hand being thrown up to catch the edge of the jammed block; instantly the right hand joined it, then a pull, and the right knee was thrown up on the slope of the overhanging chockstone, the body thrust for a second against the slope of the left wall, while the hands were transferred to an upper block; it proved firm, and a hitch was found about 10 feet higher up the gully. The ice-axe, the moment the steady pull was relaxed, slipped off, and bounded away down the gully and was lost.

The rest of the gully proved straightforward, and at 4.45pm they reached the summit in the gloom. Thirty minutes later, after a struggle with the wind and wet, Rennie's candle lantern was lit. They gave up trying to find the path and after – '*... toiling for hours over screes of boulders, besides which the worst and largest of Skye and Glencoe are but a handful of pebbles*', they eventually found a burn which they followed, leading in the dark to a waterfall and a precipice. One of them made the happy suggestion of afternoon tea, so they had bread and jam, chocolate, raisins, and, last but not least, acid drops. Cheered up, they continued down, eventually finding they were on the left bank of the Glas Allt. They sat down to dinner at 10.45pm. The mention of a candle lantern is an early one. Dent's *Mountaineering*, first published in 1885, describes a foldable tin lantern designed by the Italian Alpine Club, with the transparent windows of talc or horn.

They had made the first summer ascent of *Raeburn's Gully* (200m Severe). It was not until 1928 that a second summer ascent was made, using aid at the crux. It gives a very poor summer route, but is an excellent, atmospheric route in winter condition, when its grade can vary markedly. Raeburn's techniques to overcome the crux have a modern feel about them, involving, as they did, hand-jamming, a dynamic move, and a hooked ice-axe. The ascent seems to have raised no eyebrows at the time, at least in print, and given the lack of protection then prevalent, using an ice axe for a hold or clearing a rock of debris was taken in its stride, much as combined tactics were. Collie's infamous move in Moss Ghyll in 1892, when he cut a rock step with his axe, also seems to have passed without comment.

With a self-disciplined sport such as mountaineering, where a climber's peers would soon criticise anything out of the accepted norm, abuse of the known techniques was minimal and short-lived. A rope might be thrown over a flake now and then, but only because there was no other protection possible. Sadly, the crux of Raeburn's Gully has fallen down, at least once, so those hoping to emulate Raeburn's moves will have to try elsewhere.

❄ ❄ ❄

The 1899 Easter Meet of the SMC was held at Kinlochewe, from 30th March to 6th April. As in recent years the weather was poor, and as George Tertius Glover wrote in an excursion report – *'It seems hardly credible that fourteen of us were there for three days, and not a single assault was made on the cliffs of Coire Mhic Fhearchair'.*[18] What did occur was the 'booking' of Lawson, Ling and Glover by Murdo MacDonald, the head keeper at Torridon. He had followed the trio into the mist on Beinn Eighe. This was of course in the bad old days, when almost any walking on the hills was regarded as trespassing. Years later, with easier access, MacDonald mellowed with the times, sufficiently enough that he was given a brief obituary in the SMCJ.[19] However, William Clark had been exploring the region, returning with a report of potential rock. This he found on the cliffs of Allt na Mhuinidh, on the north shore of Loch Maree, visible from the hotel, and marked by a fine waterfall. Clark spent Sunday 2nd April studying and photographing the cliff, and thought he had a route marked out.

On the Monday, three climbers set out from the hotel with 60ft of Alpine rope and 60ft of 'cable ply'. Glover, Clark, and James Gall Inglis, who was a cousin of Clark, headed for the waterfall and Clark's planned route. As Glover remarked – '*…as climbs sometimes do, it looked harder than it really was.*' Combined tactics were used at one point, much heather and other vegetation had to be cleared, and due to poor protection from the quartzite rock, minor variations were made to avoid the steeper and more serious-looking sections. Despite this, the rock was generally helpful with small but incut holds, and the team was very pleased to find a route, the *West Climb* (90m Severe), on such a steep cliff.

The West Climb was, for its time, a bold initiative. Photography was then very popular with Clark an acknowledged expert in the technology; as a professional chemist he became a pioneer of colour photography. His use of photographs to plan a route was also a pointer to the future. Glover (1870–1953), a Locomotive Engineer, would have a long and happy membership in the SMC, joining in 1898 and President from 1928-30.

James Gall Inglis (1865–1939) was an Edinburgh publisher and keen astronomer, publishing *Norton's Star Atlas* and his own updated version of *An Easy Guide to The Constellations*. He was also a Fellow of the Royal Society of Edinburgh. *Norton's* is now in its 20th edition and is the indispensible guide to the night skies for amateur astronomers. The company of Gall and Inglis of Edinburgh and London, also published *The Contour Road Book of Scotland* in 1898, a highly popular guide especially for cyclists, showing distances and gradients (graphically) for all the principal roads. The Internet Archive has digitised it.[20]

Other excursions were made from this Easter Meet at Kinlochewe, and much potential climbing was noted such as on Beinn Eighe, Liathach, Alligin, Sgurr Dubh, Slioch and, perhaps most tantalising of all, on the mountains round the Fionn Loch. With the train service on the Highland Line and a station at Achnasheen about 15km to the east, Kinlochewe was voted to have – *'super-excellence as a climbing centre'*. Several members had cycled in from Achnasheen, The Gateway to Wester Ross. The evenings in the hotel had been – *'...enlivened by Rennie at the piano and the sweet tones of the ex-President's* [Munro's] *flute.'*[21] The Meet had been the first formal visit to this area.

❄ ❄ ❄

On 17th May 1899, the roof of the Summit Hotel on Ben Nevis was barely visible above the snow. (See *Ben Nevis: Britain's Highest Mountain* for details of this, and the Summit Observatory.) Anti-cyclonic weather set in and by 5th June the Hotel was open for business. In an SMCJ article,[22] Inglis Clark described how he and his wife Jane decided that – *'... in the absence of a Club hut at the foot of the Tower Ridge, an excellent if not better substitute could be found in the hotel on the summit itself.'* This comment would turn out to be eerily prescient, as such a hut would indeed be built just over a quarter of a century later, with funds supplied by the Clarks in memory of their son.

So the Clarks waited for a good weather forecast and on Monday 12th June boarded the afternoon train to Fort William for an evening ascent. They arranged their luggage in four rucksacks to go up by horseback the next day, and by 10pm they had gained the half-way hut on foot. They found the views too interesting to sleep however, and wrapped in flapping bed-clothes, attempted to photograph the view. All this activity and lack of sleep naturally lessened their energies, and an easy day was taken on the 13th, including a visit to the Great Tower. This was an early outing for Jane Clark, who would rapidly develop her experience and become a pioneer of female mountaineering in Scotland.

The following day they climbed their primary target on the mountain, North-East Buttress. They descended from the Carn Mor Dearg arête into Coire Leis and used the sloping ledge of broken ground which leads to the First Platform as a shortcut to the crest of the ridge. Their ascent went easily until they reached the 10ft barrier of the Man-Trap. Here combined tactics were normally used to gain higher hand holds, but on this occasion, climbing with his wife, this was deemed to be impracticable. They took instead a variation down and right. This led to a very steep corner which corresponded in many ways to the 40ft corner as described by William Brown – '*...but apparently quite different...*' There were nail scratches at its foot, but not further up, while some of the holds were covered in undisturbed moss. Up this nonetheless went Clark, followed by the rucksack, then Jane.

Clark decided that although Tower Ridge offered the finest climbing, its views were mostly confined to the north-east face, whereas North-East Buttress provided a more extensive outlook. The Castle Ridge and gullies had poorer rock, though Clark felt that nowhere in Scotland had he witnessed finer rock scenery than that to be found in Castle Corrie. The following day they descended Castle Ridge, with progress constantly delayed by steep faces. The aim of the day was to obtain photographs of the face, and here we should recall that as well as Clark's personal interest in that hobby, he would be thinking also of the guidebook work at which the SMC was now beavering away.

They finally gained the fork of the gully on the east flank of Castle Ridge, where North and South Castle Gullies begin. The Castle rocks were too high for a good photograph, but Clark recommended that photographers should cross the avalanche screes to the edge of Carn Dearg Buttress, from where, with its stupendous walls above, there would be superb views of the cliffs. This spot, Clark continued, could easily be gained from below. They now descended into the valley of the Allt a' Mhuilinn and so down.

They recommended the Summit Hotel – '*The charges (previously arranged) were remarkably moderate, the food ample, fresh, and excellent, and our general comfort attended to in every way.*'

❄ ❄ ❄

The remainder of 1899 seems to have passed with very little climbing being recorded. It was as if a first great wave of exploration had finally broken on a rocky shore and the waters were calm again. Some of this calm can be explained by a succession of SMC meets experiencing poor weather. There was also a feeling that 10 years of the SMC presented a time to pause and look back at what had been accomplished. The article by Maylard referred to above did just that. At this time, various active members of the SMC were also sitting at their desks with pen in hand, writing up sections for the first SMC guidebook.

In proposing this guide, the SMC might just have bitten off a lump too far. In the January 1901 issue of the SMCJ,[23] Willie Douglas, who was the guidebook editor in addition to being journal editor, was honest enough to confess that he had – '*...met with insuperable difficulties in completing the work in the form originally contemplated...*' He therefore proposed to publish portions of it in the pages of the Journal. This would at least, he wrote, allow members to have the use of what had already been written and allow him to have the benefit of corrections and suggestions. The difficulty may have included a shortage of funds with which to publish a separate guidebook, the data for which was not complete in any case. Douglas would have been under pressure from impatient mountaineers to publish material, wishing to know what had been done and where.

There was certainly a continuing hint of competition in the air as it was known that the Abraham brothers were making visits to Scotland, including Skye, in May 1896, taking many photographs for commercial purposes. But perhaps the most devastating visit made by the Abrahams was in May 1900, when with James W Puttrell and Ernest A Baker they made the direct line up Crowberry Ridge on the Buachaille Etive Mor in Glen Coe, taking the difficult rock which Naismith had looked at four years earlier but declined to climb. Before that event is described however, lay two SMC Meets; the 1900 New Year Meet, held at Inveroran, and the 1900 Easter Meet, held at Kinlochewe.

❄ ❄ ❄

On Thursday, 28th December 1899, the West Highland Train reached Bridge of Orchy just before 7pm. It had a snow plough on the engine, so deep was the snow, as four passengers were set down. JG Inglis was there, with L Inglis, his cousin and member of the New Zealand Alpine Club as a guest. HT Munro was also present, as was a Perthshire protégé of his and the reporter for the meet, John Gilbert Hay Halkett, a barrister who joined the SMC in 1900. Such was the amount and quality of the snow that no routes were climbed, but several of the popular mountains were laboriously ascended over the weekend. On the first morning, the entire establishment slept in. That evening, Robert Ernest Workman arrived from Glasgow.

On the Saturday 30th, Stob Ghabhar was the target. While Halkett and Munro walked, the two Inglis cousins and Workman attempted the Upper Couloir but were rebuffed by difficulties near the top. Munro cheered up

Halkett by stating that he could not recall snow in worse condition, being deep, soft, and very tiring. That evening Henry Lawson arrived from Edinburgh. No other mountaineers arrived by the evening train; in their place was a letter and a plum pudding sent by President Maylard from the Loch Awe Hotel, where '*...a contingent of renegades*' were staying. When the letter made it clear that two other Office Bearers were there as well, those on the official meet arranged for Munro to send an indignant New Year's Day telegram.

Sunday 31st saw even worse weather; high winds and heavy rain. The party even agreed it was not a day for the hills. However, Halkett, who was obviously thinking about his membership application, with Lawson walked the 19 miles to Kingshouse and back in rain and sleet, while the others stayed cosily at the Inn. At dinner the plum pudding appeared as a peace offering, and later Munro played on his flute. New Year's Day was slightly better, and Meall a' Bhuiridh and Clach Leathad were ascended. The Meet broke up the following day. Halkett, whose proposer for the SMC was Munro, seconded by Lawson, joined the club the following September. He eventually moved south, resigned in 1919 and became a magistrate in London.

The 1900 SMC Easter Meet, as in the previous year, was held at Kinlochewe, from Thursday, April 12th through to Tuesday 17th. The highlight of the meet was the first winter ascent of the Northern Pinnacles on Liathach, on Monday 16th. This was made by five on the Meet, followed by a traverse east to Glen Torridon. The actual section with the Pinnacles is a short and sharp 200m II. The five were Naismith and Mackay on one rope, Raeburn, Inglis and Willie Ling on the other. The Meet report was by Mackay, a light-hearted, lightly-written account, which began with a down-to-earth dig at Munro – '*The Easter Meet lasted from Thursday evening to Tuesday morning,... Munro forming a fringe of one at each end. (He was found in his slippers and left in bed.)*'[24]

William Norman Ling (1873–1953) was a Grain Merchant from Carlisle, and SMC President from 1919-22. In 1901 he had been rejected for membership in the Alpine Club as being insufficiently qualified. He thus joined a select group of mountaineers who would be rejected by this club but who would later prove to be more than worthy. Later on the AC did recant, and he ended up as Vice-President from 1929-30. He was active on the mountains right up to the year he died, and was particularly active with Raeburn as a regular partner, making notable guideless climbs in Norway, the Alps and the Caucasus. He attended over 100 SMC Meets, probably a record.[25] It is quite possible that climbing with the more prominent Raeburn may have limited the development and recognition of his own substantial mountaineering talent.

❄ ❄ ❄

The following month, the Abraham brothers had driven up to Glen Coe by car from Arrochar, where they had climbed and photographed on the Cobbler. Initially they stayed at the Kingshouse Inn, having met up with Jim Puttrell and Prof Ernest A Baker who arrived by train at Bridge of Orchy. Puttrell is regarded as an important pioneer of gritstone climbing,[26] while Baker, who joined the SMC in 1916, also climbed on gritstone and was the author of *The British Highlands with Rope & Rucksack* (1933). On Wednesday 23rd May, the quartet felt they were ready for Crowberry Ridge. The party stayed at the Clachaig Hotel from the 26th-29th May, and it is in the Visitors' Log that Ashley left the first description of the crucial section from the ledge. The climb begins easily, about 65ft leading to a ledge. Naismith's Route and other variations lie to the right, while above is a steep wall. The steep crest of the ridge is on the left –

> ...a traverse was made, from a small platform, to the left (looking upward) along the perpendicular face for about 6 feet; then some awkward steep slabs follow for about 25 ft. Easier rocks lead up to a good platform where the leader can anchor the rest of the party...the traverse from the small platform & the slabs beyond it, were found to be difficult. With wet rocks it is questionable whether this part would 'go' but with dry, warm rocks it is to be recommended to strong parties.[27]

More details are to be found in George Abraham's book –

> The hand-holds were scanty for the traverse along this narrow way, and only just sufficient to make the balancing of the body possible. To add to the sensational uncertainty, the rocks were slightly moist at this point. After working carefully to the left for a few feet the foot-holds dwindled away to nothingness, and the only means of obviating the defeat was to tackle the smooth bulge of rock that slanted upwards in an almost hopeless-looking manner.[28]

And lastly, Ernest Baker recalled the moment in his 1933 book, finally identifying the leader –

> George Abraham led up in brilliant style. Anxiously we watched him quit the platform, stepping out upon a tiny ledge with his left toe, and, moving cautiously leftward and gradually up, disappear from our sight. The rope went out by inches, and we waited in dead silence for a shout to say that the distant platform was won. The shout was a long time in coming. At length, the eighty-footer was nearly all paid out, and then the welcome cry came from above with a summons to the next man.[29]

The 225m climb, known as *Direct Route*, is still graded Severe and given three stars, an accolade in the climbing guides published by the SMC and defined as – '*...an outstanding route of the highest quality, combining superb climbing with line, character and situation.*' There is no doubting the rock which is of excellent quality, nor the situation which would find many a leader shaking, while the line takes a soaring ridge up one of Scotland's finest mountains. Its ascent was mentioned with a telling final comment in an SMCJ review of a series of photographs taken by the Abrahams in May of 1900. The initials would be those of William Douglas –

> Messrs Abraham, of Keswick, have very kindly given me the opportunity of looking over an excellent series of photographs which they obtained in Scotland last May…it goes without saying that they are nearly all good…
>
> Among the climbs which they did and illustrated were the Church Door of Bidean nam Bian and the Crowberry Ridge of Buchaille Etive. Of the latter climb Mr Ashley Abraham speaks in most enthusiastic terms. It was done for the first time directly from the foot of the ridge, and not joined by the gully at the side as had previously been the route. He is quite of the opinion that they have "nothing so continuously good in the Lakes." This, taken with the offer to swop Buchaille for Great Gables (S.M.C.J., Vol. IV., p. 149), looks as if the great climbers of the Lakes were beginning to realise that there are hills in Great Britain outside Cumberland. W.D.[30]

Ashley Abraham sent in a description of several climbs to the Editor of the SMCJ. His notes were published in the May 1902 issue, and included Direct Route. The description mentioned that a diagram published in the SMCJ (Vol.5, p.235) misled the party considerably, as the written descriptions were at variance with the diagram.

He must have enjoyed both the Clachaig Hotel and the climbing in Glen Coe, for he was back in October 1900 for a honeymoon holiday with his wife Winifred. In the same note as Direct Route he described first ascents of *Lady's Gully* (200m Very Difficult) on the Buachaille, and *Winifred's Pinnacle* (30m Difficult), a rocky pinnacle found in the Amphitheatre in the basin high on the west face of Aonach Dubh.

An important variation to a popular climb was made on 6th September. 1900, when Willie Naismith and the Rev AE Robertson worked out the *Eastern Traverse* on the face of the Great Tower on Tower Ridge.[31] Until then, climbers had followed the original route on the western face, technically harder with an awkward crux. Instead, the new variation followed a narrow grass ledge to the left, went through a cleft bridged by a huge block (which to date has remained), then climbed straight up broken rocks to the top of the Tower.

As Naismith suggested, if so wished the Tower could even be completely avoided by a traverse into what is now named as Tower Gully (which then was still referred to as the easy right branch of Gardyloo Gully, itself now known as Observatory Gully).

❄ ❄ ❄

The New Year 1901 SMC Meet was held at Loch Awe Hotel. On the night of Saturday 29th December, six inches of snow fell but the threatened rain held off. On Sunday morning a large contingent walked to Dalmally, where they divided their attentions between–

"The Auld Kirk, the cauld kirk, the kirk withoot the people,

And the wee kirk, the Free Kirk, the kirk withoot the steeple."[32]

The verse above was a popular rhyme at the time of the 1843 disruption. This was a schism within the established Church of Scotland, in which 450 ministers of the Church broke away over the issue of the Church's relationship with the State, to form the Free Church of Scotland. It was a climax of a bitter conflict within the established Church, and had huge effects not only within the Church, but also upon Scottish civic life.

Meanwhile, Raeburn, George Sang and Mackay headed for the Black Shoot with a 60ft rope and ice axes. Raeburn described the ascent in an SMCJ article,[33] and, obviously disappointed by fellow members' disparaging comments on the poor quality of the route, wrote that subsequent visits to the climb since its first ascent were, in his opinion, fewer than the merits the climb deserved. He did qualify this by explaining that the conditions of the climb for their ascent, although not making the climb any easier, probably accounted for the comfortable cleanness and practical dryness with which the party arrived at the summit.

Raeburn remarked that 60ft of rope was inadequate, and that 80ft would have been a better length. It would, of course, be heavier, a point which almost certainly held back the use of longer ropes, especially in wet conditions. The three climbers took 95 minutes for this first winter ascent, for what is now down as a Grade III. When the Abrahams and their companions made the first ascent of Direct Route on Crowberry Ridge, they were using an 80ft rope, though it is unclear whether this was for all four climbers.

Returning to the SMC project for a Guide to Scottish Mountains, Willie Douglas included in the January issue of 1901 an outline of the guide. It would fall naturally into six divisions, the first being the Southern Highlands. The divisions were then broken into groups; the Southern Highlands was considered to have 36 groups, the first being Ben Lomond, the second the Arrochar group and so on. Some 11 groups of that first division had so far not been allocated, and the Editor inserted a journal note asking for information. A full description of the first group, Ben Lomond, then followed, and included a fine diagram of the North-East Face of Ben Lomond with routes indicated.

The May 1901 issue of the SMCJ contained groups 2 to 5 from Division 1 of the guidebook, including the Arrochar Group and prominent hills in the Southern Highlands. These were accompanied by photographs taken by Inglis Clark, as well as line drawings (artist unnamed). The Southern Highlands continued in the January 1901 and May 1902 issues, while in September 1902 the Ben Nevis section was published. This production line approach continued through to September 1907, when the long-awaited section on Skye came out. The three issues of 1908 saw the other islands described.

There the matter stalled, as the SMC found that although it had amassed sufficient data to produce a healthy guidebook, it lacked the funds to do so. There would be some revision required, some hills were not described and the estimated cost of publishing what they thought could be a 1,000-page book with illustrations was £300. This approximates to about £31,000 in 2014 terms, and as the only income of the SMC was through subscriptions, the cost was too high.

Then, in January 1911 relief arrived, when the club received a letter from AA Mitchell, Secretary of the Gaiter Club, along with a cheque for £100. (The Gaiter Club has been described in Chapter Two.) The donation was sufficient impetus for the SMC to form a sub-committee consisting of Clark, Goggs, Raeburn and Russell, as well as six sub-editors for the six area divisions. The outcome of this will be treated in a later chapter.

❄ ❄ ❄

The third visit to Fort William for an Easter Meet took place from the 4th to 9th April, 1901. By Saturday night some 31 climbers were present at the Alexandra Hotel. Highlights included the second ascent of Observatory Gully by Raeburn and Lawson. This was the original name for what is now Gardyloo Gully, as the early climbers regarded it as the north-east branch of Observatory Gully.

Raeburn's ascent of Gardyloo Gully is a pointer to how far Raeburn had come as a winter climber when on Saturday 6th, with Lawson, he had made the second ascent. Leading the crux of the day, with Lawson safely belayed in an ice cave, Raeburn had to tackle the ice-fall above, and, let us not forget, with the overlong ice axe then used. Raeburn described the crux moves –

> The difficulty was to get at the ice-fall. It was so steep in a direct line overhanging, that pulling-in handholds were absolutely necessary; these had to be made. I managed to work up the jaws of the cave far enough to get a good undergrip for the right arm, below a great spout of ice that shot out over the overhanging lip, and then cut a handhold and toestep for the left hand and foot out on the face of the ice-fall to the left. The strain was severe, and I had to

> twice descend to the cave for rest. Ascending for the third time, I stepped up and out to the left, and now with axe in the right, worked at the weakest part of the fall above. Luckily breaking right through here into a hole behind the ice, I thrust my hand in, and felt with satisfaction the magnificent hold given by a clenched fist.[34]

What we have to recall is that the long axes then in use were designed to be used for cutting steps with both arms; it demanded much strength and a huge effort to cut steps using one arm as Raeburn described above. Looking back at the equipment and techniques, it seems almost ludicrous that shorter axes were not adopted, but these mountaineers were coming from an Alpine background, with long approaches over glaciers and a preference for snow over ice. Additionally, on descent, either walking down or glissading, a short axe would not be fully practical. As late as the early 1960s in the UK, it was not possible to purchase a short axe suitable for steep snow and ice; one bought a wooden shafted axe then had it shortened. The balance might not be ideal, but at least one handed cutting was less of a trial of strength and stamina.

Raeburn was not ignoring new equipment; he had tried Kletterschuhe on the Salisbury Crags, finding that they made the climbing easier but wore down too easily. These rope-soled shoes had been described in OG Jones' book *Rock-Climbing in the English Lake District*. Arranging some climbing in the Lakes with John Bell, Raeburn decided that Slingsby's Chimney on Steep Gill would provide a good test for these climbing shoes. His findings were that they were only useful for a short steep climb on pure rock, where it was essential not to slip.

> There is usually too much moisture, moss, and grass on our average British climbs to render it worth while to carry these shoes, evolved as they have been to suit a special district [i.e. the Dolomites]. In Skye they are not required, and indeed would not last more than a couple of hours on the razor-edged, crystalline rocks of the Coolins.[35]

The day was approaching when climbers would find that safe climbing could advance no further without better equipment; lighter, stronger ropes allowing longer pitches to be climbed, and some method of protecting a pitch for the leader in between belays. The best a leader could do was to make use of the occasional hitch, carefully making the rope run over a suitable rock projection in the hope that it would lessen the height of any fall. Raeburn's book *Mountaineering Art* was published in 1920, though he had completed it several years earlier, the war delaying its publication.[36] (Apparently, after the war he could not find the manuscript, and had to re-write the book. This he completed in three months.[37]) We may consider, therefore, that his book summed up his take on the state of the art as practised at the end of the first decade of the 20th century.

There have been several comments on his book, stating that it was out of date on publication. As mountaineering practice did not markedly advance until the 1920s, as a general criticism this can be taken with a pinch of salt. We have already noted his style of rock climbing as differing from others, but there had been no real advance in equipment, and certainly none in protection. Commenting on Scotland between the wars in *Mountaineering in Britain*, Clark and Pyatt quote a reviewer of Raeburn's book, who stated that –

> Raeburn is weak on the use of the rope in British climbing – 'he omits to mention how the active rope should be held by the man above when the party is moving singly, and the succeeding climber is attacking a difficult pitch'.[38]

In this respect, Clark and Pyatt concluded – *'Mountaineering Art was undoubtedly somewhat out of date as far as some aspects of technique are concerned.'* Reading Raeburn's section on Rock Climbing, it does go to some length to describe how the climbers move on a rock climb, and how the rope should be handled so as to safeguard them. It is true that only once does Raeburn remark just where the rope runs with a belayer, and this was when assisting a second climber up a very steep section, when the rope runs behind the small of the belayer's back. The reviewer may have missed this.

From the frequent use of hitches in the early days, the preferred method of belaying while bringing up a climber, was to pass the rope over or behind a rock, using the friction there should it be necessary to hold a fall. If there was no hitch, it would seem that the belayer held the rope in his hands, keeping it taut so that should a second climber slip or fall, there should be little movement of the rope, the stretch of the rope and the belayer's strength of grip hopefully being enough to hold the climber. Obviously, the belayer's feet would have to be suitably braced. All in all, it was a very high risk method. We have earlier seen how, on an ascent in Arran, Raeburn had run the rope over his tweed-clad knees for more friction, while fielding the second man.

Raeburn suggested that 80ft of rope would suffice for a party of three; he thought that should a longer rope be used, a longer fall would cause serious internal damage to the climber, assuming the rope did not break. He would certainly attest to this personally, given his accident on Stuc a' Chroin in 1910. (See Chapter 14.) There was no mention of protection while leading a pitch, other than the use of hitches. Combined tactics, standing on a second's back, shoulders, or even head, though widely used in earlier decades, was regarded by Raeburn as a potentially dangerous practice. He mentions in his book that —

> I can personally vouch for the fact that the only occasion, during many years' climbing as leader, on which I got into a position where advance was impossible

> and retreat dangerous, was when I had accepted assistance from "combined tactics." [39]

As for ice axes, Raeburn commented that he felt the gradual shortening of the axe had gone far enough, recommending a length of 41 inches (1.04m). '*Indeed,*' he wrote – '*the extra short pattern of axe, evolved by a well-known amateur, has only succeeded in becoming quite useless as an alpenstock, while of very small service as a hatchet.*' [40] [The 'well-known amateur' was unnamed by Raeburn, though one good candidate was Oscar Eckenstein (1859–1921), a prominent English alpinist, innovator in winter equipment and techniques, and by no means an amateur at mountaineering.] This was of course before the use of crampons for safer movement over snow and ice became common in Britain. The great majority of axes were still made in the Alpine countries, where one of their functions was in sounding out crevasses.

Eckenstein assisted Geoffrey Winthrop Young in the compilation of Young's book *Mountain Craft*, published in 1920.[41] In that book, JP Farrar recommends an axe of 39 inches (99cm), but this was given as the length of the stock or handle. Adding a typical two inches for the height of the head would lead to some 41 inches (104cm) overall, the same as that given in Raeburn's book. Young mentions that his personal axe measured 36 inches (99cm), which although better for step cutting, made it short for downhill work. He continues to describe Eckenstein's axe, which was 34 inches (86cm) overall, with a much smaller head. '*The few who have used it in conjunction with the special crampons claim for the combination advantages in difficult ice.*' Indeed, on steep snow and ice, the seven-inch difference would make an appreciable impact on the effort involved in cutting steps. The author, who started climbing before front pointing was introduced, used a wooden shafted axe which after being shortened twice was 21 inches (54cm) long overall.

Finally, in Young's book, which at some 603 pages was one of the most detailed techniques book ever published, there is a section on the use of axe on rocks. In this, Young describes how one or two guides in the Alps perfected a useful trick.

> When a vertical or sloping crack in a slab gets too small even to admit a finger, and all other holds are lacking, they force the point of the pick into the crack above their heads, and give a slight outward and upward twist to the shaft with the wrist, so that the point of the pick and its square edges are jammed slantwise and upwards in the crack. Holding the shaft rigid in this position, they then raise their weight by sheer strength inside the bent arm which holds the shaft…[42]

So there is nothing new about torquing, as this technique is now called. Young continues to note that this demands exceptional strength and skill.

What is mentioned occasionally in early Scottish mountaineering is the use of an axe in summer not only to help clear vegetation and loose rocks, but also as an extra hold above the head, jamming the pick in a suitable crack when nothing else is found. The use of an axe as a belay when nothing else was available was avoided by Young, preferring not to fall.

Despite these limitations, on this Fort William Meet the main item as regards history was an outrageous attempt on a winter ascent of Observatory Buttress. *'To some it is given to achieve success lightly; to others, after strenuous efforts, to fail nobly is the reward.'* So began a report by Willie Ling, of a long day spent on Ben Nevis by Ling, Raeburn, Douglas and Rennie on Monday 8th April.

The quartet walked into the corrie on Nevis on a pleasant, warm morning. Soft snow was pouring down over the rocks as Ling attempted the start of the buttress. This consisted of very steep rock, with holds covered by sheets of ice. Ling had to retreat and Raeburn took over the lead, finally gaining a ledge. Continuing up and right via ledges they gained an ice-slope about 200ft up the buttress, which they used to traverse left to the buttress edge. Conditions were now worse and it was late afternoon, making a finish before nightfall impossible.

They retreated the way they had come up and decided to head for the Observatory via the Carn Mor Dearg arête. On reaching this they found themselves in a full-blown blizzard, but struggling upwards they gained the Observatory just after 5pm. The wind, they were informed, was blowing at 40mph. After an hour's rest they continued down into the teeth of the gale, which, despite careful compass work, blew them off course further south and into a rough gully. Luckily they were not too far south and reached the road in Glen Nevis safely, and the hotel about 11pm.

Observatory Buttress was not climbed in winter until 1960, and the easiest route is still a Grade V. The 1901 party was a strong team but even so the boldness of the attempt and the fact that they managed 200ft in poor conditions with the minimal equipment of the day is impressive.

The last two years had seen Scottish climbing reach a cusp in its development; there was a feeling that changes had, and were, taking place. Despite the continuing lack of protection on rocks, the leading climbers were becoming more confident on steeper ground. Mixed climbing, taking in iced or snow covered rocks, was a growing trend, perhaps best demonstrated with the audacious attempt on Observatory Buttress. There was a group of leading climbers with Raeburn at its pinnacle, and a series of published and continuing guide sections pointing the way. Competition was also in the air, and the hunt was on.

References

1. Bell, J.H. *The "Church-Door" Buttress on Bidean nam Bian*. SMCJ, 5, 27, Sept. 1898, 135-140.
2. Jones, Owen Glynne. *Rock-Climbing in the English Lake District*. (London: Longmans, Green & Co., 1897.)
3. Clark, Ronald W., Pyatt, Edward C. *Mountaineering in Britain*. (London: Phoenix House, 1957), 117.
4. Maylard, Ernest A. *Scottish Mountaineering: Retrospective and Prospective*. SMCJ, 5, 30, Sept. 1899, 308-314.
5. Maylard, Ernest. '*Memories and Musings of a Hospital Surgeon*' (Glasgow. Maclehose, Jackson & Co., 1920)
6. <http://en.wikipedia.org/wiki/Laparotomy>
7. Collie, Norman. *A Reverie*. SMCJ, 5, 27, Sept. 1898, 93-102.
8. Fraser, Andrew A. *Personal Communication*, Dec. 2013.
9. Douglas, W. *A Week's Climbing in the Ben Nevis District.* SMCJ, 5, 27, Sept. 1898, 126-134.
10. Nisbet, Andy. *Scottish Rock Climbs*. (Scottish Mountaineering Trust, 2005.)
11. Wilson, Ken. Classic Rock (London: Bâton Wicks, 2007, 2nd edition.)
12. W.W.N [W.W. Naismith] *Entry in Visitors' Book*, Clachaig Hotel, for 8th-10th April, 1898.
13. Proceedings of the Club. SMCJ, 3, 16, Jan. 1895, 228-230.
14. Gibbs, G.Bennett. *August at Sligachan*. SMCJ, 5, 28 Jan. 1899, 164-175.
15. Drummond, Peter. *Scottish Hill Names*. (Scotland: Scottish Mountaineering Trust, 2nd Edition, 2007, 88.)
16. Clark, W. Inglis. *Lochnagar and Ben Nevis*. SMCJ, 4, 22, Jan. 1897, 218-223.
17. Raeburn, Harold. *A November Evening on Lochnagar*. SMCJ 5, 28, Jan. 1899, 176-181.
18. Glover, Geo. T. *Allt na Mhuinidh Waterfall: West Climb*. In: Excursions, SMCJ, 5, 29, May, 1899, 257-260.
19. Glover, G.T. *Murdo MacDonald*. In Memorium, SMCJ 24, 139, May 1948, 65.
20. <https://archive.org/details/contourroadbooko00ingl> (Accessed 2nd June 2014).
21. Hinxman, L. *The Easter Meet at Kinloch Ewe*. 30th March to 6th April 1899. In: Proceedings of the Club. SMCJ 5, 29, May 1899, 254.
22. Clark, W. Inglis. *Four Days on Ben Nevis*. SMCJ, 5, 30, Sept. 1899, 287-297.
23. *S.M.C. Guide Book*. SMCJ, 6, Jan. 1901, 34, 111.
24. Mackay, A.M. *The Kinlochewe Meet – April 1900*. In: Proceedings of the Club. SMCJ 6, 31, May 1900, 59-60.
25. Jeffrey, Robert. In Memorium: *William Norman Ling*, 1873-1953. SMCJ, 25, 145, May 1954. 255-256.
26. Craddock, J. *Jim Puttrell: Pioneer Climber & Cave Explorer* (Troubador Publishing Ltd., 2009.)
27. *Ashley Abraham's record for May 23rd 1900*, Clachaig Hotel Visitors' Book, 1889-1904, property of Mr & Mrs Gourlay, (S.M.C. archive, National Library of Scotland. Acc. 11538/14.)

28. Abraham, George. *The Complete Mountaineer*, (London: Methuen, 1907, Third Edition, Revised 1923, 223.) Also available on archive.org <https://archive.org/details/cu31924029876566> (Accessed June 2014).
29. Baker, E.A. *The British Highlands with Rope & Rucksack*. (Witherby, 1933)
30. Douglas, W. *Review in Mountaineering Literature* of Abraham's Series of Photographs of the Cobbler, Buchaille Etive., Bidean nam Bian, and Ben Nevis, 6 by 8, in Platinotype.1s. 6d.Each.
31. Naismith, W.W. *Ben Nevis, Tower Ridge*. In: Excursions. SMCJ 6, January 1901, 131.
32. *The New Year's Meet at Loch Awe, 1901*. In: Proceedings of the Club. SMCJ, 6, 35, May 1901, 204-209.
33. Raeburn, Harold. *The Black Shoot – In White*. SMCJ, 6, 35, 161-166.
34. Raeburn, Harold. *Ben Nevis—The Observatory Gully*. In Excursions: SMCJ 6, 36, Sept. 1901,251-252.
35. Raeburn, Harold. *Kletterschuhe in the Lakes*. Ibid.
36. Raeburn, Harold. *Mountaineering Art*. (London: T. Fisher Unwin, 1920.)
37. Quoted in *Harold Raeburn – The Final Journey*. Mike Jacob, SMCJ 40, 199, 2008, 41-51.
38. Reviewer. R.C.J. 4, 173 (1921).
39. Raeburn, Harold. *Mountaineering Art*, 191.
40. Ibid. *Mountaineering Art* 22.
41. Young, Geoffrey Winthro *Mountain Craft*. (London: Methuen & Co. Ltd., 3rd edition 1934, 92). (Mountain Craft has been digitised and may be found at: <http://www.scribd.com/doc/30624009/1920-Mountain-Craft>).
42. Ibid. 206.

10

The Aristocrat of Climbs (1901-03)

TOWARDS THE END of June 1901, William and Jane Inglis Clark decided to explore the cliffs of Nevis, using the summit hotel as a base. Accordingly, they informed Raeburn by telegram then walked up the mountain on Friday 21st. They had been on Skye in appalling weather, exploring several faces including the eastern faces of Clach Glas and Bla Bheinn. Their outings there had given their confidence a boost.

The weather was still changeable and by the time they gained the hotel they had been completely soaked by a passing thunderstorm. Indeed, the storm raged all night, and Clark notes that – '*...so saturated was the atmosphere, that even in bed one's hair dripped with moisture, and the walls and ceiling streamed with water*'.[1]

The use of the summit hotel, though it meant the total ascent of the mountain, paid off if staying for more than one night, as it was usually easy to drop down off the summit to the start of a route. The Clarks would often climb together, and later this would include their daughter Mabel and son Charles.

Raeburn meanwhile took advantage of the new Mallaig Railway, as an early train now left Edinburgh at 4.30am, reaching Fort William before 10am. However, he was unable at such short notice to find a climbing companion, and walked alone through a heavy rain shower, to gain the foot of Observatory Ridge as the mists began to rise.

This fine ridge had obviously been his target, and he decided to make a solo attempt, traversing a steep snowfield until he was able to step onto the rocks of the ridge. He found that it gave a more defined route than its neighbour, the North-East Buttress, though with no section as awkward as the Man-trap on that route.

Observatory Ridge (420m Very Difficult) was the last of the great Nevis features to be climbed, but oddly it was addressed by Raeburn in lesser terms, possibly as it was not a plain and obviously prominent route all the way to the summit, merging into the main bulk of the cliff below the plateau edge. Still, he wrote – '*One might as well say that the Zmutt or Furgg Ridges were not the obvious routes up the Matterhorn, but are they any worse as climbs for that?*'[2] He noted three distinctly good bits on the ridge: the slabby rocks near the foot, a hand traverse a few hundred feet up, and, most time consuming of all, over half-way up where a very steep tower spanned the ridge. He tried a direct approach to this, but judging it too risky, found an alternative on the right. Even this involved climbing a '*slightly sensational*' corner, which other than a small ledge had a direct drop of several hundred feet.

At the top he built the traditional cairn then basked in the sun. His happiness at completing this fine route, the hardest of the three great Nevis ridges, was compounded by hearing an initially strange bird song. A keen ornithologist, Raeburn recognised it as being that of the snow bunting, (*Plectrophenax nivalis*), a popular bird well known to winter climbers on Nevis. Raeburn's companion was a splendid male in full summer plumage '*…singing sweetly, with utterly unbunting-like notes, from a rock projecting from the snow below the brow of the cliff.*'

Meanwhile, the Clarks were eventually tempted out by improving weather and in the afternoon descended Number Four Gully and traversing under the Carn Dearg Buttress scrambled up Ledge Route, first climbed in 1895. At the top they met up with Raeburn. That night it stormed again, but cleared the next morning. The trio descended Tower Ridge, climbed up the short side of the Douglas Boulder, then made their way down to the corrie via the East Ridge of the Boulder and faced the North-East Buttress.

By now they felt they were on a roll, and decided to attempt a first ascent of Observatory Buttress. Unfortunately, just after they had started the climb the weather broke again and they abandoned the attempt. Raeburn of course had attempted a winter ascent the previous April.

They then made for the North-East Buttress, climbed up to the First Platform by a combination of Slingsby's Chimney and the rocks on its left, and carried on up the ridge. Inglis Clark acted as a ladder to help overcome the Man-trap, but unable to second it due to its slippery wetness he managed to climb rocks on the left.

At the summit, the staff at the Observatory informed them that the temperature was one degree Fahrenheit above freezing. This set them in agreement with the observers that wind and rain, at this temperature, are more trying than a snowstorm with several degrees of frost. And so ended their summit holiday.

❄ ❄ ❄

On 14th July, Raeburn turned his attention eastwards, to make yet another attempt at climbing Douglas-Gibson Gully on Lochnagar. On this occasion he was accompanied by William Garden and George Duncan. Duncan was an almost exact contemporary of Garden, and an Aberdeen advocate. He had been proposed for the SMC by William Brown, who had been his classmate at University. He died in September 1949, in his 80th year.

Despite battling in the gully for eight hours, they failed near the top. Their descent in the gully was made more perilous by the fact that earlier they had made traverses to avoid an overhanging block. This they finally managed to descend by rope, which then jammed and had to be cut. All this while wet rocks and water in the gully made their incarceration all the more miserable.

It would be some time before advances in equipment and techniques allowed safer mountaineering to be practised. In the meantime, as the following first ascent illustrates, some routes were pioneered by sheer perseverance, combined tactics, tolerance of, and skill at overcoming rotten rock, loose vegetation, running water, and, occasionally, matrimonial anxiety.

❄ ❄ ❄

Lehmann James Oppenheimer (1868–1916) was a Manchester man who learned his climbing on gritstone. Studying art at Manchester College, he became an expert at ecclesiastical design and renovation, excelling in mosaics. He left several first ascents in the Lakes, of which *Bowfell Buttress* (110m Very Difficult) is probably the most popular. A member of the Climbers' Club and the *Fell & Rock Climbing Club* of the English Lake District (FRCC), he was on holiday on Arran in August 1901, with his wife and brother. Spotting the gullies on Beinn Nuis from the shore, he determined to investigate further, describing the outcome in a detailed and entertaining article in the SMCJ.[3]

He made an initial investigation with his wife, climbing one of the easy gullies on the left of the face, and traversing rightward below the top to enter the final section of a great curving chimney which had caught his eye from below. He had found an earlier description of the face by William Clark,[4] during which Clark and Raeburn had undergone a dangerous experience while trying the granite slabs on the face. This defeat spurred on Oppenheimer, particularly as he was about to be joined by two other hard English climbers, Baker and Puttrell, who would drop in on the island for a day before heading north to the Cairngorms.

On 18th August, a party of six headed up the hill. Oppenheimer's wife Edith, with Mrs Baker and Oppenheimer's brother, decided to walk round and join the trio at the top, after which they could all follow the ridge to Cir Mhor. Baker and Puttrell thought that a maximum of two hours would suffice for the ascent of the curving chimney. With the ladies waiting below to watch the start, the climbers moved into the gully. From a grass ledge some 15ft up, Puttrell and then Baker failed to climb the next section of 20ft – *'Altogether it was an ignominious performance before the ladies…'*. Baker then steadied Oppenheimer, as Puttrell stood on his shoulders and with a great effort with the flat of his hands and his right boot digging into grass, pulled over the top of the slab – *'Here he rested, spread-eagled over the bend in the slab, while we watched the water, deflected from its natural channel, pouring from his knickers and boots.'*

The route continued with a narrow chimney topped by chockstones which went with care, then a rounded knob of disintegrating granite blocking the gully climbed with more care and leading to what, from the foot of the cliff, looked to be the worst section; another chimney with jammed stones. On gaining this, they agreed that it was not feasible, and that a traverse out of the chimney had to be made. While Puttrell, who seems to have been the leader of choice on the day, was back and footing, the other two made themselves as secure as possible. They stood in the steep chimney-bed and wedged themselves in with back and knees.

Puttrell was now in a difficult situation; he had gained the right edge of the chimney but in order to continue he had to rotate his body in order to use his hands to exit, all the while keeping wedged fast in the chimney. He succeeded, and the other two climbed up with much assistance from the rope, Oppenheimer slipping at the top.

They now had to regain the chimney above the jammed stones, which meant taking in steep slabs with no handholds, but with a few tufts of grass along a few incipient cracks. Puttrell took to Oppenheimer's shoulders again but retreated, being fearful that the grass tufts would not hold him. Baker being the lightest then had a go, and after threading through a hole in the rock and climbing up a corner managed to return to the chimney above his companions.

More mixed climbing led eventually to a 50ft chimney, split by a thin rib. The chimney on one side was rotten, the other too smooth. A 50ft traverse gave no sure escape, and although Puttrell wished to continue for another 50ft, he was dissuaded as there were no hitches over which the ropes could be run for protection. At this point there were shouts from below, as the ladies had returned to the foot of the route. The climbers' reply that they were only making moderate progress did not help diminish their anxiety, and they asked if the climbers wished a rope to be lowered from above. Disgusted with their performance, they tried the chimney again, with Puttrell making a determined effort to no avail. The ladies persisted with their effort and a consultation took place between the climbers. They had been in the chimney, not for the two hours as estimated, but for six hours, and had only climbed some 240ft out of the over 400. They relented, and Oppenheimer's brother set off for Glen Rosa for help, the ladies returning to the top.

Baker then volunteered to try climbing the grass tufts on the left wall. Some of them showed signs of collapsing, but he succeeded in gaining steep grass, and further up a good ledge. This, Oppenheimer realised, was the traverse line which several days earlier he had climbed with his wife. The way became easier and they soon unroped, to gain the ridge some 30 minutes after having agreed to be rescued.

At this point, while the climbers were greedily devouring their lunch, the ladies lectured them on the folly and madness of the sport. Oppenheimer thought that Puttrell had escaped this, but afterwards he told him that on putting his head out of the final cave, Mrs Oppenheimer – '*...had addressed him in most uncomplimentary terms, and when he emerged unroped, without Baker and me—we were coiling the rope lower down—there was a scene for half a minute.*'

Continuing along the ridge to Cir Mhor was of course abandoned, and they descended Glen Rosa in the twilight, meeting Oppenheimer's brother with two gentlemen volunteers and a couple of keepers with ropes and lanterns. By extricating themselves Oppenheimer was afraid he had disappointed their would-be rescuers. The lady at the first farm was also disappointed – '*We heard that she had threatened to stay up, have a good tea ready, and horsewhip us afterwards. So we missed more than one adventure that night.*'

Oppenheimer found the route stiffer than the '*far more magnificent*' Church Door Buttress proved ten days later. It had disappointed the climbers to find that many of the difficult parts in the chimney were the least interesting, and some of them even looked easy. The large scale of Beinn Nuis, Oppenheimer felt, deceived the eye, with what seemed to be short walls broken by ledges proving to be higher and lacking in holds. He finished his article by confessing that although description may ruin the fascination of a climb for the few, it had advantages for the many, which he had too often experienced to depreciate. In the First World War Oppenheimer enlisted in the Artist's Rifles and died a lieutenant in November 1916 following gas poisoning. He was buried in Boulogne Eastern Cemetery.

The current guidebook to Arran has the route as *Nuis Chimney* (*Gully* 3, 130m Very Severe, V 6). It describes the route as one for the *serious body contact enthusiast*. A brief note on this ascent also appeared in the Climbers' Club Journal, where Puttrell was acknowledged to have led the route bar the two traverses which the lighter Baker made.[5] Baker and Puttrell continued on to the Cairngorms, but with poor weather and long approaches could not enjoy much rock climbing. They did find one route of 200ft on Creag na Leacainn (Lurcher's Crag), at the north end of the Lairig Ghru, but

– '*...most of the granite in this region is unsuitable for climbing.*' Oppenheimer, on his return home, made some enquiries as to ascents on the Nuis face. Green and Boyd had climbed Number Five Gully in 1895, while Clark and Raeburn had climbed the easier Gullies 1 and 2. The latter pair had then attempted the slabby face further right, where they ran into terrible difficulty, details unknown. All of this contributed to the air of deception which many granite cliffs possessed.

On 20th June 1908, Harry MacRobert and William Morrison attempted Gully 3 on the A' Chir Ridge. They described the gully as being divided in its lower part into two gullies by a rib of rotten granite. They failed to climb the first pitch in the left branch, and after climbing some distance up the right branch they admitted defeat and moved out of the gully and on to the ridge. MacRobert returned in July 1911 and climbed the right branch with A Arthur.

❄ ❄ ❄

The Cairngorms had so far, with the exception of Lochnagar, been almost ignored by mountaineers; the Cairngorm Club had few Ultramontane members, so information was scarce. Good climbing tended to lie in distant corries, or on steep and obviously very hard rock. Climbers with a few days to spare headed for Skye or Ben Nevis for the most part, where much more could be done in a day. What exploration had been done so far had not been encouraging, with mainly wet, crumbling gullies, or vegetatious, crumbling faces. There is little in the literature to suggest that access due to restrictions by the shooting sports was any more difficult than in the west, and we have to surmise that the slow development of Cairngorm climbing was in the main due to a lack of information, the small number of local climbers, and topography.

This state would slowly improve however, but in the interim and for the first time, the SMC planned to make the Easter Meet of 1902 at Aviemore, as June 1901 saw the opening of a new hotel there. Easter Friday in 1902 was on March 28th, but Raeburn and Henry Lawson beat the rush by going to Aviemore on March 7th. The previous week the pair, with Mackay, had been on a wet but enjoyable a visit to Arran, and planned on another trip together. Unfortunately Mackay could not make it so Raeburn and Lawson went ahead without him. Both of them were keen on a certain line on Lochnagar, but mindful of a vested interest which an Aberdeen section of the SMC had in the same climb (almost certainly Tough and Brown were the climbers), they decided to respect the others' plans and climb elsewhere. That climb was probably Douglas-Gibson Gully, which eluded an ascent until 1933.

Lawson later penned an article on their visit, during which they climbed a pinnacled ridge on Sgòran Dubh whose crags overlook upper Glen Einich.[6] Whether they were more keen to make a first ascent or to be able to educate the Easter Meet of the cliff's potential, Lawson coyly refused to say; but in the end they scrambled up to the pinnacle clearing vegetation as they went, attempted to continue directly with Raeburn being egged on by Lawson, and ended up with Raeburn insisting he was misunderstood by the club and was in fact a good Salvationist. Accordingly they found an easy if treacherous route up the needle which they duly climbed. It was sleety and windy as they gained the ridge above and dutifully made for the summit. There was very little snow on their ascent of *Original Route* (150m Moderate).

The information that Raeburn and Lawson provided at the meet led to visits every day by various SMC parties, conveniently taxied to lower Glen Einich by cars organised by William Clark. Of the four days of the meet, only one had good weather, with blizzards on the Saturday and Monday. For all that, some five more first ascents were found. In all, 34 members and guests were present, the largest on record to date. The mucky, loose, vegetatious and indeterminate Sgoran Dubh buttresses had done little to raise the estimation of Cairngorm climbing, and the subtle beauties of the Cairngorm glens would remain undiscovered for a few more years. Later that year the SMC received a shock when on the 25th October Lawson died suddenly. Henry Lawson (1867–1902), described by Mackay as the *long-legged walker of formidable achievements,* had recently become the SMC Librarian and was an actuary in Edinburgh. He was in his 35th year.

❄ ❄ ❄

Throughout 1902 other areas in Scotland received attention, most notably the Southern Highlands, with the Arrochar hills and the Tarmachan cliffs receiving ascents by Clark, Gall Inglis and Mackay. On Creag na Caillich, the western Tarmachan crag, Mackay introduced Geoffrey Winthrop Young to Scottish winter climbing. On 6th January, along with a 24-year old law student, Stair Agnew Gillon, the trio marched up the frosty slopes and into Coire Fionn Lairige. The cliffs were in fine winter garb, and more snow was about to be delivered. They committed themselves to the left-hand of two gullies on Meall Garbh, *Mackay's Gully* (100m II), the right-hand one having been climbed by Clark and Gall Inglis on 28th December 1898, *Clark's Gully* (100m II).

Finishing their gully, they traversed the ridge westwards, finally deciding to examine Craig na Caillich. Gillon, another strong walker, joined the SMC that year and went on to be an advocate. He became a close friend of John Buchan after they met as students at Oxford, and survived World War I in France, and Gallipoli, dying in 1954 aged 76.

They fell victim to the sight of an obvious central gully on the face – '*It had never been done. It had to be done. And here the great cloud swept over the ridge above, and the snow began to fall. We started up at 2.55 P.M.*' [7] This being the 6th January, they knew full well that they would be heading for a finish after sunset. To honour their guest Young, they allowed him the lead. The day was already darkening and soft snow was pouring down the gully faster than they were climbing it. To their right was an awesome rocky buttress, overhanging them above. They exited the gully to gain the face of the cliff, with several tiers, draped with blue icicles, dripping water, rising above them. The leader stood on the head of his second, who was perched on the highest grass ledge, and managed to reach a narrow ledge sloping out to the left. This led to the finish of *Great Gully,* (150m III).

It was only after this ascent that Mackay discovered that the gully had been attempted by Raeburn and Lawson on 19th February 1898, that pair being forced to make a traverse left at half-height before finishing upwards to the left of the gully (see Chapter 8). This cliff, along with neighbouring crags of the Tarmachan Ridge, often provides winter climbs early in the season when days are short and the sun's rays feeble.

Elsewhere in the Southern Highlands, during 1901-02 various parties were working out lines on the cliffs above Creag Tharsuinn's Coire Sugach above Arrochar. Maclay, Workman, Inglis, Clark, Rennie and Raeburn were all busy at some point climbing the various schist buttresses and gullies in this quiet, secluded corrie. The early summer routes here are 'traditional', i.e. mainly wet and vegetatious and providing much better sport in winter conditions. In more recent years, several excellent rock climbs have been recorded.

❄ ❄ ❄

The weather towards the end of June 1902 must have been at its best; Saturday 26th June had been set for the Coronation of Edward VII and would have marked the start of Coronation Week, but that was postponed until the 9th August due to the would-be King's illness. Raeburn and the Clarks arranged a few days' climbing on Ben Nevis, with the Clarks arriving at Fort William on Wednesday 25th in what turned out to be the start of five days of glorious weather following a period of biting winds and frequent rain. Raeburn, yachting in the Firth of Forth in a 40-mile race on the Friday, was delayed by calm and caught the train on Saturday morning.

The plan was for Raeburn to meet up with the Clarks and Glover on the Saturday at 2pm, at the foot of Observatory Buttress. Once Raeburn had his eye on a route, stubbornness, that character trait of many a Scot set in, and he would make determined attempts to climb the route.

Inglis Clark, who was just finishing a six-month convalescence from some undisclosed illness, had arranged to meet up later in the week with Raeburn. Before that, Clark left Fort William at 5.30am on Thursday morning, and walked up slowly, alone, to meet up with his wife and Glover at 1pm below Carn Dearg Buttress. Both Clark and Raeburn later wrote an article on their respective ascents, with each covering their waiting period below the cliffs with musings about mountaineering.[8,9] On Thursday, Glover and Clark's wife Jane had eventually joined him. The trio decided to climb Staircase Climb. This route climbs the rocks on the right of Waterfall Gully, and had first been climbed by John Bell, Maclay and Naismith in July 1898 (see Chapter 9). The lure of a recent climb close at hand was too much to resist. In the event, they thoroughly enjoyed the climb with excellent rock, fantastic scenery on all sides, and all in a sensational position.

In his article, Clark remarks on one finding which makes mountaineering so appealing to many of its adherents: the all-demanding focus which shuts out extraneous feelings and recent events. On Staircase Climb they had gained a little recess overhung by an 8ft step. Glover was leading, with William second.

> No thoughts of business or secretarial duties forced themselves on the mind, but a steady stand with muscles braced and a side hold in the crack, were the prelude to the contact of fierce hobnailers with but lightly protected shoulder blades. No unsteady backer for this spot, for the holds above are trying. Yet it is done, and the leader is launched alone on the top to overcome the still difficult pitch ere the safe hold is reached. What a spot for middle-aged folks to be in!

On Friday 27th, Glover and the Clarks began by exploring the eastern face of the Great Tower. They descended to gain the traverse ledge which Naismith had discovered in 1900. Continuing further along this ledge towards the Gap, they found it harder, and part of the traverse was made on all fours. It was the western face which most interested them however, and in particular the stupendous chimney which plunged down from the gap, eventually forming a gully lower down. This they thought could be climbed, assuming the start was feasible. Clark admitted to having an old ambition to climb to the Tower in this way, and that many heroic plans to do this had been upset in the past.

Glover was very keen to do some new, difficult climb, so after a leisurely halt for afternoon tea under an awning on the summit, at 6pm all three descended Number Four Gully into Coire na Ciste, the air of which was cooled somewhat by great snowfields. Crossing the corrie they could see the gully above, filled with snow and ending in a waterfall. After finding a holdless wall of rock above a bergschrund, they were forced to climb a corner on the left, before traversing right again and through the waterfall to gain the gully. All were soaked, but so warm was the evening that they were not uncomfortable. Snow and rock pitches led into sun-warmed rocks above in the gathering darkness. It was after clearing loose rock from the final chimney that they emerged onto the Gap at 11.15pm and the pet dream of years was accomplished by *Glover's Chimney* (150m Difficult).

On the Saturday they had an understandably late start, having finished their day at 1.20am. It was therefore too late to make the rendezvous with

Raeburn under Observatory Buttress. They had their eye however on another new climb: this time the buttress to the left of Glover's Chimney. Known as *Pinnacle Buttress of the Tower* (230m Very Difficult), a steep lower wall leads to a terrace above which a steep prow of rock finishes below the Great Tower. When they approached the upper section they could see on its summit one of the observers from the Observatory looking down at them, holding an 80ft rope. The west face looked formidable.

On reaching the foot of the Tower, they now felt that they should climb it by the most direct route, to save time. The observer lowered his rope and hauled up Clark's heavy rucksack, containing his photographic equipment. Thus lightened, they romped up the dry rock, reaching the cairn on the Tower at 4.15pm. Looking down, they spotted a moving speck on the rocks of Observatory Buttress.

> It was that solitary climber, who amid the great immensities of the place seemed to traverse invisible ledges, and to climb where foot and hand holds could not be seen. Our chance of a share in his great enterprise was gone, and the reproachful glance of my wife who had waited for us for two and a half hours at the "Gap" was such as to make us hasten aloft to bury our disappointment and well-merited but silent reproof in the business of afternoon tea.

Walking up on the Saturday, the weather was so good that Raeburn made the greater part of the Allt a' Mhuilinn in bare feet, as far as the foot of Tower Ridge. His clothing was as loose as possible, without actual removal. True to his nature, he arrived at the meeting place on the hour of 2pm, but there was no one in sight. But inevitably the shadow of Tower Ridge alerted him to time passing. There appeared a solitary figure on the Great Tower, possibly one of the observers from the summit Meteorology Station, but not the friends Raeburn had been waiting for. It was time for him to face the grim-looking slabs of Observatory Buttress.

> Below, was the fast flowing shadowtide; above, the blaze of sunlight, and oh, blessed thought, perhaps afternoon tea. It was enough, I went up, and, fifteen hours from the Sea, stood upon the summit.

The summit party was about to start their fourth cup of tea when Raeburn appeared, intensifying their disappointment by his accounts of '*pulling in holds, and overhanging pitches.*' For whatever reason, most probably his habitual modesty, Raeburn wrote his article with the three lines quoted above being the only reference to actual climbing on *Observatory Buttress* (340m Very Difficult).

Glover now had to leave, but the Clarks and Raeburn were not finished. On the next day, Sunday 29th June, they made another first ascent, this time on the South Trident Buttress, the most southerly and best defined of the three Trident Buttresses bounded on the left by Number Four Gully.

As Clark remarked in his article, '*The lower part of the buttress is what is usually called impossible; but after the experiences of this week, who can say what is impossible?*' A fine new route was climbed, *Pinnacle Arête* (150m Very Difficult). On the best section, requiring a full 80ft rope by the pioneers, Clark remarked that it was as vertical a climb as he could remember in this country, with the rope in places hanging parallel to the face. The holds were perfect, and the rock good.

Flushed with success, and looking across the corrie at The Comb, they decided that although it had often been pronounced impossible, they thought it was at least worth an attempt, so accordingly they climbed the easy steep ledges at the foot of the Comb and followed the slanting rake of slabs leading to a corner at the right. (This corner was eventually climbed in 1921 at Severe.) The corner overlooked the water-worn gully to the right, and into this they were forced by a lack of good holds. The gully then forced them to climb even further right, making a return to the arête of the Comb unfeasible. Looking up the gully, they decided not to attempt it, perhaps due to a large cornice, of which there were a number on the mountain even at the end of June. They rescued the day however by making a rising traverse across *Number Three Gully Buttress* (150m Moderate) in summer, and now a popular winter Grade III.

The weather continued serenely on, with more afternoon tea enjoyed on the summit. They had one more day to climb on Nevis and as it turned out it resulted in an inspiring route. For the curious, there is very little information regarding the first ascent of *Raeburn's Arête* (230m Severe), as it is now named; Raeburn wrote no article, neither did William Clark. In fact, in his article Clark does not even mention the day, never mind the route, presumably expecting that Raeburn would pen an account. The bare route description, with no name given to the route, appeared in the guidebook to Ben Nevis, mentioned below.

In essence, the Clarks and Raeburn made the ascent on Monday 30th. This outstanding route climbs the arête on the left of the north-west face of the First Platform, the clean, slabby face which looks down the Allt a' Mhuilinn. It has some of the best rock on Nevis, and was a fitting and climactic end to a wonderful five days of climbing.

There is presumably some private explanation as to why Raeburn was silent regarding this ascent; conjecture is easy but facts non-existent. To this point he had shown no real reticence about describing his exploits through the pages of the SMCJ. For a man deeply attuned to nature around him, I believe he was making a statement, that climbing was not everything, no matter how good the route. He did write the article covering his solo of Observatory Buttress in the same week, but with no details about the actual climbing. It is hard to explain why he covers his other principal climbs on paper, but not one of his very best summer routes in Scotland. The SMC, in the guide to Ben Nevis, award the route three stars, and they are very parsimonious with their stars!

For 1902, it was certainly a very difficult route, and this is made clear in Clark's description, included in the first guide to Ben Nevis.[10] This was published in the September 1902 SMC Journal as Section 'E', along with other areas. The Ben Nevis section was compiled by William Clark and in its 42 pages are contained history, flora and fauna, geology, meteorology, photographs (many by Clark), diagrams, and descriptions of the known climbs. It was part of the ongoing publication of guides to the Scottish mountains through the pages of the club journal. It sold for five shillings.

Raeburn supplied notes on the fauna and climbs, with information on early ascents of the ridges coming from Collie, Hopkinson, Haskett Smith and Slingsby. There was also a map, and two pull-out panoramas, the latter by Clark and Lamond Howie. It would inevitably spur on more activity on Scotland's highest mountain. Raeburn's Arête is described by Clark, who includes such passages of text as – *The angle was very great, but the rocks were of superb description…the absence of hitches rendered a traverse for twenty feet to the right essential …the whole climb consisting of vertical slabs requires careful attention …*

Clark finished by stating that –

> From a climbing point of view this ranks among the steepest on Ben Nevis, and would be impossible but for the magnificent nature of the rock. This party took 2 hours 40 minutes from the bottom corner to the first platform, taking no rest during this time.

It is worth explaining here that Clark's mention of vertical slabs indicates a change in word useage, as currently a slab is recognised as being rock at a fairly easy angle, much less steep than vertical. The route does indeed take in steep slabs, with even steeper rock walls adjacent. In Clark's day, a slab could be a smooth piece of rock, at almost any angle, including vertical.

❄ ❄ ❄

Three SMC members were back in the Cairngorms in October 1902, when Goggs, Raeburn and Mackay visited Lochnagar. The target was, no surprise, the unclimbed gully now known as Douglas-Gibson, which appears to have been a line which particularly appealed to Raeburn's stubborn nature. Goggs was a staunch Salvationist, the other two well known Ultramontane members. He wrote a humorous article from his point of view for those –'*…wishing to gain experience of the ways and methods of that eccentric section of the SMC.*'[11]

On the first day, it being too late to attempt an ascent, the party were content to allow Goggs to 'bag' the summit of Lochnagar, and also to inspect the gully from above, Raeburn tying on to two 60ft lengths of rope. He reported that he had descended to within 30ft of the highest point previously reached, that he saw a way up these 30ft, and that they would have to try from the bottom the next day. Suffice it to say that the next day the gully was deemed to be too wet for an attempt. They then attempted the ridge on the left, but after climbing some 250ft of mixed rock and vegetation gave up on reaching seemingly holdless rocks.

Still not discouraged, Raeburn then announced an attempt to drive a route through the Tough-Brown Ridge traverse, which declaration worried Goggs – '*I had a hazy idea that the Tough-Brown Ridge was something desperate, but I preserved a quiet outward demeanour, and once again my good fortune prevailed.*' Raeburn failed at 40ft and retreated. Still undaunted, the next target was West Gully on the Black Spout. This they managed to climb, but not before Goggs' rucksack fell down the gully. They descended in the gloaming.

The next day, presumably having removed all mud and grit from their fingernails, they were back in the corrie, searching fruitlessly for the rucksack. It was added to a list of clothing and equipment which had been lost on previous visits. Another target was set by the Ultramontanes, the Black Spout Pinnacle. Once again, defeat was on the menu, with Raeburn failing to jam up a chimney. Even after a pause for lunch Raeburn realised he could never climb the overhang above. Goggs saw his chance and pounced, insisting that he absolutely must be at his business the following day.

A difficult descent was eventually made. Finding that they had 10 minutes to spare before leaving for the last train from Ballater, the trio rushed over to where the Pinnacle is separated from the summit by a little col. They scrambled up the Pinnacle and so could at least claim a record of four defeats, two successes, and one lost rucksack.

In his comprehensive history of the first 100 years of mountaineering in the Cairngorms, Greg Strange remarked that – '*...with four failures and more lost gear it is surprising that Raeburn returned to this corrie, but as others have found, granite climbing can be addictive, especially when there are new climbs to be discovered*'.[12] Knowing the determination that Raeburn could show when chasing a route, it may be rather that his special addiction was to climb prominent lines, wherever they were found.

The 1903 New Year Meet of the SMC was held at Killin. Much snow made crag approaches hard work, but several teams were busy on the Tarmachan cliffs, including Raeburn, Charles W Walker and his cousin H (probably Harry) Walker. Three days' worth of snow and wind reduced the numbers attending until on Sunday 4th January only seven remained from the original 23 members and several guests. The above trio were rewarded by their persistence as it partly cleared and snow could be seen blowing from the top of Meall Garbh. One year before, Mackay's party had made a direct ascent of the wide chimney running up the crag; Raeburn's rope succeeded in climbing the right arête of this chimney, starting up a series of snow couloirs and ending up a series of steep walls, one of which they measured at an angle of 73 degrees. *Great Gully Arête* (150m III)

Easter Friday 1903 fell on the 10th April, with 21 members and guests of the SMC attending the Meet at Sligachan Inn. Munro was present, claiming to have travelled 800 miles to be there. The weather was severe, and as the meet report by President William Charles Smith stated – '*Probably not the oldest member of the Club ever saw the Coolin range under such acute Alpine conditions.*'[13] There was a great accumulation of old snow, and new snow fell during the meet. Step-cutting was required during several expeditions, and such was the icing up of rocks that two experienced parties failed on the Pinnacle Route.

The expedition highlighted in the report was that by Raeburn, the Walker cousins, and Willie Ling. On Friday 10th April, starting early from Sligachan, they gained the foot of Sgurr Dubh by the long glen, traversed all the tops of Sgurr Dubh, crossed the gap, over Alasdair and Sgumain, and down to Glen Brittle. The last of the club departed Skye on Monday the 20th.

In a later article on Skye, Raeburn recalled the dreadful weather during this Easter 1903 Meet. He ascended Dearg from Glenbrittle with Donald Stewart Campbell and HT Munro. For several years, Raeburn had an understanding that he would lead Munro up the Inaccessible Pinnacle, but it seemed as if the weather gods were aware of this and were not in a cooperative mood.

> In the corries even were we obliged to hold on to the rocks occasionally to prevent being blown away. The writer has a vivid recollection of being spread-eagled and clinging with every available portion of his anatomy to the ice-covered "easy" ridge of the "Inaccessible" – truly so to-day – while the level hail drove fiercely past, expecting every moment to see his legs raised in the air, his hobnailers crack together once or twice like the tails of a pennon, and then,…hurled away into Coruisk…Needless to say we did not get up…[14]

They tried again two years later in 1905, but if anything conditions were even worse. Munro never did gain the summit of the Inaccessible.

An alternative Easter Meet in 1903 was held at Inveroran, where 12 members gathered. On the Friday, six headed for the north-east face of Stob Ghabhar, traversing soft snow towards the Upper Couloir. Below this the party split into two ropes of three. Maclay, Oscar Röhde and Solly decided to attempt the rocky buttress on the south flank of the couloir, so far unclimbed, while Naismith, Thomson and John Waugh moved further left to try a short snow gully.

After finding the very steep start directly up the buttress too difficult, Solly's rope began slightly further left and succeeded in climbing the buttress, moving up and right but never quite seeing into the Upper Couloir. On the Solly-Maclay route, at one point a glove was accidentally dropped and fell clear of the rocks for 200ft or more. Naismith's party also moved up and right, finishing just left of the other route. Oddly enough, neither climb has been recorded in a guidebook, although there is a more modern winter route, *Hircine Rib* (130m Grade VI, 7), first climbed in 1989, following the line of an earlier Severe in summer (1961). Hircine Rib also takes the buttress just left of the Upper Couloir, and it seems likely that the earlier climbs start a little further left and rise up and right, with the Solly-Maclean line perhaps finishing up as for Hircine Rib on the easier, final section.

The following day the wind had increased, and parties on the hill often had to stoop or even lie down until a squall had passed. Nonetheless, several snow gullies were climbed in the Bridge of Orchy hills, while a party led by Thomas Edward Goodeve (1876–1919) found a mixed route up the south-east spur of Stob Coir'an Albannaich. Goodeve, an engineer with the army, joined the SMC later in the year. Always fit, he was a popular member and good companion on a climb. A specialist on railways, he served in Palestine, and sadly was killed by a train on 26th January 1919 while on an inspection tour, somewhere north of Baghdad. He was by then a Major. He is buried in the Damascus Commonwealth War Cemetery, Syria.

On the Monday, Maclay, Naismith, Röhde and Solly made for Beinn Dorain. They headed for the col between that hill and Beinn an Dothaidh, and en route they examined the cliff on the right of the corrie. This was almost certainly Creag an Socach, which was to be developed mainly during the 1980s and 90s, especially with hard winter routes. Recognising that the climbing was too difficult for them, they climbed a steep crack at the left of the crag. Their route sounds very much like a climb recorded in 1988 as *False Rumour Gully* (60m, IV,4), though without more details this is impossible to corroborate. What is certain is that the pioneers certainly had the skill and abilities to make such a climb in 1903, given that it had been relatively free of ice.

❄ ❄ ❄

Into this story now appears one Alfred Harker (1859–1939), an English geologist who spent a decade exploring the Cuillin and investigating its igneous rocks for the Geological Survey. He became an SMC member in 1900, proposed by Colin Phillip, that other aficionado of the Cuillin. His application records only his intensive explorations of the Skye mountains; he may well never have climbed any other mountains. It is intriguing that he was never made an Honorary Member of the SMC when other notable early geologists – Geikie, Peach, Heddle – were accorded that distinction. Nevertheless, among his various other honours there is the singular one of having a geological feature on the earth's moon named after him (Dorsa Harker, a 197km wrinkle ridge in the Mare Crisium). The mineral harkerite, first found on the Isle of Skye, is also named after him.

Continuing the space exploration theme, he discovered another mineral on Skye, mugearite. In 2012 the NASA Mars vehicle Curiosity landed and began analysing soil and rock. One analysis by X-ray spectrometry was held on a rock named Jake (named after a NASA engineer who died not long after Curiosity had landed). Jake has much higher amounts of alkali elements, metals such as sodium and potassium, than previously analysed Martian rocks. When pushed for anything similar to that found on Earth, the NASA geologists came up with a possible candidate - the mineral mugearite. In 2013 it was confirmed that the Mars analysis was similar to Harker's mugearite, which was named after the nearby croft Mugeary. If only Harker were alive to learn of this finding.

Harker's vast experience on the ground allowed him to mark on a copy of the SMC four-inch map the major walking routes in the Cuillin. In varying degrees of thickness, and in red ink, these show the ways over the moors, the passes, and other routes which, although not climbing routes, involve some scrambling. Willie Douglas had this map bound into the Sligachan Climbers' Guide in 1904. As we will see later, all this work would lead to a surge in climbing in the Cuillin and to the first SMC guidebook.

The Sharp family had been tenants of Sligachan. William Sharp had died in 1895, and Mrs Sharp continued to manage the Hotel until 1903, when she moved to the Golf Hotel, Montrose. It is not recorded whether she appreciated the drier climate of the east coast, or missed the midges of Skye. We should be grateful to her memory however, as the Sligachan Climbers' Book, which recorded climbing in the Cuillin between 1893 and 1903, was presented by her to the SMC. The Hotel's Visitors' Book (1885-1905) was also held in the SMC Archives, and may well have also been presented to the club by her.

The SMC made a typewritten copy of the Climbers' Book, added a four-inch map, and later a complete guidebook by Willie Douglas, with photographs. These were given to the Hotel's management for the use of all climbers. It is worth mentioning the four-inch map in more detail. William Douglas, Editor of the SMCJ, had been carefully collating information on climbs in the Cuillin. With permission from the Ordnance Survey, he had published the four-inch map, based on the OS six-inch map. This appeared in the issue of the SMCJ for January 1898.

There was further progress on mapping at this time, as the Ordnance Survey had been engaged in a re-survey of Scotland, and had issued new six- and one-inch maps. The old one-inch maps had been based mainly on surveys undertaken between 1850 and 1880, and other than a few of the new railway lines, little updating had been done since. A new survey was started in 1890, with the new issue, the Second Edition, released between 1894 and 1904. Accordingly the SMC began purchasing a complete set for the club library. The maps were reviewed by James Gall Inglis.[15] As a professional cartographer, he obviously had a keen interest on what was evolving with maps. One point of which he was always proud was his discovery in 1928, along with John Rooke Corbett, that Beinn Tarsuinn was a Munro.[16] His review was especially critical on the naming of features, usually Gaelic ones, with many discrepancies between the six-inch and one-inch maps.

❄ ❄ ❄

The combination of Raeburn and the Clarks continued to be fruitful, as June saw them meet up at the Kingshouse in Glen Coe. William Clark described the weekend in a delightful article – *The Motor in Mountaineering*.[17] Glen Coe remained more difficult to gain than Fort William, with the railway and hotel in the latter's favour. Clark had however overheard a remark about his Ben Nevis articles, suggesting that he had written all there was to say about that venue, so he and his wife decided to return to Glen Coe, particularly as he barely knew its climbing delights.

The Clarks, being well-heeled, had purchased the first car to be registered in Edinburgh, S1. They passed this registration on to Lord Kingsburgh, first President of the Automobile Association, and kept the registration S2 for their own use, running an Arrol-Johnston 'Dogcart'. George Johnston was a locomotive engineer who teamed up with Sir William Arrol, an engineer on the Forth Bridge, to form the Mo-Car Syndicate. This Scottish company would produce the first car manufactured in the UK, beginning in 1895. The first Arrol-Johnston car was a six-seater 'Dogcart' (it had two transverse seats placed back to back), which went into production at a factory at Camlachie, in the east end of Glasgow.

The Clarks slowly drove up to Glen Coe on Friday 12th June, leaving Edinburgh at 5am. Stirling was gained at 7am, and breakfast enjoyed soon after 8.30am at Strathyre. The 'Baa Pass', just below 1500ft above sea level and complete with stony pitches, was taken with relief, and the Kingshouse Inn, under new management, was a welcome respite. They decided the following day would be an expedition to Sron na Creise, where a wall of attractive buttresses facing the Inn beckoned. In the end they climbed rocks on an easterly buttress, as JS Napier had recently written to inform him that he had climbed the central buttress. Their route was enjoyable, their only regret being that it had not been longer. A heavy hailstorm hastened their descent, and an anxious night followed, as Raeburn was due to meet them in the morning and the weather was unsettled.

Raeburn was yacht racing in the Forth on the Saturday afternoon. This allowed him to catch the night train to Tyndrum and cycle up to Glen Coe for a 6am rendezvous. He arrived at 5.45am, in clearing weather. A few hours of sleep and they set out for the Buachaille at 10am. The target of the trio was no less than the Crowberry Ridge, that '*…very aristocrat of climbs*.' Clark's intention was to repeat the original route by Naismith and Douglas, first climbed in August 1896. He felt that the more recent direct ascent in May 1900 by the Abraham's party was quite beyond the powers of himself and his wife. Raeburn of course had a more ambitious plan; a second ascent. As is often the case, Clark had misgivings during the approach, but once he gained the rough rock at the foot of the buttress and his boots clicked onto the excellent holds, his spirits rose. The Clarks probably needed little encouragement from Raeburn to attempt the harder climb. Clark's knowledge of the route taken by the Abrahams and their companions was hazy, being confined to a report in an earlier SMCJ and a popular article in *Pearson's Monthly* in 1902.

The crux pitch begins at a ledge which had a reliable belay, albeit one with problematical safety. By this, Clark meant that there was a solid flake or spike of rock, though whether or not the rope would remain there should the leader fall was another thing. Despite the awkward position, while Jane belayed Raeburn, Clark attempted to photograph him on the crux moves to the left, the leader having switched from boots to Kletterschuen. '*I endeavoured to stand on my head and focus the camera on a 12-inch tripod.*' Sadly, the photograph would have been ideal if it were not for the fact that the lens' focal length was insufficiently wide to capture the entire scene, Raeburn's head being missing from the final image. '*An anxious and silent interval was only broken by the slow movement of the rope, but soon it moved more rapidly, and after 35 feet were out my wife followed out of sight to take her turn.*' Finally it was William's turn.

> With the confidence of the rope I was able to balance myself with the right hand on the trifling pinnacle, and standing on the meagre extremity of the ledge, to reach sufficient holds to prevent falling backward; but for some 8 or 10 feet higher I was not ashamed to call out, "Hold me firm," and to feel gratified at the response from above.

The summit was gained and more photography done, but on the descent Clark realised he had left his Dallmeyer lens on the summit. It would have to be recovered the following day. Accordingly, all three were back on the Buachaille on the Monday. But Raeburn would not be satisfied with an easy route, and he suggested an attempt on The Chasm, in which a strong party had earlier failed to climb. This great gully cuts a deep gash in the SE flank of the mountain. In July 1898 John Bell and James Maclay had succeeded in reaching the foot of the 100ft pitch (pitch 8). Raeburn and the Clarks decided to drop into the gully above this pitch. This they did, and battled their way up rocks and old snow to gain a point about two hard pitches below a feature known as the Cauldron. This would be at a point named Pitch 12 in the current description; the crux pitch 15 is known as The Cauldron, and is often unclimbable depending on the amount of water coming down.

Raeburn had to catch the evening train at Tyndrum, the going had been strenuous and stressful, and so they made for an escape on the left. Even this was difficult, leading to the ascent of what they named the Lady's Pinnacle. Eventually Raeburn scampered down the hill for his return home, and the Clarks continued to the summit, where they recovered the errant lens. Looking back at this attempt, Clark regarded it as the most prolonged piece of difficult climbing in his British experience. It would be some 28 years before a complete ascent of The Chasm would be made.

At the end of October 1903, Raeburn and the two Walkers, Charles and Harry, decided to attempt a route on the cliffs of Corrie Ardair, on Creag Meagaidh.[18] In April 1896 Raeburn, Tough and Douglas had failed to finish the Central Post or gully, defeated by increasingly dangerous avalanches. The persistent Raeburn had returned, presumably choosing the last month before snow began falling.

Unfortunately, in place of snow there was foaming water, the rain having been almost continuous for weeks before. The Central Post being very wet looking, they headed for the Pinnacle Face. As the first 300ft were deemed hopeless, they made for the sloping gully on the left (now *Raeburn's Gully* I), from which they might access the face via one of its many horizontal ledges.

Three separate efforts to climb the face were made. In each case the ledge would fade away to a smooth and impassable gap. They ended up having to climb the gully all the way to the top. As none of the party was keen to attempt to find the summit in the thick fog that had rolled in, they descended to Aberarder and cycled back to their hotel at Loch Laggan.

The following day, November 1st, arrived with perfect autumn weather and they resolved to attempt the Central Post. For several hundred feet the climbing went well, though steep in places. The gully was initially more of a scoop, but about half-height it deepened, forming a triple pitch and leading into a chasm with overhanging walls and the drifting smoke of water spray. The party was so far dry, and wished to remain so, and accordingly they looked for a way out on the buttress to the left. Several pitches of grass and rotten rock eventually led to a ridge and so to the top.

On the final day they cycled to Kingussie, investigating the steep cliffs of Creag Dubh en route. They found two routes here, finishing up above the steep rocks by steep and rotten grass ledges. Ice axes were found practically indispensable there, as well driven into turf they formed the only belays found. This crag would later become the haunt of those in search of steep, hard rock. One of the routes climbed in 1903 was later recorded in 1965 as *Fred* (100m Very Difficult).

In a brief article in January 1904 one of the early tigers of the SMC, John Bell, analysed what he thought his perfect climb should consist of.[19] He thought there should be four points: it should be new, continuous, difficult, and once started should be the easiest available. He expanded on these four points. A new climb had its special charm, he thought, though it did not lessen the enjoyment much if others had done the climb before '... *provided that one doesn't know exactly where and how they did it. Difficulty is always relative'*, he continued, it did not matter what its absolute standard was as long as it was difficult for the climber. Continuous was ideal, so that once started it had to be finished or else abandoned and a retreat made. His final point, *the way should be the easiest found*, might puzzle the modern climber. He probably meant if not the easiest, certainly the easiest logical way up a difficult mountain.

> In its highest form we should have a whole mountain before us and know of no easy way. As we all know, there is no such mountain in Scotland (except under bad weather conditions), but while this is so, there are many climbs on which if a man is once started, he may spend many hours in the attempt to find the easiest way to the top.

In more modern times, climbers may often regard parts of a mountain rather than its whole; they enjoy route finding up a complex buttress for example, perhaps winding their way up with more difficult rock or ice on either side. What is interesting is what Bell left out of his analysis: he did not specify that his perfect climb should finish at the summit. He may of course have been taking this for granted.

There are clues that mountaineering in Scotland was beginning to mature as a sport; Bell's analysis is one, and in a way Raeburn's attempt to climb the Central Post is another. He knew that for a summer attempt snow would be an obstacle, and accordingly he attempted the climb at the very end of the season. That year, 1903, had been a very snowy one. Additionally, and going against the practice, when his party came up against very wet conditions in the gully they backed off, preferring to remain dry. Accounts of climbing before then would have seen heroic attempts to climb obstacles, water or no water.

As a meteorological aside, the chaotic and unusual weather experienced throughout the UK in 2012 prompted the Met Office to look back through their records for a similar year. They came up with 1903 as the year which approached the weather of 2012 for its 'weirdness'. It was certainly a wet one, the worst that England had on record, with Scotland not far behind.

Ironically, as this was being written, the winter of 2013-14 has just been confirmed as being the wettest on record for the UK.

By the end of 1903, when the SMC held their 15th AGM, the club numbered some 160. Some 57 of those were AC members, indicative of an active interest in alpinism. The number of books in the library had risen from 30 to 300, and there were 900 slides in the club collection. At that AGM, Alex Fraser made a motion to reprint the first two volumes of the club journal. They had been printed in small numbers, had long sold out, and contained the Tables of Scottish Mountains as compiled by Hugh Munro, part of their appeal. This motion was vetoed by Mr Munro, who claimed copyright on 'Munro's Tables.'[20]

Faced by this awkward moment, the SMC seems to have given in to the legal entitlement of Munro. It has, of course, meant that to those enthusiasts who collect such items, Volumes 1 and 2 remain scarce items, with a correspondingly high price in the collectors' market. One other item from the AGM was the decision to make available life memberships for the SMC. Correspondence followed, with various costs proposed. There was a letter from William Clark, then Secretary, which included an analysis of membership so far. He found that many of those who had joined the club in the early years 1889-92 did so from sympathy, and to assist the young association in its start. Once the club was firmly launched, they withdrew after a few years. Of 137 who joined during these years, only 103 remained for five years, 84 for 10 years, and 70 were remaining in 1903.

As time went on, those joining tended to remain members. Clark then made the reasonable assumption that present-day candidates would remain for a longer period in the Club than original members had done. This had a bearing on the subscription costs, the reason for his analysis, but it also tells us more about the makeup of the Club in these early years. What also has to be borne in mind is that many mountaineers then were alpinists, keeping their precious summer holiday time for the Alps, and exploring the mountains of Scotland at other times outwith the best of summer.

There were exceptions of course, with some members in the professions able to choose days, or even weeks, here and there, but it helps explain why for many years the SMC held their climbing meets at Easter and New Year, two periods when snow and ice might well be available, but dry rock and good weather would be a scarce commodity. The social aspect of these meets held them firm for many decades, throwing logic to the winds. Indeed, the SMC Easter Meet continues as a regular event, even if at the mercy of the phases of the moon.

It is easy to underestimate the importance of these meets, particularly from a modern outlook. They brought together climbers who otherwise might not have met, and so new climbing partnerships were formed. They stimulated interest in far-flung areas of Scotland, opening up new climbing grounds, and were often aided with organised accommodation and perhaps transport. Indirectly they would have introduced some element of competition, which, tied in with an exchange of information about climbs, equipment and techniques, could not have failed to support safe mountaineering alongside rising standards. Without these early meets, the SMC, and no doubt other clubs, would have been in danger of fading away.

References

1. Clark, W. Inglis. *Stormy June Days in Skye and on Ben Nevis.* SMCJ 6, 36, Sept. 1901, 213-230.
2. Raeburn, Harold. *The Observatory Ridge, Ben Nevis.* SMCJ 6, 36, Sept. 1901, 213-217.
3. Oppenheimer, Lehmann J. *Ben Nuis Chimney.* SMCJ, 7, 37, Jan. 1902, 1-9.
4. Clark, W. Inglis. *A Day on Cir Mhor.* SMCJ 5, 25, Jan. 1898, 29-36.
5. Climbers' Club Journal. *Kyndwr Club Notes.*1901, 13, 35-36.
6. Lawson, H.G.S. *Sgoran Dubh Pinnacle.* SMCJ 7, 38, May 1902, 57-60.
7. Mackay, A.M. *Tarmachan and the Craig na Caillich Gully.* SMCJ 7, 38, May 1902, 61-65.
8. Raeburn, Harold. *From Sea to Summit.* SMCJ 7, 40, Jan. 1903, 194-198.
9. Clark, W. Inglis. *New Climbs on Ben Nevis.* SMCJ 7, 40, Jan. 1903, 199-211.
10. SMC Guide Book. *Ben Nevis.* SMCJ 7, 39, Sept. 1902, 134-176.
11. Gogg, F.S. *A Salvationist on Lochnagar.* SMCJ 7, 40, 185-193.
12. Strange, Greg. *The Cairngorms – 100 Years of Mountaineering.* 2010, The Scottish Mountaineering Trust, 19.
13. Proceedings of the Club. *Sligachan Meet – Easter, 1903.* SMCJ 7, 41, May 1903, 280-284.
14. Raeburn, Harold. *Ridge-Walking on the Coolins at Easter, 1905.* SMCJ 9, 50, 59-70.
15. Notes and Queries. *The New Ordnance Survey Maps.* SMCJ 7, 41, May 1903, 294-297.
16. Inglis, J. Gall. *Mullach Coire MhicFhearchair and a new "Munro".* SMCJ 18, 107, April 1929, 269-275.
17. Clark, W. Inglis. *The Motor in Mountaineering–A Visit to Buchaille Etive Mòr.* SMCJ 7, 42, Sept. 1903, 313-322.
18. Raeburn, Harold. *The Cliffs of Corrie Arder.* SMCJ 8, 43, Jan. 1904, 4-11.
19. Bell, J.H. *A Purely Climbing Ideal.* SMCJ 8, 43, Jan. 1904, 1-3.
20. Proceedings of the Club. SMCJ 8, 43, Jan. 1904, 73-74.

11

Stormy Weather (1904-06)

THERE WAS little snow in the 1903-04 winter season; the ground was iron hard and the wind often a biting southeaster. The SMC New Year Meet of 1904 was based at the Alexandra Hotel, Fort William. Some 30 members and guests were present, including five original members and six new members. John Bell wrote the report of the meet, with various climbers adding notes on their ascents.[1] Raeburn, along with the Walkers and Maclay, made the first ascent of *North Trident Buttress* (200m III) on the Friday, New Year's Day. It gives an enjoyable mixed route in winter. On the Saturday, John Bell, Graham Napier, Raeburn and John Rennie succeeded in making a day trip to Ardgour where they made the second ascent of the Great Ridge on Garbh Bheinn.

The tireless Raeburn was out again on the Sunday, this time with Rennie and a new member, John Wigner. Their plan was to climb the North-East Buttress, but they found the wind too strong and made instead for Tower Gully. Here Rennie decided that he fancied some rock climbing for a change, so making a traverse on steep and treacherous snow they moved to the foot of Tower Gap Chimney which they climbed to gain the ridge above via the Gap. Apparently this was the first time this traverse (*Eastern Traverse from Tower Gully* is 120m III in the current guide) had been made.

Monday 4th January found Percy Unna, Maclay and Robert Parr exploring the cliffs of Stob Ban on the other side of Glen Nevis, where the latter two made a first ascent on the Central Buttress – *Gendarme Ridge* (150m IV,4). Raeburn meanwhile was making a first ascent on Meall-an-t-Suidhe, climbing the middle of three gullies seen from the bridle path. This was with two new members, James Burns and William Newbigging. In climbing with new members, thereby possibly missing out on a better climbing day, Raeburn was showing a typical generosity of spirit.

Unfortunately, Wigner, who had an impressive climbing record in the Lakes and Alps, would leave the club within two years. He moved south to Widnes to follow a successful career as an industrial chemist, but not before he proposed Percy Unna for membership. Parr died suddenly in 1904. Newbigging however, would go on to leave his name on other new climbs. James Burns was a solicitor from Falkirk.

Earlier, we described William Inglis Clark photographing Raeburn on the second ascent of Crowberry Ridge Direct. Clark was a pioneer in photography, and often struggled up the hill encumbered with the heavy and bulky equipment of the day. He penned an amusing sketch indicating what his companions thought of him on such days.

> The philosopher, regarding the mountain photographer, sees in him one of the most miserable of beings. He toils on gloomy or misty days, with a battery of lenses and superfluous plates, while the wind capsizes his camera, and the focussing cloth flies out to leeward. There he is on the coldest part of the ridge, with frozen hands and rucksack half filled with drifting snow. Where are his companions? Crouching in some sheltered spot and calling on him to "Hurry up, for it is cold." Well he knows it, and recognises that they look on him as a camera fiend, a veritable Jonah….Who can measure out the reward to the photographer? Our Hon. Librarian tauntingly said to me that he supposed one per cent. of successes would be good work. But, in all this musing, think of the great effect on character. No big D—— is uttered even when some grand catastrophe occurs; and witnesses can testify that mountain photographers, although the most chastened, are amongst the meekest, most hopeful, and enthusiastic of climbers.[2]

Clark's training as a chemist would have been an enormous help with his photography, with much of the work demanding careful processing with chemical baths. He was also an early experimenter with colour photography, and his four colour prints of September 1909 were the first to be published in the SMC Journal.[3] He followed these with several more in the October 1914 SMCJ. In Clark's time, the photographer also processed his or her own colour work.

He was not the only competent photographer active on the Scottish hills; there was William Lamond Howie (1846–1918), FRSE and FCS (Fellow of the Chemical Society). Howie provided the SMCJ with but one article, which was on photography.[4] He gave the occasional lecture, including one to the Edinburgh Photographic Society on the 16th December 1891 entitled *'To Ober-Ammergau and back in 1890'*.

❄ ❄ ❄

Easter Day 1904 fell on the 3rd April. The Sligachan Hotel, under new management, was about to undergo a makeover which would temporarily deter expeditions to Skye for a period in 1904. The SMC decided to hold their Meet at Aviemore, which immediately split opinions in two; one side held that the eight mile distance from the climbing ground, the absence of good rock (with the dubious exception of Sgoran Dubh), and the risk of chill if travelling home by car were all negative points. The other side argued that the palatial hotel, superb scenery, and a greater certainty of finding snow to climb outweighed the negative. In the end, despite a constant gale of some 50 to 100mph and blizzards unsurpassed in the Club's history, the meet was held to be one of the most enjoyable.

The weather at the end of March 1904 had seen an anticyclone over Scotland. However, this broke on the morning of Thursday 31st and thereafter the meet was plagued by raging winds and blizzards. Several club photographers watched from a sheltered spot as the surface of Loch an Eilein was torn into spindrift, blowing from the castle to the other end of the loch in nine seconds. They calculated this as indicating a wind velocity approaching 100mph. Munro succeeded in climbing Sron na Lairige, the north-east top of Braeriach, and described the blizzard as exceeding anything in his experience. He may not have been a full-blown mountaineer in the technical sense, but he was certainly an experienced and hardened hill walker.

By Friday morning, there were 22 members heading for the hills, with several ascents accomplished despite the gale. On the Saturday, the buttresses of Sgoran Dubh were targeted by several parties, with the Walker cousins and Thomas HB Rorie having a hard time on Pinnacle Buttress. (Rorie, a Dundee man like the Walkers , would be killed in 1916 on the Western Front, as a captain in the Black Watch. He had the unusual distinction of having brought his wife to the 1908 SMC Meet at Braemar.) Sunday was just as stormy, with only one party out walking.

On the Monday a strong party headed for Sgoran Dubh. The quartet consisted of Godfrey Solly, AE Robertson, James Rose and Alexander Moncrieff. After some delay in choosing a route, they decided on a ridge on the second buttress. The climbing, with Solly as leader, went well for the first 800ft, becoming more difficult for the next 200ft, after which a col was gained. Above this Solly made a hard lead up a steep and narrow shelf with no protection, as was often the case at this time. It was now 4pm, and as an easy traverse could made into a gully on the south they decided to descend. From what they could see, the remaining section of the ridge appeared to be easier than what they had just climbed. They eventually reached the hotel just before 10pm.

It seems that Solly had tagged onto the above party by accident, as due to a misunderstanding his intended climbing partner had not met him in Glen Eunaich. The route was described in more detail by Solly, who mentions their crux of the day.

> Just below where we stopped was, I thought, the most difficult place. We had to get up some slanting slabs with nothing much to hold by, except that for the right arm there was a bulging-out piece of another slab a little higher. To the left was a sheer drop.
>
> Comparing this with other climbs that I know, it lacks the interest of the scenery such as there is on some of the Ben Nevis routes, but as a gymnastic climb I know nothing in Great Britain to equal it for long and continuous interest.[5]

This was high praise indeed from one of the best climbers around, and considering that much of the rocks were covered in snow, their partial ascent was another notable event. In the current guide it is down as IV,5. This attempt certainly prompted some of the young tigers in the SMC to make a visit. On Friday 29th April, WC Newbigging, WA Morrison and AE Robertson left Edinburgh at 4.25am, bound for Aviemore. William Alex Morrison, whose profession was given as 'Analyst', and William Corrie Newbigging, who had joined the SMC the previous year as a student, were both about 21, while the Rev Archibald Eneas Robertson, well known to later Munro baggers, was 34.

Morrison described the first complete ascent of what they named *Rose Ridge* (260m Very Difficult), in honour of James Rose, a member of the first attempt party on the Easter Meet. They found the pitch below which Solly's party had decided to abandon their attempt to consist of a 40ft climb up a stretch of piled blocks, the first of which required a determined effort. After this pitch the climb degenerated, with easily avoided scrambly pitches.[6]

What of Raeburn, who was on this Meet? The report summary by Clark briefly states that on Friday 1st April, Raeburn, Garden, Roth and George Almond climbed a snow gully in Coire an t-Sneachda.[7] In the current guide they are credited with the first ascent of *Pygmy Ridge* (100m IV,5, Very Difficult. More details from Clark has them avoiding iced rocks at the foot which forced a traverse right to gain a '*...fine little pinnacled ridge to the east of the central gully.*' At almost the same time, another SMC party, with Goodeve, Russell and Robertson, were heading up and left for the same ridge. Robertson wrote – *'It was not judged sportsman-like to pass in front of them, so traversing back to our original line, we gained the ridge* [here Robertson was referring to the plateau edge]. *The small cornice was easily surmounted.'*

Whether we accept that Raeburn's climb was made in mixed conditions or was free enough of snow and ice to be a rock climb, it was certainly a fine ascent. Greg Strange, in his history of climbing in the Cairngorms, remarks of this route that '*...it is certainly, by modern standards, a better climb than anything done in the Cairngorms up to that point.*'[8] It was also, along with the easy gully credited to Goodeve's party, the first route recorded in the Northern Corries. Raeburn then left Aviemore with Euan Robertson (1880–1975), an AC member who had joined the SMC in 1902, and was the son of Robert Augustus Robertson, an original member who was President 1897-1899, and also an AC member.

Raeburn and Euan Robertson headed for Achnashellach. In an article in the SMCJ some eight years earlier, Lionel Hinxman had praised Strath Carron as a climbing centre.[9] References in his article to the *'absolutely perpendicular'* precipices of Fuar Tholl would have been like a red rag to a bull for Raeburn, who was by now reaching peak form. The weather, if anything, was even worse than that suffered in the Cairngorms. On Saturday 2nd April, as the pair entered Coire Lair, there was *'...dense mist, a howling sleet-laden gale, and under foot eight to ten inches of slush. Nothing of course was visible of the corrie.'* [10] The Sunday was even worse for weather, though they managed an ascent of An Ruadh Stac, now a Corbett.

On Monday 4th April the wind shifted slightly to the north-west and the temperature dropped. More snow had fallen overnight and they slogged through a foot or so of it to enter the corrie with lifting clouds to view the fine north-east face of Sgurr Ruadh. To that date, the only known climb on Sgurr Ruadh was an ascent by Robertson and a friend on 26th May 1898 of the SE Face, partly by a gully and partly by a buttress. These are now named after Robertson, with both graded separately at IV,4. Robertson himself does not seem to have left any description of his climbing.

Raeburn chose the north-east buttress for an ascent, starting up a chimney left of the ridge as the initial rocks were iced up slabs. After 80ft they gained the ridge by a good ledge, pleased to find some shelter from the wind, which was being deflected over their heads by the rock wall. They gained the top after 80 minutes, and Raeburn commented that due to conditions the climbing was *'...not very easy, but the icy snow usually adhering to the steep grassy walls gave good hitches, and handholds could also be cut where required.'* As they made the final descent home via the Coulags Glen the rain was a deluge. Raeburn however was content, and confirmed Hinxman's view that the district was a fine one with some excellent climbing to be had.

The route is now named *Raeburn's Buttress via Narrow Gully* (350m II). Raeburn certainly had an eye for a good line, and the direct start is V,6 in winter, Severe in summer. It would, however, be another 44 years before the next climb was found. The Strathcarron Hotel, where Raeburn and Robertson were staying, was small but comfortable. It was also probably too distant to be convenient for a club meet, given the travelling times by train; for example from Aviemore to Achnashellach alone took Raeburn from 8.30am to 12.52pm.

❄ ❄ ❄

The Clark family must have been energised in April 1904, making several ascents in various combinations. Firstly, William, Jane and their son Charlie made for Ardgour, climbing the *Great Ridge*. Snow and ice near the summit gave them some exciting climbing before finishing the route. On 18th April, William, Charlie and Raeburn made for the North-East Ridge of Aonach Beag, and enjoyed a glorious day, finishing through a line of unbroken cornices stretching for several miles.

Next came the turn of Ben Nevis, with Jane, Charlie, and Raeburn teaming up for a first ascent of *Central Gully* (240m III) on South Trident Buttress. A steep ice pitch was avoided by the party, before finishing up the wide snowfield and the sun above. This last climb was recorded in the SMCJ with an article by Jane Inglis Clark.[11] The route is described in the current guide as a fine climb with an alpine feel. Elsewhere on Nevis, on 11th June the Walker cousins Charles and Harry found a climb right of Carn Dearg Buttress, *Cousins' Buttress* (275m Very Difficult). It has a wet start up a watercourse and gives better opportunities in winter conditions at Grade III.

On Sunday 12th June, the Walkers climbed a route starting at the foot of Slingsby's Chimney, and taking the rocks about 150ft to the left. This would place it close to a modern Severe (*Rain Trip* 180m Severe), and possibly near *Green and Napier's Route* of 1895 (150m Difficult). Writing this chapter in 2013, a year in which several fatal avalanches have occurred, it is salutary to note that in approaching their route, the Walkers narrowly missed being wiped out by a huge avalanche which crashed down what was to become Zero Gully.

> …it fell into the large snowfield, and thundered down into the valley below. Many large blocks of hard snow bounded down until the screes were reached, when they burst like huge shells, scattering the stones in all directions. Any party caught crossing to Slingsby's Chimney would have been most effectively wiped out.[12]

In August, James Burns, Morrison, Newbigging and Robertson spent several days in the Fort William area. A sally to Garbh Bheinn of Ardgour via the ferry and cycle hit the notorious wet weather streaming in from the sea, and they were unsuccessful at finding the *Great Ridge*, let alone climbing it. Excellent cycles, Robertson noted, were available for a day hire in Fort William, at 3s.6d. per day. In 2013, this sum roughly equates to £16. In 2013, day hire of cycles in Fort William would appear to be around £20.

Robertson and his climbing friends were mostly from the group which would shortly be recognised as middle class. In several of the mountaineering clubs there was also a sprinkling of the upper class. The person responsible for devising the social class scheme was THC Stevenson, a medical statistician in the General Register Office of England and Wales, using a combination of occupation (title or role) and the industry in which the individuals in the population worked. While Stevenson conceived society as divided into three basic social classes (the upper, middle and working classes), in fact he produced a much more complicated classification that subdivides these three. Sticking with the triumvirate, we may regard Raeburn, Robertson, Brown, Clark etc as members of the new middle class, which was only given that name around 1913.[13]

Robertson *et al* moved on to Ben Nevis, where they had more success, climbing the *South-West Ridge* (180m Moderate) on the Douglas Boulder, while the next day they enjoyed Raeburn's Pinnacle Arête on the Tridents, probably making the second ascent. Burns then left, the remaining trio climbing Staircase Climb before spending the night in the Summit Hotel. The next morning they made a taxing descent of Observatory Ridge. In his report, Robertson described this as being both difficult and tedious. Robertson had made the first descent of this fine ridge the previous year with Raeburn, and then had also run into route finding difficulties. He finally concluded that it was a magnificent ridge – *'...for continuous difficulty and interest I think it is the best climb on Ben Nevis.'* [14] We can only surmise that he preferred to ascend the route.

One sad event occurred in October 1904, with the closing of the summit meteorological observatory on Ben Nevis. It had been chronically underfunded by the government of the day, and eventually this situation became unsustainable. Apart from its scientific endeavours, many mountaineers had enjoyed a good day on the mountain, with the extra knowledge that on a dark afternoon or evening in winter they would always find hospitality and shelter there. The observatory made its final log book entry on the 1st October, and after a week of decommissioning, the key was turned for the final time and the observers went their various ways. The nearby summit hotel, which opened shortly after the observatory in 1885, continued to operate in the summer months but finally closed in 1916. It too was used by mountaineers as a summit base from which to explore the Nevis cliffs. [The full story of the Observatory may be found in *Ben Nevis, Britain's Highest Mountain*[15].]

With judicious timing, William Kilgour published his book on life at the observatory the following year.[16] He was not a permanent observer, and most likely acted as a relief observer. His book was reviewed in the SMCJ, possibly by Willie Douglas.[17] The reviewer was unimpressed, mentioning interesting if haphazard chapters, and carelessness in the use of words –

> One can guess what is meant by the "Broken" spectre, the "missives" hurled about by the wind, and the ski-runners "deporting" themselves on the snow, but"caligenous" glens are rather staggering. The expression is "caligenous," [sic] if it means misty or anything like it.

[Here we have an amusing typographic error, as the SMCJ Editor, Douglas, should have written caliginous, unless, of course, he meant to be careless himself as a joke.] The reviewer concluded –

> Most of our members will doubtless concur heartily in the opinions expressed regarding the closing of the Observatories, and the terribly lame apologies which were made on behalf of the Government.

❄ ❄ ❄

In October 1896, Tough and Raeburn had been exploring on the Cobbler. On the North Peak they had attempted what would eventually become Ramshead Gully (60m Very Difficult), failing due to ice. A right traverse on Halfway Terrace then took them to The Fold, the crux pitch of *Recess Route* (85m Severe). Declining to attempt this, they retreated, and made the second ascent of *Right-angled Gully* (35m Very Difficult), The first ascent had been made by Naismith and McGregor the previous month. They boldly tried the Direct Finish, '*...but the last fifteen feet proved too much for us, and, under the conditions, was clearly impossible, a snow cornice several feet thick overhanging its outlet.*'[18]

As we have learned by now, Raeburn was persistent in his climbing and was back on 30th October 1904, this time in a '*...large and merry party, including two ladies,* [who] *had the pleasure of completing the climb.*' This climb was *The Fold*, which was later recorded by Jock Nimlin in 1935 on his first complete ascent of Recess Route. He was obviously unaware of the 1904 ascent. In the 1997 SMC guide, Recess Route was elevated to Severe, mainly due to some holds being polished as a result of the route's popularity. It is also given a winter grade of V,6.

The overall poor weather of the previous year or two seems to have continued, and the New Year Meet of 1905, held at Loch Awe, found the hills with virtually no snow on them at all and rain or sleet throughout. Despite 28 members being present, including John Bell, Inglis Clark, Raeburn and a host of other good climbers, the only new route found was a gully on mixed rock and grass on Beinn a' Bhuiridh, a southern outlier of the Stob Diamh peak of Cruachan lying just east of what is now the Cruachan Reservoir. The party was Morrison, Robertson, and Thomas Goodeve. Morrison was the acknowledged and actual leader on this climb, which had been attempted during earlier meets at this venue. Morrison's lead was the central of three gullies, and provided a wet ascent with several rocky sections, sufficient to satisfy the party on an otherwise barren meet. It was recorded, without name or grade, in MacRobert's 1934 guide to the Central Highlands. Perhaps it could be named *Morrison's Gully* in some future guidebook. Another party made an ascent of the Black Shoot, though their names were not published.[19]

❄ ❄ ❄

To the good of the general morale of mountaineers in Scotland, Easter 1905 had somewhat better weather and some snow. The SMC Meet took place between Thursday 20th April and Tuesday 25th, and was held in two venues: Sligachan on Skye, now refurbished, and the Kingshouse, Glen Coe. The Cuillin could have been described as being bipolar, with snow in the corries and ice crystals on the northern flanks, while the south-facing rocks were free of ice and dry. Most of the activity was ridge walking and traversing, with Raeburn showing his considerable energy on a route from Camasunary to Glen Brittle via Garsbheinn, Sgurr nan Eag, Sgurr Dubh na Da Bheinn, Thearlaich-Dubh Gap, Tearlach, Alasdair, and Sgumain.

On Friday 21st April, a team of tigers entered Harta Corrie via the Bloody Stone, climbing two routes en passant. Raeburn, Slingsby, Solly, and a Swedish guest, Herr Erik Ullén, were headed for the East Face of An Caisteal, selected as a possible shelter from the fierce north-west blizzard. This face is made up of three slabby buttresses of ice-smoothed gabbro. An initial attempt on the south buttress was rebuffed by an overhang, and the party retreated to try the central buttress. Raeburn, leading, gained the steeper section and found the rocks to be free of ice, dry and clean. Here he removed his boots and put on cloth-soled Kletterschuhe.

> A traverse had soon to be made to the left, across and up some steeply inclined slabs. This, none of the party would have cared to attempt, and would have considered it unjustifiable to lead up in boots.[20]

This route is in the current guidebook as *Raeburn's Route* (360m Difficult). The party eventually gained the ridge and the summit, enjoying an enchanting view of the snow- and ice-plastered Cuillin. As their night was to be taken in Camasunary, they decided to descend via Lota Corrie. A short, standing glissade down a steep gully, a traverse out of this before it plunged down more steeply and after entering Harta Corrie, Camasunary was gained at 8.15pm after a weary tramp. One wonders what Ullén, an experienced alpinist, thought about this day, and for that matter the next, when he and Raeburn traversed from Camasunary to Glen Brittle including Garsbheinn to Sgumain via the Thearlaich-Dubh Gap. Large, sticky snowflakes were falling, plastering the rocks, the abseil rope displayed its common failing and stuck, while poor Ullén was half-blind through his necessity to wear spectacles. Despite this they climbed the Gap in 30 minutes, Raeburn leading with gloves. As a forlorn footnote, Ullén, despite being sponsored for the SMC by Raeburn, failed in his application for unknown reasons.

Camasunary Lodge and Farm had been reserved for six participants on the SMC 1903 Easter Meet, from the landowner, an RL Thomson Esq. That meet had been brilliantly organised by William Clark, who for the current meet in 1905 managed to book spaces for about eight Members at a time. The guide John Mackenzie also did some guiding from Camasunary.

On the other venue at the Kingshouse, a gathering of 15 were '*…packed tightly into an unpretentious but most comfortable inn…*', hosted by Donald Stewart, the lessee. On the Friday, Maclay, Oscar Röhde and John M Macharg made what must have been an attempt at climbing Crowberry Direct. They were back at the hotel and while gathering more information, realised that they had traversed right instead of taking the Abrahams' traverse left to the crux. The following day, bolstered by the addition of Naismith and Thomson (Macharg had to leave early), Maclay and Röhde had another attempt, but the weather continued its tricks and a fall of snow prevented an attempt on the crux. Oscar Röhde was a Cheshire cotton merchant who had joined the SMC in 1898; he resigned in 1914, possibly due to an increased work load from the huge increase in demand for cotton goods with the Great War.

Maclay later wrote an article on the Crowberry Ridge, describing the routes, including his own inadvertent variation.[21] The infamous Abraham direct route had so far received one repeat ascent, led by Raeburn, who described it as one of the most difficult climbs yet done in Scotland. As Maclay commented – '*It involves certain disaster to the leader should he slip, and is, in the opinion of the writer, at least on the verge of the unjustifiable even for the very best climber.*'

Maclay's variation avoided the Abraham traverse by traversing left at a higher point. The article was accompanied by a diagram drawn by Naismith, who with Thomson had made the original ascent of the ridge by an easier route. Maclay modestly prefaced his description by stating that he was not describing a new route, but merely indicating how the grand climb which is the Crowberry Ridge '*… may be enjoyed by any party of competent climbing capacity, instead of being reserved for an occasional one of exceptional skill and boldness.*'

Meanwhile, Burns, Morrison and Newbigging had been exploring the North Buttress on the Buachaille, firstly starting from Crowberry Gully, while Naismith and Thomson climbed the same buttress but on the side close to Great Gully. This was on the Friday. On Sunday, Burns, Macalister, Morrison and Newbigging climbed another route on the North Buttress, this time as close to its left edge as possible.

❄ ❄ ❄

On Skye, on 16th June one of the Sgurr nan Gillean gullies, *Third-Fourth* (100m Very Difficult), finally saw a complete ascent, by Robertson Lamb, Henry Bowron, Walton Tattersall and Henry Heap. The gully had in fact been climbed by Norman Collie (and John Mackenzie?) sometime before 1890. However, a subsequent rockfall left a section of the route very dangerous and very loose. The gully is best avoided, having slimy pitches and a loose section, which gave the leader, Lamb, a seriously hard time. Surprisingly, Lamb's party had to kick their way up a huge snowdrift before gaining the foot of the first pitch. It may be worth quoting from an account Lamb gave, if only to forewarn climbers and provide an indication of some of the antics which some cruxes forced on the pioneers –

> At the foot is a narrow ledge with an upright slab. Three of the party climbed on to the ledge and the fourth got into a cave close below and safely belayed. The leader now proceeded to make stepping accommodation of his two colleagues, first on to the back of one, then on to the shoulders, head, and finally on to the out-stretched hands of the other. Still he was almost three feet short of any safe hold. After spending over an hour in vain efforts to overcome the difficulties that side of the gully had to be relinquished. One of the party (Mr Tattersall) then noticed another possible route at the extreme end of the ledge. This was a rotten-looking dyke, and after a short rest, the leader (Mr Lamb) tried again. After displacing a great quantity of loose stones and débris he struggled over the main difficulty, which is very stiff for about fifteen feet, was able to find a good anchorage, and the rest of the party followed.[22]

Tattersall's arms were so tired from holding up other climbers that they were almost useless when it was his turn for the crux. About half-way up this section, he stood on a small resting place, which five seconds later crashed down the gully. *'There go I but for the rope,'* Tattersall remarked to himself. In his Skye manuscript, Pedlar writes that the Abrahams, although crediting the Lamb ascent, gave the route scant space in their Skye book. Perhaps, Pedlar suggests, Ashley Abraham was secretly miffed at being pipped to the post. The Wayfarers' Club hut in Langdale, purchased in 1930, is called the Robertson Lamb Hut, and has been the venue for the SMC September Meet since the mid 1990s.

❄ ❄ ❄

In July 1905, WA Mounsey and G Bennett Gibbs mounted an expedition by car to Glen Coe and the Fort William area. Mounsey's car was a 10-14HP Renault, with the registration BR 68 (i.e the 68th car to be registered in Birmingham). Their holiday proved to be an exciting one, with poor roads (for example the road to Ardgour round Loch Eil was too bad to be driven), and dodgy makeshift ferries: the Ballachulish Ferry relied on two planks of wood balanced across the boat, while the car was kept in place by wooden wedges, the only fixings.

They met up with an SMC party staying at the Kingshouse, consisting of Morrison, Goggs and, as Gibbs irreverently referred to him, the 'sky-pilot', AE Robertson. This resulted in a classic photograph showing

Goggs and Morrison at the crux of Crowberry Direct. The photograph was used to illustrate the dust jacket of the 1934 SMC guide to The Central Highlands. Unfortunately it was posed, as none of the party would lead the Abraham route, taking instead Maclay's variation. Indeed, Morrison was lowered by rope down the crux section. At least Robertson may have learned from Clark's unfortunate lens choice and had the right focal length on this occasion.

> It was agreed with singular unanimity that the pitch is not justifiable for the ordinary run of climbers. Morrison was let down from above, and although he climbed up with only the moral support of the rope, he concurs in the general verdict, and describes the pitch as 40 feet of "boulder" climbing, without the slightest possibility of safeguarding the leader after the first few feet.[23]

The use of the motor car in mountaineering slowly began to increase. Its pioneers included William Clark and the Walker cousins from Dundee. (Charles and Harry Walker were Spinners and Manufacturers of Jute based in Dundee, and obviously had the healthy financial means then necessary to purchase a motor car.) In July 1905 Clark continued his exploration of the Arrochar Alps when with Charles and Mabel he drove up Glen Croe and explored the cliffs of The Brack – *'Massive, dank and sun-starved, the Upper Buttress of the Brack is the antithesis of The Cobbler's sunny South Peak, which it faces across Glen Croe.'*[24]

Not only is The Brack somewhat 'sun-starved', facing as it does east, its geology has lent it an often subterranean air, with many deep fissures, cracks and mysterious caverns on the hillside, and on its crags. One such fissure is to be found at the right-hand end of the main crag, where a conspicuous black chasm cuts deeply into the rocks. It was first climbed on 30th May, 1906, by three young climbers; Alastair Campbell McLaren (1880–1950), a Gaelic-speaking sheep farmer from Inverardran, just east of Crianlarich, SG Shadbolt, and OP Shadbolt. There is a puzzle here, as McLaren climbed with a Leslie Garnet Shadbolt (1883–1973); the other two Shadbolts were probably his sister, and brother Osmund. Both McLaren and LG Shadbolt were to join the SMC in 1911, while Shadbolt became a Vice-President in the Alpine Club. The black chasm would eventually gain its name of Elephant Gully, as the following accounts explain.

Shadbolt left a note in the SMCJ with minimal information.[25] *'There is a good deal of grass in this gully which renders it rather bad on a wet day, but it is an interesting climb and in a most beautiful situation.'* The note was in fact inserted following an article by William Clark, in which he and his wife Jane had explored the cliffs of The Brack, travelling there by motor car.[26] And the reason that Clark was prompted to explore The Brack was due to Norman Collie telling Clark that it was a scandal that the SMC should allow so noble a mountain as The Brack to remain unexplored, *'...seeing that it possessed finer cliffs, climbs, and precipices than the Cobbler, &.'* This may well have been Collie's impish sense of humour of course, but it certainly had the desired effect. The two Clarks were there in 1905, sometime before the Easter Meet in April, but conditions were so wintry as to preclude any ascent. They did attempt the deep fissure on the right of the main cliff, but it was very icy, with avalanches of ice or snow from above, forcing a retreat.

The Clark family returned on the 14th July 1906, with William, Mabel and Charlie, and succeeded in climbing a buttress route on the left of the face, which they christened the Knife-Edge Buttress. Their route, for some unknown reason, was re-named the *Inglis Clark Arête*, and so it has remained ever since. However the guidebooks, including the current edition, have introduced a date error, as they have the first ascent as being 1895. Young Charlie Clark made his first climb in 1900, and was to join the SMC in 1906. In 1895 he would have been seven years of age.

Details of the Elephant Gully climb are fortunately supplied by Raeburn, who climbed the gully with Charlie Clark in 1912.[27] He was unaware of the first ascent by McLaren and Shadbolt when he approached the route on the cold, frosty morning of 3rd November.

Raeburn, in one of his literary diversions from the usual reportage, also poetically described the approach round the head of Loch Long, on this still winter morning –

> Keen frost the previous night, and this morning an absolute dead calm, left the whole visible extent of the surface of Loch Long unruffled by the faintest ripple. The water was of extraordinary clearness, and more extraordinary still, seemed to possess in full the double capacity of perfect reflection and absolute transparency. At once every detail of the boulder-strewn shore, the bracken-clad lower slopes, the snow-tipped peaks, and the deep blue sky were mirrored in its polished surface. At the same time the rocks, the sands, and the seaweed of the loch bottom were visible through the upper pictures of the surface. The effect struck one as though the water was not real. Something airier, lighter, more alive than the somewhat heavy and very inelastic substance which we know results from the marriage of the fiery oxygen to the volatile hydrogen.

Here, Raeburn had exposed his education, having a chemistry degree from the Watt Institution, Edinburgh. Below the gully they gathered for lunch. The bold Raeburn, always with an eye for a future line, spotted that the slabby buttress to the left of the gully looked promising. On the day however, its summit was fringed with plates of ice, while great icicles hung from the jutting ledges of the upper part. No one, therefore, even thought of trying it. As it happens, several hard lines would be found there in future years.

Raeburn and young Charlie started up the gully. It was a wide one, the underside of the first chockstone fully 20ft across, and wholly impossible to climb directly. The two began to burrow underneath, finding that after about 80ft from the entrance the way became narrow, slimy, and very steep. They retreated and, roping up, climbed the right wall. This provided the route leading on to the turf-covered summit of the second, and great, chockstone.

This monster chockstone also provided the name for the gully –

> Especially huge is the upper of these. One does not quite realise this till close at hand. In fact, doubts were expressed by someone of the possibility of getting behind the chockstone, whether the aperture, which was evidently there, would prove large enough. Another made the remark, "I believe an elephant, were he a rock-climber, would probably be able to get through."

Above lay the crux of the route. From its turf-covered top, a neat horizontal ledge led out on the right wall. The ledge was overhung above and just wide enough to stand on without falling over. At its outer end was a small recess, at head height and about 18ins wide with a sharp-angled crack in clean rock. The crack was the key hold, but Raeburn could not quite reach it. A gentle heave from the powerful shoulder of Charlie and the key was in hand. When Charlie followed he found that his extra height [he was 5ft 11in] enabled him to reach the hold without any jump. A final, mossy tunnel led to an exit, a neat green hole in the turf some way back from the cliff edge. Then they saw the cairn – *'However, we did not grudge it to the then unknown pioneers. We had enjoyed the climb to the full, and the uncertainty of the issue had kept up our interest to the very last.'* Today, *Elephant Gully* (90m Difficult) is probably better in winter, at III/IV.

❄ ❄ ❄

Raeburn was comfortable enough with his status, and certainly knowledgeable enough, to write a long and serious paper on 'Scottish Snow.' It was published in the September 1905 issue of the SMCJ.[28] It included two photographs by Gilbert Thomson of Willie Naismith demonstrating glissading, and a photograph by Raeburn of a Scottish bergschrund, the topmost section of a snowfield where the snow ends and the steeper rock above begins, often with a gap between the two. In his introduction, Raeburn acknowledged his indebtedness both to Naismith's 1893 article on *Snowcraft in Scotland*,[29] and Claude Wilson's book *Mountaineering*.[30] The paper is interesting not least because it indicates some of the climbing practices prevalent at this time.

> He [Naismith] boldly claimed for British winter climbing that it approached in many respects to good summer work in the Alps. The present writer goes further, and considers that winter mountaineering in Scotland is in many respects a better training and a more strenuous sport than most of the ordinary Swiss work, where one plods behind a guide up a well-known route by what is often a plainly marked track.

Raeburn mentioned the great spike versus pick controversy that raged for some time in the SMCJ, following an article by Naismith which was criticised by John Gibson (see Chapter 5). He sided with Naismith in this instance, regarding that balance was the fundamental secret of safe climbing, whether on rocks or ice. Just as importantly, given the popularity of glissading, Raeburn warned of the need for caution in steep places should glissading be planned, citing a fatal accident in the Lake District which occurred on 26th December, 1903, described below. [Raeburn actually refers to Easter 1903, but the details correspond with an incident in December.]

Alexander Goodall of Keswick, and Fred Botterill of Leeds arranged to ascend Scafell Pinnacle, via Steep Ghyll and the ridge route, on December 26th 1903. (The older spelling was Gill, and the weight of opinion has now returned to that. Seemingly Ghyll was a Victorian affectation, as they thought it more romantic.) Ten minutes were afterwards spent at the summit of Scafell, and the glorious sunset they witnessed being immediately followed by another snow shower, the two men made their way back, intending to descend Deep Ghyll by the West Wall Traverse. (Botterill, one of the best Lakes climbers in the period leading up to WWI, made the first ascent in 1903 of Botterill's Slab climb, one of the first rock climbs to be graded Very Severe. He suffered TNT poisoning while working in a munitions factory during the Great War, and died in 1920.)

Just below the top of the gully Goodall began to solo down a patch of soft snow that was followed by about 12ft of scree. Another patch of snow lay below. Botterill asked Goodall for the axe, but Goodall was determined to continue. Both climbers carried a rope but had not roped up. Goodall began to glissade in a standing position until he reached the scree. Three or four steps then led him to the second snow patch, where he sat down and began sliding down, using the axe as a brake. He then seemed to stop for an instant but the next moment Botterill saw him on his back, arms outstretched, and accelerating downward and over a steepening. He had lost hold of the axe and was found dead below by another climbing party who had witnessed the fall.

Goodall was fairly competent on rock, but apparently unknown to Botterill had little or no experience on snow and ice.[31] In fact, Botterill had intended to investigate the descent himself but Goodall insisted that he wanted to do it. There had been several close calls to SMC members while glissading, including that of Professor GG Ramsay at Easter 1894, when on Ben Achallader he lost both control and his ice-axe and was lucky to escape losing nothing further than his cap and a little skin.[32]

Raeburn's paper included slope angles in winter, snow arêtes, and other aspects of snow and ice slopes including avalanches. Several of the latter are listed, including one witnessed on the Ross-shire Ben Dearg, which had a width of over 100 yards. This event was seen by HGS Lawson and Hugh Munro, as they were exploring Beinn Dearg and the Fannichs area.[33] Even Munro, who had much winter experience under his sporran, had never seen anything like it. We have previously noted the 1904 avalanche on Ben Nevis, which narrowly missed killing the Walker cousins. There is a description in his paper of an incipient avalanche in which Raeburn himself was involved, fortunately with no injuries to the party of three. It occurred at New Year, 1904, on Ben Nevis.

> Ascending the Observatory Gully on Nevis, the snow was found to be very hard. Higher a layer of powdery snow, with a slight surface crust, lay on the hard. Shortly after adopting the precaution of cutting right through this upper snow, and making steps in the solid underneath, and when at a good height above an unpleasant iced wall, the whole upper surface suddenly cracked right across the gully, here about 40 yards wide, just above us. It did not at that time move farther, but the precaution of cutting into the under layer was a very necessary one, and should invariably be adopted in like circumstances, even though it involve considerably more labour.

Here Raeburn must surely have been using his hard-earned Alpine experience, though modern climbers would probably have avoided the slope altogether, once they had seen, by digging an exploratory trench, that they were in a zone of slab formation. Bob Barton, one of the authors of the standard British book on avalanches,[34] makes the following comments on Raeburn's observation.

> Raeburn has written a very clear description of the kind of conditions that often precede a windslab avalanche (including the one that got me in Coire an t' Sneachda, also at New Year) being a soft windslab over a hard base. The "slight surface crust" may have been a wind crust or, less likely, a sun crust but the fact that the crack propagated across the whole slope is a strong indication that Raeburn had encountered a windslab.
>
> His decision to cut into the under layer was a sound one since it put the additional loading of his body weight onto the stronger under layers but it also suggests that the slab was relatively shallow; it becomes impracticable to cut or kick into the under layers once the soft slab reaches half a metre or even less. Typically, as one ascends a gully, the slab deepens in a kind of reverse taper towards the peak accumulation zone, which is often just under the cornice. The climber in such a place tends to progress as the slab deepens from climbing on hard snow, to being able to penetrate through the soft slab to the firm under layers, to climbing on the slab itself, the hard under layer having become inaccessible. This is when the avalanche is likely to release.[35]

Cornices, the overhang of snow sometimes found at the top of gullies or on the flanks of ridges, was another topic Raeburn touched upon. These can block the egress of climbers if sufficiently large or formed of hard snow. Numerous ascents have finished with a tunnel having to be dug through a cornice: hard, tiring, and uncomfortable work at the end of an ascent. Raeburn's own researches through the pages of the SMCJ found that the maximum size found by mountaineers in Scotland seemed to be about 20ft in height and with a 10ft overhang. One of the observers at Ben Nevis Observatory, however, informed Raeburn that he had measured a cornice at the head of Observatory Gully which was 40ft in height.

Raeburn's description of ice-axe braking is very different from modern teachings, but we have to remember that he and his contemporaries were using a much longer axe. He advocated placing the upper hand on the shaft near the head, palm turned up, and the lower hand on the shaft, palm turned down. The ice-axe was then put behind one, with the spike dragging through the snow, as in a boat's tiller through the water. This method allowed an immense braking power to be applied, by widening the space between the hands, and raising the body on the lower hand. The climber would of course be leaning back, facing down the slope in this method.

Belaying on snow in Raeburn's days meant driving the shaft of the axe into the slope and taking a turn of the rope round the shaft. Unless the belayer was adept at using a dynamic belay, allowing the rope to run for some distance round his waist should a climber fall, the outcome would usually mean the belayer and axe being pulled down the slope, or the wooden shaft snapping with the same result. Again, the mantra instilled on every mountaineer's consciousness was that *'the leader shalt not fall.'*

In his summing up of Scottish snow, Raeburn stated his case quite simply that safety above all was the main objective of a mountaineer, and that balance was the primary technique. On hard snow or ice, while nailed boots were capable of upward motion they would not be as secure as crampons. These would eventually become universal in winter but until then, there was always the risk of a downward slip if the foot was not placed correctly and it was therefore crucial that the climber retained an upright stance whenever possible.

> Above all he should have learned, if he is capable of learning, the great lesson of balance, to stand up straight and to plant the feet firmly in the steps. He must also remember, however, that though his conquest of the snowy gully, with its 10 or 20 foot ice pitches, is probably a more difficult and risky bit of climbing than almost anything usually done in the Alps, still there everything is on a much greater scale, and endurance of long-continued exertion is much more valuable than any other climbing qualities, except balance and caution. Balance is the most valuable quality because it in reality doubles at least a climber's endurance. All three qualities spell safety on long and difficult expeditions, and safe is the highest qualifying adjective we can bestow upon the mountaineer.

This point was also well made in Dent's *Mountaineering*, where in the chapter on *'Snowcraft'*, he explains the techniques required on a traverse.

> There is no time at which it is of more importance to stand properly in the steps than when a man immediately in front or behind has slipped badly and fallen clean out of his step on a steep ice-slope. If in attempting to check a man who has fallen, those who are still in their steps follow the natural inclination and try to get a handhold by leaning towards the slope, the feet are almost sure to be jerked out by the pull...The body may be bent forwards or backwards, but must not lean towards the slope.[36]

❄ ❄ ❄

The early weeks of April 1906 were marked by a good spell of weather. The preceding New Year Meet, held at Tyndrum, though popular and enjoyed by some 29 members and six guests present, was not marked by climbs out of the ordinary. By the time the Easter Meet came round on Friday, 13th April, the weather had been superb for the preceding 10 days, with a drought under a cloudless sky. This did not go unnoticed by Raeburn, who had his eyes on an ascent of The Chasm on Buachaille Etive Mor.

The Easter Meet at Glen Coe was so popular that it was held at the Kingshouse, Clachaig and Ballachulish Hotels. One enduring memento of this meet is the group photograph taken by Archie Robertson in front of the Clachaig Hotel on the Saturday morning. This has some 29 of the great and the good (plus one 'gatecrashing' local), and has been reproduced many times, including in Clark and Pyatt's *Mountaineering in Britain*. In total some 38 members and 11 guests were in attendance.

The Chasm, at 450m and Very Severe, is one of the best gully climbs in Scotland. Its deep cleft defines the left boundary of the mountain's south-east face. It almost rivalled Church-Door Buttress in its attention from the early pioneers, with John Bell and James Maclay climbing it as far as the '100-foot pitch' in 1898, and William and Jane Clark with Raeburn exploring its upper pitches in June 1903. When Raeburn and the Clarks finally exited from high up the gully in 1903, they did so by climbing Lady's Pinnacle, several pitches below the Cauldron.

One has to be careful in reading accounts of early gully and chimney climbs, due to the earlier climbers using 'true' left and right, meaning left and right when facing down the route, following standard geographical practice for describing watercourses. At a later date, left and right became to mean the more logical terms when looking up a route.

With the spell of drought conditions, Raeburn and Ling, who by now had formed a formidable climbing rope with successful Alpine seasons under their belts, had high hopes of ideal conditions in the gully. There was however much snow in the gully, so much so that the lowest section was a uniform slope of hard snow. At one pitch, faced with a potentially dangerous fall into a space between snow and rock, the leader removed boots and climbed in wool stockings. Raeburn remarked here in his report that double stockings, while the essential wear for walking, would have been useless for rock climbing.

The lower half of the '100-foot pitch' was taken up by snow so they found themselves standing on a huge mass of snow, which stretched half-way up the crux pitch. Raeburn calculated that the depth of snow here would have been close to 100ft.

> Still high above us loomed the remaining 100 feet of the pitch, a black slimy slit of smooth rock, down which hissed and gurgled enough water, in gallons per minute, to furnish an ample supply to a fair-sized town. Even if we had thought of tackling this, which we did not, the walls were quite inaccessible, several yards of black vacancy, save for water-spray, separating them from the thin tongue of snow on which we stood.[37]

The necessity to retreat back down the gully was avoided by gaining a narrow crack on the left (south) wall. This was too narrow to enter and follow, but the leader jammed himself in it which allowed some security for the second, who could then gain another ledge on the left. They eventually exited the gully, finding themselves at the col which separated the pinnacle Raeburn had climbed in 1903 from the rest of the mountain. When they gained the summit, it was so windless that a match burned unsheltered. All around, muirburn veiled the distant hills in a blue-grey haze of smoke. Finally, hunger beckoned and the pair scampered down to the Kingshouse and dinner.

In the current guidebook, indeed in guidebooks since that of WH Murray's in 1949, the partial ascent of The Chasm (i.e. an ascent exiting below the crux at the top of the Devil's Cauldron) has been credited to Noel and Mona Odell, and RF Stobart in April 1920, exiting by the South Chimney. In his first ascent listing, Murray explains why he did not credit Raeburn and Ling with their partial ascent in April 1906 –

> The climb has not been admitted as a first ascent, on the grounds that the extraordinarily great volume of snow robbed the gully of everything, apart from situation, that distinguishes it as "The Chasm". Exit was made by the South Wall.[38]

This seems a bit harsh, considering the efforts which Raeburn had been making to climb this fine gully.

There is another hangover from the 1906 Easter Meet in Glen Coe, that of the mention in the Meet report of ascents of a 'central gully' on Stob Coire nan Lochan. On the Saturday, 14th April, the report states that – *Messrs Collie, Naismith, and Slingsbys (père et fils) climbed the central gully on Stob Coire nan Lochan.*[39] This might refer to what is now SC Gully, a popular Grade III route, the first ascent of which is ascribed to Baird, Leslie & Fynes-Clinton in March 1934. Collie's party was competent enough to have made an ascent in 1906, given good conditions, but there appears to be no account of the ascent. Two other possibilities exist; one is that 'central gully' was then the name referred to what is now Broad Gully, the easy snow gully right of Summit Buttress, and a commonly used route of descent. The second is that the 'central gully' was *NC Gully* (180m I/II), normally a straightforward and pleasant snow gully.

Further on in the same report is another, connected puzzle –

> On Tuesday there was a general exodus homewards. Some of the contingent from England remained over. Messrs Glover and Worsdell had a good climb in one of the gullies on Stob Coire nan Lochan. They found some of the pitches difficult, and had five hours of step-cutting. As a result they did not put in an appearance at Ballachulish until 11 P.M.

Again, Murray has a note in his first ascent list, in which he has given the above ascent as being of North-West Gully on Stob Coire nam Beith, stating that the name of the mountain was misprinted. There is, unfortunately, no explanation given as to how he came to this conclusion. It is possible that Glover and Worsdell did make an ascent of North-West Gully, particularly if they climbed the lower pitches more directly. Perhaps Glover and Worsdell had climbed SC Gully on the Easter Meet. Unless more information is found however, we will never know, and this interesting 'what if' must remain as conjecture. We leave a final word to Robin Campbell –

> Murray was not immune to error or bias: he overlooked Raeburn's ascents of *Crowberry Gully* in winter and discounted his ascent of *The Chasm*, "…it has not been admitted as a first ascent…" and he buried MacRobert's all-but-the-last-move, 1910 winter attempt on the *Shelf Route* in a footnote. Glover and Worsdell were perfectly capable of climbing *SC Gully* in 1906, and might well have done so.[40]

References

1. Proceedings of the Club. SMCJ 8, 44, May 1904, 100-109.
2. Clark W. Inglis. *Garbh-Bheinn of Ardgour and the North-East Ridge of Aonach Beag*. SMCJ 8, 45, Sept. 1904, 139-148.
3. Clark W. Inglis. *Photography in Colours for Mountaineers.* SMCJ 10, 60, 294-306.
4. Howie, W. Lamond. *Mountain Photography*. SMCJ 2, 5, May 1893, 249-253.
5. Solly, G.A. *Another Account of the same Expedition* Proceedings of the Club. SMCJ 8, 44, May 1904, 119-120.
6. Morrison, W.A. *The Rose Ridge of Sgoran Dubh*. SMCJ 8, 45, Sept. 1904, 152-156.
7. Proceedings of the Club. *Thirty-Third Meet of the Club, Aviemore, Easter, 1904.* SMCJ 8, 44, May 1904, 110-115.
8. Strange, Greg. *The Cairngorms. 100 Years of Mountaineering*. (Scottish Mountaineering Trust. 2010), 19.
9. Hinxman, Lionel W. SMCJ 3, 16, Jan. 1895, 218-222.
10. Raeburn, Harold. *Sgurr Ruadh and Coire Lair.* In: Excursions. SMCJ 8, 46, Jan. 1905, 221-223.
11. Inglis Clark, J. *Three on the Centre Grid of the Trident Buttress, Ben Nevis.* SMCJ 8, 45, Sept. 1904, 149-151.
12. H.W. [Harry Walker]. *The North-East Buttress*. In: Excursions. SMCJ 8, 45, Sept. 1904, 180-181.
13. Rose, David. *Official Social Classifications in the UK.* Social Research Update, Issue 9, July 1995. University of Surrey.
14. Robertson A.E. *Ben Nevis in August*. In: Excursions. SMCJ 8, 46, Jan. 1905, 220-221.
15. Crocket, Ken & Richardson, Simon. *Ben Nevis - Britain's Highest Mountain.* (Scottish Mountaineering Trust, 2nd Edition 2009.))
16. Kilgour, Wm. T. *Twenty Years on Ben Nevis,* (Paisley: Alexander Gardner, 1905.)
17. Review of '*Twenty Years on Ben Nevis.*' In: Mountaineering Literature. SMCJ 8, 48, Sept. 1905, p.334.
18. Raeburn, Harold. *The Cobbler.* In: Excursions. SMCJ 4, 22, Jan. 1897, 248-249.
19. Proceedings of the Club. *Thirty-Fourth Meet of the Club, New Year, 1905, Loch Awe*. SMCJ 8, 47, May 1905, 249-250.
20. Raeburn, H. *Skye—The Castles from Harta Corrie*. In: Excursions. SMCJ 9, 50, May 1906, 101-102.
21. Maclay, James. *The Crowberry Ridge of Buchaille Etive Mor*. SMCJ 8, 48, Sept. 1905, 304-308.
22. Lamb, Robertson. *Sgurr-Nan-Gillean: Direct Ascent of the Gully between the Third and Fourth Pinnacles*. SMCJ 9, 51, Sept. 1906, p.288.
23. Bennett Gibbs, G. *More Motoring Among the Mountains and a Kingshouse Meet in July*. SMCJ 9, 49, 9-18.

24. Prentice, Tom. In: *Arran, Arrochar and the Southern Highlands.* (SMC Rock and Climbers' Guide. 1997.)
25. Shadbolt, S.G. *The Brack.* In: Excursions, SMCJ 9, 51, Sept. 1906, 144.
26. Clark, W. Inglis. *The Motor in Mountaineering – The Brack.* SMCJ 9, 49, Jan. 1906, 19-24.
27. Raeburn, Harold. *The Brack: Elephant Gully.* SMCJ 12, 70, February 1913, 209-214.
28. Raeburn, Harold. *Scottish Snow.* SMCJ 8, 48, Sept. 1905, 285-298.
29. Naismith, W.W. *Snowcraft in Scotland.* SMCJ 2, 4, Jan. 1893, 157-167.
30. Wilson, Claude. *Mountaineering.* (London: George Bell & Sons, 1893).
31. *The Accident In Deep Ghyll.* Yorkshire Ramblers' Club Journal, 2, 5, 79-82.
32. Ramsay, Professor G.G., *The Formation of the Scottish Mountaineering Club.* SMCJ 4, 20, May 1896, 73-91.
33. Lawson, H.G.S. *Beinn Dearg and the Fannichs.* SMCJ 6, 35, May 1901, 152-160.
34. Barton, Bob, and Wright, Blyth. *A Chance in a Million?* (Scottish Mountaineering Trust, 2000, 2nd revised Edition.)
35. Barton, Bob. *Personal communication,* 14th March 2013.
36. Dent, C.T. *Mountaineering.*(London: Longmans, Green and Co., Second Edition, 1892), 176.
37. Raeburn, Harold. *The "Chasm," Buchaille Etive Mor.* In: Excursions, SMCJ 9, 51, Sept. 1906, 149-151.
38. Murray, W.H. 1949. *Rock-Climbing Guide to Glencoe and Ardgour.* (Edinburgh: SMC, 1949), 150.
39. Proceedings of the Club. *Thirty-Seventh Meet of the Club, Easter, 1906. Ballachulish, Clachaig, Kingshouse.* SMCJ 9, 50, May 1906, 81.
40. Campbell, Robin N. *Glover and Worsdell's Gully, April 1906. Was it SC Gully or North-West Gully?* In: Miscellaneous Notes. SMCJ 40, 197, 2006, 402-403.

12

Nevis Highlights (1906-07)

George Mallory (1886–1924) has a special significance in British mountaineering. Speculation about his death on the 1924 Everest Expedition, with the perennial question of whether or not he and his companion Irvine succeeded in their summit bid, continues to this day, and has made him a household name. It provides an interesting contrast then, to recall his final mountain outing on Everest, the highest mountain on earth, with an early one on Ben Nevis, Britain's highest mountain.

In this account, Mallory was in his 20th year, a first-year student at Cambridge. While he was at school at Winchester College, one of the schoolmasters, Graham Irving, had introduced him to climbing, Irving was 29 and in 1904 had formed the Winchester Ice Club. Mallory had befriended another pupil, Guy Leach, who was one year older than himself. The Minute Books of the Ice Club include an account of the trio's ten-day expedition to Fort William, including five days spent exploring Ben Nevis, which were written up by Irving. The Books surfaced in 2009 and eventually found their way to the Alpine Club in London; in addition to an article in the AJ,[1] we are grateful to Peter Gillman for providing a copy of the pages from the Volume of the Minute Books which describes in detail their trip.

They arrived in Fort William on Tuesday, 3rd April 1906, Mallory having decided to make part of his journey by boat from Birkenhead to Clydeside. Basically, they alternated their days by climbing on the Ben and taking to a rowing boat on Loch Linnhe, with one other day spent climbing Stob Ban in the Mamores (becoming lost on the return when attempting to continue via Mullach nan Coirean.) What seems incongruous is their almost total ignorance of existing routes and mountain features on Nevis. Some four years earlier the SMC had published a guide to the mountain in their Journal. This lack of knowledge, which to some would suggest overconfidence (and there is a fine line between overconfidence and arrogance), would certainly have increased the challenge they faced on the huge expanse of cliff that was the north-east face of the mountain. Gillman suggests as one possibility that this lack of research may have been deliberate, Irving wishing to maximise the forthcoming adventure.

As Gillman also notes, Irving as leader knew of only two features: the 'North-east Ridge', (i.e. the North-East Buttress), and Tower Ridge. On the 1902 OS six-inch map, only two mountain features of interest to climbers are named: Castle Ridge and Tower Ridge. The North-East Buttress is not named. When the SMC published their Ben Nevis guide in 1902, it included the same map but it had been updated by the SMC to include some 25 named features, including the North-East Buttress. Irving was in the Alpine Club but for some reason their library then did not subscribe to the SMCJ, which goes some way in mitigating his lack of knowledge of the mountain. His consistent naming of the North-East Ridge instead of Buttress, and the fact that the trio made up several names for other features, makes one presume that he had no sight of the SMC Guide.

On Wednesday, 4th April, they sallied out for their first experience of Nevis. They were possibly over-confident. They were certainly going into the unknown. They had a feature name that was to be their target – the Tower Ridge. They gained the foot of the Douglas Boulder at 12.45pm and had a leisurely 35-minute lunch for before roping up and cutting steps up Western Gully. None of these names were used by the Winchester trio, and we rely on their topographical descriptions here for working out where they went.

They gained the Douglas Gap and climbed the steep rock pitch leading to the ridge. Progress went easily at first until they reached the foot of a steep mass of rock –

> ...which appeared to be the Tower: as this was completely wrapt in a thick coating of ice, further advance that way was seen to be hopeless; but when tracks had been retraced for a short distance, a possible route to the right showed itself.

They had been caught in the potential trap which is the steepening on the ridge known as the Little Tower. This is best climbed at its left end, but it gently persuades one to continue moving right until a parallel ridge, lower than the main ridge, is gained, a feature known as Secondary Tower Ridge. They followed this for some distance before realising their error. Being unable to find a way back on to the main ridge as all rocks were sheathed in snow and ice, they abandoned the ascent at 5pm, making a tedious descent, Mallory going first and clearing out their steps, Leach next, with Irving as the leader coming down last.

When they finally regained the Douglas Gap, they decided to descend via the Eastern Gully, the normal approach route, and one they found much shorter and safer. Here Leach found some difficulty in using the steps prepared by Irving in the failing light and slipped, being held on the rope by Mallory. They eventually reached the glen in one piece at 8pm, and their lodgings at 10.30pm, to be met by their anxious landlady. Fortunately, a search party had not yet been organised. During their outing, there had been a strong wind, but otherwise conditions were close to perfect.

They returned to the Ben on Friday 6th April, and from their description climbed Tower Gully (120m Grade I). The snow was good, and the angle allowed progress by kicking steps. When some soft snow with a hard base was gained, Mallory took a turn –

> ...and with his usual energy kicked some ample steps. At this moment the two figures, to which reference has previously been made, appeared in the valley below: the first was evidently that of a man, the second, following a short distance behind, probably that of a woman.

A brief, shouted conversation took place, before the unknown figures passed out of sight. For some reason the name Solly was raised as possible identification, but we know that the Rev AE Robertson was based in Fort William during this time, and it is quite feasible that it was he and his wife Kate. Throughout their stay in Fort William, these two figures were the only mountain users the trio saw.

Continuing up Observatory Gully, the left-hand gully above, Gardyloo Gully, was considered, but was thought too hard. Both that, and Tower Gully, had received their first winter ascents in 1897, by three AC members. As mentioned, Irving seems to have been unaware of this. They roped up and Irving cut his way across a steep slope, with a small rock face below and right. They were aware of the serious position, and their leader cut ample steps, '*...sloping inwards, were made in the hard névé beneath the fresh snow, which varied in depth from 0 to 15 inches.*' Irving overcame the steep wall and cornice at the top of the gully and by dint of vigorous thumping succeeded in raising an arm on to the plateau. It was 3.20pm, and they had climbed Tower Gully.

Back on the mountain on Monday 9th April, they climbed Carn Mor Dearg then descended into the glen and headed for the Trident Buttresses. Dropping down into the glen they observed that both the North-East Buttress and Tower Ridge were '*...still hopelessly ice-bound.*' They therefore climbed what may have been North Trident Buttress (200m III), first climbed by Raeburn's party two years earlier. They topped out on Carn Dearg at 6.25pm, before continuing to the summit of Nevis to witness a superb sunset. On Tuesday 10th, after the rucsac they had accidentally dropped down the route the previous day had been recovered, it was the turn of the easy *Ledge Route* (450m II), to be climbed.

The climax of their stay came on Thursday 12th, with an ascent of the North-East Buttress. Majestically commanding the skyline, they would have found its line just as attractive and dominating as had members of the SMC and others in previous visits. Their confidence had been boosted by their successes following the Tower Ridge débacle and they decided to leave most of their food and other equipment at the foot of the buttress. They also had a plan to descend by the Tower Ridge, the hot sun of the previous trip making them think that sufficient snow and ice would have lifted off the rocks.

North-East Buttress had received its first winter ascent by Naismith and four others in 1896 (see Chapter 8). He left no details of the ascent however, and it was not until 1925 that in a retrospective article he provided one paragraph on its ascent.[2] This dearth of information, coupled with its obvious forbidding outline, length and steepness, probably precluded any subsequent winter ascents until Irving's party stepped on to the rocks at noon. There is also a good argument that the early Scottish pioneers did not consciously separate summer from winter ascents of particular routes; they climbed a route following their Alpine experience, because it was a good line.

As they climbed in all weather and conditions, a route was a route, and they did not differentiate between summer and winter ascents for some years to come. A route first climbed as a rock climb was not generally regarded as an automatic candidate for a winter ascent until equipment and attitudes changed following the First World War.

Irving changed the order on the rope, with Mallory swopping places with Leach and taking the middle. In the Minutes Book there are several mentions of Mallory being an excellent 'windlass'. We can surmise that Irving had more confidence in Mallory than Leach as a belayer. The arête was gained at 3.30pm and progress went well for some distance. Irving dropped his axe when clearing ice off a rock but continued once another axe was passed up.

More hard cutting led eventually to what sounded very like the crux pitches of the buttress, as vertical rocks and ice were reached. This was possibly the notorious rock feature known as the Man-trap. Irving attempted to bypass this on the right, the way Brown and Tough had gone in their summer ascent, but abandoned this in favour of a snow ledge to the left which led up a perpendicular rock face about eight feet in height, scaled with some difficulty. The leader, after so much step cutting, was obviously tiring, but they felt that the top could not be too far off. A traverse right led to what they found to be the *'greatest feat of the whole climb'*, an ice-chimney.

With the increase in altitude, the ice was becoming thicker, as an impassable wall seemed to loom ahead. Irving found a couloir however, which led to a still steeper, broad ice-chimney, vertical at the top. This section, which was probably the '40ft chimney' pitch, took Irving about 1hr 15minutes. *'Again and again it seemed that the leader must be baffled despite his vigorous efforts.'* Finally he wriggled his way over the top onto the flat surface above. The remainder of the route went more easily, with Mallory checking a *'slight slip'* by Leach before the weary party gained the plateau at 8.25pm. They had taken just over eight hours for the ascent. Naismith, in a party of five and with some knowledge of the route, had taken just under seven hours. All thoughts of crowning the day with a descent of Tower Ridge were, of course, forgotten.

There is no doubt that a heavy load was placed on Irving; he had led all the roped climbing in good if icy conditions, with two relatively inexperienced seconds. The expedition by this trio showed a strong bond of three young men perfused with determination and self-confidence; features which Mallory would later take to the higher mountains. They were fortunate to survive their Ben Nevis trip with no serious outcome, given their lack of local knowledge or for that matter a map. The weather and conditions were kind to them, and they must have been physically fit. It had nonetheless been a remarkable display of mountaineering. Irving continued at Winchester, retiring in 1937, and died in 1969, in his 92nd year. Guy Leach also became a teacher and won a Military Cross in the First World War. He died in 1957, aged 72.

Nine days later, on Sunday, 22nd April 1906, Harold Raeburn arrived in Fort William. In Scotland the wet sou'wester had backed to a strong, cold wind from the north-east, providing flurries of snow. Raeburn had arranged to climb with the Rev AE Robertson, but to their mutual regret Robertson was unable to accompany Raeburn owing to a slight indisposition –

> I was saved the necessity of climbing the "Comb" solus, however, as he introduced me to a Genevese gentleman, a member of the Swiss Alpine Club, Monsieur Eberhard Phildius, who was staying in Fort-William, and who proved a pleasant companion and a keen and capable climber.[3]

These few words, from Raeburn's article on his ascent of Green Gully, provide much insight into his character. The weather had broken, if still wintry; his intended companion for what he knew would be a difficult outing had dropped out; and yet he was determined enough to mount a solo attempt on the intended route, which was Comb Buttress. That another competent mountaineer was on hand was a stroke of luck. Phildius was possibly in the Fort to meet up with Robertson, as both had an interest in the Christian Youth Movement.

There is more than a touch of coincidence here however, perhaps even synchronicity; Phildius had made first ascents in the Alps, climbing with Marcel Kurz, the noted Swiss topographer and guide book compiler, including two routes on the Grande Rochère in the Aosta Valley, Italy (the North

Wall and East Arête, 19th August 1905, and the North East Arête, 21st August 1905). Raeburn and Ling had contacts with Kurz, who gave them useful information for their alpine trips, while Robertson had contacts with Phildius through their interest in YMCA and theology matters.

John Quinton Eberhard Phildius (1886–1961) was nine days away from his 20th birthday when he met up with Raeburn, who was twice his age. His mother was Scottish; Eliza Mackinnon, his father Christian Phildius, a naturalized Swiss citizen with important connections in Berlin, was General Secretary of the World Alliance of YMCAs from 1896 to 1922. Eberhard followed his father into YMCA work as secretary of YMCA Switzerland, later volunteering to support War Prisoners Aid work for Allied prisoners of war in Austria-Hungary. He began work with Italian POWs at Mauthausen in Upper Austria (Oberösterreich) in May 1916 and maintained operations there for four months. Phildius was also active in supporting war morale work for Austro-Hungarian soldiers in the Imperial army.

The impression one gains from two photographs taken on the summit of Nevis, was that Phildius was then a tall, athletic mountaineer. The other climber in the photo is Hugh Smith Ingram, a banker from Edinburgh who would join the SMC the following year. Ingram's application form was sponsored by Goggs and seconded by AE Robertson. In a companion photo, Phildius is shown with Alfred Smith, who also joined the SMC in 1907, sponsored by Goggs and seconded by James Buchan. In Smith's form, he mentions that his ascent of Nevis in April 1906 gave him almost 1000ft of hard snow, requiring step cutting. The Ben was obviously in good condition.

The Comb, an elegant and striking buttress at the head of Coire na Ciste, is named from its resemblance to a cock's comb. The buttress is flanked on the left by Comb Gully, and on the right by Green Gully. The Comb had been the target for an earlier attempt by Raeburn, when at the end of June 1902, in superb weather, he had joined William and Mabel Clark on an attempt to climb the rocks of the Comb. They had been unable to find a way up the steep edge overlooking the gully, while water-worn, slabby rock in the gully and possibly the sighting of a cornice finish had forced them to descend after 100ft on the right wall of the gully before continuing a traverse right. This led to the first ascent of Number Three Gully Buttress (150m Moderate), and a popular III in winter conditions. As was so often the case with Raeburn, he was determined to succeed. There is a mention in the 1902 Guide to Ben Nevis that he had descended the upper section of The Comb, presumably as a reconnaissance for an ascent, finding that the upper and middle sections were easy.[4]

With Phildius, the plan was to head up towards Number Two Gully, then traverse right under the overhanging rocks of the Comb to enter the

Coire Mhic Fhearchair, May 1905. Collie climbed on the Central Buttress here around 1898 but left insufficient details to pin the line down precisely. The (left) East Buttress and the (right) West Buttress were climbed in 1907 and 1919 respectively (AE Robertson © SMC)

Stob Garbh. Cruach Ardrain in the background, April 1905. Unrecorded route, climbers unknown (© SMC)

'Rock on Stob Binnein' The climber is demonstrating how to glissade using an alpenstock (© SMC)

1906 SMC Easter Meet held at Ballachulish, Clachaig & Kingshouse. A large, dispersed meet, with some 38 members and 11 guests in all. *'The President [John Rennie] was gratified at finding himself supported by a galaxy of past and present office-bearers...'* (AE Robertson © SMC)

One of the most attractive sections of crag on Ben Nevis, the dominant feature on the left is The Comb, named after a resemblance to a cock's comb. Green Gully bounds it on the right, with No.3 Gully Buttress extending further right (© Simon Richardson)

On 22nd April 1906, two aspirant SMC climbers were on Nevis. They met Phildius and Raeburn at the summit, who had just made the first ascent of Green Gully. This montage, from two photos, shows L to R: Phildius, Hugh Smith, & Alfred Ingram (© SMC)

Green Gully on Ben Nevis, James H.B. Bell leading during the second ascent in 1937. The only real difference in equipment compared with Raeburn's ascent in 1906 would have been the shorter axe used by Bell (© JHB Bell Collection)

Raeburn (top) & Willie Ling on an unrecorded route on Suilven, 30th March 1907 (Ewen B Robertson © SMC)

The West Face of Tower Ridge, Easter 1909. Glover's Chimney is the obvious gully just left of centre. Just right of centre, a prominent snowy recess lies below steep, hanging ice, making a useful landmark. Raeburn's Easy Route runs up and right beneath this, finishing well right of the top of Tower Ridge (AE Robertson © SMC)

Sketch of Goodeve's Route from Charlie Clark's account of his 1908 ascent, drawn by his sister Mabel. The snowy recess is obvious (© SMC)

Diagram from the 1954 Macphee Guide to Nevis. The snowy recess lies above the third 'K' from the right. The 'Ks' mark the Macphee guess as to the line of Goodeve's Route. The 'Rs' indicate Raeburn's Easy Route (© SMC)

Thomas Goodeve was the leader on the eponymous route on Ben Nevis in 1908. His high level of fitness would be a crucial point on the ascent (© SMC)

The North-East corrie of Ben Lui was a favourite destination for the early pioneers, in part due to its Alpine-like slopes with long routes of snow and ice. In suitable conditions, a glissade could be made of the face in a few minutes (Possibly by AE Robertson c. 1908 © SMC)

An action shot taken on Salisbury Crags, Edinburgh. Lucy Smith and Pauline Ranken, June 1908. The route is possibly 'The Long Stride', which has a Very Severe variation (© LSCC)

The LSCC's First New Year Meet, held at Crianlarich, 1908-09. L to R: Lucy Smith, Kitty Stuart, Ruth Raeburn, Jane Inglis Clark, M. Eckhardt, I. McBride, Pauline Ranken (© LSCC)

Probably taken between 1911 and 1913, this photo is a rare, and extremely well-preserved example of the Autochrome process, which was the first practical method for producing colour photos with a single photographic plate. Collie is looking at a glowing neon gas discharge tube, and is credited with making the first such device
(© University College London)

Portrait of John Mackenzie by ER Hughes, July 1908. Gifted to Norman Collie by the artist
(© Sligachan Hotel)

Barrel Buttress in Sail Garbh, Quinag. The Raeburn route, climbed on 1st April 1907 with Ling and Mackay, takes the obvious chimney right of the sunlit patch of rock. In winter it is Grade VI
(© Noel Williams)

The occasion was a Joint LSCC-SMC day at Easter, 8th April 1909. The group on Beinn an Dothaidh was composed of (Men L to R): Harold Raeburn, George Lissant Collins (AC), Alexander Mackay, William Garden, Willie Douglas, Willie Ling.
Women include: Mabel Inglis Clark (Back, 2nd L), Joan Smith (sitting, 2nd R) and Lucy Smith, Pauline & Anna Ranken, and Daisy Gillies. Ruth Raeburn took the photo. A very enjoyable day was had, with two new routes, not recorded in guidebooks and mistakenly thought to be first ascents many years later (See Chapter 14)
(Alpine Club Photo Library, London)

'EPB on Stob Garbh, AP.' April, 1909.
Wearing what appears to be a handkerchief on his head as protection from the sun, EPB is Eric Paton Buchanan. AP stood for 'Absolutely Perpendicular.'
An unrecorded climb
John Bell (© SMC)

One of the spectacular pinnacles of Torridonian sandstone on Stac Pollaidh. (Gael. *Steep rock of the pool*, from the many lochs and lochans around it). This pinnacle is known as the *Lobster's Claw*. It lost a little height some years ago due to natural erosion. Photograph date unknown but predates the slight loss in height. Willie Ling, Godfrey Solly and George Lissant Collins were active on this hill at Easter 1907, climbing a route which has so far not been described in a guidebook (© SMC)

Sligachan, Skye, September 1911. Leslie Garnet Shadbolt and Alastair Campbell McLaren, both smoking a pipe, are on the left, and had made the first continuous traverse of the Cuillin Ridge on 10th June the same year, taking 12hrs 18 minutes from Garsbheinn in the south to Sgurr nan Gillean in the north, the usual direction for the traverse. Back: Shadbolt, Amphlett, Tomkinson, Rule, Scoones. Middle: Mrs Amphlett, Miss Tomkinson, Arnold Brown, Prof Baly. Front: McLaren, MacRobert & 'E.M.' (© SMC)

Refreshment on Ben Lui. 5th March 1911. Figures recognised here include: REW= Robert Ernest Workman, RW=Robert Watson, JRY=James Reid Young, WGM=William Grierson MacAlister, PAH=Percy Archibald Hillhouse? M=? Workman was on the first ascent of Crack Climb (Difficult) on Stob Coire nam Beith in Glen Coe in 1912 (James Cornwallis Thomson © SMC)

William Norman Ling (1873-1953) has been described as *'one of the most outstanding mountaineers of the turn of the century',* with several good, early, guideless ascents in the Alps, new climbs in the Alps, Norway and the Caucasus, and of course numerous first ascents in Scotland especially with his frequent companion Raeburn. A corn merchant by profession, he was active in the mountains up until a few months before his death (© SMC)

The Cuillins from Bruach na Frithe, with the prominent peaks of Sgurr Alasdair and Sgurr Dearg on the far skyline (© abrahamphotographic)

'Looking South from Cruach Ardrain'. February 1912. The climber here is obviously embarking on a sliding descent in fairly heavy snow conditions (James Reid Young © SMC)

The West Ridge of Sgurr nan Gillean. The pinnacle right of the figure, known as *'The Gendarme',* was a well-known, awkward obstacle. It finally fell down in March1987, a victim of natural erosion (© abrahamphotographic)

Lochearnhead, 1912. Mabel Inglis Clark, Mrs Watson, Robert Watson, Harry MacRobert and Charles Inglis Clark. Perhaps one of the last photographs of Clark before he joined the war. He was 5ft 11ins, which probably prompted MacRobert to stand on the step! (© SMC)

Right: Graphic from an advert dated 1912 in an SMC Journal. The subject was Gaberdine clothing for mountaineers, produced by Burberry. The belayer has not even deigned to use the flake at his right hand for a belay (© SMC)

Left: A gully on Beinn Eunaich, 2nd January 1911. Henry Watson & Allan Arthur. Both were on the 1911 SMC New Year's Meet at Loch Awe. Unrecorded, and may have been an attempt at the Black Shoot (© SMC)

'After the blizzard' The only recognisable climber here is Naismith, centre. Taking early photographs in such conditions verged on the heroic (© SMC)

Relaxing in July 1910 at the Hotel de Mont Collon, Arolla, Switzerland are L to R: Natalia Yovitchitch, Harold Raeburn, Ruth Raeburn, Willie Ling, and far right Stuart Cumming. Raeburn had just recovered from his climbing accident in Scotland, and had climbed with the Serbian-Scot Natalia since 1908. She was experienced enough to join Raeburn, Ling, Ruth Raeburn and Edith Gray on an ascent of the 13,790ft Rimpfischhorn, the day following the Fluhalp. She was 14 years younger than Raeburn (Ling Diaries © SMC)

'Lunch in a snow squall'. Having a title implies that this image was used for a slide show. Several members of the SMC were very competent photographers, including the Rev AE Robertson, 2nd left here, and sitting next to William Garden, 3rd left. One point which is consistently clear from the literature of this period is the tendency to climb in all weathers, with an emphasis on winter excursions. (© SMC)

The Thearlaich-Dubh Gap in 1906, the first major obstacle encountered on the Cuillin Ridge on a south-north traverse. It was first climbed by Collie and W Wickham King in August 1889. Graded Severe, it can be a bottleneck on a busy day should a struggling climber be jammed at the crux, when it can be bypassed by a descent into Coir' a' Ghrunnda. Raeburn made the first two winter ascents in 1903 and 1905 (© SMC)

gully. They would use this, they hoped, to climb up until it became possible to gain the rocks of the Comb on its left flank. From his description of the approach, negotiating up and around masses of fallen cornice, snow conditions were excellent, with hard snow into which a struck axe would stick firm –

> The only way to make an impression on this toughest of snow is to cut a groove with the blade and then drive the piece out with the pick. There is one advantage about this toughness for the climber, that handholds and footholds once made can be relied upon. They are practically as good as if cut out of rock.

They found the ledge under the Comb and traversed right towards the gully. One to two feet of soft snow lay upon harder material, and as they were on steep ground and avalanching was highly possible, they dug down until they could cut steps in the harder snow below. Finally they gained the gully and could, with difficulty, then look up to see what lay ahead –

> From above one could, to a certain extent, take cover beneath the shield of our cone-pointed, brim-turned-down felt hats, but occasionally the snow that fell mixed with the seldom ceasing stream that poured down the gully, was caught by the powerful ascending eddy and rushed up, thus taking us behind our defences. The pain of a stream of icy snow in the face is so great that work must stop, and the face covered till breath is regained.

As to the angle of the slope in the gully, the two pitches ahead Raeburn estimated to be about 70° to 75°, with small portions approaching 90°. He was experienced at using a clinometer to measure such slopes, and though he was not carrying one on this day, his estimates were probably fairly accurate. To a climber who is cutting steps and clinging on to handholds, and at such angles handholds are a necessity, 75° feels as if it were vertical, with anything steeper feeling as though it were overhanging. Occasionally Raeburn's pick broke through an icy curtain, revealing soft snow or black vacancy, backed with green bulbs of ice. This produced a 'pigeon-hole' hold, easy to hold on to.

Without such quality snow-ice as met by the two climbers, Raeburn considered that the steep pitches would have been impossible. As it was, the going was exhausting; hanging on with one hand and trying to cut steps with the two-handed axes then in use, quickly produced severe cramps. It was much harder work, noted Raeburn –

> ...than the free open swing on the hard splintery ice slopes of the Alpine peaks. I suggest for climbs such as this going back to the original Swiss icemen's tools, the iron-shod straight "baton," and the light tomahawk-like hatchet stuck in the belt when not in use.

The second ice pitch almost defeated Raeburn, but he succeeded at the third attempt, at which point Phildius relieved him. From this height in the gully, it was evidently possible to traverse out left and so gain the arête, but the climbers saw that the sharp edges were so fringed and crowned with unstable looking cornices of ice and snow that they decided to continue on up the gully.

Above their heads, at the top of what was now a shallow scoop of hard snow, lay a threatening cornice. It had grown in stature as they approached, and was now seen to be more than twice the height of a man. On the right was a rib of ice-covered rock, running up to buffer into the cornice, thus halving its height. Here it was only slightly overhanging, as Raeburn took over the lead for the final pitch. He ran out of steam and holds, on the last, vertical, snow wall –

> I must confess to a feeling of helplessness for a moment as I stood on my ice-axe, driven horizontally into the vertical snow wall, some hundreds of feet of little less than vertical ice-plastered rocks stretching away down into the depths of the mist beneath, while my fingers slid helplessly from the glassy surface of the cornice *névé*, in the vain endeavour to find or make a hold by which I might haul myself up. The problem was solved by a retreat, until Phildius was able to pass me up his axe. Then the ice-plating was quickly shattered, and with fingers well crooked in the tough *névé*, a steady drag landed the body over the cornice lip, and Phildius soon followed.

The drive and confidence shown by Raeburn, that he had Phildius pull out what was almost certainly the only belay they had beneath the cornice, an ice axe driven into the snow, was impressive. Even more certain than before, a fall at this point would have meant certain death.

Raeburn and Phildius had taken about five and a half hours to climb the 450ft or so of the gully. The usual time, as given in the 1960s, before front-pointing, but obviously using crampons, was a suggested 4-8 hrs. Some three months later, in the Alps, with his friend Ling as a companion, Raeburn climbed the Zmutt Ridge on the Matterhorn. In comparing the two climbs, he thought that in everything but vertical height (the Zmutt is some 4,000ft), the Nevis climb was the more difficult and sporting. With his diffidence in recording the route he also helped to consign their ascent of the Nevis gully to near oblivion for over 60 years –

> Objections may be made to this climb that it is not the actual climb of the Comb. This is true, for we were never once on the exact arête. But what does this really matter? Phildius and I came out for a climb, and we got one, up one of the steepest cliffs on Nevis, in as icy condition as I have ever seen the old berg.

The route had a passing mention in the 1920 revised second edition of Clark's Ben Nevis Guide, of which only 1,000 copies were printed. Within one year 600 copies had been sold, mainly to the outside public, at a selling price of five shillings. The Ben Nevis Guide was Section E of the SMC

Climbing Guide to Scotland. Included in the paragraph on The Comb was the following –

> Raeburn made an icy ascent on 22nd April 1906, which, although not on the arête, yet led to the summit of the Comb. The climb was, however, almost entirely on snow and ice.

The 1920 revision was by Harry MacRobert (1880–1954) and other than adding some new routes it varied only very slightly from the Clark 1902 edition. The third edition of this guide, published in March 1936, was edited by Graham Macphee and included a description of Green Gully, '*...so named from the bright green moss in its lower section...It does not appear to have been climbed throughout its entire length.*' This is followed by some details from Raeburn's article, (wrongly dated as the 23rd April.) The Macphee guide, with 101 pages and including diagrams, photographs and a revised version of the 1895 panorama from the summit by JE Shearer, was published as a fully bound book, with what was to become the familiar red, textured, cloth covers of the SMC.

MacRobert knew Raeburn, and indeed did at least some climbing with him. He was a Chartered Accountant who joined the SMC in 1905, later serving as President (1932-34). He must have had some conversations regarding Raeburn's climbs, though there is no record of this. The point that Raeburn had intended to climb The Comb and had been rebuffed by conditions, climbing instead the adjacent snow and ice gully, led to a drastic reduction in the impact the route might have had. No doubt Raeburn, with his customary modesty, would have downplayed his ascent. In his article, we have seen how he felt obliged to make an apology for his failure to climb The Comb.

Subsequent guidebook authors appeared to have followed suit, without climbing the gully, to the extent that in 1954, with the fourth edition of the Ben Nevis guide, also edited by Macphee, the route is described in detail with the first ascent ascribed to Jimmy Bell, who made the second ascent on 4th April 1937. Bell, in his recording of the ascent in the New Climbs section of the SMCJ,[5] makes no mention of Raeburn, presumably also assuming that the gully had not been climbed before in winter. MacRobert had some history of overlooking or downplaying significant ascents, and appears to have done likewise here. Later authors and editors seemed to have ignored primary source material, a not uncommon failing.

In averagely good conditions *Green Gully* (180m IV,3) is well protected with modern equipment and is an enjoyable romp with several interesting steeper pitches, normally of hard snow or ice. Raeburn would have had no means of belaying other than pushing his long axe into the slope and passing the rope round the shaft. A fall longer than a few feet would have been fatal. In conditions such as that on the first ascent with spindrift, it is often difficult to concentrate on making hard moves on an ice pitch, all the while fighting for breath in a cloud of snow and ice particles. The long axes of Raeburn and Phildius would have been exhausting on a route with so much one-handed cutting required. Raeburn had already climbed routes at least as difficult as Green Gully, though perhaps not with as many difficult pitches. He was very obviously on top of his game.

In Phildius too, Raeburn had the solid backing of an experienced alpinist, albeit one with no experience of Scottish winter conditions. It would be an historian's dream to know what he thought of the ascent, but we have no knowledge of any account by the Swiss climber.

Green Gully was not the only first ascent by Raeburn to be forgotten or overlooked; Crowberry Gully on the Buachaille Etive Mor was to suffer a similar neglect, being recorded as a first winter ascent by Bill Mackenzie's party in 1936. Post-war, this situation did not change, and it was not until much later that it slowly dawned on mountaineers that the early pioneers, the Victorians and Edwardians, had been severely underrated. As Robin Campbell wrote in a seminal 1972 SMCJ article, describing winter climbers immediately before the Second World War –

> ...with the exception of Bell's partial ascent of Zero Gully in 1936...and Mackenzie & Murray's ascent of Garrick's Shelf in 1937...the pre-war group's main achievement was to *re-establish* ice-climbing in Scotland at the former high standard attained by the Victorians.[6]

Campbell went further some 11 years later, writing about Raeburn in Green Gully in '*Cold Climbs.*' –

> ...it is already clear that he was climbing at the turn of the century at a standard which was not surpassed until the renaissance of Scottish climbing led by Marshall and Patey in the fifties – a judgment fully sustained by examination of Raeburn's prowess in the Alps which included such exceptional ice-climbs as the Spigolo Inglese (sic!) on the North Face of the Disgrazia, climbed with Willie Ling in 1910.[7]

Let us also not forget the high standard of winter climbing which had been forged in the Lake District towards the end of the 19th century. There would be more outstanding climbs yet to be found in the few years left before the dark abyss of the First World War swallowed all. Raeburn, with others, would be involved in these climbs, as before.

❄ ❄ ❄

When a youth in 1872, William Inglis Clark had undergone a long walk across Scotland. This left him with vivid memories of Sutherland, and in particular Quinag, that large and complicated mountain with its stunning Barrel Buttress standing out as the most tempting target for mountaineers.

The difficulty of access to this remote part of Scotland was alleviated somewhat when Clark became a car owner; consequently, in June and July of 1906, a long-planned tour was accomplished, first with his wife Jane and daughter Mabel, and latterly with his son Charlie.

There remained still the nerve-wracking use of ferries, with Loch Carron in particular providing much angst. Clark removed his outer clothing for this, in case he had to swim for his life, and apparently some 23 men held his 10-H.P. Humber car by wheel and footboard, mudguard and nameplate as it was manoeuvred onto the planks provided – '*...unsecured and oscillating to and fro.*' The car was only prevented from capsizing at one point by being pushed bodily sideways back on to the planks.[8]

In June 1906, Clark and the two ladies made for the north-east buttress of Quinag. (The Water Stoup, from the Gaelic *cuinneag*, a milking pail or stoup. See the SMT publication *Scottish Hill Names* for more details on this, and many other hills.[9]) The climb that they made was never recorded, and as a consequence does not appear in a climbers' guidebook. It is probably the Grade 3 scramble described in *Highland Scrambles North* and found on the east buttress.[10] In winter it is a Grade III climb. They then descended and climbed the buttress between the V-Gullies, also a Grade III in winter. Neither route has a summer ascent on record.[11] The rock, Torridonian Sandstone, was a new experience to the party. They had found it to be scarce in good hitches, often very steep, but rough to the touch with ample handholds. Some care was needed with loose blocks, but otherwise it gave good climbing.

The next expedition was to Stac Pollaidh, where the family, without Charlie, was to meet up with Charles Walker from Dundee. There is a photograph in the SMCJ dated 11 June 1906, so we may take that date as being the day they made the ascent of the *West Buttress* (90m Difficult). The photograph appears in the guide to the Northern Highlands, published in the SMCJ, where there is also a description of their route.[12] They were not, however, the first to explore the area, as both Norman Collie and Godfrey Solly had made climbs near here. Stac Polly, as it was then commonly named, is now referred to as Stac Pollaidh, and, as the SMC 1906 guide described –

> This curious little mountain, though barely reaching 2,000 feet in height, is remarkable for the extraordinary character of its summit ridge, which rises abruptly on all sides from steep talus slopes, and is broken into a succession of excessively sharp *aiguilles* or pinnacles of shattered sandstone. It has been graphically compared by Professor Mathew [sic] Forster Heddle*to "a porcupine in a state of extreme irascibility."[13]

*Professor Matthew Heddle (1828–1897), an Honorary Member of the SMC from 1893, was an eminent Scottish mineralogist and geologist, who built up one of the finest collections of Scottish minerals. Some 5,700 specimens from his collection are now housed in the National Museum of Scotland and the National Museums Collection Centre.

The Clarks elected Charles Walker as the leader, with William second and the two ladies next. They chose to attempt the skyline, which was a more broken face left of the vertical section. Their route was practically free of grass and was essentially a rock climb with great slabs of the red, pebbly sandstone which provided excellent friction grips, but lacked belays where most needed. At about halfway up, difficulties increased to the extent that Walker exchanged his nailed boots for Clark's plimsolls or tennis shoes, commonly known as rubbers, which the latter had found suitable for climbing in the Dolomites. A small foothold high on the left, and a sharp handhold above were the targets, and with the help of William's shoulder a few minutes of strenuous struggle saw Walker on a small ledge –

> It was no easy matter to dispose of two ladies, two rucksacks, and the writer on the meagre ledges of the face, and the presence of a two-foot cubical block poised on the only standing space, made it difficult and even dangerous for the leader to handle the rope at all while the writer joined him above the pitch.[14]

On the summit the party enjoyed lunch and the superb view, which Clark gave a good description of. Following the building of a cairn, the party then approached the top of the great cliff a little to the south-east. A column of rock stood here, isolated from the summit mass by a narrow cleft.

> It must have measured at least 15 feet high by perhaps 6 feet by 2 feet, and no doubt as to its stability occurred to us. I was photographing near the edge when Walker, his rope held by my wife, put his foot across, and barely rested on the column preparatory to crossing. At that instant, a weird sound issued from the base of the rock, which had doubtless changed its point of support, and we hastily moved to a safer position in case of developments. The sound somewhat resembled a very deep-toned drum, the pitch of the note being about the lowest audible to the human ear.

❄ ❄ ❄

Elsewhere in Scotland that summer, the mossy crags of Coire Sugach in the Arrochar Alps were being probed. The Arrochar section of the SMC Guide had been published in the SMC Journal of May 1901, authored by William Clark, but it concentrated on the obvious attractions of the Cobbler, with no mention of Coire Sugach, on the quiet and retiring north-east flank of Beinn Narnain. It was not long before exploring climbers made their way into this corrie, with James Maclay leading the pack in 1900 and 1901.

In April 1900, Maclay decided to attend the alternative Easter Meet at Arrochar, staying at the Colquhoun Arms Hotel on Friday night the 13th, all by himself. Hearing that there were ice axes at the other hotel, there he found Euan Barclay Robertson (1880–1975), FS Goggs, both of whom would join the SMC the following year, and two members of the recently established Climbers' Club, Nettleton and Marler. The latter foursome had enjoyed a stormy day on the Cobbler, and following introductions and several hours of chat the five decided the next day to head for the hills to the north of the Cobbler.

From Maclay's description in his report of the Meet,[15] the weather was poor with a strong wind and some rain. They eventually found a sheltered spot in the corrie and from there they observed several gullies. The main buttress at the southern end of the corrie is now called Creag Tharsuinn; this is named as Tarsuinn in Jock Wilson's 1949 SMC District Guide to the Southern Highlands. From where the party were enjoying lunch, a perpendicular cut in the cliffs, about the midle of the corrie, seemed attractive, and they made for this. A steep streak of snow led to the foot of the rock pitches, where a small stream was pouring down. As Maclay wrote, the gully proved a tough job.

> By putting a leg right into the water, the first landing was reached, and after removing a lot of turf and stones, and with the assistance of the second man at two difficult points, the worst part was passed and the third man was told to come up. The operations had, however, already occupied one and a half hours or more, the others meanwhile sheltering in a position not safe from stones, and within the reach of spray. In view of this, and of the increasing danger from stones and the inadequate length of the rope (said to be 100 feet), it was reluctantly decided that the two last members should go round an easier way. After they were out of the line of fire the climb was completed without much delay. The moral is that five is too large a party for such a climb.

The climb in summer, not often repeated we suspect, is *Maclay's Gully* (60m Very Difficult), and Grade III in winter. Like many of its companions gullies and other routes in this corrie, it is better in winter conditions, usually found early on in the season. Maclay, an aficienado of such climbing, would return in May the following year, with his friend AE Workman, to find and climb two further routes, while Inglis Clark and JG Inglis found *Original Buttress Route* (75m Difficult) in November 1901. On New Year's Day 1902, the formidable trio of Rennie, Raeburn and Maclay recorded two more gullies in winter condition at II and III. Finally, rounding off this early period of exploration, and bringing us up to date, in June 1906 AC McLaren and the two Shadbolts climbed the hardest route to date with *McLaren's Chimney* (60m Very Difficult).

❄ ❄ ❄

There is an intriguing mention in an SMC Abroad report, where Ling and Raeburn describe a successful three weeks in the Alps, in July 1906.

Climbing in the Val Ferret, they made the first ascent of an Aiguille of the Rouges de Dolent, which they named La Mouche (The Fly). The final 350ft was steep and difficult, and boots were removed. A rope ring was used at one point on the descent. We may assume that this was a rope sling used for protection and/or abseil.[16] As for climbing bootless, Raeburn had recommended earlier that while it was normal practice to wear two pairs of socks for walking or climbing in boots, one pair only should be used for rock climbing without boots.[17] This would be because two layers of sock tend to slip over each other, making for an insecure feeling on rock.

The New Year Meet of 1907 was held at Corrie on the Isle of Arran, and was notable for the exceptional amount of snow on the hills. Raeburn severely bruised a knee walking in heather covered in deep snow when he hit a hidden boulder. This prevented him climbing for the duration of the meet. The snow was too deep in any case for any safe climbing, and outings were in the main confined to stumbling along the ridges in varying degrees of blizzard conditions.

❄ ❄ ❄

The contrast of the New Year Meet with the Easter 1907 Meet, held at both Inchnadamph and Arrochar, could not have been greater. Not only was the weather gloriously sunny, there was virtually no snow on the mountains. Held at the end of March, conditions were ideal for rock climbing, and both Quinag and Stack Polly received the attentions of the resident tigers. On Friday 29th, Solly and George Lissant Collins (non-member), climbed the eastern buttress on Quinag, probably making a second ascent of the Clark route. Clark, Douglas and Harry Walker climbed a steep, snow-filled gully immediately right of Barrel Buttress. This is very probably *Cooper's Gully* (300m II), later recorded in 1979. Saturday saw Clark, Goodeve, Raeburn and Walker climbing a fine gully on the western face of Quinag, but lack of details makes it impossible to determine which one.

On Stac Polly, on Saturday 30th March, Ling, Solly and Collins climbed '*...a very fine arête at the north-west corner of the mountain.*' Solly provided more details of their route in an article in January 1909.[18] There is a calendar error in his article, where he gives the 30th March 1907 as a Monday. They skirted the cliffs, moving westwards and passing under the foot of the climbs made by Collie, and by Clark's party. Rounding the western extremity of the mountain, they saw the cliffs of the north-west buttress, describing them as being tremendously steep. Solly mentions that Charles Pilkington had been there some years ago and had made several starts, but finding the rocks so steep that he came down. This was in mist, so Pilkington had been climbing blind.

The Solly party roped up, and deciding that the lead demanded a young climber sent Ling, who was then 34, to the front with Solly in the middle, and Collins last. From the description of the route, it seems as if they were attempting an arête or ridge. This went direct initially, until overhanging rocks forced them left towards a gully. Before reaching this they were able to move back right to their original line, now above the overhang. Shortly above came the crux. A narrow ledge led to a small platform on the extreme edge overhanging the cliff. Just below the platform Collins wedged his shoulders into a kind of letter-box. Solly kneeled on the platform, and Ling climbed on to his shoulders. As the slightly built Ling struggled up, Solly, a solidly-built man, raised him upwards, at first with his shoulders, then with his hands holding on to his feet.

> From my shoulders he got into the chimney, then hanging by one hand he swung his right foot on to a hold on the edge of the chimney, and grasping some heather pulled himself up to a large platform.

Solly made some general remarks on the nature of climbing found in the area, indicating how the geology of the area gave them a different type of climbing.

> It is difficult to generalise upon the climbing of a district after only one visit, but my first impression is that, except on Stack Polly, few distinct climbs of much difficulty will be found. There are many magnificent ranges of cliffs and steep mountain faces, but the climbs seem for the most part to be either impossible or too easy.... I saw nothing at all comparable to the distinct ridges and gullies of the north side of Ben Nevis.

Their route does not seem to have made it into the climbing guides, unless it has something in common with *North-West Corner* (100m Very Difficult), recorded in 1962. It had been, as Ling remarked in his diary, *'A most enjoyable day, and a good climb.'*[19] Collins, a Rochdale solicitor, would join the SMC in 1908.

It is worth pointing out here that in describing climbing rock features, the term 'corner' has slowly morphed from meaning an outer edge, to the modern term meaning the inner angle formed by two faces, hence the mention of the arête at the corner. Inchnadamph and Arrochar were venues for the official meet, but contingents of SMC members had mutinied on learning of this, being averse to the lengthy, shoogly train journey, so that an unofficial Easter meet was held also at Fort William. At Arrochar, the cliffs of Coire Sugach were poked at, with no memorable route being climbed, while at Fort William, Number 3 Gully and Castle Ridge on Nevis were the highlights.

The high point of the Inchnadamph meet, in climbing terms, was the ascent on Monday 1st April of *Barrel Buttress* on Quinag, by the elite team of Raeburn, Ling and Mackay. And here we have a mystery, as although their ascent was mentioned briefly in the official report of the meet by Herbert Boyd,[20] where he wrote that the climb would probably be fully described elsewhere, no account of it was given anywhere until November 1928, when Alexander Morrice Mackay (later Lord Mackay) described their day fully in a retrospective SMCJ article.[21] It may be that Raeburn decided not to describe the route, being dissatisfied with the manner in which it was climbed. Having said that, he had been modest in the past, barely describing the actual climbing on his solo ascent of Observatory Buttress, or the first ascent of Raeburn's Arête as two examples. Certainly Mackay himself could offer no explanation for this omission. With some poignancy, the 1928 article was basically written as a memorial to Raeburn.

Mackay was reappearing on the climbing scene after his accident on Cir Mhor in 1903, which had resulted in a very bad break of his leg. On the Friday of the meet, with two others he climbed Suilven by Pilkington's Gully and traversed it, getting there and back directly from the hotel over the north-west shoulder of Canisp. The following day he traversed Stac Polly, while on the Monday, he was on the first ascent of Barrel Buttress of Quinag, described below. Nothing much wrong with his leg then!

Raeburn had seen this buttress two days earlier, when coming past Sail Garbh and not surprisingly decided it worth exploring. We have another source of information, as Ling kept a diary of his mountain days. In his article, Mackay writes of referring to Ling's notes, to remind himself of the events of that day. The team crossed the moor and gazed up at the great, barrel-shaped buttress.

> For me, I had been trained in a school, the school of Geoffrey Winthrop Young, to whom it was a faith that no climb was impossible, yet I remember me well wondering there and then if *this* one was to falsify all our fond theories. From below, the sense of that bulging centre, ribbed almost around with a broad belly-band of smoothed, spreading rock-girdle, was overpowering...the centre of the Buttress seemed actually to impend, while the sharp side outlines of the massif indubitably formed on either hand the bowed line that would correspond to such a shaping of the centre. Nothing so like the upward cast of a hogshead, hooped and coopered at the middle, narrowing after that to the top, could well be figured.[22]

Mackay thinks he led the comparatively easy first section, a steep staircase of alternating rock and grass; Ling records that they –

> ...clambered up steep grass and rocks for some distance till we came to the foot of the final chimney. We roped, Raeburn, self, Mackay. The first portion of the chimney was a narrow crack overhanging quite impossible, so our leader took to a ledge on the R. This was very narrow & rose sharply. On it were large blocks of rock which had to be swarmed over and were none too secure. The leader reached a small platform above which a shallow chimney led to another ledge which would take us back to the chimney but the angle was against us & the leader could not get purchase off the heather to raise himself.[23]

This problem was solved when Ling passed up a stone which Raeburn stood on and was just able to pull himself up into a nasty place without much of a hitch. Above was a wider ledge on to which all three gathered. Raeburn then attempted the overhanging chimney above, but after two tries admitted defeat and came back down. Ling wrote that they had climbed about 150ft before being defeated, which Mackay thought was an underestimation. Additionally, where Ling describes their attempt as being in a crack or chimney, Mackay thought it was more like a sheer round open face –

> The Barrel was not gullied in the usual sense; it rounded, goggled, sprang out like the tracery of a vault. It is true, perhaps, one stave has slipped a bit and overlaps its neighbour most of the way up, making a perpendicular black line; the overlap being to eastward. But the first long struggle we had was, in my memory, an open-faced climb to reach the taut belly-band of the affair; and at the last the upper edge of the centre hoop when attained was thus: a promenade – we walked, all three walked, along a flat corridor, left side against a sheer wall, ledge not over 1½ feet wide; below the underhang; landing ground a sward 300 feet below. Gorgeous! Exhilarating!

Raeburn had tried the overhang for three-quarters of an hour, sending down over Mackay showers of mingled groans and splinters of misguided rock. Meanwhile, Mackay was awkwardly clinging to one of the large blocks of rock *'which had to be swarmed over'*, with neither handhold or foothold, his right arm jammed into the crack behind a flake, and using a *'jockey grip with the knees on the neck of that stony steed.'* Mackay wondered why he was not taken up to join the other two but eventually-

> When they did really begin to despair, they had me up. Profound relief to muscles and mind. But the mind sprang incontinent at the problem ahead. No route – it seemed plain – unless, by returning to the cracked stave, one swarmed the flat and opening crack. It was really not a "chimney," but at least afforded two splayed walls by whose help to utilise the subtlest of all climber's arts – carefully distributed counter-thrusts, all with a subsensed resultant of equipoise.

Mackay recalled that he urged the attack, he even offered to try it. He insisted that Raeburn could do it, but his more experienced leader *'...said no - would not push his attack with utter seriousness. Ling and he ordered retreat, so down we went.'* Mackay urged that no problem should defeat a party of strength and courage until it had at least prospected the enemy from each end, so without much need for such persuasion they soloed up the eastern gully which divided the Barrel from Buttress II. Lunch had given them a fresh heart. They roped up at the top and Ling began descending the face, at first easily, then with more difficult descents from ledge to ledge until finally he traversed over the top of the chimney to a roomy plateau from which sprang the second chimney, a desperate looking affair.

They were now some 35-40ft above their former high point. There was a jammed block, gained from the westward by a perilous open traverse, nearly on knife edge of barrel-bulge. At Ling's suggestion they made a rope ring round it and decided to descend. Ling went first, then Mackay swarmed down. *'First over a blob of rock split by the crack, then down a perpendicular splay, some 30–40 feet…'*, as Mackay recalled. And here, in his retrospective article, Mackay reveals an interesting observation about differing rock climbing techniques.

> Ling, as always, seemed to be a sinuous being, climbing close to the rock corner. I, on the contrary, adopted the methods we had so often developed in the South, and climbed out. I hope climbers of to-day know and love the delights of *"climbing out."* You eschew holding-in; you abandon the precarious safety of body friction. Feet spread, finding far out counter-pushes, hands not used as hooks from which a heavy body hangs pendant, but balancing, distributing, controlling. In this form of rock work the arms are hardly weight-carriers at all and do not tire. Viewed so, from above, one doubtless looked like a straddled spider, dangerously out-topping the void below. Harold disliked the method. His words were, *"No, no, not that way. Keep close in."* But I begged (rope above relieved all fear perchance) to have my own way…

Mackay successfully descended this perilous passage, and afterwards reclimbed it in a similar manner. Raeburn came down last, in his own classical method, and confessed that it was not quite so impossible as it had looked before lunch. All three were together again at the foot of the chimney. They had pulled the rope through the rope ring above, the rope was down on the ledge, and they had eaten the last of their dates. The die was cast, as Mackay raised the absolute necessity of forgetting the preceding defeat, and climbing upward again as if for the first time. They all agreed, and Raeburn led magnificently up.

Ling and Mackay again insisted on ignoring the traverse of the upper Barrel by which they had gained the chimney, instead climbing the black cleft throughout. It made a magnificent finish. Raeburn had to enter it off Mackay's shoulder and head. Ling helped Mackay to overcome the bulge, and then Ling was persuaded to dangle free under the chockstone, and at a word, to kick himself violently off into the void, while the pair above heaved and hoisted the swinging man over the stone before he could swing back under.

> *Ce n'est pas la Guerre*, perhaps, but *magnifique* it was, and it succeeded. Doubtless a stirrup rope or other more ponderous device will, when it is done again another time, bring the last man up. And so to the top by more grand open climbing. And so over Quinag, and so to great triumph at Inchnadamph.

> And so, finally, is a great joy fulfilled, a memory achieved, and a dear duty done.

And thus Mackay finished his article, referring near the end to '...*the meeting over our dear friend Harold Raeburn's last farewell that caused these ancient memories to be stirred up a little, and to grow into a desire to live for others too.*' He found Ling in a similar mood, and gradually, together, they were able to fulfil their duty and tell their tale. We must assume that the meeting Mackay was referring to was Raeburn's funeral in 1926. It was, in any case, not only a useful service to mountaineering history which Mackay had performed, but a touching tribute to a lost friend and popular member of the SMC.

The current guide has an enigmatic entry for this climb, when it describes the summer route as being '...*graded Very Difficult and even in modern terms is very difficult.*' In winter it provides a starred route of 270m at VI,7 - VI, 8 if the chimney is climbed direct. As regards the summer line, the guidebook editor, Andy Nisbet, makes the following comment –

> I wrote that note, having climbed very near it and looked at it. And I was convinced it was more than the V. Diff we use nowadays. In fact it didn't look any easier than the VS I was on at the time! Though I presume it is. And the other winter routes of VI,7 on the cliff are winter ascents of summer VS's. So yes it was a warning to anyone wanting to try it.[24]

❄ ❄ ❄

In September 1907, the SMC published their guidebook to the Island of Skye.[25] This was a continuation of the guidebook sections to the Scottish mountains which the club had been publishing in the pages of their Journal, with the Skye section being edited by the Editor Willie Douglas. It was a comprehensive look at this much-loved area, with history, geology, bibliography, natural history and so on, and with two earlier articles reprinted as appreciations of the Cuillin. The first was the introductory part of an article by the late William Brown on climbing in the Cuillin in 1896,[26] while the second was the article by Norman Collie, *'A Chuilionn'*, reprinted in full.[27]

This guide was significant in several ways for climbers in Scotland; firstly, it brought together much of the knowledge concerned with the Cuillin of Skye, a highly popular area which was the closest thing in Britain to the Alps. Secondly, for the first time in Scottish climbing, it contained a classified list of routes with grades of difficulty. The latter was based on the publication in 1897 of *Rock Climbing in the English Lake District* by Owen Glynne Jones, and gave four Courses, or grades; 1. Easy, 2. Moderate, 3. Difficult, and 4. Exceptionally difficult.

In the Douglas guide, there then followed a list of the peaks with their respective routes and grades. As examples, the Tourist Route on Sgurr nan Gillean was 1, its Pinnacle Route was 2, while the gully between Pinnacles

3 and 4 was a Grade 4. The only other route in the guide given a 4 was the Water-pipe Gully on Sgurr na Fheadain, if all the pitches were climbed direct, otherwise it was given a 3.

The guide also recommended rope-lengths, with all climbs in Grade 3 being recommended an 80ft rope for a party of three as well as a spare 60ft rope mentioned as being useful. For Grade 2 routes – '*...a 60-foot rope will, as a rule, be found quite sufficient for a party of three.*' On Sgurr Dearg, the Pinnacle (not named by Douglas as the Inaccessible Pinnacle, but so named in a description of its climbing history by Charles Pilkington and reprinted in the guide) was given a Grade 3, which we assume was by the shorter but harder west side. There is virtually no climbing described for the Sron na Ciche face of Sgurr Sgumain, as at the date of publication only three routes had been climbed, including Cioch Gully and the Cioch by Collie's party, Western Gully, and Central Gully.

There is in the guide only a passing reference to that amazing rock feature on the face of Sron na Ciche, The Cioch –

> Between the eastern and middle gully is a large pinnacle of rock (Cioch a Sgumain). The traverse of this Cioch from the eastern gully to the small central gully affords an exceedingly interesting climb, and was made first during July 1906.

Perhaps one reason for this was the disinclination of Collie to properly record his climbs; there may well be more than a handful of routes on the Cuillin which he never bothered to record. There was also the fact that in the early decades of climbing on Skye, the only accommodation was at Sligachan. Although Collie discovered the Cioch in 1899, he then embarked on a series of expeditions to other ranges and countries, and it was not until he returned to Skye in 1906 when he discovered to his surprise that there was still no record of that feature (See Chapter 3). As Ben Humble wrote in his book *The Cuillin of Skye* –

> ...climbers usually descended by Coire Lagain late in the day with a long trek to Sligachan before them. Those who took Coire Lagain on their way to the hills were intent on higher peaks, while the position of the sun would not cause such a shadow early in the day.[28]

Willie Douglas and the SMC were not the only guidebook authors in town however, as the Abraham brothers from Keswick had been surreptitiously climbing, photographing, and building up their own material for a book. The SMC were aware of this, and certainly regarded the Abrahams as guidebook competitors. As we will shortly see, their publication of an illustrated book on climbing in Skye would trigger another wave of exploration on that island, one dominated by climbers from outwith Scotland.

The first wave of climbing had broken on the serrated crests of the Cuillin; now, with improved travel, an increase in outdoor activities and the publication in September 1907 of the SMC Guide to Skye, a second tsunami was about to hit. The climbers would be, in the main, from England. There was already a good amount of interaction between the Scottish and English clubs, with many climbers having membership of clubs in both countries. Climbers from Scotland were, for the most part, not shy in extolling the virtues of climbing in Skye, while many of the rock climbing venues in England were increasingly seen as being overworked. This feeling was on several occasions also remarked upon in the SMCJ, with some of the popular climbing grounds regarded as having given up their best climbs. The thirst for new routes was growing, and it was blindingly obvious that the Cuillin of Skye was a prime source. As for the home-grown Scots, the Northern Highlands was being slowly opened up, particularly for those who owned that new-fangled device, the motor car.

On the surface, it might seem that in Scotland there was a sense there was nothing much left to do on the crags, but we should remind ourselves that with the very limited equipment and techniques available for protection, the climbing of steep walls was basically taboo. Once the prominent gullies and ridges had been climbed, interest moved on to other gullies and ridges. With what appeared to the early pioneers as a diminishing supply of these, this may well help explain a slowing of first ascents on the mainland.

There were also the inevitable effects of time, with the original activists no longer in the prime of youth and a hiatus before fresh apprentice climbers arrived to fill the gaps. William Brown and John Gibson were deceased; William Clark and Willie Naismith were in their 50s, with others not far behind. In the main, winter climbing remained the focus of much of the exploratory climbing, partly due to the Alpine background of many mountaineers active in Scotland, and partly due to the hold which landowners of areas with sporting interests had on access. The Cuillin of Skye not only had a vast area of climbable rock up for grab; its rocky nature precluded much of the game shooting which would otherwise have excluded mountaineering in the non-winter months.

One exception to the ageing cross-section was Harry MacRobert (1880–1954), who had joined the SMC in 1905 as a 25 year-old accountancy student. He quickly became involved in the publications side of the club, and was also an assiduous promoter of new members, introducing at least 17 other members. From Kilmacolm in Renfrewshire, during the First World War he served as a captain in the Highland Light Infantry, with the special duty of training in map reading and compass work, a post surely suited to his personal skills and one which, with luck, might have helped keep him safely distant from the mayhem of the front.[29] One of his routes which did not appear in any guidebook was a 1907 winter solo of *Gully 4* in deep snow on Beinn Nuis, Arran, an island which he obviously liked.

❄ ❄ ❄

William Clark was now increasingly reluctant to lead boldly, but he was obviously still happy to follow, especially when the leader was a climber of the calibre of Raeburn. So it was on 14th April 1907, when Raeburn led the Clark family up a winter first in Glen Coe. Clark and his wife Jane, along with son Charlie had come up by car, meeting Raeburn at the Kingshouse. Their goal was the cliffs of Stob Coire nan Lochan, backing one of the most attractive corries in the area and with several buttresses and gullies, so far as we know, still pristine at that time.

When the party gained the corrie, they were faced with three well-defined buttresses, with an easy, broad snow couloir on their left. *'All looked formidable, and but for the presence of Raeburn in our party we might have been content with a general inspection.'*[30] The party found the central buttress the most attractive, and as it projected further into the corrie, they considered it would afford a longer climb.

Clark took photographs, from one of which his daughter Mabel made a rough but useful sketch. They could see that the finish of the buttress reared up to form a tower, but several snow-filled cracks in this promised a possible finish. They made their way to the buttress, finding the rocks steepening on approach. The lower nose was unpromising, so they moved up slightly left to start in a recessed corner.

> With Raeburn leading we were soon enjoying the thrilling delights of vertical strata, with, at places, enough of difficulty to make extreme care necessary. The handholds, at times filled with snow, were on the whole satisfactory, and the whole party in due course foregathered on the narrow ridge.

The next section was easier, climbing steep snow, and here the irrepressible Raeburn – '*...used a little of his superfluous energy in climbing a crazy pinnacle on the ridge, the descent from which was best accomplished by a long jump into the snow.*'

The party had now gained the foot of the final tower, with no apparent way up on the right. While the family ate a frugal lunch on a narrow ledge, Raeburn soloed leftwards to explore possibilities. Clark was becoming anxious as time wore on, but eventually Raeburn returned to announce that he had found the way ahead and had in fact reached the summit of the tower. Clark described this crux section –

> We poor mortals...can only look on such a climber with astonishment if not with envy...I am convinced that the next passage is one which should only be dealt with by a strong party. Turning the corner to the left... you look down a considerable depth over the steep face, but attention is immediately concentrated on a little saddle of rock which requires to be crossed to get into the corner between the tower proper and the big block which had partially sheltered us...The holds are excellent, and the climber can thoroughly enjoy

> the giddy outlook into the corrie far below. The next step requires more care… it consists of a long stride round a slightly bulging rock, the ledge being but of slender proportions.

Clark ended his description of the route by stating that the section from their lunching spot was one of the most enjoyable in the Glen Coe district. *Ordinary Route Central Buttress* (150m III/IV,4) is a popular way to the summit, with a harder variation, *Pedestal Variation* (IV,5) starting from the gap between the tower and the upper section. Presumably this is the way the pioneers took, with the indefatigable Raeburn in the lead.

He finished his article with an amusing example of the way in which '*motor accidents*' were manufactured for the newspapers. On their arrival in the glen, they had left their car in a stone-breaker's layby, in order to explore the Aonach Eagach. Clark's son Charlie, who had cycled alongside the car, and had to leave from Bridge of Orchy by the evening train, had put his bicycle beside the car. From the hill above they had seen two cyclists examine the car and cycle.

When Charlie later reached the Kingshouse, he heard how a motor car had been driven furiously down the road, had smashed into a bicycle, injured the driver, been run into the stone-breaker's recess, and the injured people had in all probability been taken to Ballachulish and were at that moment in the doctor's hands. Whether any were killed or not was a matter of doubt.

Clark's article raised one interesting cartographic point, when he mentions that the corrie below the cliffs, containing several tiny lochans, did not appear to have a name; Coire an Lochan, he stated, was on the south-west flank of the Stob. On the OS six-inch maps from 1843-1905 the title Coire nan Lochan appears to sweep down from the lochans and into the glen below. The corrie lying to the south-west is the upper corrie of Coire nam Beithach, unnamed on the map.

However, on the OS one-inch map of 1885-1900, which gives the spelling Coire an Lochan, a sizeable lochan is clearly indicated in the small corrie south-west of the Stob. This is a mapping error, as in subsequent maps of all scales the lochan disappears, leaving a burn which appears to follow a triangular course, with one arm impossibly contouring the hill.

Presumably the OS deleted the lochan markings, recognising that it was non-existent, but left the triangular outline of the non-existant lochan. Additionally, Clark refers to Coire an Lochan throughout, and not Coire nan Lochan as it appeared on the six-inch map. This indicates that he would have been using the OS one-inch map, which used the spelling Coire an Lochan. [On the modern OS 1:25K map, the Coire nan Lochan label has moved downhill somewhat, and appears to be naming the glen below the corrie.] Some names are obviously a moveable feast.

References

1. Gillman, Peter. *Mallory on The Ben.* The Alpine Journal, 2010/2011, 199-205.
2. Naismith, W.W. *Early Winter Climbing.* SMCJ 17, 99, April 1925, 124-132.
3. Raeburn, Harold. *A Scottish Ice Climb.* SMCJ 9, 52, Jan. 1907, 153-158.
4. W.I.C. [William Inglis Clark]. *Ben Nevis.* SMCJ 7, 39, Sept. 1902, 118-176.
5. Bell, J.H.B. *Green Gully—The Comb—Ben Nevis.* In: New Climbs. SMCJ 21, 125, April 1938, 350-352.
6. Campbell, Robin N. *The First Scottish Ice Climbers.* SMCJ 30, 163, May 1972, 48-57.
7. Campbell, Robin & Raeburn, Harold. *Green Gully.* In: Cold Climbs, 90-93. (London: Diadem Books, 1983.) Compiled by Ken Wilson, Dave Alcock and John Barry.
8. Clark, W. Inglis. *Quinag and Stac Polly.* SMCJ 9, 52, Jan. 1907, 175-191.
9. Drummond, Peter. *Scottish Hill Names.* (SMT 2007)
10. Thow, Iain. *Highland Scrambles North.* (SMT 2006.)
11. Nisbet, Andy. *Personal Communication*, April 2013.
12. SMC Guide, *Coigach Group.* SMCJ 9, 51, Sept. 1906, 137.
13. Ibid.
14. Clark, W. Inglis. *Ibid.*
15. Maclay, James. *Arrochar Meet - April 1900.* In: Proceedings of the Club, SMCJ 6, 32, May 1900, 61-63.
16. Ling, W.N. and Raeburn, H. In: Excursions, SMC Abroad. SMCJ 9, 51, Sept. 1906, 220-222.
17. *Ibid.* Raeburn, Harold. *The "Chasm".*
18. Solly, G.A. *A Climb on Stack Polly.* SMCJ 10, 58, Jan. 1909, 179-182.
19. Ling, William. *Diaries*, NLS. Book 6, 30.
20. Herbert C. Boyd. *Thirty-Ninth Meet of the Club - Easter 1907, Inchnadamph, Sutherland.* In: Proceedings of the Club, SMCJ 9, 53, May 1907, 254-258.
21. The Honourable Lord Mackay. *Sail Garbh: Its Barrel Buttress.* SMCJ 18, 106, November 1928, 207-213.
22. Ibid.
23. Ling, William. *Diaries*, NLS. Book 6, 33.
24. Nisbet, Andy. *Personal communication.* May 2013.
25. SMC Guide Book. *The Island of Skye.* SMCJ 9, 54, Sept. 1907, 293-367.
26. Brown, W. *The Coolins in '96.* SMCJ, 4, 22, Jan. 1897. 193-213.
27. Collie, Norman. *A Chuilionn.* SMCJ, 4, 23, May 1897, 259-266.
28. Humble, B.H. *The Cuillin of Skye.* (London: 1952, Robert Hale, 56.)
29. J.S.M.J. *Late Mr Harry MacRobert.* The Glasgow Herald, August 28, 1954. [The initials are almost certainly those of Stuart Jack, a friend and fellow SMC member.]
30. Inglis Clark, W. *The Cliffs of Stob Coire an Lochan.* SMCJ 10, 59, May 1909, 240-245.

13

Epic on Nevis (1907-08)

THERE WAS a new game afoot on Skye. A letter from SMC member Fred Jackson to Willie Douglas on 5th May 1896 waved a red flag –

> Two brothers Abraham, professional photographers, are now in Skye photogr[aphing] & climbing, for they do both. They wrote to me for guidance, having got my address.[1]

Jackson had joined the SMC in 1893 and had various addresses in and around Manchester. He made several contributions to the SMCJ in the form of crag drawings and reviews. The Abraham brothers, from Keswick, had earlier illustrated Owen Jones' book on Lakes Climbs. With an eye on the business potential, after the death of Jones in 1899 following an accident on the Dent Blanche in Switzerland, the brothers published a second, extended edition of his book on Lakeland climbing in 1900 and picked up his plan for a Welsh volume, with the publication *of Rock-Climbing in North Wales* in 1906. Their next target would be the Cuillin of Skye.

Climbing as a team, the Abrahams were highly efficient; George was a natural leader, and his climbing style was described by Geoffrey Winthrop Young –

> George Abraham was another climber who interested me at this time by his different if equally finished style of movement. He was graceful to watch and, as I understood it later, he was one of the earliest of the home school to climb consistently by balance rather than grip.[2]
>
> By contrast, Ashley was built to belay, with a heavyset physique and a calm temperament.

The brothers' first expedition from Sligachan in 1896 was the classic traverse of Sgurr nan Gillean by the Pinnacle and Western Ridges on

Saturday 2nd May; they also climbed the Inaccessible Pinnacle, by the harder, western edge. From its summit, they lowered themselves by a doubled 80-foot rope.

> The only stretch that could be called difficult was about half-way up, where it was necessary to draw the body upwards from a diminutive standing-place on to a sloping slab which was provided with meagre hand-holds. At first there was an unsettling feeling that these excrescences were not sufficient to prevent one sliding backwards off the slab into space, but a few feet higher a deep crack accommodated the whole of one's fingers, and ample holds were soon available on the right.[3]

During their next visits, in 1906 and 1907, George, Ashley and various friends covered not only every peak, but also every rock climb that had been done, as well as making many fine new routes. The first of these exploratory visits was made at Easter 1906, mid-April, when Ashley was joined by AE Field, RA Milligan, and George Woodhouse. The party made three attempts to reach the summit of Sgurr nan Gillean, the conditions being very wintry, despite the *'balmy weather of the preceding fortnight.'* They finally succeeded on the third attempt, climbing by the easier third ridge.

> …ere long we were shaking hands around the cairn with as much enthusiasm as though our peak possessed 15,000 feet greater altitude than it actually did. Mere height is often a secondary consideration, however, and these Coolins afford a fine instance of how much greater a factor of a climb is its technical difficulty than its size. We looked over at the Pinnacle Ridge and its Western relative, looming through the mists like silent white ghosts, and then retraced our steps downward and across the moor to Sligachan.[4]

Ashley later used this article, published in the *Manchester Guardian* and pasted on to pages 86/87 of the Sligachan Climbers' Book, as a basis for the chapter on Sgurr nan Gillean in *'Rock-Climbing in Skye'*. Ashley returned to Sligachan later that summer in 1906 with Henry Harland and Alfred Binns. Harland (1870–1948), a very competent climber from Hull, often acted as leader on the Abrahams' routes in Skye; Ashley commented how *'we never had a moment's uneasiness as he moved safely and deliberately over their difficulties.'* Alfred Henry Binns (1871–1960) had climbed in the Lake District with many of the original pioneers including Harold Raeburn – in 1898 the pair had been defeated on the Central Chimney (Very Severe) of Eagle Crag, Buttermere (eventually climbed by Bill Peascod in 1949).

Ashley left an entry in the Sligachan Climbers' Book, but by now he was writing his *'Rock-Climbing in Skye'*, and for commercial reasons was withholding any real climbing information. In late June, Harland led Binns and Ashley Abraham up the first free ascent of the South Crack of the Inaccessible Pinnacle. This had been climbed on a top rope by William Wickham King on 23rd August 1898, during an SMC Meet at Sligachan, and is a

30m route currently graded at Hard Very Difficult, an unusual grade which is currently not a standard in SMC guidebooks. It implies that the grade is very close to Severe. The route, which climbs the wall left of the easy classic East Ridge, is a good alternative when the latter is traffic-bound, as increasingly it is now. Ashley, who had moved away some distance in order to capture the ascent with his camera, described the hard moves –

> He stopped for a good while with his feet on the "dyke" and shouted down to us that the next step appeared difficult. There are plenty of holds, but they are somewhat awkwardly placed... A small foothold on the right wall is the key to the situation and, after testing this well and determining as far as possible the necessary distribution of the balance a foot or two higher, Harland moved slowly upward and soon gained the wider part of the crack, where he again disappeared from my sight.[5]

On his return visit in June 1907, Ashley was accompanied by Harland, Binns and Geoffrey Bartrum (1881–1960), a merchant, and regular participant of Geoffrey Young's Welsh meetings in Pen-y-Pas. Bartrum was to join the SMC after the Great War. Ashley went looking for Collie's Climb on Sgurr Alasdair with Harland and Binns. Following what they felt was the most interesting start they again gave Harland the lead on a route which lay left of Collie's Climb and took a line first up and left, then made a detour back right under a steep headwall before climbing more directly to the summit. *Abraham's Climb* (300m Difficult) is slightly better and less loose than the earlier climb. That day they stayed overnight in Coire Lagan, where they enjoyed a quick swim in the lochan before supper and a comfortable sleep in their sleeping bags. On the same holiday, the quartet climbed the Nose and North West Gully of Sgurr an Fheadain, now known as *The Spur* (Grade 2) and Summit Gully (150m Difficult). (The Grade 2 refers to a scrambling grading. See *Skye Scrambles*, an SMC Guide.[6])

One high water route of the 1907 holiday was *Slanting Gully* on Sgurr a' Mhadaidh, whose seductive-looking precipices had first caught Ashley's eyes some 11 years earlier. Returning with Harland, Binns, and Bartrum, the plan was to take their tent and equipment in by pony and camp high in Coire na Creiche. They planned the expedition carefully, allowing a week's provisions. Harland built a tent especially for the trip and they believed June could be relied upon in Skye to provide mainly good days. They looked forward for months to their visit, but day after day it poured with rain. After a week of this it finally cleared, and they chartered a pony and ghillie. The pony would take their equipment almost to the foot of Waterpipe Gully, above which the ground became too steep.

Two trips with the pony saw their camp set up on a carpet-like expanse of sloping grass beside the burn. Gradually the day became darker, and they had just got all their gear in the tent when the rain began. It soon became obvious that climbing that day was out of the question. Ashley Abraham wrote that they had abandoned the comforts of Sligachan for the discomforts of one small room eight feet by six feet, at the mercy of a deluge of water at any moment. And yet they were happy. Why? He asked.

> Perhaps the reason is to be found in the fact that, in spite of our veneer of civilisation, there is still something in us that responds to the outdoor, natural life that was the lot of our early ancestors ; a primal, elemental faculty that has lain dormant for generations, but which is still alive in every healthy man. Whatever it is, it is something very deep-seated and genuine, as all those who have experienced it well know. For myself it will be a sorry day when increasing years and "the ills that life and time oppose" step in and prohibit all but civilised comforts.[7]

Twelve hours later the incessant rain finally poured water into the tent, flooding across the waterproof ground sheet and ejecting the inhabitants. They wrapped their dry clothing and food into the sheet and after re-trenching round the tent and fixing an extra climbing rope splashed their way back to Sligachan.

The storm abated three days later, and Harland and Bartrum went up to see what damage had been done. The evening turned out fine and as the pair had not returned, it was concluded that all was well. Accordingly, Binns and Abraham set off early the next morning. As they contoured into Coire na Creiche, they spotted the small white dot of their tent. After all four met up they climbed a route straight up the western spur. They then descended into Coire a' Mhadaidh, intending to try the North-West Buttress, first climbed by Collie, Howell, Naismith & Parker on 5th September 1896.

Binns, however, persuaded the party to attempt *Slanting Gully*, successfully as it turned out, and providing a 210m Severe route which Ashley considered to be the hardest of his *'Difficult Courses'*. Abraham, in his book, had listed routes by grade, using *Difficult*, and *Exceptionally Severe*, as his two grades. He was also at pains to point out that when he described left and right, such as the sides of a gully, he meant while looking up, excepting a few cases where a descent was described.

> Directly above…was a beautiful narrow chimney, surmounted at the top by a small chock-stone. Above it, receding one beyond the other as far as we could see, were chimneys, chock-stones, pitch after pitch, and the clean-cut walls of a gully of most alluring appearance. A great black cave, high up, completed a picture that was calculated to gladden the sight of any rock-climber worthy the name.[8]

The ascent of the gully was described in great detail by the Abrahams, with photographs where possible. Poor Bartrum volunteered to carry the camera equipment at one point, so that Ashley could be there to assist

Harland should it be required. This was required several times, with a steady shoulder being used by the leader. They found the gully remarkably dry and clean and with little scree, almost resembling climbs in the Lake District. They emerged from the lower section of the gully, gaining the Foxes Rake, and looked up to see what fate awaited them in the gully's upper stretches.

> ...even the most rash of us was somewhat taken aback. And not without cause, for two thin vertical cracks, each about 40 feet high, and both overhanging at the bottom, were what we saw. These converged at their upper extremities into a small cave, which also overhung. Above this rose the narrow continuation of the gully, which dwindled again higher up to an overhanging crack which scarcely needed a second glance before being pronounced unclimbable.[9]

Time now entered the equation; it was 7.30pm, but as one of the party remarked, it would do them no harm to spend a night out – a week's enforced idleness in a hotel had lent much enthusiasm – so they settled down and studied the cracks. Ashley spotted a chance here for a photograph, and used this to persuade Harland to attempt it. Harland then asked Bartrum for more shoulder support and the pair crossed the rake to attack the crack.

Several difficult sections were climbed, with Harland accepting the use of Bartrum's shoulders, and finally they reached the foot of an overhanging crack at the top of the gully. At this point there was also an outward sloping ledge running up and right to an edge on the cliff face. Harland attempted the crack but could not reach a hold above, even standing on Ashley's shoulders. He was exhausted and the decision was made to take to the sloping ledge. This eventually led in the twilight round a corner and so to a vertical arête of rough gabbro and up to the screes on the breast of the mountain.

The happy quartet had still to descend to their camp, and as Ashley noted, although some people hold a fond delusion that it never becomes dark in Skye during June, it was as dark a night as any he had seen. They slipped and tumbled down the screes into the corrie, past Deep Gash Gully. Half an hour of more or less painful progress saw them reach their tent at 11.30pm. A quick bowl of soup and they crept wearily into their sleeping bags, after as grand a day on the rocks as it had ever been Ashley's good fortune to share. *'The second ascent was made by Mr. L. G. Shadbolt and his sister, who endorsed our opinion that the finest gully climb yet done in Skye is that of the Slanting Gully of Sgurr a' Mhadaidh.'* [10] This was in September, 1911, and more anon of Leslie Shadbolt.

Perhaps the most outstanding climb found by the Ashley-Harland rope was that of *Cioch Direct* (150m Severe), which leads to the Terrace beneath the Cioch. In writing of their ascent in June 1907, Ashley Abraham was quite straightforward in stating that the route was *'...the most exciting, and but little short of the most difficult, in which I have been concerned.'* [11] Not completely happy with the usual way of gaining the Cioch, by wandering all round and then pouncing down upon it from above, he asked himself why a direct approach from below should not be looked for. His initial search was not encouraging, as apart from a steep chimney the face looked impregnable and had a line of perpendicular rock about half-way up the buttress.

Ashley's companions had stayed away due to wet weather, while Harland had extended his stay on purpose, hoping for a successful ascent of what they already knew would be a very fine climb. They had enjoyed the hospitality of the SMC climber and water colourist Colin Phillip at Glen Brittle which gave them a shorter approach, and as they reached the rocks below the Cioch, which were dry and warm, they also benefited from three weeks' strenuous climbing in the Cuillin. They were supremely fit and this boosted their confidence. Harland even went to the extent of building a small cairn at the foot of the route rather than wait until a successful ascent.

The climbing led to a widening at 40ft, where a branch led up to the right. This turned out to be a dead end, and they returned to the left fork which led to a steepening at 70ft. The continuing chimney was blocked with long spikes of rock, but the place was so steep that they could not be adequately tested, and so they were left alone. A good belay a few feet up on the right wall allowed Harland to climb up past them, where some 30ft higher he landed on a small ledge at the top of the chimney.

> To the left the rocks overhung considerably, and away to the right also they were obviously quite unclimbable. Immediately above us, however, they looked more hopeful and presented a steep nose of rock, at the top of which there appeared to be a small ledge. Above this ledge two thin cracks, about a yard apart, sprang upward for about 10 feet, where they ceased just below the foot of a short chimney.
>
> Nowhere else was there the ghost of a chance of getting higher, so I stood out against the nose with the rope passed round a small belay, which most fortunately existed, and Harland climbed onto my shoulder. This he soon left, and ere long attained the foot of the cracks. What had looked from below like a ledge proved to be the sloping top of the nose. Hereabouts the holds were very unsatisfactory, and he stayed for some time.
>
> "Is there no hold inside the cracks?" I asked him. "Can't you get an arm in each and wedge them?" His answer was sufficiently startling — "Yes; there's splendid hold in both, but I'm wondering whether the rock dividing the cracks is safe!" [12]

Ashley described the large chockstone as being about 10ft high, and perhaps a yard across. He thought it must have weighed well over two tons. Nervously he asked whether it moved or quivered at all. Harland replied that it did not, although he could not see what held it in place. They decided that Harland should continue, but pull on the stone as little as possible. Two loose stones were wedged against each other in the chimney, as Harland, with great difficulty, managed to climb past them without disturbing them. Ashley also had great difficulty in avoiding touching the loose stones, and once past these and safely positioned above, he decided to remove them so that they would not annoy future parties. The two rocks fell away at a slight touch, and fell about two feet on to the top of the large chockstone.

> To our intense surprise this moved appreciably, giving a harsh, grating rumble, and then seemed to remain stationary. Only for a moment, however, for immediately afterwards the whole mass slid down a few inches, and then heeled slowly over. It disappeared from my sight almost without a sound, until it struck the rocks about 50 feet below. The impact seemed to shake the whole face of the Cioch; then the silence was broken by a thunderous crash and roar as it bounded down the steep rocks to the corrie below, leaving in its wake a cloud of sulphurous dust. We gazed at each other in astonishment, not unmixed with awe, and then down at the vacant place. The deafening noise, the clouds of dust, the great ugly leaps the rock took, and the thought that we had just climbed up the outside of it, left us not a little shaken.[13]

For the rest of the day, Harland gave anything in the shape of a loose block a very wide berth. Above, another wedged block was climbed, then a 10ft chimney which was overcome with combined tactics. They then took to a traverse on the left, under some poised boulders, to gain a ledge. A horizontal crack now led right to a small recess at the foot of two steep cracks. These ran upwards and parallel for about 30ft, about six feet apart. Harland was delighted when he joined Ashley and spotted the cracks.

> A shoulder simplified matters at the start. After leaving it he struggled up the right-hand crack for about 15 feet, where it became necessary to cross over to the companion crevice. This proved a very ticklish performance. His left leg could just reach across and enable him to press against the vertical face with the sole of his boot. A fairly good handhold for the left was also found, but directly the swing across should be effected, the push of the left foot would be downwards and it would slip off, leaving him hanging by the hands alone.[14]

It was a not untypical hard move for a leader; he knew what to do, but realised that it would probably commit him, with the chance of reversing the move uncertain if not impossible. He made the move with left hand and foot, then hesitated. Ashley shouted at him to move across before tiredness overtook him. The belay was good. Harland's mind was made up when his left foot slipped off. His left hand held firm and he got his right hand above his left which enabled him to pull up on his arms and gain a higher hold. A pause for breath on a small ledge then he continued to gain a sloping ledge beneath a great slab.

Following Harland's pitch, Ashley exulted in the feeling, as his left hand supported his weight, the muscles tightened, and the final struggle upward on both hands took him up and on to a safe rest in comparative safety. The slab above was steep and rough, with several cracks enabling upward progress, until after 40ft they landed on a broad ledge with, immediately above, the overhanging nose of the Cioch. The two climbers congratulated each other, and swore that it was the best, stiffest and most interesting climb that either had done.

As to what other climbers thought of this route, here is Bill Birkett, a Lakes climber, describing the crux pitch some 80 years or so later –

> After two long pitches, providing high exposure, the difficulties begin. Within a few feet, an awkward exit into a chimney is effected with poor handholds and a reasonable degree of commitment. This is thought-provoking enough, probably the crux of the climb, but those with any failing in their chimneying technique will be struggling above; I got positively jammed solid and made upward progress only by prising the crack open with a brutish display of ineptitude![15]

There is a dark side to Cioch Direct however, which partly explains why it is given a solitary star in the current SMC guide. The area of unstable rock on the crux third pitch had threatened climbers for many decades, from Harland onwards. The striking, protruding pinnacle of rock on pitch four known as the Yardarm fell sometime in 2000. The worst incident occurred on 31st May 2011 when a lead climber accidentally dislodged a chockstone leading to the fatality of the second.

Following their first ascent of Cioch Direct, Harland and Ashley descended the buttress and made their way back to the foot of the climb –

> The evidences of the recent fall of rock were very plentiful. The cairn, built by Harland four hours before, had been swept away, and a great ugly gash in the screes indicated the spot on which the main mass had fallen. After re-building the cairn we followed the base of the cliff for about 60 feet downwards, and then struck up a shallow scoop, which brought us into the somewhat indefinite lower part of the Cioch Gully.[16]

Not being content with one good first ascent, the pair then climbed a route up the western edge of the Cioch. Now known as *Cioch Nose* (45m Very Difficult), it provides a short climb in a superb situation.

Other climbs were pioneered by the Abrahams, in various combinations of partners. Both brothers were back again in October 1907, with two friends from Kendal: Arthur Wakefield and Andrew Thomson. Wakefield would later climb with Bower and make the first ascent of six Severe routes on Gimmer Crag. He would also climb in the higher ranges, and was on the 1922 Everest Expedition, climbing as high as the North Col. Thomson is credited as being the first climber to describe laybacking as a technique on rock.

Rock Climbing in Skye was published in 1908. The SMC Guide to Skye, published in the club Journal the previous September, had already sold out. Ashley's guide contained additional routes to the SMC guide, which had been withheld by the Abraham brothers for sound (i.e. selfish!) commercial considerations. It was reviewed in the SMCJ of September 1908 by Willie Naismith, who on the whole was generous.[17] Their new guide was a completely different concept to the SMC guide – a substantial and richly illustrated volume that reads more like a series of adventure stories than a guidebook and appealed to a wider audience. The Abrahams never reprinted it, and the first edition is now scarce, commanding a good price on the antiquarian book market. Naismith wrote –

> This is a most important contribution to Scottish climbing literature, and it will be welcomed by the whole climbing fraternity. S.M.C. members will feel no jealousy of Mr Ashley Abraham for his genuine admiration and love for the Coolin... Some of the descriptions of rock climbs — the Cioch direct ascent for example — are abundantly exciting, and will be apt to cause the reader to wedge himself across his arm-chair while he gropes about for a good hitch.
>
> ...The author's generous recognition of his friend, Mr Harland's plucky leading in some of these stiff climbs, is pleasant to read, and leaves one with the impression of a cheery party who worked well together and backed up one another loyally.
>
> ...Owing apparently to the rough surface of the paper which has been used, the illustrations are just a trifle disappointing. The success of the snow views in "The Complete Mountaineer," by Mr George Abraham, had led us to look for great things in this volume. Moreover, Messrs Abraham's Skye photographs are so perfect in definition that we were not prepared for the haziness shown in some of the reproductions. Many of the rock views are, however, first rate, and the diagrams of routes are admirable, as is also the map.
>
> John Mackenzie's numerous friends will be glad to have a good portrait and appreciative notice of a worthy man and agreeable companion.
>
> If one were in a critical mood, doubtless a few defects and omissions could be found in the book. The wall of Blaven can be climbed from the gap behind the Pinnacle, although the description on p. 296 seems almost to imply the contrary. Speaking from memory after twelve years the route starts opposite the place where the Pinnacle is most easily climbed from, and goes up a slab set at about 45° without obvious holds.* The way to Blaven from Sligachan does not lie *down* the glen (p. 285), and "Nae, nae, sir" (p. 9) hardly sounds like the expression of a Skye man. "Still and all," as they say in the West Highlands, any flaws that have been detected are trifling, and we are happy in being able to congratulate Mr Abraham unreservedly on producing such an excellent book. W. W. N.
>
> [Footnote] * Mr MacRobert, who has been climbing at Sligachan this summer, reports that Mr Abraham's "Deep Chimney" of Sgurr nan Gillean is the same

> as the S.M.C. "Jammed Block Chimney." Climbed in 1898 ; and that Mr Abraham's "Jammed Block Chimney" is evidently a new climb, further south.

The act of photography when the Abrahams were active was, as we have touched on earlier, fairly heroic. One of the photographs in Ashley's book was of the difficult 80ft pitch in Waterpipe Gully, the taking of which almost led to disaster as the wind blew the camera towards the gully. Ashley made a grab for the camera then lost his balance. Fortunately, he had tied himself to a rope which he had attached to the top of a pinnacle and he ended up suspended over the gully. A small ledge held his camera securely while he sorted himself out. The successful photograph showed Harland and Binns with the second back and footing up the narrow gully. It is reproduced in Ben Humble's book, *The Cuillin of Skye*.[18]

❄ ❄ ❄

On 15th June 1907 Raeburn was invited north to Kingussie by his friend Frank Sidney Goggs (1871–1941), then the SMC Librarian; in later years he was also the Journal Editor and President. Goggs was an Insurance Secretary. It was some 20 miles from Kingussie to the Shelter Stone Crag, which Raeburn had admired from a distance some years earlier. He had to catch the 5.16pm train south the following evening, so obviously an alpine start had to be part of the plan.

> Goggs, with his usual sublime disregard for distance, and confidence in his sleeping powers — born of his success last June, prone on the rugged cobble-stones of an empty hay barn — voted for the Shelter Stone itself. With vivid recollections of miserable nights spent — by others — in that damp and dismal hole, and considering my inability to sleep out, even on rock ledges 11,000 feet above sea-level in the Alps, I vetoed that vote. The "noes" had it, such is the power of "passive resistance." [19]

This small fact given out by Raeburn, his inability to sleep during mountain bivouacs, was a rare personal admission. As for the comfort or otherwise of the famous Shelter Stone, the only night the author spent under its massive bulk was spent trying to deter a wee mouse from dining on his loaf of bread (naturally the mouse won).

Luckily for the two climbers, there was a bothy at the foot of the Lairig Ghru, which Raeburn vaguely remembered from 11 years previously and Goggs had found open the previous week. They cycled in from Kingussie and reached their bothy at 8.40pm. Heather for a bed, wood for a fire in the morning and they settled to sleep by 10pm. A 1.30am rise, breakfast, and they were off by 2.40am. There was more than a touch of frost in the air as they climbed over Creag na Leacainn, pools of water thinly skinned with ice. The top of the Shelter Stone Crag was reached at 6am, and they decided to descend the rocks bounding the right flank of what is now Castlegates Gully, which separates Carn Etchachan from the Shelter Stone Crag. (Castlegates Gully, an easy scramble or snow climb, was first ascended on 19 July 1904 by Hugh Stewart and AB Duncan.) Their route became steeper as they descended but gave them a pleasant scramble of 55 minutes. It is named Castle Wall and is now a 210m Difficult in summer, and Grade IV in winter.

They gained the Shelter Stone for 'lunch', which they finished at 7.30am, Raeburn then falling into the sort of half-sleep enjoyed by outdoor people. Finally, the pull of the rocks overcame their torpor and they scanned the crag for a line. To the right of the rib they had descended was a gully, now named Breach Gully, and on its right a well-defined, very steep rib. This latter feature tempted them, and they thought it should be possible if the lower part could be climbed. They roped up at 9.15am. They found the start, and indeed the lower two-thirds of the route, extremely steep. From a height of about 300ft, Raeburn thought – '*...a moderate outward leap would have, apparently, been enough to land one on the screes at the foot, without touching anything on the way.*'

They found the rocks good, but with holds obscured by moss and earth, adhering in places at angles approaching the vertical. They had to make a short traverse left at 60ft, almost to the edge of Breach Gully, to find a '*... very neat little chimney, with overhanging ledge at the bottom, and somewhat difficult and exposed exit at the top.*' This allowed them to regain the arête. The next section, reading between the lines, was obviously an unpleasant pitch, with 40ft of slabby rock '*...which Goggs wishes me to label as dangerous.*' Another steep bit, a short traverse, an overhanging chimney, more steep ledges, two *'balance corners'*, one with a mantelshelf, led them eventually to a steep grass gully and so to the arête again. Here were superb views, and an almost level shoulder, above which easier angled ground and scrambling led to the top, 1hr and 40 minutes after starting. The current guidebook is quite unequivocal, describing Raeburn's Buttress (240m Severe) in summer as vegetated and dangerous. It is more popular as a Grade IV winter climb.

❄ ❄ ❄

On a technical note, an article in the SMCJ by Gilbert Thomson highlighted several technical problems facing climbers of the day.[20] The first problem concerned using the rope to pull up a climber, hold a climber, or hold a falling climber. In the first instance, Thomson advocated the stirrup method, whereby using either a second rope, or a length of the sole rope lowered from above, the climber needing to climb using the rope would step into a stirrup loop. Using alternate ropes to hold his weight, the climber holds his own weight while the other rope is pulled tight, so avoiding the near impossibility of pulling him up using one rope alone.

Friction alone over an edge would be the problem here, hence the use of two ropes. The climber being raised of course has to be uninjured. Thomson cites the Welsh climber OG Jones as describing this method in his book *Rock Climbing in The English Lake District.*

The second instance was that of holding a climber in position. Here we are reminded that there was still no use of belaying equipment; not even that as simple as a sling, let alone a karabiner, the steel ring which would allow a rope to be firmly tied onto a sling round a spike of rock. The leader belaying at the top of a pitch would hope to find a good 'hitch', preferably a sound flake of rock over which the rope could be thrown and safely taken in as the second climber came up. Failing that, an ice axe driven into turf or jammed in a crack might be used. To date, mountaineering in Scotland and elsewhere in Britain for that matter, relied almost completely on the leader not falling. As Thomson pointed out however –

> The weight of a man on a rope is a horrible drag, physically and mentally, and could not long be supported without some help, that of friction being usually the handiest.

As for the third instance, of holding a falling climber, Thomson, as with his contemporaries, was under no illusions. He referred to John Bell's pioneering paper on ropes and falling weights, published in Volume 4 of the SMCJ, which clearly demonstrated just how little force was needed to break a rope.[21] (See Chapter 3.) Thomson was quite clear on this point –

> The safety of the rope is entirely illusory in the case of a clear fall from any height. The falling body has acquired energy of motion, due to gravitation having acted on it through a certain space. To stop the motion, a pull in an upward direction must be applied with equal power through the same space, or, if the space is smaller, the power must be proportionally greater. This is in addition to the pull which is required merely to support the weight. If, therefore, a man has fallen ten feet, he could be stopped in the distance of another ten feet, if an upward pull equal to his weight were applied throughout that distance, in addition to the pull required to counteract his weight. If he had to be stopped in, say, one foot, the pull would be such as few ropes and fewer ribs would stand.

There were, of course, no climbing harnesses or belts which could take some of the load off a falling climber's body. It is salutary to record that when the author began climbing in the 1960s, for the first year or so a waist line was used. This was a length of hemp cord of about six metres or so, which was wound several times round the waist. A karabiner was then clipped into this to which the climbing rope (hawser-laid at first) was then tied. The waist line was probably just as illusory as in the days before, and most climbers were aware that even if a fall did not kill, hanging for any length of time would, through asphyxiation. A year or two on and a waist belt was designed and sold commercially. Finally, in the early 1970s, the climbing harness appeared, and climbers breathed a sigh of relief – even while hanging in space. In an earlier SMCJ, a note appeared which related the sad story of a quarryman who died in a fall, despite being roped.[22] The quarryman was a convict, a Henry Hanley, and the accident occurred in Peterhead, where he was clearing rocks. The note was signed with the initials WB, and was probably written by William Brown –

> …Hanley slipped, and, his rope being slack at the time, he fell ten feet before it tightened - sustaining injuries, which are described as "the fracture of the breast bone in three places, the breakage of several ribs, and a double fracture of the left leg." The medical man, who conducted the examination, was of opinion that; apart from the injuries to the chest, the other injuries would not have proved fatal. Probably the left leg was broken after death. His view was that the sudden jerk of the rope, when it became taut, snapped the ribs and crushed them into the lungs. He was unable to say what distance of a drop would produce the injuries above described; but he thought that in the case of a man of 149 lbs. (Hanley's weight) it would begin to be very serious after six feet….
>
> …If the above opinion is correct, a new terror is added to mountaineering, and fresh testimony furnished of the absolute necessity of keeping the rope taut. It seems also to point to a possible danger in hitching a bight of the rope round a projecting knob of rock as is often done by way of additional security.

Thomson ended his interesting paper with a discussion on ice axe braking and glissading. It was very obvious to him that braking with the adze of an axe could easily end in disaster, with the axe being wrenched out of a climber's grip. He relates that when photographs of glissading were taken for use with Raeburn's article on *Scottish Snow* some experiments were performed on stopping a slide.[23] On a slope and using a sitting glissade it was easily possible, even at the maximum rate of descent, to come to a halt in about six feet. When the slide was repeated and the stop made using an rope hitched around an axe, just as could happen in a real event, one trial of this was more than enough

> The stop, which was easy and pleasant when spread over six feet, was exceedingly unpleasant, and involved possibilities of, at least, minor injury, when made in, perhaps, a foot. And the force was a mere trifle compared to what would be acquired even in a short fall.

Thomson lightened his otherwise grim article with an amusing story involving a cornice –

> Once upon a time a party came up to a snow cornice, and resolved to tunnel through. A was an experienced mountaineer, B was well up in navvy work. A and C started to tunnel, B and D sat under some poor shelter, watched,

> shivered, and criticised. The two busy axes nibbled out the snow in spoonfuls, but the tunnel had made considerable progress, when B's disgust at this method of working, combined with the cold, led him to hustle D out to drive with him an opposition tunnel. In a few minutes its mouth was marked by four deep grooves, and in a few more minutes, a cubic yard (more or less) of snow had been prized out, and went thundering down the slope. Another and another chunk followed, and when A and C got their heads out of their tunnel, B and D were sitting at the top. There are few applications of science that the mountaineer may not, with advantage, lay under contribution.

❄ ❄ ❄

On the Scottish mainland the Cairngorms was not the only area seeing exploratory climbing in June 1907; the Northern Highlands saw some action when a trio decided to explore the cliffs of Coire Mhic Fhearchair.[24] George Bennett Gibbs (1864–1937), Wilfred Arthur Mounsey (1871–1950), and Edward Backhouse (1876–1922), formed a close-knit group within the SMC. All three worked in finance on Teesside.

Gibbs, who joined in 1896 and is best known for discovering Curved Ridge on the Buachaille, suffered from a heart affliction for the last 15 years of life; this probably accounted for his death while searching for flints, the interest of his later years. Gibbs proposed Mounsey – who seems to have taken up skiing latterly – for Club membership in 1901; and in 1907 Mounsey in turn proposed Backhouse, who married Mounsey's cousin Lucy, but in 1922 was killed on the Leiterspitz above Zermatt along with his guide Thomas Biner.

When the trio turned the corner on the approach and viewed the immensity of the triple buttresses of Coire Mhic Fhearchair, the records contained only one climb – and a descent at that – by Collie's party, when an earlier attempt was made on the Central Buttress. Lawson, Glover and Ling had walked in during the SMC Easter Meet of 1899 to attempt the buttresses but bad weather made this impossible, and as a consolation they climbed Sail Mhor by a gully, Lawson, Ling and Glover's Route (400m II). This was on Sunday 2nd April.

Gibbs' party, for he led the entire route, decided on the Eastern Buttress, which looked to be at an easier angle than its companion buttresses. The initial, sandstone section they climbed from ledge to ledge, always being forced leftwards, so that they ended up on the ledge below the quartzite rocks and at the left end. They then moved back right until they reached the right flanking gully, up which they started. A chimney led to snow. Having no axes, and with their original target being the buttress, they stepped back on to its edge, and by choosing the easiest route up this enjoyed a delightful climb, *East Buttress* (210m Difficult) up superb rock. An open chimney gave them the hardest section of the route. On their return to the Inn at Kinlochewe, the storm had arrived, with indigo and purple clouds above.

❄ ❄ ❄

The SMC New Year Meet for 1908 was set for Fort William, at the favourite watering hole, the Alexandra Hotel. The Meet became the setting for an extended winter climbing epic on Nevis, fortunately one in which no serious injury was involved. On the evening of Friday, 27th December, three young climbers sat in the Alexandra Hotel, the first arrivals of the Meet. Thomas Edward Goodeve (1876–1918), probably the oldest at 31, was a Mechanical Engineer in the Royal Artillery. John Henry Aitken M'Intyre (d.1933) was a Lecturer in Engineering Drawing at Glasgow & West of Scotland Technical College, and Charles Inglis Clark (1888–1918) was the son of William Inglis Clark and a student aged 19. Clark had joined the SMC the previous year, M'Intyre and Goodeve in 1903.

Unusually, but then it was quite an epic, we have no less than three accounts of this story, from three different perspectives; young Clark wrote the main article,[25] his father William wrote an account of the search,[26] and M'Intyre, who was the reporter for the Meet, gave his version.[27] The following is an amalgam of all three accounts. The unusual spelling of M'Intyre follows his usage, as indicated in his application form and elsewhere.

M'Intyre had been up the Allt a' Mhuilinn earlier in the day, checking out conditions, and reported that as far as he could see, the lower rocks were practically free of snow, the upper rocks being in the mist. The trio must have been feeling somewhat constrained by the more elderly members from previous meets, as Charlie Clark wrote –

> …felt that we had the exclusive use of Ben Nevis. This was due to the absence of the Hon. Secretary and other habitués of the Ben, who might forbid an attempt at anything difficult under the prevailing conditions.

That evening, they decided on an early start, ordering a call at 5.30am, with breakfast at 6. Accordingly, the next morning, they left the hotel at 6.45am and made their way to the 'Lunching-Stone' below the Castles area. The Lunching Stone is the huge boulder below the north face of Castle Ridge on the approach path from the Half-Way Lochan, which was in the early days a popular spot for a brief halt and refreshments. Here Goodeve and Clark discussed the options, and decided that Tower Ridge was feasible. M'Intyre, recalling the origin of the name for the Douglas Boulder, requested that he be treated as luggage, labelled with great care. (On the first ascent of the Douglas Boulder, Willie Douglas was the *luggage* on the party.) Goodeve, designated leader of the day, placed Clark as second man, and M'Intyre the *Light-weight third*. None of the three climbers had done Tower Ridge previously.

Goodeve and Clark had not climbed since August, but felt extremely fit after a good season's dances and other energetic amusements. Tower Ridge seemed to have less snow on it than the North-East Buttress, and while they were aware of a ledge which avoided climbing the Great Tower direct, and felt that they could find this, as it turned out they were wrong on both accounts. Additionally, though having both an 80ft and a 60ft rope on the climb, they used the latter, which Clark later admitted was stupid, as it rather cramped a party of three. The cold being intense, they did not change the rope on the route, which consequently slowed them down.

They climbed the Western Gully approach with hard snow and gained the Douglas Boulder Gap at about 10am. According to Clark –

> The Gap between the Ridge and the "Boulder" was reached without serious difficulty, but soon afterwards we were confronted with an almost vertical face of rock above us, shaped somewhat like a mantelpiece. Owing to all the holds being glazed with ice, and having to be cut out, a long time was taken in attempting to force a way up the centre and at both sides. This proved unsuccessful at first, and from the last point reached, Goodeve was lowered down to the right (west); he then made his way along a narrow ledge. After disappearing round the corner, he was stopped by an icy chimney about 30 feet high. A long time was spent cutting steps up the face of this, but, as the second man had no first-class hitch, and there being a big drop below, it was decided to be too unsafe to persevere.

Clark's account now has Goodeve returning to the central part and standing on Clark's head succeeding in climbing it to the ridge. Following which - *'A narrow arête was cut up to the foot of the Little Tower.'* This would seem to clearly indicate that the party did attempt an alternative to the chimney at the Gap, and were aware of the Little Tower.

M'Intyre's account humorously remarks that Goodeve, apparently not satisfied with the difficulty of the climb, thought he would like to try a variation. The appearance of the steep chimney leading out of the Douglas Boulder gap must have come as a shock to the climbers, but it does not reflect well on Goodeve's leadership at that point. The trio were in trouble already. As M'Intyre put it –

> Meanwhile the second man and the third man, each of whom had the rope securely hitched, occasionally tramped their feet and clapped their hands, not by any means as encouragement to the leader, but simply to put heat into these extremities. At last, disgusted with the variation, he retraced his steps, apologised for the delay and reascended.

The Little Tower is the ledge which provides a slight steepening of the Ridge and, to many parties, a subtle puzzle, if not trap, in route finding, as it gently persuades climbers rightwards. M'Intyre thought, rightly, that the route led up the left-hand, or eastern side, while the other two thought that the west was the only possible way. Goodeve decided to try the western side, unfortunately as it happened, but again with combined tactics saving the day. Finally, the foot of the Great Tower was reached after much step cutting. Here they were dismayed to find that it was 4pm with darkness rapidly setting in.

Below the Great Tower they made their third, and most serious navigational error. Clark wrote –

> Another consultation was held, and in consideration of the late hour, we decided to avoid the Tower if possible, and to make the straightest possible line for that dinner waiting us at 7.30 P.M., at the Alexandra. Easy as it is to suggest such a course of proceeding, we found it a most difficult one to carry out. We had a hazy impression that an easy ledge ran round the west side, enabling one to reach the Gap, without climbing the Tower itself. Certainly, when we looked to the east, there seemed no feasible ledge, as all the rocks were plastered with ice.

M'Intyre again gives a slightly different version of this event, and one begins to wonder whether during or after the epic there was some friction between the climbers –

> The so-called easy ledge to the left did not appeal to Goodeve, as seen by him, to be sufficiently difficult for the party. The leader accordingly worked round by the right to the north-western comer of the Tower, from whence the various routes up and traverses around were surveyed. It was agreed upon by all to force none of these routes, they were much too difficult.

By now, darkness had set in. Much time had been taken up by Goodeve attempting to climb up the Tower by what turned out to be cul-de-sacs. Clark describes what he called a slight haze, which made far objects appear much closer than they were. Goodeve was heard to remark *'This looks like defeat, Charlie.'* The third man [M'Intyre] thought a great deal, but offered no comment. After several hours of this groping in the darkness, they at last imagined that they were secure, as they had reached a snow gully which they could see descend about half way down to Coire na Ciste. The snow was extremely hard, with some patches of ice, and the party took great care in their descent, with the end men on the rope alternately anchoring and glissading. Their anchors would have been driven axes for the most part.

When they had descended 350ft or more, M'intyre, who then was the lowest, came across a vertical wall of iced up rock. They lowered him for 12 feet, where he found a three-foot space. Clark then descended, cutting large steps for Goodeve, who would have had no protection in descent. Eventually all three were safely on the ledge. Twenty foot lower, they came across a –

> ...terrible-looking icefall which was absolutely impossible, having a tremendous overhang. We now realised that we were in the Tower Gap Chimney, and that this icefall was the waterfall described...in the account of the original ascent by Glover and Clark.

They were close to the foot of the gully, but with no safe method of reaching safe ground in the corrie. They finally had to take the only choice available to them at this juncture and climb back up again, but this time moving out of the gully and on to the slope to the west, or right. Clark's article includes a diagram of this section of cliff, drawn by his sister Mabel, while events were clear in his mind, and it is abundantly obvious where they climbed next, paralleling the gully and taking to the face on the immediate right of Glover's Chimney, as the gully leading up to the Tower Gap is now known. Up until this point they had weak visibility from the stars, but now clouds had moved in and darkness was almost complete. They headed up for a ledge which was visible above and there they stopped for some food.

After their snack, they made their fourth error. The ledge they had stopped at was very likely the sloping terrace which runs up and right under the steep headwall above. The darkness was obscuring this, along which easy climbing could have led them to the plateau or down in to the corrie. The precise line taken by the embattled trio will never be clear, but they were now on mixed ground at modern Grade IV, and literally climbing for their lives. (The terrace was eventually climbed by Raeburn and Arthur Russell in September 1911, as part of a route eventually named Raeburn's Easy Route. It was first climbed in winter by an unnamed SMC party in 1920 and provides an elegant Grade II.)

Clark again described the optical illusion whereby far objects appeared close, as he thought the summit cornice was about a rope's length above Goodeve. To his dismay, although they climbed steadily for half an hour, it never came any nearer.

> In reality, it was still far above our heads with much more formidable objects to traverse than easy snow slopes… At one place, after cutting up an exceptionally steep slope, we were faced by a rocky pitch which was impossible. So steep was this slope, that one looked almost vertically down on the head of the man below. There was a ridge of icy rock on our right hand side, and this had to be traversed. For the first three feet there were some fairly good holds, but after that a distance of about ten feet had to be done practically by friction alone. The rock was deeply undercut at the level of the feet, and one had to take a tremendous stride on to a slippery surface. Holding on with the left hand, the leader had to lean over and cut steps with the right, and then pull himself slowly across by means of a very small finger-grip. We all took a sigh of relief when the party got safely across.

They now headed for the cornice marking the plateau edge; it was either that, Clark wrote, or be frozen to death. A rib of rock rose above them, about 20ft high and almost vertical. The ice here was also very steep, but hard snow in the corner allowed Goodeve to worm his way up and so gain a small ice arête which joined the top of the rock and the ice slope leading to the plateau. Clark needed a pull from the rope to second this pitch, as most of the snow had been kicked down by Goodeve; Clark completed this demolition job and M'Intyre had to be bodily pulled up by the two above. It was now, M'Intyre thought, at least midnight. Happily, the cornice proved to be fairly easy, and soon after midnight they were at the top of Tower Ridge. They had gained the plateau, and had been climbing for at least 15 hours –

> All three shook hands, each one fully realised the brilliance of the experience, and each felt truly grateful that the ascent had been carried out without mishap. The defeat which Goodeve thought he had received at the Tower was converted, by hard work and anxious leading, into a memorable victory.

Meanwhile, in Fort William anxiety levels were understandably rising. The various mountaineers on the Meet had been arriving all day, and as time drew on and Goodeve's party did not appear a search plan was organised. At 11.30pm, Morrison, Sang and another (probably William Clark) left the Alexandra, rucksacks filled with bandages, wraps, restoratives and tempting food. They headed up the pony track and continued past the Halfway Lochan and on to the upper slopes. Morrison had knocked the bottom off a wine bottle and employed this as a trumpet. He also had an 'electric flash light' (a battery torch). At 4am they stood at the top of Number 3 Gully and began to search along the lip of the plateau.

> …the plateau was hurriedly traversed, while Morrison, with lantern lowered to the snow, scanned every crystal for the welcome sign. We were nearing the top of the Tower Ridge, when "What's this — a footprint — and leading from the cornice?" Hurrah ! ten feet farther, other prints — a second man — the mark of special nailed boots —the recognition of C. I. C.'s footprints. Where is the third? Twenty feet farther they are found, and we hurry back along the converging tracks till we look over the edge of the ghastly cornice, where the grooves in the snow tell of the rope and the escape of our friends from the dangers down below.

Morrison tracked the footprints, and while the others tried in vain to light a second lantern, he disappeared down the slope. It soon became apparent, however, that the lost party had descended the rocky slopes towards Glen Nevis, for the rescuers were looking at lower Carn Dearg, in the direction of Polldubh. Believing that the lost ones were safe, the rescuers returned up the slope and retraced their route to the Halfway Lochan. There they rested, and on continuing their descent about 7am they met the other rescue parties – Raeburn, John Bell, Harry Walker, Ling and others, which they then directed onwards after the lost sheep.

On gaining the plateau, Goodeve, who must have been close to exhaustion having led the entire climb, handed over the lead to M'Intyre who was still at the other end of the rope. Having reached the main plateau, they found one of the guide cairns, and M'Intyre set out in a westerly direction, hoping to find the next guide cairn. The strong wind prevented them from lighting a lantern, so they could not use a compass in the dark. The Summit Observatory had been closed for three years, so they could neither shelter there nor send a reassuring telegraph to the hotel. The other two repeatedly shouted *'Keep back from the cornice!'*, so that M'Intyre deviated too much to the south. As a result, they made their fifth error of the day, and unwittingly began to descend into Coire Eoghainn, the vast corrie which lies immediately east of lower Càrn Dearg on the Glen Nevis side of the mountain. It could have been much worse, as many parties have found themselves in serious trouble further to the west, on the steep slopes funnelling them into Five Finger Gully.

It was here that the only real injury of the day occurred. They ran into very treacherous snow which forced them to cut steps for many hundreds of feet. M'Intyre had just negotiated an almost vertical slope of iced rock when he slipped. This jerked the rope and Clark's ice axe was pulled out causing him to lose his steps. Goodeve's axe belay held for a second then he too was pulled down the slope, knocking his head rather severely against a rock. Despite a bad cut, his strong constitution held firm and he quickly recovered. It was now about 4am, and being very tired, progress became extremely slow. With increasing dawn light, they could finally make out landmarks, and headed for the col between lower Càrn Dearg and the western flank of Ben Nevis.

They had just reached the col when the search party under Raeburn sighted them. It was now 9am, when a figure came bounding down the slope at a very rapid pace. It was Raeburn in person. A few minutes later he was heartily shaking hands all round and handing out sandwiches. He piloted them down through the difficult and narrow gorge which leads down into Glen Nevis and after an easy walk they reached Fort William just after 1pm on the Sunday afternoon.

The trio had been fortunate as regards weather conditions; the wind was not too severe, and they were usually mist-free. It was however bitterly cold, and both Goodeve and M'Intyre received frostbite to their hands and fingers, so that Clark thought that had it been any colder it would have been disastrous. The Meet report ended with the following coda –

> Some of the members present offered an opinion which might profitably be enlarged to the following: —
>
> It is a courtesy due from every party to their fellow-members to make sure before leaving the hotel, either that someone connected with the hotel, or that some of their fellow-members, then resident, are conversant with their intentions for the day. J. H. A. M'I.

Following this event, the remainder of the Meet was understandably somewhat muted. On Monday 30th December, Harry Walker, Ling and Raeburn headed for the Ben. The target was a winter ascent of Staircase Climb, the Very Difficult which climbs the buttress right of Waterfall Gully, first climbed by John Bell, Maclay and Naismith in 1898, with a variation added by Raeburn and Archie Robertson in 1903. The party found ice on the rocks, and at the pinnacle, where it would be necessary to use a shoulder, the ice was adhesive and they decided to retreat.

> Raeburn was anxious to try his crampons, so Walker and I put in a couple of Mummery spikes & we started over to the Castle. The gullies were evidently just a snow grind, so we made for the Castle itself. There was a good deal of step cutting and scraping to be done but we progressed steadily upwards, along ledges, up steep hard slopes with most impressive scenery till at last we came to the slight cornice at the top of the Castle.[28]

On the Tuesday Raeburn made a solo ascent of the north face of Castle Ridge, by an unknown route. M'Intyre walked up Ben Nevis with several others. Bell, Ling and Walker had an 'off day', and walked to Ardgour and back, some 26 miles. On the Wednesday Bell, Ling, Raeburn and Walker climbed the Great Ridge of Garbh Bheinn. George Ednie and Willie Naismith had done the round of Carn Mor Dearg, the Arête, and Ben Nevis, and Naismith had persuaded Ednie to descend via Castle Ridge when he learned that a party led by Harry MacRobert was having trouble on the upper part of The Castle. Naismith and Ednie waited on top but MacRobert managed to finish in the dark without help. Epics besides, the Meet was deemed to have been a great success. As for Goodeve's party, errors notwithstanding, it was a superb exhibition of general fitness, determination and careful climbing under exceptionally difficult conditions.

There is one last point to discuss regarding the Goodeve epic; the fact that despite the original descriptions and a clear diagram showing their line, within a few years the full significance of their climb became diminished to the point where it was assumed that they had in fact wandered up the much easier line now taken by Raeburn's Easy Route. This diminution began with the publication in 1936 of Graham Macphee's guide to Ben Nevis, where in the description of Goodeve's Route he dismissed it thus –

> …crossing the gully, they traversed along a ledge to the west and climbed up to the summit plateau…The route calls for no special mention.

Macphee himself admitted in both editions that the exact route was not known with certainty. Worse still, the very poor diagram illustrating this part of Tower Ridge in Macphee's 1954 edition has Goodeve's Route marked too far to the right, in effect suggesting that it takes the upper ledge of Raeburn's Easy Route. In his graded list of Nevis routes in the 1954 edition, Goodeve's Route is listed in the Moderate climbs as being the easiest, easier even than the Eastern Traverse on Tower Ridge.

Macphee's description was continued in the editions by James R. Marshall (1969, 1979), with no diagram, then after the author raised the matter, it was more properly recognised in the 1981 edition of Lochaber and Badenoch by Colin Stead and Marshall, where it was given a Grade III and at least finished close to the top of Tower Ridge. This last point is mentioned in William Clark's article on the search for Goodeve's party, where the summit search party working their way along the cliff edge, found the footsteps as they were '*...nearing the top of Tower Ridge*'.

Finally, although we will never know the exact line taken by Goodeve, their climb has been recognised as having finished up the buttress on the right of Glover's Chimney, where there are several routes at Grade IV. This area was fittingly named *Goodeve's Buttress* in Simon Richardson's 2002 edition of the SMC guidebook, in honour of their ordeal. It does not qualify as a route in its own right, as it is incomplete through not having a unique beginning, but it fully merits its narrative here as yet another positive indication of the standard of climbing which could be found over a century ago, a standard which would not be regained until after the Second World War. It's also a good story of what was a comedy of errors, just avoiding becoming a tragedy.

❄ ❄ ❄

The SMC were back to the Cairngorms for their Easter Meet in April 1908, based at Braemar. It was a large gathering, with 36 members and 15 guests. Some 20 present were members of the Alpine Club, including their President, Hermann Woolley. Even the report in the Journal by William Garden admitted that the Meet would not be long remembered for the climbing, with heavy snow cover and blizzards setting in.[29] The Meet ran from Friday 17th April, to Tuesday 21st.

On Good Friday, Goodeve, Ling and Raeburn attempted the Douglas-Gibson gully, but were driven back by a sudden thaw and its subsequent avalanches. Disappointed but not downtrodden, they climbed *Black Spout Buttress* (250m Difficult, III,5). They made no comment on climbing conditions on the buttress, and their ascent was assumed to be as a rock climb. Knowing the calibre of this rope, a winter ascent was just as likely. On the Saturday, William Clark, James Greig and the two Walker cousins attempted a route on Carn-an-Turc, climbing directly up from Loch Kander. They failed, but then climbed a steep gully '*... with a very sporting ice-corner, and came out at the summit just to the right of the main top, Clark having led up this gully.*' This gully has not been conclusively identified but has probably been recorded at some later date.

Goodeve, Ling and Raeburn were joined on the Saturday by William Garden and Henry Watson, an Edinburgh Chartered Accountant; the team headed into Coire an Dubh Lochain of Beinn a' Bhuird. There they made two climbs, one of which, according to Greg Strange,[30] may have been *Slab and Arete* (150m Difficult), the current guidebook recording it as having a 1948 ascent.

On the Sunday several parties attempted routes in the teeth of blizzards and were beaten back. The sensible ones kept to low-level walks. Garden, Goodeve and Henry Kellas climbed Cairn Toul by the right-hand arête of the Soldier's Corrie, in the height of a tremendous gale and snow blizzard, and after much hesitation as to navigation, descended into the top of Glen Geusachan and so back to Derry and Braemar, reached about 8pm. On the way they had spotted an enormous snow avalanche which had fallen from the rocks of the Devil's Point, some blocks of which were part ice and part snow and weighing an estimated several tons each.

The day after the Meet's end, Wednesday 22nd April, the cold was intense, registering 10°F (-12°C) at Braemar, and a stinging 4°F (-15°C) at Balmoral. The last of the climbers staying on left in wretched weather, on Sunday 26th April. [Kellas was the younger brother of AM Kellas.]

There was an alternative Meet for Easter 1908, held at Tyndrum. Participants included Naismith, MacRobert, Morrison, and AE Robertson. The weather seems to have been somewhat better than in the east, and Ben Lui and the Upper Couloir of Stob Ghabhar were successfully climbed. Above the cornice of the north-east face of Ben Lui, the climbers were met by a large party from the Manchester Rucksack Club, which had been founded in 1902.

❄ ❄ ❄

On Saturday, 18th April 1908, while William Clark was cutting his way up a snowy gully on Carn-an-Turc, his wife Jane, daughter Mabel, and Lucy Smith, (the daughter of former SMC President William Smith, Sheriff and Advocate for Ross & Cromarty) were engaged on an Easter outing of their own, based at Killin. The Clark family were all keen mountaineers and Jane and Mabel had accompanied William for Alpine holidays. The three ladies found themselves sheltering by a huge boulder near the Lix Toll, and there and then decided to form a Club. And so the Ladies Scottish Climbing Club was born.

The history of the LSCC is entertainingly told in a book celebrating their centenary.[31] The philosophy of the club is formally summed up as – '*...to bring together women who are committed to mountaineering in Scotland and to encourage an interest in all aspects of mountaineering at home and abroad*'. It is the oldest all-women's climbing club extant; the Ladies' Alpine Club was founded in London the previous year, which may well have spurred on the Scottish ladies to form their own national club. The LAC merged with the Alpine Club in 1975.

The September 1908 issue of the SMCJ included a note by William Clark, introducing the Club and outlining its origin, organisation and aims.[32] The first officials were: President, Mrs Jane Inglis Clark ; Hon. Treasurer, Miss Lucy Smith ; Hon. Librarian, Miss Ruth Raeburn ; Hon. Secretary, Miss Mabel Inglis Clark. After the model of the SMC, a Committee consisting of Mrs Douie Urquhart, Mrs Wm. Douglas, and the three officials was formed. The LSCC maintains two climbing huts in Scotland, Blackrock Cottage near Glen Coe, and Milehouse near Kingussie.

The first Meet of the LSCC was held in May 1908 at Arrochar, attended by seven members. The Cobbler, Crois and Narnain were climbed by various routes, with the ladies returning to Arrochar soaked but happy. By the time of Clark's note there were 14 members, with monthly walks in the Pentland Hills throughout the year, and other meets as arranged. The LSCC continues strongly to this day. As for other clubs at this time, some had ladies as dinner guests, and some, like the SMC, did not. The following short excerpt is from the 4th Annual Dinner of the Fell and Rock C.C. (founded in 1906), and indicates that in at least two of the other clubs, such matters were somewhat more advanced.

> The toast of "The Ladies" was proposed by Mr. Godfrey A. Solly, who after expressing his pleasure at such a unique gathering, mentioned the example of the Alpine Club of Canada, which had a large proportion of lady members, a lady Secretary, a number of ladies on the Committee, and had even had a lady Editor. This was the first mountaineering dinner at which he had had the pleasure of meeting ladies. "My first experience of a lady climber was on the Montanvert, where I was asked to give a lead on a climb with which I was totally unacquainted. After some time, I could not see a good route ahead, and said so. The lady demurred, at which I suggested, that as she had done the climb before, she had better take the lead—which she did most successfully."[33]

The SMC could possibly have started life as a mixed club, but as we know from the records no ladies turned up at the first meeting in 1889 and it remained a men only club until, following several attempts and AGM voting, women were admitted to the Club at the AGM in the Nethybridge Hotel on 1st December 1990.

❄ ❄ ❄

On Skye in 1907, the Abrahams, with Harland and Arthur Wakefield or Andrew Thomson, were winding up an October holiday. From a base at the keeper's cottage in Glen Brittle, they climbed Window Buttress and the Inaccessible Pinnacle. Perhaps the best route of this autumn foray was *West Buttress Route* (300m Difficult) on Sgurr Mhic Coinnich, which is a scramble until some 50m below Collie's Ledge. The climb was made more exciting when a fierce storm hit them. Hail pounded the rocks, and Ashley, seconding a pitch, had to make a step to the right.

> As fast as I cleared a foothold, the half-thawed hail came rattling down from above and covered it. Had the rope been directly above me I might have pocketed my pride and used it, but it led away horizontally and was therefore useless. My position was most uncomfortable, and all my attention was needed to retain it.[34]

Just as his fingers were about to lose all feeling, the storm abated, and he was able to clear holds of hailstones and make the moves to the belay. There were more trials of weather to meet above however. As George led up the final steepenings he came to an edge near the top of a corner and ground to a halt. The wind was too strong for clear communication, and those below could only guess what was going on. George's foot would move right to the edge and quickly be withdrawn. Finally he stepped right and was out of sight, just in time to miss a gust of wind which came roaring round the edge, striking the place he had just vacated like the crack of a whip.

In turn, each climber discovered the wind on reaching the edge, about the only place Ashley could recall where the wind was too strong to allow movement unless it dropped its speed. The numbed climbers gladly gained the sheltered side just past the summit cairn where an intake of food raised their spirits. A proposal to descend to the col via King's Chimney was vetoed and they scurried along the ridge to reach An Stac, which they had hoped to climb. The weather however, prevented that, and they continued into the corrie and on to Glen Brittle.

George Guy Barlow (1878–1969) was a physicist at Birmingham University. He was a junior to Professor JH Poynting, the two collaborating on research into the pressure of light. He started climbing through OG Jones, under whom he had read Physics at London University. He first visited Skye with his friend Harry Buckle in 1906, making the first ascent of Cioch Gully on 8th August. They also made an independent discovery of the Cioch, which Collie had found a few weeks earlier, finding the cairn there made by Collie and Mackenzie. Sadly, on meeting Collie, they found him to be so off-putting that they said nothing about their day. It would be another year before Barlow could find any information about the Cioch and that was from a meeting with Abraham in Wales.

❄ ❄ ❄

Before delving more deeply into the climbing on Skye, a brief step on to the mainland reintroduces two names; Leslie Garnet Shadbolt (1883–1973), and Alastair Campbell McLaren (1880–1950). Both joined the SMC in 1911, and in time they would leave their mark on the Cuillin. Outwith Skye, on 9th June 1908, they climbed a Severe route on the north face of Aonach Dubh, taking in a prominent chimney on the left of Ossian's Cave. *Shadbolt's Chimney* (210m Severe), as it is now, provides a climb with, as the current guide states in that somewhat dreaded phrase occasionally found in climbing guides, '*distinct character*'.

On 28th September 1908, a threesome started up a first ascent on the north buttress of Càrn Dearg on Ben Nevis. Raeburn and David Sloan Arthur (1880–1924) had met up with Harry MacRobert, who had spent the night under the cliffs, testing a tent of his own design. North Buttress was the original name suggested by Raeburn, lying on the left of South Castle Gully. Following the ascent up its fine arête by the three climbers, it is now known as Raeburn's Buttress (250m Very Difficult). They had already done several routes on Nevis, including Observatory Ridge and Tower Ridge, but Raeburn had promised them a new route, and felt that there must be unclimbed rock in the hanging corrie of Carn Dearg.

A fine rain began to fall as they started up steep rocks with outward sloping ledges. These also had sheets of moss easily slipped on, so they took to a water-slide on the left. The holds improved and they were soon 100ft up. The gully divided, the right fork running up a deep chimney for another 80ft before ending in a passageless crack where they moved right on to a slightly overhanging wall. Superb holds on this allowed it to be climbed easily. Another move right and a crack splitting the arête permitted progress on easing angles.

The rock on the arête was very rotten in places, and many large blocks were cleared by the last man. One block, over half a ton in weight, and as it struck the rock, about 100 feet down, it caused a perceptible tremor to shake the whole of the great buttress. As it ascended, the arête became ever steeper and narrower, and at length actually overhanging, and not more than a few feet in thickness. On its right it presented a smooth slab, rushing down almost vertically, "straight as a beggar can spit" – as MacRobert, quoting Kipling*, said – for several hundred feet.[35]

> *There's a wheel on the Horns o' the Mornin', an' a wheel on the edge o' the Pit,
> An' a drop into nothin' beneath you as straight as a beggar can spit:
> With the sweat runnin' out o' your shirt-sleeves, an' the sun off the snow in your face,
> An' 'arf o' the men on the drag-ropes to hold the old gun in 'er place -- 'Tss! 'Tss!
>
> For you all love the screw-guns . . .[36]

There was a steep drop into a black chimney on the left, with a small foothold on the slab side of the arête and another, very high and badly sloping, for the left foot on the chimney side. Handholds at first appeared non-existent, but with an effort, the *mauvais pas* was passed and the leader gained security astride a knife-edge on the top of the slab. The route had been climbed. *Raeburn's Buttress* is a Grade IV,5 in winter. Although not entirely solid or clean rock, the guide states that it is a good climb still worth doing. As for David Arthur, he died at the early age of 44 on 19th April 1924, having been twice wounded in the Great War; the second occasion being at Glencorse Wood, in action with the Scottish Rifles in 1917, and during the third Ypres battle, for which he was awarded the Military Cross. He finished the war a Major.

Raeburn finished his article by remarking that on the day of the climb, 28th September 1908, he had never seen so little snow on Nevis. All that remained were a few patches below The Comb, and along the foot of North-East Buttress. Not a flake of snow or crystal of ice was left in Observatory Gully.

> To me, Nevis is much more familiar in snow and ice conditions, and I must confess to a feeling of something wanting, a gauntness and raggedness of the great crags. There is a flowing grace of line lent to their beauty by the far-flung shining drapery of the snow-fields, that enhances, to my mind, the pleasure of a visit to the north-east face of Ben Nevis in the early summer.

There are three recorded dates when snow could not be found on Nevis, one of which was on the 28th September 1935. The year 1933 was another snow-free recording, as was early October 2006. Graham Macphee personally vouched for the 1935 incidence, as he was then in the throes of writing a climbing guide to Ben Nevis and he personally visited the usual sites which carried snow through the year.[37]

References

1. *Letter* from Fred Jackson to Willie Douglas, dated 5th May, 1896. Bound between pages 140/141 of Douglas' annotated copy of the SMCJ, Vol.4. (SMC Library, Special Collections Department of Strathclyde University Library, Cathedral Street, Glasgow. See <www.smc.org/publications> for current access restrictions.
2. Young, Geoffrey Winthrop. *Mountains with a Difference*. (London: Eyre & Spottiswoode, 1951.)
3. Abraham, G.D. *The Complete Mountaineer*, (1907).
4. Abraham, Ashley. *A Wintry Ascent in Skye*. Manchester Guardian, 6th May, 1906.
5. Abraham, Ashley. *Rock-Climbing in Skye*. (London: Longmans, Green & Co. 1907, p.188.)
6. Williams, Noel. *Skye Scrambles*. (SMC, 2nd Edn. 2011.)
7 – 14. Abraham, Ashley. *Rock-Climbing in Skye*. (London: Longmans, Green & Co., 1907.
15. Birkett, Bill. *Classic Rock Climbs in Great Britain*. (1986, OUP, 154.)
16. Abraham, Ashley. *Rock-Climbing in Skye*. (London: Longmans, Green & Co., 1907, 255.)

17. W.W.N. *Review* of Rock-Climbing in Skye. In: Mountaineering Literature, SMCJ 10, 57, Sept. 1908, 175-176.
18. Humble, B.H. *The Cuillin of Skye.* (London: Robert Hale, 1952.)
19. Raeburn, Harold. *A Cairngorm Climb – The Shelter Stone Crag, Loch Avon.* SMCJ, 10, 55, Jan. 1908, 6-12.
20. Thomson, Gilbert. *Some Mechanics of the Rope and Axe.* SMCJ 10, 55, Jan. 1908, 17-25.
21. Bell, J.H. *The Strength of Climbing Rope.* In: Correspondence. SMCJ 4, 24, Sept. 1897, 347-349.
22. W.B. *Fatal Accident due to Rope.* In: Notes and Queries. SMCJ 3, 13, Jan. 1894, 44-45.
23. Raeburn, Harold. *Scottish Snow.* SMCJ 8, 48, Sept. 1905, 285-298.
24. Backhouse, Edward. *The Eastern Buttress of Coire Mhic Fhearchair.* SMCJ 10, 56, May 1908, 67-70.
25. Clark, Charles Inglis. *Thirty Hours on Ben Nevis.* SMCJ 10, 56, May 1908, 73-81.
26. Clark, W. Inglis. *A Nocturnal Meet.* SMCJ 10, 56, May 1908, 71-73
27. M'. J. H. A. *Fortieth Meet of the Club, New Year, 1908, Fort William.* In: Proceedings of the Club, SMCJ 10, 56, May 1908, 112-119.
28. Ling, William. *Diaries.* Book 7, p.9, Dec. 30th.
29. W.G. [William Garden] *Report of the Easter 1908* Meet. In: Proceedings of the Club, SMCJ, 10, 57, Sept. 1908, 144-153.
30. Strange, Greg. *The Cairngorms – 100 Years of Mountaineering.* (SMT, 2010, p.22.
31. Steven, Helen. *Rising to the Challenge.* (SMT, 2010.)
32. Clark, W. Inglis. *The Ladies Scottish Climbing Club.* In: Excursions and Notes. SMCJ, 10, 57, Sept. 1908, 173-174.
33. *The Fourth Annual Dinner, Coniston.* FRCC Journal, Vol.2, 2, Nov. 1911, 252-257.
34. Abraham, Ashley. *Rock-Climbing in Skye.* (London: Longmans, Green & Co., 1907, 198.)
35. Raeburn, Harold. *The North Buttress, Càrn Dearg of Nevis.* SMCJ 10, 58, Jan., 1909, 183-189.
36. Kipling, Rudyard. *Screw Guns,* (Verse five.) 1890. A screw gun being a Rifled Muzzle Loader built in two halves – breech and chase, which could be carried on mules and rapidly screwed together when needed.
37. Macphee, G.G. *Snow on Ben Nevis.* SMCJ 20, No. 120, Nov. 1935, 451.

14

Skye Redux (1909-10)

The winter of 1908-09 presented an almost endless series of snow, wind, and rain-storms; the 42nd Meet of the SMC was the New Year Meet held at Killin and Inveroran, and continued this pattern as the weather exhibited itself in the role of a quick-change artist. On Tuesday 29th December, the Killin Hotel proprietor reported a foot of snow on low ground, some SMC members musing that perhaps the meet would be confined to Glen Ogle, that pass being the major geographical barrier from the south in bad winter road conditions. Some would travel by train, a more reliable method. As it turned out, those arriving on 31st December were witness to a record thaw; by Saturday 2nd January, some of the 3,000ft tops had no snow showing.

As a consequence, with rain and strong westerly gales, the Meet saw no major routes done. Much of the activity took place on the Tarmachans. On New Year's Day 1909, five members including Naismith and Raeburn, drove to the watershed above Lochan na Lairige and skied over Tarmachan, about half of the time on grass. Another party, walking over the ridge, had several members blown over by the wind, despite trying to keep their heads below the skyline.

The LSCC were holding a parallel New Year Meet based at Crianlarich, with eight members and one guest. On Saturday 2nd January, Boyd, Ling and Raeburn climbed Stobinian from the north-east corrie with seven members of the LSCC, by a steep rock gully, iced, with two pitches. There were three ropes, all led by the ladies, with the gentlemen there to provide advice if needed. There is no patronising in this statement; the ladies of the nascent LSCC were fulsome with their thanks and appreciation for the encouragement, backup, friendly company, and occasional tutelage provided by their friends in the SMC – the early writings by the LSCC makes this very clear.

On the Saturday two snow gullies were climbed on Cruach Ardrain, led by the ladies, with Charlie and William Clark present as 'teachers', as a report of the LSCC Meet later noted. In the formative years of the LSCC, while many members, most notably from the Clark family, had an impressive list of climbs behind them, the SMC were especially helpful in providing advice and if needed leadership, some of the LSCC members being novices in the game. Raeburn was particularly prominent in this respect. Oddly, the SMC report has no mention of this outing, and indeed Saturday has the Clarks on separate hills for walks. It has to be said that the ladies were often more concerned with their enjoyment of the hills than the tedious task of accurate reporting, and that the dates may be incorrect.

On Sunday 3rd January, Boyd, MacRobert, Raeburn and guest Austen Thomson headed for Craig na Caillich, the buttress at the western extremity of the Tarmachan Ridge. They were intent on climbing Great Gully, which had seen ascents by Raeburn and Mackay in 1898 and 1902 respectively. Almost certainly, as Raeburn had not succeeded in making a direct ascent but had instead traversed off left at half-height, he was determined to make amends. As the Meet report by Alfred David Smith has it –

> There was a fair waterfall to begin with, but after the first plunge was over, things were not so bad. Very little snow was found in the gully, but some ice was encountered in the central pitch. At the nasty, grassy pitch about half-way up a new traverse was made to the right and then back again before the final difficult pitch. The top one is climbed by the left side, gradually working out on to the steep grassy face. The direct ascent was tried with a rope from above and pronounced impossible.[1]

At Inveroran, breakfast on the morning of the 31st December was delayed by a flood in the ground floor of the hotel. Problems on the hills included slushy snow and of course swollen burns. Excitement was confined to a near disaster on Loch Tulla, as two guests along with Charlie Clark and James Reid Young approached Beinn Achallader by boat, having to put back to search for the boat's bung which no one, including engineer Young, had thought about. Luckily they all made it before the boat foundered, including Young who later became SMC Guidebook General Editor from 1919-20.[2]

In Aberdeen, March 1909 saw 29 rainy days, while it was not much better in Edinburgh. The days leading up to Good Friday of 1909 saw high pressure, slowly falling, as some 45 members and eight guests began to arrive at Fort William for the Easter Meet. Before that meet properly began however, another meet was on-going a little further south, with the LSCC at Inveroran. A profitable joint day was held on Beinn an Dothaidh, with members of both clubs, including Douglas, Garden, Ling, Mackay, Raeburn and George Lissant Collins from the SMC. The latter had joined the SMC the previous year, and was a solicitor from Rochdale, Lancashire. He was an original member of the Climbers' Club, and a member of the Alpine Club. He had visited the Alps regularly since 1893.

Members of the LSCC were: Joan F Smith, Lucy Smith, Ruth Raeburn, Mabel Inglis Clark, sisters Anna and Pauline Ranken, and Daisy Gillies. Three winter routes were climbed on this Thursday, two of which have since been recognised as being first ascents, the routes being forgotten, overlooked, and quite simply missed by subsequent guidebook authors including, shamefully, Ken Crocket (Southern Highlands section of *Arran, Arrochar and the Southern Highlands*, SMC, 1997). Fortunately, we have club archivists such as Robin N Campbell, who has been bringing into the daylight such corrections to history. That these routes were overlooked is perhaps understandable as Campbell explained in a Journal note –

> The original Guide Book article to Beinn an Dòthaidh appeared in Volume 7 of the Journal – seven years beforehand, and the Club didn't get around to publishing a district guidebook until John Wilson's guide of 1949, by which time these enterprising efforts had been forgotten.[3]

Willie Ling's diaries have been instrumental here in finding out who went where for the most part, while Mabel Inglis Clark, daughter of William Clark, described the ascent she was part of some 20 years after the event. Ling, and presumably the other gentlemen, had caught the early train to Bridge of Orchy, meeting there with the LSCC ladies on 8th April. On entering the corrie, Ling mentioned '*…a fine buttress cut off from the main mass by a slanting gully or couloir.*'[4] The gully would have been West Gully, dividing North-West Buttress on the left from West Buttress on the right. The group split into three parties, each party having two gentlemen. They tossed a coin for routes, and Ling having won he chose the buttress on the right, which had an obvious stepped arête overlooking West Gully. In his party were Lucy Smith, Joan Smith, Ruth Raeburn, and Alexander 'Sandy' Mackay. Ling's party roped up with Lucy Smith leading, followed by Ling, Joan Smith, Mackay and Ruth Raeburn. The description is from Ling's diary entry for the day –

> There was a very steep & awkward corner to start with in our climb which our leader managed very well. The turf on the ledges was hard frozen & difficult. The angle throughout was steep. The climbing afforded plenty of variety some of the situations were quite sensational and in parts the rock was [un]stable and required great care.
>
> Half way up we came to a snow platform where we were in the sun & could all halt for a few minutes. Here the leadership was changed, Miss Raeburn & Miss L. Smith reversing ends. There were some steep rocks here and a very tricky balancing corner which Miss Raeburn negotiated with great confidence

> in spite of the uncertain condition of the snow. It was quite difficult. Then steep rocks led to a platform where we could all gather and as it was now 4 o'clock we had some food.[5]

Above this, the angle lessened, and they were soon at the top of the buttress. The route was recorded in 1982, and named *Stairway to Heaven* (135m III), and as Robin Campbell suggests, whoever edits the next Southern Highlands Climbers' Guide should perhaps rename it Ladies' Arête.[6] As for the other overlooked new route, the second party with Collins, Mabel Inglis Clark and two or three others, headed for '*...a long narrow icy ~~chimney~~ gully.*' This was the gully which shoots out and up on the left from West Gully. Ling had written chimney then scored it out to replace it with gully, probably because at one section the gully does narrow to almost a chimney. Mabel Inglis Clark described the ascent but unfortunately omitted the other names of the party. It would have included either Douglas or Garden, and perhaps two from the LSCC.

> All went well with my party until we were faced with a very steep rock face, entirely plastered with ice, and slightly overhanging at the top. Here my leadership skills broke down entirely, and Mr Collins had to take the lead. He cut handholds and footholds on the icy face, and as if by magic he was soon over what appeared to me to be an insurmountable difficulty. After bringing me up, he left me to reassume the responsibilities of leadership, while he unroped and traversed to the right across a narrow sloping ledge of snow, and so gained the summit of the mountain.[7]

Above the difficulties in the narrows of the route, the climb is split by a steep buttress at the top, with the line as first recorded by Arthur Ewing and Sandy Trees as *Taxus* (240m III) in 1969 moving left then up. A steeper Icefall Finish climbs up more directly, and it seems likely that Collins took a right exit beneath this to gain the finish. Somewhat gallantly, the brief note in the SMCJ for the Easter Meet does not mention the exchange of leadership. *The Icefall Finish* (90m IV,4), was first recorded by SMC members from Greenock in January 1976 led by Bill Skidmore, and received a second ascent the following month by Crocket and Ian Fulton. Raeburn probably climbed West Gully with several LSCC. As mentioned by Ling, we can confirm that in freezing conditions the turf on Stairway to Heaven can be as hard as a brick. While this can be a bonus with modern ice gear, in nailed boots it would have added to the difficulty.

❄ ❄ ❄

Once the Meet proper at Fort William got under way, Friday morning started with morning mist on the hills, which soon burned off to produce one of those perfect spring days. Following breakfast at 6am, several parties trotted past the Halfway Lochan and over the shoulder to enter the Allt a'

Mhuilinn. For those visiting Nevis for the first time the view of the cliffs was *'astounding, marvellous'*.[8] The Meet Reporter was John Reid Levack (1870–1940), a physician from Aberdeen specialising in radiology, who had joined the SMC in 1908. Levack was also a staunch member of the Cairngorm Club, being President for six years, and was a prominent promoter of the scheme to erect a view indicator on his favourite mountain, Lochnagar.

On Nevis, Raeburn, Ling, Gibbs and Mounsey had a 12hr 30 minute day, climbing the Douglas Boulder by the west arête then Tower Ridge, taking in the Great Tower by the Recess Route on its western face. The west arête of the Douglas Boulder is the *South-West Ridge* (180m Moderate in summer, III in winter, and probably undergraded at that). The arête was probably free of snow at that altitude, as it was mentioned that the rocks were in good condition. The higher rocks on Tower Ridge in contrast, were quite icy, and a photograph by Mounsey indicates a good covering of snow at the Gap. Another party from the Meet had watched as Raeburn busily chopped ice holds in the 'Recess' –

> ...the chip, chip of his axe being plainly heard, whilst every now and again a shower of ice could be seen to shoot out and rattle down the cliffs, indicating what was being done to get the road clear.[9]

Meanwhile, Goodeve, Workman and Young, just arrived by train from Glasgow, started at once for the Ben, intending to climb The Castle. Unfortunately, the sun was by then warming the cliffs, and they were not far up the climb when a large ice-fall from above narrowly missed them. They debated their position, and decided to continue, keeping as close as possible to the North Castle Gully edge. A second fall took place, and then a third, a large ice block missing the leader's head by inches. Enough was enough, they decided, and retreated immediately.

The next day, Saturday, Raeburn, Goggs, Gilbert Thomson and Unna climbed North-East Buttress –

> The route followed was by slabs to the right of Slingsby's Chimney, and, thereafter, the arête was very closely followed. No serious difficulty was met except at the forty-feet corner, where every hold was thickly caked with ice, much more so than was met with on the Tower. By afternoon the snow began to show signs of slipping off the underlying ice.

Immediately right of Slingsby's Chimney is a summer route, *Slab Rib Variation* (150m Difficult). This provides a IV,5 in unconsolidated snow or powder conditions, recorded as such in 1982, though it would seem possible that Raeburn's party made the first ascent, snow conditions being more amenable. As far as the written record shows, this would have been the third winter ascent of North-East Buttress, and the second by a Scottish party, Irving's party having made the second winter ascent in 1906.

Tower Ridge and the western arête were climbed by Workman, Young, Goodeve, William Grierson MacAlister and MacRobert, thereby making the second ascent of the South-West Ridge. This party found the snow on Eastern Traverse and on the final section of the ridge above the Gap very loose and dangerous in the warming sun. M'Intyre led Nelson and Macmillan up Number 3 Gully, while Naismith and his guest Allan Arthur (1884–1963) walked up with skis to the summit via the Coire Leis arête and enjoyed a superb run down for 2,000ft, almost to the half-way house. Arthur joined the SMC later that year. An electrical engineer, he was a Vice-President in 1935-37. As his obituarist Stuart Jack wrote –

> There must be but few members alive who knew Allan Arthur, and fewer still who ever climbed, or rather raced with him; for he seemed to be possessed by some demon, and while the party with which he had started was reaching its first top, Allan had long since passed it and was racing ahead for the next and the next again.
>
> And this demon seemed to follow him into his business, till, at last, it brought on a nervous breakdown from which he never recovered.[10]

Castle Ridge saw several ascents over the weekend, while the popular mountains in the area, including Garbh Bheinn of Ardgour, were visited. On the Sunday, Raeburn cycled to Glen Coe, where the following day, with two English guests, he made a winter ascent of Crowberry Gully (see Chapter 8 for details of all three ascents of this classic route by Raeburn).

The weather gradually deteriorated during Sunday, and Monday dawned dull and rainy. Despite this, Collins, Ling and Naismith climbed North Castle Gully in a snowstorm, while Unna, Workman and Young drove to the road end in Glen Nevis, and traversed the Aonachs over to Glen Spean. En route they experienced very high winds and driving snow, along with a strong electrical brush discharge which appeared on their ice axe points.

This electrical phenomenon is also known as St Elmo's Fire, and was quite often seen as a strange light playing on the upper spars and masts of sailing ships. The author has experienced it once, when, with his axe strapped on to the back of his rucsac a hissing sound was heard during a walk in Glen Coe, a day with occasional falls of hail. Every time he turned, the sound remained at his back, and soon the penny dropped! St. Elmo's fire is a plasma. The electric field around the object in question causes ionization of the air molecules, producing a faint glow easily visible in low-light conditions and a hissing or buzzing sound. Sharp points lower the required voltage because electric fields are more concentrated in areas of high curvature, so discharges are more intense at the ends of pointed objects such as an ice axe spike.

Also on Sunday, Goodeve, Glover, Ling, the Walker cousins and Worsdell drove up to the head of Glen Nevis and set off from there at 8am, intent on taking the long approach to climb the *North-East Ridge* of Aonach Beag, roping up in two groups at 1.15pm. The rain came on as they started. This was a slow start, due to the pilgrims becoming lost in the mist and having to partly retrace their steps. Ling's diary records that his aneroid was questioned, but vindicated itself. Below the final gendarme, Ling, Glover and Harry Walker decided to try a new variation to the right, with the others taking the normal route.

> The face was uncommonly steep but we thought that by traversing to the foot of a shallow gully we could regain the ridge. The conditions were very bad. First we crossed some steep soft snow & then came a little traverse to a short ice chimney which took some cutting. Above that was a sensationally narrow ledge to balance along & then a short descent over icy turf to a little platform. In the conditions it was very doubtful whether we could get to the ridge & as it was now 4.30 and our teeth were chattering with cold, we decided to return. The other three had gone the ordinary route to the left & called to us from the ridge above. With great caution we retraced our steps and descended the ridge again to the lunching place 6.15.[11]

They then toiled up to the col between the Aonachs, gaining that at 7.05pm and down the other side into the corrie. Descending this, they reached Steall at 8.20pm (this was Steall ruins on the north bank of the Water of Nevis). At Polldubh they found their welcome trap waiting for them at 9.25pm which took them down to Fort William at 10.20pm – '*... quite ready for an excellent dinner at 10.50.*'

Officially, the Meet was over by Monday night, but a few lingered on, loath to return to everyday routine. Castle Ridge was climbed under a foot of new snow by William and Mabel Clark, the latter leading, while Jane and Charlie Clark, along with Morrison, climbed North Castle Gully. A small splinter Easter Meet was also held at Crianlarich, with various hills and easy snow climbs being done.

❄ ❄ ❄

With an avalanche on Beinn Achaladair on 10th April 1909, the nascent LSCC almost had half its membership wiped out. The President, Jane Inglis Clark, tells the story. Climbing a snow gully to the right of the broad gully leading to the col above the north corrie, Mrs Douie Urquhart, Jane Clark, the Misses Stuart, and I McBride moved steadily upwards. They moved carefully, one at a time, with axes driven into the snow and the rope hitched. About an hour into the climb, a curious hissing sound announced an avalanche coming down the gully, which missed them by about a foot. The snow to this point was '*rather treacherous*', being soft on top and quite hard below. They thought that by keeping close to the rocks on their left they would be safe. Higher up, the snow worsened, and accordingly they decided to move on to the rocks. Just as the leader turned to move across, the snow beneath her gave way. They pushed down on their axes but to no avail, as they were carried down the gully.

> Down we went, and to my horror the ropes began to tighten round my neck. In another minute I would have been strangled, but with a big effort I managed with my left hand to get the ropes pushed off, holding on to my axe with the right. I dared not think what might be happening to the others. Then came another danger; we were making straight for an island of rocks. I really gave up thinking then, and expected to be crashed into bits. To my astonishment we sailed over the big boulders. What a relief! I then did all I could to stop our wild career, and finally we came to a halt. I was afraid to look round on my companions. I can never forget how thankful I felt when I found that they had not a scratch! only the ice-axes left in the gully! The snow of the avalanche had been in such quantity that it acted as a cushion to carry us safely over the rocks. We did think of going up again for the axes, and actually started to do so, but decided that we had had enough for one day, and that the axes might be rescued another time.[12]

As a final note to this tale, of what had presumably been yet another slab avalanche, the extreme stress and worry felt by the Edinburghians by the potential loss of two ice axes was somewhat allayed by the finding of one of the axes by an SMC party and its subsequent return to its owner with much rejoicing. As to the sense of a winter party of five carrying two axes, we can only state the obvious and say that all need to carry an axe and know how to use it.

❄ ❄ ❄

On Skye, with limited places to stay close to the Cuillin, camping was also increasingly employed; not just in Glen Brittle, but as wild camping in the corries for those energetic enough to carry the necessary gear. The only real downside to Glen Brittle, apart from the nearest bar being at Sligachan (and the midges, oh the midges!), were the dark volcanic sands of its beach, which always seem to have a sombre look even in bright sunshine.

Guy Barlow became one of the Cuillin's most prolific climbers, often roping up with Everard Wilfred Steeple, and also Harry Buckle and AH Doughty. With these partners, Barlow would pioneer 37 first ascents in the Cuillin, some 16 of which were climbed before the First World War. Nineteen of these first ascents are starred in the current SMC guide, an indication of the general quality of his climbs. Steeple (1872–1940) was described by Showell Styles in *Classic Rock* as being –

> …retiring to the point of unsociability…I found myself walking across moorland with a small insignificant stranger, large of nose and drooping moustache, who could hardly have been more unlike my idea of a great climber and was probably (I thought) a very moderate hill-walker.[13]

On 20th June 1909, Henry E Bowron and Steeple climbed *Median* (355m Very Difficult), a line up the Western Buttress of Sron na Ciche. It was a long and fairly direct route up the centre of this huge buttress, of which the guide introduction states – *This excellent climb is serious for the grade and needs good route finding ability in order to avoid considerably harder variation. Normally 4 hours.*

At the time of its first ascent, writes Pedlar, Median was the Cuillin's most serious route for its grade. The name was not the original, indeed the first ascenders did not give it a name, being unaware of any other climb on the buttress. The name Median first appeared in the 1923 SMC Guide to the Island of Skye, with rock climbing information compiled by Steeple and Barlow. It was probably Steeple who supplied the name, as being both fitting and convenient, in order to separate the routes on the face.

The next day, Robertson Lamb led Steeple and Bowron up Cioch Direct. When Lamb reached the parallel cracks, at the point where Harland had had to swing over to reach the left-hand crack, Lamb could not reach far enough, and – '*...was obliged to climb straight up, over a bulge of smooth rock, a rather trying operation. Bowron and I, with a slight advantage in the matter of reach, found the transfer to the left more satisfactory.*'[14] The same volume of the Climbers' Club Journal had an article by Barlow and Buckle, describing routes in Coire Lagan.[15]

Steeple and Barlow climbed on Skye from 1906 onwards, missing out only the war years. They usually stayed at Mary Campbell's *Cuillin Cottage*, where, as Ben Humble wrote – '*Countless climbers have happy memories of that little cottage nestling in trees by the burnside*',[16] or camped in the high corries. Their imminent arrival on the island could be divined by the arrival of their paper-wrapped parcels at the Glen Brittle Post Office. These contained both food and equipment, with each parcel painstakingly made up so that it almost, but not quite, exceeded Post Office parcel regulations for weight and size.

There is an amusing insight to life at Mary Campbell's, at least while Steeple and Barlow were in residence. Dorothy Pilley, climber and author of *Climbing Days*, was on Skye in August 1919. She described the different approaches which rock climbing pioneers had, including Steeple and Barlow –

> Among such wily and experienced experts none has been more successful or added more useful new climbs, both in Wales and Skye, than E.W. Steeple and Guy Barlow. Indeed they had even then added so many that it was idle for them to pretend ignorance or absence of ultimate design if found near any attractive crag. ...So when we met them, looking like Vikings, in Coire Lagan, with Holland intent on 'something new near the West Wall of the Cioch', some shrewd glances seemed to be being exchanged.

Pilley, along with Cecil Holland and Herbert Carr, did in fact climb a new route that day in 1919, *Cioch West* (215m Severe) in the current guide, which describes it as '*A fine climb giving constantly interesting climbing with a splendidly exposed crux.*' The new climb seemed to Holland's party as being rather harder, on the whole, than Cioch Direct –

> We noticed at the top that Steeple and Barlow had watched our proceedings and it was kind of them to break through their polite reserve far enough to remark that our climb was 'Very pretty'. Later they thawed so far as to entertain us, with the utmost hospitality, in Mary Campbell's once famous den. This was a rival establishment, frequented only by the most courageous at Glen Brittle, a dark cabin with cupboard-like, shut beds in the walls. Here when a large meal ended, tea and eggs in dozens would appear. But Steeple and Barlow beat this. Not content with the tea and eggs in surplus, their hospitality produced a plum pudding boiled in their own billy. It had been gurgling therein succulently all through the meal. Whether it had come to Glen Brittle in one of their locally notorious parcels or had been somehow created by them there I never knew.[17]

According to Humble, Mary Campbell died in 1947, with her nephew and his wife continuing to run Cuillin Cottage. Since Pilley's visit, the bed recesses had been removed, making for a more spacious lounge.

❄ ❄ ❄

Climbing on the Scottish mainland continued, albeit at a much quieter pace than on Skye. The Cairngorms saw very little climbing, although a new area was opened up with the exploration of Glen Clova in the south-east.

> The upper waters of the Dee have cut a deep valley extending far into the most elevated mass of land in Britain. That part lying to the north is now known as the Cairngorm Mountains, while the portion to the south, an only slightly inferior range, is known in its different parts as the Lochnagar Range and the Braes of Angus.

So began the introduction to the Braes of Angus section of the SMC Guide Book, published in the SMCJ for May 1904 and edited by Hugh Munro.[18] When he came to the section headed Climbs, his succinct comment was '*There are none.*' Greg Strange remarks in his history –

> On the south-east edge of the Cairngorms overlooking the wide fertile farmlands of Strath More [sic] are the Braes of Angus. This plateau area of rounded hills is cut by several long roughly parallel glens whose rivers flow south-east into Strathmore then into the North Sea. Perhaps the finest of these is Glen Clova, the upper part of the valley of the South Esk.[19]

The rocks in the main glen have granite giving way to schist, gneiss, diorite and epidiorite. Heather gives way to grass, and the vegetation is richer and more varied than in surrounding areas. Botanical hunters have long been attracted to this area, but for the next wave of explorers, the climbers, the target was unclimbed rock accessible to those from the east. Munro was not aware of any recorded climbs, but at least he recommended, for the ambitious, Glen Doll and especially Craig Rennet, a bold bluff on the south-west side.

Taking up this challenge were two climbers from Aberdeen: James Alexander Parker (1864–1946), a Civil Engineer from Glasgow, and Howard Drummond, a merchant from Aberdeen. Parker gained employment with the railways, and was responsible, while working for the South-Eastern and Chatham Railway, for putting a new roof on London's Charing Cross Station. In 1906 he moved to the Great North of Scotland Railway Company based at Aberdeen, where he was involved in building Aberdeen Joint Station (1913-16). A member of the AC, and an enthusiast for the Pyrenees, he joined the SMC in 1908 and was President of the SMC 1925-26, and of the Cairngorm Club 1928-30. He was Editor of the SMC Guide to the Western Highlands (1931). As his obituary remarks, he was a man who took some knowing. *'Some may have thought him somewhat brusque and severe, but behind that outer crust there was a wealth of no ordinary sincerity which made his friendship, when obtained, well worth while.'*[20] With his friend William Garden, he compiled the Index to the first 10 volumes of the SMCJ, a task which all who have done such drudgery will instantly recognise as truly heroic and ever useful.

On New Year's Day 1910, Parker and Drummond approached Craig Rennet, and climbed an easy winter line on the left of its east face, taking in steep steps of mica schist and vegetation. The following day they were joined by J Bruce Miller, a Manufacturing Chemist from Aberdeen. Thwarted on an attempt to climb the large buttress known as the Scorrie, they eventually climbed a gully in Winter Corrie, *Backdoor Gully* (200m II). Winter Corrie is the hanging corrie on the north-east flank of Dreish, lying on the left side of Glen Clova. In future years, it would become a popular winter crag especially for those in the Dundee and Angus areas, with conditions often good earlier on than in the higher hills.

❄ ❄ ❄

In February, Harold Raeburn was injured in a climbing accident. It would not be fatal, but there is the possibility that it would turn out to be life-changing. We have the details from Ling's Diary 8, which covers from 9th April 1909, to 8th August 1910. On 27th February 1910, a party of seven set out from Strathyre Hotel and motored to the foot of Glen Ample. The seven were: Edith Gray, Ruth Raeburn (Harold's sister), Lucy Smith, John Bell, Harold Raeburn, Robert Hope and Willie Ling. They walked up Glen Ample (probably from the north) and at the shepherd's cottage, possibly Glenample, Bell left them and returned home. The six continued on to the bealach and after dropping down the other side had lunch before roping up. The weather was excellent; it was hot in the sun. The snow was in good condition, and they aimed to climb a buttress in order to gain the top of Stuc a' Chroin. We assume that they were climbing on the eastern flank of Stuc a' Chroin, having entered the corrie to the north of the peak.

The first rope was Raeburn, Smith, Hope and Gray, with Ruth and Ling on the second rope. Smith was unfit, so on reaching the same height as the pass they decided to continue by an easier route. To the left of this was an open chimney above a steep slope of hard snow. There was a crack at one side, with a leaf of rock at the side of a large slab. This was topped by a stone without holds. Raeburn, who was leading, tried the stone but it would not go. He then traversed across the slab by a frozen turf foothold, and from another foothold gained the top platform above the slab.

Smith followed to the further foothold, then Hope climbed on to the grass hold. He had not made himself firm there before Gray slipped on her hold and dragged him down. Smith was then torn from her stand and Raeburn, unable to hold all three was pulled after them, shooting right out to land on the hard snow below with a sickening thud, after which all four slid down the slope, Raeburn in front.

Ruth and Ling at this point had been just below the first rope. Leaving Ruth where she was, Ling untied and dashed down the slope. The higher three were apparently unhurt, but Raeburn was lying helpless and head down. When Ling reached him he was barely conscious and groaning, but he came to when Ling raised him. His ribs were broken and he was in a bad state. Hope came down and between them they bandaged Raeburn with puttees, then slid him down the slope through a narrow gap between rocks. He then stood up and supported between them they reached the bealach at 4pm, the ladies following.

Ling left his hat and coat for Raeburn, then raced down to Glen Ample Farm in 25 minutes. With the two shepherds, Tam and John Hunter, a makeshift stretcher was prepared from two poles with a large wool bag nailed to them and two blankets. Ling sent a message off for a doctor then set off up the hill. Just before 6pm they met Raeburn, almost dead beat and supported by Hope and Ruth. Smith and Gray they had met earlier, descending. Raeburn was suffering from the cold, and wrapping him in the blankets and all the coats they got him on the stretcher. The going, as anyone who has ever helped on a stretcher carry will know, was very hard, and halts were of necessity frequent. By now it was dark, and it was difficult to pick ones steps. Ruth went on ahead and came back with a lantern, and finally the cottage was reached at 8.30pm.

In bed, and even with hot water bottles, it took Raeburn a long time to feel warm again. The doctor had arrived just after 9pm and bandaged Raeburn properly. With broken ribs combined with shock and cold, he was feeling intense pain. Ling does not say, but Raeburn's ribs could have been broken either by the fall, or, more likely, by the rope. Ling finished his account in his diary, writing –*'Truly a sad ending to a joyous day.'* [21] On March 20th, Ling went back up Stuc a' Chroin himself and recovered the axe [presumably Raeburn's]. He gained the summit and descended by the ridge.

A letter written by Raeburn to Geoffrey Young dated 13th April 1910 provides more information on his accident[22] –

> ...My accident though bad enough for me was less so thro' the actual injury than to the digestive troubles ensuing. It kept me 6 weeks on my back however & of course I am still very weak & not able to get about much.
>
> The place was not a definite climb & was not difficult & only about 25 feet high. My injuries were caused more by the fearful jerk of 30 stones [190Kg] weight on the rope round my waist than by the fall.
>
> The others luckily were quite unscathed. One thing the accident has demonstrated to me & that is the kindness & consideration of my friends. I am profoundly grateful to all of them. I am glad to say that I am mending so fast that I have hopes of not only getting out to the Alps but of being able to do smaller climbs if not able to tackle anything of the calibre of Monte Rosa's East face.
>
> I am
Yours Sincerely
Harold Raeburn

The accident explains why Raeburn was absent on the SMC Easter Meet in 1910; the report of the meet expressed much regret that Raeburn, then a Vice-President of the club, was unavoidably absent as was the President, Gilbert Thomson, and the Secretary, William Clark.[23] There may well have been a positive note to Raeburn's convalescence; he may have found more time to work on his book *Mountain Art*, which, but for the economic stringencies of the war, would have been published sooner, or perhaps he used his convalescence to actually start the project. In either case its publication was delayed until after the war. As to his injuries, his *'digestive troubles'* may well have been a source of future ills.

❄ ❄ ❄

The Easter Meet was blessed with generally good weather, probably the best since 1894, and the old members present regarded it as one of the most successful meets ever. It was a multi-centred affair, being held at Kinlochewe, Glen Coe (Kingshouse), Dundonnell, and Inveroran. Good Friday of 1910 fell on 25th March, and there was a reasonable amount of snow on the high peaks. In many ways, it would in hindsight be a high-water mark as regards early SMC Meets.

From the Kinlochewe party, on Friday the Walker cousins, with Ling and Robert Corry (a guest from the Alpine Club who joined the SMC later in the year) attempted a route on the West Buttress of Coire Mhic Fhearchair but ran out of steam below a steep wall, traversing right into a snow gully. Matters were better the next day, when two ropes made first ascents on Martha's Peak on Beinn Airigh Charr. The previous year, in May, Glover and Ling had climbed a Moderate here, and had obviously spotted the potential for more. Ling, Corry, Glover and Harry Walker found *Face Route* (330m Difficult), while Charles Walker, Charlie Clark and Robert Wordsell climbed *Walker's Route* (250m Very Difficult) Both routes are on the main face, rising above Loch an Doire Crionaich. The latter route was climbed in winter in 1999 at IV,5.

George Glover wrote an article following the ascent of these two routes which provides more details than in the meet report written by Collins. The crafty climbers, for example, approached the hill by boat, rowing across Loch Maree from Loch Maree Hotel to a pebbly beach about a mile west of Letterewe. They joined the stalkers' path from Letterewe to the Fionn Loch and continued along the Strathan Buidhe, dropping down below the cliffs and passing Loch an Doire Crionaich, the party dividing into the two ropes as above.

Ling led his route throughout, finding that although the general angle was steep, much of the rock sloped inwards, providing secure holds. The only drawback the party had, as Glover wrote, was four ice axes (too many) and 80ft of rope (not enough). About 20ft from the top of Martha's Peak they saw the footprints of the other party, the three bachelors Clark, C Walker and Worsdell having successfully climbed their route, which lay as closely as possible on the centre of the curve of the buttress where on the west it swept round into the corrie. The bachelors' party were not quite finished however, as they went on to a group of crags of the east of the summit of Beinn Airigh Charr –

> …where without axes they landed on frozen turf at the top of the westernmost chimney, and the leader, after a very difficult run out, was heard making use of such expressions as are the property of fishers – which prompted Ling to let down a line and land the party to save time.

Also on Saturday 26th March, seven from the meet, including William Garden and Percy John Henry Unna (1878–1950), had a tentative look at the Coire Mhic Fhearchair Triple buttresses, but like the party the day before were forced off the rocks and completed their ascent by an easy snow gully. Unna, born in London and of Danish origins, had joined the SMC in 1905. An engineer, he served as President from 1936-38. He died of heart failure on Beinn Eunaich while walking alone during a New Year Meet, and was buried in Pennyfuir Cemetery near Oban. He is revered for his Principles of Mountain Management, and for his major contribution to the purchases of Glen Coe South and Dalness, donated to the National Trust for Scotland.[24]

Several other ascents were made from the Kinlochewe section of the SMC Easter Meet; Charlie Clark and Charlie Walker avoided church-going on the Sunday and instead headed for Beinn a' Mhuinidh, at the north-east end of Loch Maree. They reported making an ascent on steep rocks and vegetation, on a Creag Roy, where the line of cliffs turn up Glen Bianasdail. This would be somewhere to the north of Waterfall Buttress, but no map seen has a Creag Roy marked.[25] There is a Creag Ruadh marked on the current OS 1:25K map, about 1km north-east of Kinlochewe and plainly visible from the hotel there; possibly Clark had enquired as to the name of the line of crags visible on the south flank of Beinn a' Mhuinidh and had been given that name. Unfortunately the current guide is in somewhat of a guddle, as the first ascent list has a *Double Flake Route* (75m Severe) down for Easter 1910 by William Inglis Clark and CW Walker, while in the text the route year is 1946. William Clark was not even present at the meet, and may well have been confined at home with an illness. Influenza was prevalent then, and was often a killer, requiring careful convalescence.

There were more detailed activities the following day, including the ascent of an easy snow gully on Liathach by Alexander White and his guest GK Edwards (Canadian AC), on the north-west flank of Pinnacle Buttress. This was on Monday 28th March, when they met up with Charlie Clark and Herbert Cameron Boyd who had climbed, with some difficulty due to icing, the third pinnacle on Liathach. The last pair had also met another party, consisting of Mounsey, Corry and the brothers Backhouse, who had attempted a climb on the rocks of Meall Dearg, but had been defeated by deceptively steep rocks with downward sloping holds. The two parties teamed up to climb the pinnacle, approaching by snow slopes to gain the col at the foot of the Northern Pinnacles.

Boyd, who was a lawyer, penned a fair description of what they saw when they walked in to climb on Liathach –

> The walk beneath the north side of Liathach is a very fine one. It opens out a magnificent view of a long line of gaunt terraced cliffs, relieved by bands of snow on the ledges and in the gullies, where climbing of a high order might be had. Beyond this we could see a beautiful corrie — Coire na Caime — enclosing a little lochan, and hemmed in by great walls of rock ; on the left a

> lofty range of precipices, crowned by the Fasarinen Pinnacles ; on the right the steep buttresses of Meall Dearg, the ridge of which swept round in a graceful curve, dipping to a col directly in front, then mounting in the saw-like edge of "The Northern Pinnacles," and culminating in the shapely snow-covered cone of Mullach an Rathain. In the heart of the corrie shining slopes of snow stretched upwards to the foot of the rocks, and narrow ribbons of snow gullies divided the buttresses from each other. In the bright spring sunshine the whole formed a scene of rare beauty and Alpine grandeur.[26]

The first pinnacle was a mere bump, but the second one presented an almost vertical smooth face of rock which quickly defeated them. They then traversed round to the right on frozen turf and scree and tackled the third pinnacle, the largest of the group. Mounsey led at first then handed over the lead to young Clark. The top of this was gained at 4pm, having taken a full 2hrs 30 minutes. With a close inspection of the fourth pinnacle and a look at their watches, they decided that descent would be the sensible course. A snow gully led down from the gap between the third and fourth pinnacles. As there were several ice pitches, Clark was lowered down to cut steps as he went, and was then joined by Mounsey and Boyd.

At the foot of the gully, they found themselves in the bed of a bigger gully, with hard snow. The lower section of this was not visible, and there was uncertainty as to whether or not to continue the descent. They had cut their way down a short stretch when they heard shouts from above. It was White and Edwards who, on seeing the slow progress of Clark *et al.* on the pinnacles, had decided to descend into Coire na Caime from the col then climb back to the summit of Mullach an Rathain by a snow gully. This made their decision for the Clark team, as they turned round and rapidly climbed up the gully, to find themselves beyond the fourth pinnacle on easier ground. This led to the summit where they could throw off their ropes and enjoy the view. But night was falling and they had no wish to be caught by darkness on the rocky slopes, so they traversed the jagged slopes of the Fasarinen, past which they took to a long, sloping snow gully. They encountered some difficulties avoiding the numerous rocky bluffs, but the road was finally gained just after 8pm, after some time spent in '*floundering through the darksome mysteries of some pine woods.*' By this time the stars were shining brightly, with Jupiter and Sirius blazing like glorious jewels in the heavens.

As they left the keeper's cottage, where much tea and scones were in evidence, they were graced with one of Nature's great spectacles. It is left to Boyd to describe the sight, and to wrap up one of the memorable SMC Meets in the wonderland that is the Northern Highlands of Scotland –

> As we left the cottage we were entranced by one of the most beautiful displays of the Aurora Borealis that I have ever beheld. The great streamers flashed over the crest of Liathach, shooting right up into the zenith in many coloured hues.

> The fascination of the spectacle was such that Clark and I, cycling homewards in the dark, could scarce keep our eyes off the sky, and had several narrow escapes from the ditch. We could have wished for no more fitting finale to the magnificent day we had had on the mountain, a day which was in every way ideal, — perfect weather, exquisite views, and delightful climbing, culminating in this gorgeous display of the auroral splendours.[27]

On the Dundonnell section of the SMC Easter Meet, Morrison and Sang made a first ascent of the easy and scenic *Hayfork Gully* (300m I) in the central corrie of An Teallach. George Sang joined the SMC in 1898 and was Secretary (1913-30). In his obituary for Sang, William Clark recalled that while on a rock climb, Raeburn had remarked to him that he thought Sang was one of the best climbers in the SMC.[28] He was certainly popular and hard working. His companion, William Alex Morrison, joined the SMC in 1902, and according to Sang's obituarist Alexander Harrison, '*...was one of the last of what was sometimes called the Ling Sang Fu Dynasty, which exercised such a great influence on the Club.*'[29]

The two friends had an life-threatening experience during the Great War, when, on 20th June 1916, they were working in a munitions factory at Roslin, seven miles south of Edinburgh. An explosion followed by fire trapped two girls. Between them, and with a third man, Archibald Young, they rescued the girls. While Sang, who knew their location, employed fire buckets, Morrison dashed in through dense white smoke and found one girl whom he passed on to Young. Morrison then returned and found the second girl. All the while small explosions were taking place, and immediately following the second rescue a larger explosion flattened part of the building. Twelve minutes after the original explosion, the entire building blew up. Morrison received the Edward Medal, First Class, and Sang the Edward Medal, Second Class.[30] The girls were badly burned but survived.

On a different level of excitement, while exploring An Teallach during the Easter Meet in 1910, Sang and Morrison had noticed a forked gully –

> It slanted upwards from the corrie in a dead straight, thin, white line that looked quite 500 yards long, then branched into two irregular narrowing prongs and so to the ridge. When I asked Morrison what it suggested to him, he replied without a moment's hesitation, "A Hay Fork."[31]

On the Saturday of the meet, Morrison and Sang seemed to have had a good time, with hard snow in the confines of the gully. After two hours' of hacking steps with alternating leads up ever increasingly angles, they were confronted by an evil-looking ice fall. Sang was exceedingly thankful that it was Morrison's turn to lead, and enjoyed a rest and a cigarette.

> I do not pretend to know how the leader got up that icefall, what I do know is that when I came to actual hand grips with it I happened to glance down between my legs at the valley far below, with our happy luncheon stone shining

> in the warm sunlight, and pastoral desires came thick upon me. Sitting down there by the gurgling stream the raven's liquid croak had seemed almost a melody. Now his nearer presence and harsher cry betokened the expectation of human eyes for supper.[32]

The gully forked above the ice pitch, and Sang took the right fork, which was easier. It led to some excellent looking rock, which tempted the leader off the snow.

> All that seemed obvious was perilously untrustworthy, and all that was obscure was firm and difficult. All pulling in holds pulled out promptly, nor was it possible to tell if the vegetation was rooted or merely laid on the rocks for appearance' sake.

Next came a pinnacle with a crack wide enough to admit a slim climber, before the climbing tapered off in difficulty; 200ft later they scrambled on top of the second pinnacle of the ridge between Bidein a' Ghlas Thuill and Glas Mheall Liath. Sang finished his route description with a warning to future climbers to avoid any day when rocks are falling; he had been subjected to a cannonade of substantial debris while Morrison was leading the pinnacle crack.

On the Sunday, which was wet and windy, the pair had a rest day. Morrison, who was a scientist and carried a bag of tools around with him, filled the time by mending all the clocks in the hotel, while Sang, a lawyer and Writer to the Signet, attempted to distract his friend by reciting fragments from Longfellow's epic poem *Hiawatha*. The next day, bathed in sunlight, they entered Toll an Lochain of An Teallach and after a traverse of the ridge descended to the then occupied croft at Larachantivore where they had arranged a meal and bed for the night.

Tuesday 29th March saw them heading for Beinn Dearg Mhor, where Glover and Ling had climbed the central gully in May 1907.[33] This was after attempting the central buttress and finding it too difficult, then the central gully up the buttress, where they ran into a barrier pitch, finally settling for the central gully. Like the earlier party, Morrison and Sang found the rocks disappointing, and eventually climbed and scrambled up the south buttress.[34] Their day finished with tea at Larachantivore then an easy walk back to Dundonnell.

❄ ❄ ❄

The section of this SMC Easter Meet based at Inveroran walked in the Blackmount, making ascents of favoured hills such as Stob Ghabhar and Dothaidh and Dorain. No technical climbs were attempted by the two members and three guests, who shared the tiny inn with an equal number of anglers. However, the highlight of the Easter Meet was marked by an audacious attempt on a hard winter route which almost succeeded. Some seven SMC members and five guests were mustered at the Kingshouse, including Harry MacRobert and Robert Arnold Brown. Various combinations climbed the easier routes such as Curved Ridge and North Buttress on the Buachaille, and the Aonach Eagach Ridge. On the Monday, MacRobert and Brown headed for Crowberry Ridge on the Buachaille, intent on a winter route by the line of what was known as Garrick's Shelf Route (in the current guide Shelf Route).

The North Face of Crowberry Ridge lies between the crest of the ridge and Crowberry Gully on the right, and consists of two huge parallel ribs divided by shallow gullies which lead to the crest of the ridge below Crowberry Tower. Immediately right of Direct Route is the gully taken by Naismith's Route. Hyphen Rib is right of this again, and is separated from the rightmost rib, which hangs over the lower section of Crowberry Gully, by the second shallow gully, the line of interest here. In summer it is loose and vegetatious and is not recommended. In winter it is a much sought-after route. When MacRobert and Brown approached the route it had not received an ascent, summer or winter. The Sunday had seen the worst weather of the meet, with torrential rain and wind. One party of three had in fact ventured on to the Buachaille, climbing North Buttress and finishing over all three tops. Three hours had been spent on the rocks, which were streaming with water and melting snow.

The following brief account is taken from a note written by MacRobert 10 years after his attempt. It was attached to an article by Joseph Alan Garrick, a Mechanical Engineer at the Royal Technical College, Glasgow, who had joined the SMC in 1920, aged 26; some details by Garrick are given here in order to paint the scene.[35] In May 1923, Garrick and his friend D Biggart ventured on to Crowberry Ridge, aiming to climb Direct Route. The weather had been poor and it rained overnight. Moreover, Garrick's work usually didn't allow him to climb at weekends, and although he had long summer holidays, often spent in the Alps, he was unfit for most of the year. Accordingly, when they reached the famous traverse on Direct Route, he was unhappy on seeing wet rocks and persuaded Biggart to take the easier line avoiding the crux. When they moved rightwards, they found two gullies. The one on the left, nearer the crest, was '*...wet, grassy, and altogether repulsive; the other, on the right of the first, cleaner, more conspicuous, and seductive by comparison.*'

Garrick and Biggart chose the latter, for its more gentlemanly qualities and because they thought they could see a possible traverse back left towards the crest of the ridge from the top of its first pitch. They were wrong, as the climbing turned out to be more difficult than the approach rocks climbed below. Worse, they also found that there was no traverse back left, with the only way being a continuation of the gully. Still thinking they were on Naismith's Route, they decided to continue. Passing a chockstone, they found the wall on the left unattractive in the prevailing conditions so they continued up the gully, ploughing up soft snow to emerge on to another horizontal ledge. Above, the gully steepened, and thinned down to a scoop.

The scoop lay in the angle between the ridge and a wall which, rising out of Crowberry Gully, cut right across the ridge. Biggart continued leading, and near the top of the scoop ran into a large block which looked ready to fall. He retreated some 20ft to Garrick, and they discussed the situation. Biggart had found a narrow chimney on the extreme right of the wall, and they decided he should try that. Garrick anchored himself to the ledge he was on by thrusting a leg over a sharp stone wedged in a cleft, while Biggart disappeared into the chimney. Loose rock inside it forced him out, and for a while he straddled a recess. He had to make a move on to a steep, sloping hold, well lubricated with slime. Suddenly he launched himself across, making an astonishing foot-change on the sloping hold and with swift, gliding movements crossed the top of the scoop and so on to safe ground beyond. The rest of the climb led easily to the crest and on to the summit.

Sadly for Garrick and Biggart, the climb had in fact received its first ascent in September 1920, by Fred Pigott and John Wilding who reported the ascent in the Rucksack Club Journal (4, 190). This ascent remained unknown to Scottish climbers for over 20 years.

Returning to 28th March 1910, Sunday night had seen a keen frost and when MacRobert and Brown reached Crowberry Ridge on Monday morning they found it, as expected, badly iced –

> ...the 100 feet of steep rock below Abraham's Ledge took us over an hour to negotiate. It took another hour to descend the little chimney on the right and cross over to Naismith's route. This was sheeted in ice, and so we tried the more broken-up gully to the right (Garrick's route). After a further strenuous four hours we had reached the final difficult pitch referred to by Garrick. Here the take-off was badly iced, and the second man had neither secure stance nor hitch. The place completely beat us, and we turned at 3 P.M. The descent of the ice-pitches and the glazed rocks took some time, and it was not till 6.30 P.M. that we got off the rocks on to the snow slope between the foot of the Crowberry and Curved Ridges.

As Robin Campbell points out in a note describing the history of this route,[36] the first complete winter ascent was that by Bill Murray and Bill Mackenzie in March 1937. Before that however, Murray, together with Archie MacAlpine and Kenneth Dunn, had been well and truly hammered attempting the same route in December 1936. While it took MacRobert and Brown 3hrs 30 minutes to retreat, Murray's party suffered a 12-hour epic. It only remains to confess that the author, with front-pointing gear, was defeated here in the 1970s by poor conditions, leading to a free abseil into Crowberry Gully. One may wonder why Raeburn, once recovered from his accident, did not attempt the route. There are occasions in mountaineering when a climber's name became 'connected' with a route, other climbers making a conscious decision to leave the ascent to that person. Douglas-Gibson Gully on Lochnagar may be one such example, perhaps this was another. The final remarks on this route, which is now in the current guide as *Shelf Route* (165m IV,6), will be left to Campbell –

> So the route's history is doubly ironic: it was once named for Garrick, who didn't make the first ascent, and became famous for a valiant defeat, but for the wrong valiant defeat! Since 'Shelf' is probably MacRobert's name for it, I suggest that we personify the thing again, and call it – in the tradition of the Douglas-Gibson Gully of Lochnagar – 'MacRobert's Shelf'.

❄ ❄ ❄

The next time Raeburn, recuperating following the accident on Stuc a' Chroin in February, is mentioned in Ling's Diaries was on 26th June 1910, when in company with John Bell, Mrs Bell, and Ling, they climbed Tower Ridge; Raeburn was unroped. They spent the night at the summit hotel then the next day descended North East Buttress. He had obviously recovered well enough that, as we will see below, he felt strong enough to climb in the Alps.

We have included here a description of a climb in the Eastern Alps by Ling and Raeburn, the ascent of the Spigolo Inglese, as one example of the competence of some Scottish mountaineers in the higher ranges of the world; there are other examples, such as Gibson's first traverse of the Meije, Collie's climbs above Chamonix and in the Canadian Rockies, and of course Raeburn in the Caucasus and elsewhere. Space, and the focus of this history must exclude these and others.

At the end of July 1910, Raeburn was in the Alps with Ling, meeting up eventually with Ruth Raeburn, and Natalia Yovitchitch, a Scots/Slav lady with whom he had been climbing occasionally since 1908. En route to Arolla via Berne and Chateux D'Oex, they stopped for an ascent of the spectacular Satarma Needle. Raeburn climbed this in his socks, and considered the route underrated and bordering on the dangerous. Other routes were climbed on this trip, including a first ascent of the North Face of the Disgrazia by Raeburn and Ling.

In the SMC Abroad notes for 1910, it states that this year would be known as one of the worst seasons ever experienced in the Alps. Even Ling and Raeburn were defeated twice on routes by storms. The SMCJ report from Ling and Raeburn is of necessity brief, but it has them making a bivouac at 7,000ft, having dismissed their porter.

> Leaving next morning at 1.10, the summit of the Disgrazia was gained *via* the north face – a new route – at 3.20 P.M., a severe ice climb. Rocks near summit mostly impossible and badly iced. The usual snowstorm on top, but other side easy. In Cecilia Capanna at 5.50 P.M.[37]

Another report of the same ascent provides more details. The route would not be repeated for five years, by two Italian Alpinists. It is one of the ironies of reportage that the route is still known as the 'English Route', or Spigolo Inglese.

> In the summer of 1910, the Scots W.N. Ling and H. Raeburn chose the easiest line up this shadowy wall, an elegant snow slide which leads directly to the WNW crest. They plan[ned] to reach in a couple of days the Maloja pass and hired the Guide Casimiro Albareda. They climbed from Val Sissone and Albareda thought they wanted to cross the Passo di Mello, but when Albareda understood the true objective, he exclaimed "*impossible!*" and headed back down. After a bivvy, at 1 am by the light of the lantern they walked under the Pizzo Ventina and looked for a way through the tangle of huge seracs and riddle of crevasses. Raeburn even measured the slope's gradient: 62° for a brief section and 52° on average! In just over 8 hours they reached the WNW crest and then the summit. The *via degli inglesi* or *lo spigolo (arête) degli inglesi* was the name the route would be known by.[38]

Once again, we have to be grateful that Ling kept a diary which has been saved. It is here that we have enough details of this first ascent to fully realise just how formidable this climbing pair were. The date was 8th August, and having bivvied on fir branches on a grass ledge, the pair got up just before midnight and ate breakfast, leaving the bivouac site at 1.10am. The first part of the climb was on a rocky and grassy ridge leading to the glacier. At 2.35am they were at 8,500ft and here they roped up. Huge seracs and hard snow made the going laborious, with much zig-zagging. After a five minute halt at 4.30am, they continued up hard snow slopes leading to the bergschrund below the rib of snow and ice which they intended to climb. Here, at 10,500ft, they halted for breakfast between 6.10 and 6.45am. They inserted a Mummery spike in each heel, which would have been a special nail screwed into the boot and designed for hard snow or ice work. By now the sun was up, and most welcome.

The 'schrund was safely crossed, with the angle of slope above measured as 62°. The snow, though very steep, was hard, as they kicked their way up for some distance until forced to cut steps by even harder snow. They made for a small island of very steep rocks. From the top of these a very narrow ridge of snow led out on to the general face. Here the angle was 52°. To their left was a large area of rock, but these proved to be impossibly icy and slabby with no hitches, forcing them to continue up the face.

> We had to be extremely careful, the angle was tremendous and the snow was getting very thin. A slip on the part of either would have been fatal.[39] We tried here and we tried there, but there was no easier route. Cutting in hard ice we came to a jutting out rock where we managed to clear out a hitch. Above this a very steep and dangerous slope led to the top rocks. Those above us were

> impossible and it was necessary to traverse the slope diagonally upwards to see whether the rocks were better at their other corner. I kept to the hitch as long as possible, but had to follow on to the face. Raeburn cut on and at last came to where there was just enough snow to hold him. I came to the foot of the rocks where a ledge took us to the foot of a small chimney. We tried this but further along was better and we climbed the rocks to the ridge, our first top 3 o'clock. 14 hours from the bivouac.[40]

The summit was gained at 3.35pm and after the descent the Capanna Cecilia hut at 5.50pm. The physical and nervous strain on such an ascent can only be imagined by most. No runners, no belays. A hitch was still a lucky flake of rock over which a rope could be placed. The Mummery spike would have helped prevent some slip on hard snow, but the climbers relied on cutting adequate steps and good balance throughout. (On this route we know that the 'Mummery spike' was an individual nail, while in earlier mentions the use of the name was ambiguous, as it could also have meant a pair of crampons.) The ice axe, as might be expected, was overlong and very fatiguing. It took them another two days to return to their base, where they celebrated their fine route with a bottle of Bouvier champagne.

As for Raeburn and Natalie Yovitchitch, here we must assume that a certain amount of romance was in the air. Born Natalia Rutherford Yovitchitch in 1882, she was the grand-daughter of one Robert Rutherford. He was buried in Dean Cemetery, Edinburgh, and Natalia's name is also on the grave monument, as having died in 1937 in London, aged 55. On 16th August 1909, she was tied on to Raeburn's rope along with Edith Gray, with Ling and Ruth Raeburn on the other rope –

> To prevent Messrs Ling and Raeburn from getting rusty, two members of the Ladies' Scottish Climbing Club, Misses R. Raeburn and E. Gray, with an experienced friend, Miss N. Yovitchitch, then took them up to the Fluhalp, and the next day up the Rimpfischhorn.[41]

The Rimpfischorn was given as 13,790ft. Raeburn would climb with Natalia in the 1910 season in the Alps, with their last recorded outing being on Arran in November 1910, when with Ruth Raeburn, Ling and John Bell they were on Cir Mhor on Arran. The face was impossible due to soft snow and ice, so they made for the Western Stoneshoot and avoiding a dangerous pitch in this made their way to the summit. Natalia was half Serbian, half Scottish, fourteen years younger, and a very competent mountaineer. Sadly, the relationship seems to have ended here, and with the coming conflagration that would be the Great War, does not seem to have been picked up again. Raeburn never married, nor did Natalia. Following on from this fact, as far as we know none of Raeburn's 10 siblings had children, if indeed they entered wedlock, so that the family line died out. In an age where large families were common, this seems unusual.

❄ ❄ ❄

Steeple and Barlow we introduced above; making a first ascent of *Median Route* on Skye in 1909. In September 1910 they were back, putting up two new routes on Sgurr a' Mhadaidh: *Third - Fourth Gully* (150m Moderate) and *South-East Gully* (240m Severe), and two on Sgurr a' Ghreadaidh; *Eagle's Gully* (150m Grade 3) and *Vanishing Gully* (120m Difficult).

On 12th September, along with Arnold Doughty and HE Bowron, they set up camp in Coire a' Ghreadaidh. This is a beautiful, west-facing corrie, but as per the guide contains a surprising lack of continuous rock and only a handful of recommended climbs. Of these four routes, only *South-East Gully* (240m Severe) is worth doing in summer. It lies on the Upper Cliffs of Sgùrr a' Mhadaidh, on the Coruisk Face.

On 16th September they set out for the Coruisk Face. By the time they reached the foot of the gully it was 4.30pm. They were worried by the limited amount of daylight left, but it was their last opportunity and they roped up. Two short pitches led easily to the difficult third pitch. An immense amount of effort was required to overcome a boulder in the middle and in the section above, and so much time had been used that with regret Bowron and Doughty decided to retire.

Several more pitches gave some interest before a possible escape route via a terrace appeared. They decided to continue and three more good pitches finally led to the finish. By now the moon had risen and with its help they gained the summit of Mhadaidh just before 8pm. The camp was regained at 10.30pm. It had been Steeple and Barlow's first major climb together, and one which they were pleased with.

They were obviously a party which enjoyed each other's company, with the usual, and unusual, amusing happenings which camps often provide. Some were recorded in the diaries which Steeple kept, or in later journal articles –

> September 14th. The process of dressing was enlivened by an altercation between Barlow and Doughty. The latter has kindly provided us with little home-made pillows, and Barlow, who has dreamt during the night that he was sleeping on a hedge-hog, has discovered what he avers are chicken-bones amongst the down.

> September 17th. During dressing operations a complaint reached me from the other tent that somebody's sleeping bag had, in some mysterious way, become impregnated with a very full flavour of mulligatawny. It was ultimately discovered that half a packet of Maggi soup had unaccountably strayed away from the box in which it was supposed to have been placed.[42]

References

1. A.D.S. [Alfred David Smith] *Forty-Second Meet of the Club, New Year, 1909. Killin*. In: Proceedings of the Club. SMCJ 10, 59, May 1909, 258-261.
2. Workman, R.E. *Forty-Second Meet of the Club, New Year, 1909. Killin*. In: Proceedings of the Club. SMCJ 10, 59, May 1909, 261-264.
3. Campbell, Robin N. *Two Old New Routes on Beinn an Dòthaidh*. In: Miscellaneous Notes, SMCJ 40, 200, 2009, 490-491.
4. *Ling's Diary*, Book 7, 80-81. Alpine Club Archives.
5. Ibid.
6. Campbell, Robin N. *Ibid.*
7. Clark, Mabel Inglis. *Reminiscences of Snow Climbs in the Highlands*. LSCCJ 1929, 29.
8. Levack, J.R. *Forty-Third Meet of the Club, Easter 1909, Fort William*. In: Proceedings of the Club. SMCJ 10, 60, Sept. 1909, 335-342.
9. Ibid.
10. J.S.M.J. [Stuart Jack] In Memorium - *Allan Arthur*. SMCJ 28, 155, May 1964, 51-52.
11. *Ling's Diary*, Book 8, 5-7. Alpine Club Archives.
12. Clark, Janie Inglis. *An Avalanche Experience on Ben Achallader*. In: Excursions and Notes. SMCJ 10, 60, Sept. 1909, 346-348.
13. Styles, Showell. *Gashed Crag etc*. In: Classic Rock (London: Bâton Wicks, 2nd ed. 2007, comp. Ken Wilson, p.44).
14. Steeple, E.W. *June Days in the Coolins*. Climbers' Club Journal, Vol.XII, 21.
15. Barlow, G. and Buckle, H.B. *New Climbs in Coire Labain*. Climbers' Club Journal, Vol.XII, 3.
16. Humble, B.H. *The Cuillin of Skye*. (London: Robert Hale Limited, 1952), 77.
17. Pilley, Dorothy (Mrs I.A. Richards). *Climbing Days*. (London: G. Bell and Sons, 1935), 101-102.
18. S.M.C. Guide Book – *The Braes of Angus*. SMCJ 8, 44, 125-132.
19. Strange, Greg. *The Cairngorms – 100 Years of Mountaineering*. (SMT, 2010), 22-23.
20. Garden, William. In Memorium. *James Alexander Parker, M.Inst.C.E. 1864-1946*. SMCJ 23, 138, April 1947, 432-434.
21. *Ling's Diary*, Book 8, 55-59. Alpine Club Archives.
22. Raeburn, Harold. *Letter to G.W. Young. 13th April 1910*. Alpine Club Archives.
23. Collins, G.L. Proceedings of the Club – *Easter 1910 – Kinlochewe*. SMCJ 11, 62, June 1910, 103-108.
24. *Wild Land Policy, Jan. 2002*. The National Trust for Scotland. <http://www.nts.org.uk/conserve/downloads/wild_land_policy_2002.pdf>
25. Walker, C.W. *Craig Roy, Ben Mhuinidh*. In: Excursions and Notes. SMCJ 11, 62, June 1910, 123.
26. Boyd, H.C. *Easter (1910) on Liathach*. SMCJ 11, 64, February 1911, 210-215.

27. Ibid.
28. Clark, W. Inglis. In Memorium. *George Sang*. SMCJ 19, 111, April 1931, 162-163.
29. A.H. [Alexander Harrison]. In Memorium. *W.A. Morrison*. SMCJ 27, 154, May 1963, 393-394.
30. *SMC Roll of Honour*. SMCJ 14, 82, February 1917, 197-198.
31. Sang, George. *An Teallach at Easter 1910*. SMCJ 11, 63, October 1910, 164-172.
32. Ibid. p.167.
33. Ling, W.N. *An Teallach and Beinn Dearg Mhor*. SMCJ 10, 55, Jan. 1908, 1-5.
34. Morrison, W.A. *Corrie nan Clach, Beinn Dearg Mhor*. SMCJ 11, 63, October 1910, 173-180.
35. Garrick, J.A. *The North Wall Variation of the Crowberry Ridge*. SMCJ 17, 97, April 1924, 1-10.
36. Campbell, Robin N. *Garrick's Staircase and MacRobert's Shelf*. SMCJ 38, 194, 2003, 443-444.
37. *S.M.C Abroad in 1910*. SMCJ 11, 64, February 1911, p.238.
38. UPclimbing.com *MONTE DISGRAZIA - The mountain of the British climbers. A Mountaineering History - April 23, 2012*
39. *Ling's Diary*, Book 8, 87, Alpine Club Archives.
40. *Ling's Diary*, Book 8, 87, Book 9, 1-2, Alpine Club Archives.
41. *S.M.C Abroad in 1909*. SMCJ 11, 61, Feb. 1910, 51.
42. Steeple, E.W. *A Week in Coire Ghreadaidh*. Rucksack Club Journal, Vol. II, 1. 1911.

15

The Darkness Drops (1911-14)

The New Year 1911 Meet of the SMC was held at one centre – Loch Awe. It made a pleasant change from recent multi-centre meets, and had a record number of participants, with 38 members and five guests. The weather was mixed, with rain and wind at first then fine weather by 2nd January. The LSCC were having their New Year Meet at Tyndrum, and sent a greetings telegram in Gaelic. As the SMC Meet Reporter James Reid Young wrote – *Rumour whispered that it was couched in bad language, but the lying jade was quickly routed, when it was found to be merely bad Gaelic.*[1]

Beinn a' Bhuiridh, lying south of Beinn Cruachan, was the target for the *Ultramontanes*, consisting of Raeburn, Ling, Goodeve and C Walker. They attempted a buttress on the right of the prominent gully, by which they must be referring to the hill's north face.

Icy rocks rebuffed them however, and they crossed the gully to continue up a chimney on its left. Hill walking was the main activity of the meet, while socially it was one of the most successful. Travel then, even by rail, was never a certain thing, as exemplified by a comment in the report, where a party descended the hill and gained Balquhidder Station in order to catch a train home –

> Here Workman withdrew to the waiting-room with his bag. As to the subsequent adventures which befell him there, on the unexpected arrival of a branch line train, it were perhaps better to remain discreetly silent.

Robert Ernest Workman (1879–1960), a Glasgow Civil Engineer, joined the SMC in 1899 and as a Lieutenant in the Royal Irish Rifles survived the First World War. He has a brief mention in the 1961 SMCJ as the Club's last link with the 19th century, but has no obituary there, presumably as he had outlasted his contemporaries.

❄ ❄ ❄

In the east of the country, Howard Drummond and James Bruce Miller, both members of the Cairngorm Club, had certainly found Clova to their liking, first visiting that glen in January 1910 and returning on 3rd January, 1911. On this occasion they climbed Pinnacle Ridge, a Grade II in Glen Doll. Much of the best rock climbing in Clova is on Red Craig, on the east side of the glen, described in the *North-East Outcrops Climbers' Guide* (SMC, 2003). Drummond was proposed for the SMC by James A Parker in 1911.

In 1910 Parker had spotted a pinnacle in Coire Brochain of Braeriach. Determined to climb it, he mounted an expedition in October 1911, joined by James Bruce Miller, Henry Alexander and Walter Alexander Reid, the last three having joined the SMC in 1908.[2]

The Black Pinnacle, as it was named, like the Cioch in Skye was only visible due to the shadow it cast. They soloed up a large slab below the pinnacle, leading to a scree slope. Here they found an empty meat tin, which momentarily dampened their exploratory joy, but then they reasoned that rock climbers do not usually carry large tins of meat, and it was probably thrown over the cliff top. The pinnacle was eventually gained and the plateau reached by a traverse then an easy gully. It was a modest 150m route, of Moderate grade. What was perhaps of more import was that it marked the start of an increase in exploratory climbing by local climbers in the east. Henry Alexander joined the SMC in 1908. A journalist, he was General Editor of Climbing Guides in 1931.

❄ ❄ ❄

On 2nd June 1911, Willie Ling, Mr & Mrs John Bell and Ruth Raeburn climbed Pinnacle Ridge on Sgurr nan Gillean. Ling then left for Glen Brittle, climbing Slanting Gully on Sgurr a' Mhadaidh with McLaren and Shadbolt. On 4th June, McLaren led Ling and Shadbolt up *Little Gully* (70m Difficult), thinking it was the normal route to the Cioch. It had first been climbed by Guy Barlow in 1908. As Ling's Diary notes, McLaren continued above the terrace, gaining the upper ledge by a direct variation of Collie's route.[3] As Robin Campbell comments,[4] Ling was plainly impressed by what he had seen of Shadbolt and McLaren and immediately recruited them to SMC membership with Bell as their seconder.

Winthrop Young was captivated by the Cuillin, and was to return regularly. One of his ambitions there was to make the first traverse of the Cuillin Ridge, and to this end he climbed all the peaks, making himself familiar with the difficult sections. The Traverse of the Cuillin Ridge had been responsible for a glint in many a climber's eye both then and now; Young, as described above, the writer John Buchan, and others, some of whom would have withheld their interest, so as not to encourage potential rivals. In the end Winthrop Young was beaten to this by Shadbolt and MacLaren, who made the first traverse on 10th June 1911, with a ridge time (i.e. Gars-bheinn to Sgurr nan Gillean, peak to peak) of 12hrs 18 minutes.

Staying at Sligachan, Shadbolt and MacLaren left just before 4am, gaining the summit of Gars-Bheinn at the southern end, at 6.10am. Sgurr Alasdair, although not on the main ridge, is traditionally included, and was gained at 9am. Sgurr Dearg cairn was reached at 11.15am, after climbing the Inaccessible Pinnacle, and here, with the mist completely cleared and the weather set fair, they realised that they had a really good chance of completing the traverse and in a reasonable time. At 6.25pm they stood on the summit of Sgurr nan Gillean. It had been, as Shadbolt would later write – '...*a great day.*[5] In 1971, George Roger, then President of the SMC, wrote a letter of congratulations to Shadbolt, then aged 88. Shadbolt replied –

> I was delighted to have your good wishes. Please thank the Club and my fellow members when the opportunity arises. We were very lucky to succeed on our first attempt as there were large sections of the ridge we had never seen. Fortunately it was a perfect day and quite clear. My stalwart and well-tried companion Alastair MacLaren was as always a tower of strength. He was ever at his best in his beloved Highlands – steeped in all the lore and having the Gaelic. It was a great day for us both.[6]

In the second week of September 1911, Sligachan was host to a power summit of climbers: Leslie Garnet Shadbolt (1883–1973), Alastair Campbell MacLaren (1880–1950), Humphrey Owen Jones (1878–1912), Miss Bronwen Ceridwen Jones (sister of HO), James Merriman Archer Thomson (1863–1912), and Ernest Septimus Reynolds. The first two we have met already. Humphrey Jones (no relation to the better known OG Jones) was a native of Aberystwyth, and had a successful career in the chemistry lab at Cambridge. He was a keen Alpinist, making first ascents, several with G Winthrop Young, including the Mer de Glâce Face of the Grépon. This alpinism would be his downfall; he married in 1912 and took his new bride on honeymoon to the Alps, introducing her to the mountains. On their first route together, on the Italian flank of Mont Blanc, their guideTraffer fell when a hold broke while leading, and all in the party of four were killed.

Thomson's name is on several of the routes on Skye, including the eponymous Very Difficult above the Cioch. Alongside another Very Difficult, *Wallwork's Route*, these two climbs, with their sense of exposure well above their grade, compress mind-stunning situations into their lengths. Thomson, as he was known, was a major figure in Welsh climbing from about 1895 onwards. On Lliwedd alone, his favourite home crag, he left 19 first ascents, including the first girdle traverse. A taciturn character, his lack of communication on the hills would probably have beaten the Sphinx –

> A professor from Bangor, also notoriously incommunicative, has a day out on the hills with Thomson. Neither speaks. As they're parting the professor cracks and gasps out, "I have a brother who is even more silent than myself." Thomson gives him a sharp look and says nothing.'[7]

Unfortunately, his life was plagued with bouts of depression, and in 1908 he suffered a complete nervous breakdown. Clark & Pyatt's brief comments on Thomson state –

> There is little doubt that he gained from his contacts with the mountains some pleasure that was his alone, and that may well have helped to compensate for some trouble that he kept even from his closest friends. He was only 49 when he died suddenly in 1912.[8]

As Pedlar reveals, Thomson was a homosexual, but unlike Winthrop Young, who could seemingly handle this in an age when it was not openly discussed, and achieved partial 'resolution' through marriage, he must have found this impossible to handle; while staying at his brother's house he drank a two-pint bottle of carbolic acid and was dead within two hours.

On a more cheerful note, Thomson's significance was that in the early years of the 20th century he developed the new balance technique in rock climbing, as opposed to the push-pull method, with the body kept close to the rocks, as epitomised by Raeburn and others. With rock climbers gradually moving out of the gullies and chimneys and on to the faces, this would give Thomson and his disciples an advantage, put to use on exploring the vast potential waiting in Skye. Bronwen Jones was also adept at balance climbing, and was described by G Winthrop Young as '*...the first to demonstrate how much more adept girls were at climbing on the first slab discoveries than at wrestling up throttled gullies.*'[9]

As for Ernest Septimus Reynolds (1861–1926), he was a medical man whose claim to fame, and internationally too for a while, was his discovery that there was arsenic in beer, at least in the local variety. This he divined from his patients in the Manchester area, some of whom had a symptom which could only have been caused by arsenic.[10] The arsenic was traced to invert sugars used in the brewing; made by the action of sulphuric acid on cane sugar, and to glucose, made by the action of sulphuric acid on various forms of starch. Sadly, some 115 deaths were linked to these. The original source of the arsenic was Spanish pyrites, from which the sulphuric acid was made. For Reynolds, it was a triumph for his expert diagnostic skills, which he much preferred over new-fangled techniques such as X-Rays.

Thomson and Jones had enjoyed a superb season in the Alps, and accordingly arrived fit and raring to go. In total they recorded in the Sligachan Climbers' Book 13 first ascents, eight of which could be regarded as major. Highlights included the North Face of Sgurr a' Mhadaidh, climbed on 12th September 1911. In the guide as *Archer Thomson's Route* (225m

Severe), and climbed by Thomson, HO Jones and Shadbolt, the original entry stated that '*...the climb proved to be unsurpassed in combined length, difficulty & variety by any in the district known to the party.*' The description was detailed, including one unusual pitch where above a smooth slippery slab was a basalt cube, also with a smooth, slippery surface. *'Three steps are taken up the slab & and the block is grasped at two of its corners, a knee is placed upon it & an erect position is assumed gradually. The operation requires the most care & circumspection.'*

On the same day, MacLaren, BC Jones and Reynolds climbed *Slanting Gully*, the Severe further left on Sgurr a' Mhadaidh first climbed by Ashley Abraham's team in 1907. Like them, MacLaren's rope avoided the difficult final pitch, but he returned on the 15th with Thomson, and with Jones and Shadbolt on the second rope, they made the first direct ascent, giving a 210m Severe on mainly sound rock. They climbed both the final pitch leading to the upper rake, and a continuation with two pitches above that. In between, on the 13th September two routes were made on Western Buttress of Sron na Ciche, *Zigzag* (300m Difficult), by Shadbolt, MacLaren and Reynolds) and *Chimney and Crack Climb*, (300m Very Severe), by Thomson and the two Jones). The latter is described in the guide as a hard variation to Median, which appears to take the left-hand of the fanned corners avoided by Median. The first ascent party had been attracted by the appearance of a thin crack rising above them, which turned out to be the crux. Thomson was the leader, in what was obviously a bold and serious lead by a climber at his best –

> With the right forearm and leg in the crack, I gained height by gripping the square edge with both hands, conscious the while of a gradual but constant increase of gradient. The vertical part had begun when a nick, perhaps 70 ft. up the edge, gave me an opportunity to step forth with one foot on the slabs, and thus perched leave a space vacant for Jones to arrive. The relevancy of this two-inch thick nick to the issue may be gathered from the threefold purpose it served. It was the second man's mainstay, the leader's belay, as well as his next and necessary foothold. Jones cleverly contrived to permit me the use of it for a moment; I worked upward for some 16 ft., and here found it possible with a foot out on the left wall and the back against the right to take a needed rest in a leaning position athwart the crack. The climb to this point had been exceedingly severe. The continuation was severer. A projecting boss bulged out over my shoulder. Recessed holds, required on over-arching rocks, being sought in vain the same strenuous method of gripping the right-angled edge had perforce to be continued. A period of concentrated effort ensued, then the pendent foot reached a pushing-point on the upper curve of the bulge, and finally, with an upward step, a foothold was gained on the steep slab above.[11]

The assault on the Cuillin cliffs continued the next day, 14th September, with the ascent by all six of *Archer Thomson's Route* (55m Very Difficult) on the Upper Cioch Buttress. The exposure on this route is sensational, and the author, luckily usually happy with drops below his feet, was nonetheless much impressed as a young climber on what was then graded Difficult (it is now Very Difficult. Should you wish more of the same, try *Wallwork's Route* (50m Very Difficult), an adjacent route.) The party of six were roped together for the ascent, which brings a shudder at the thought of a leader fall, but Thomson had a reputation for being an extremely careful climber and one who never had a fall, despite the breadth of his mountaineering experience.

The rock on this buttress is renowned for its quality; Thomson's party had gathered on the Cioch but had been scattered by a downpour of rain. Climbing Archer Thomson's Route had been the brainchild of Shadbolt, who – '*...had already detected what seemed to be the most promising line of attack.*'[12] They had a shock on topping out, when they came across a small cairn, suggesting an earlier party. Relief was palpable some days later, when Donald Mackenzie, a nephew of John Mackenzie the guide, informed them that it marked the limit of a descent made by a surveying party. Thomson remarked in his AJ article that it was safe to predict for the climb great popularity in the near future.

On their last day of the week, five of the six set out for the Bhasteir Tooth. At the base of the cliff Reynolds handed his new, four-strand climbing rope to Jones and promptly departed '*...in prudent haste*' for Sligachan. It was raining almost continuously, and they must have risen early, as both ropes climbed the North Chimney in the dark, and descended Naismith's Crack in the daylight, Thomson and Jones delayed '*...by exhausting wrestles with the cold rigidities of the four-stranded abomination.*'

It had been a rainy week in fact, with exceptional floods, but thanks to the general quality of the rock and the calibre of the climbing group, they had enjoyed a week on virgin rocks. As Thomson wrote in the AJ – '*...the island offers a rich and varied store to mountaineers of differing tastes and preferences. Of our party it is said that we "worked hard." It is possible we did; it is certain we enjoyed it.*'[13]

Shadbolt wrote a retrospective article for the Climbers' Club Journal, in which he commented on both the climbing and on Thomson –

> We climbed together in various combinations and the many first ascents which were made were very largely due to Archer Thomson, whose eye for new routes and whose persistence in following an undeviating line often led to the accomplishment of some hitherto neglected variations, as well as to some entirely new climbs. The Slanting Gully was ascended by four of the party on two ropes, but Thomson would have none of the traverse to the right below the final pitch and not only climbed it direct but insisted in walking across the Upper rake and finishing up the obvious continuation of the gully beyond...

> Looking back over the years I always remember this climb as the finest I ever did in Skye. I realise how much the technique of rock climbing has advanced since those days, and I often wonder how it is considered by modern climbers. – It was about my limit for difficulty, but not out of my class, although I could never had led it as I would have never been able to work out such an intricate route, or had the initiative to go on, not knowing what was coming next. Thomson's judgment was superb and his route-finding ability displayed at its best. The uncertainty of the outcome enhanced the value of every situation and the standard of difficulty remained constant throughout.[14]

Shadbolt here picks out an important feature in the making of a first ascent, particularly one in which no prior prospecting has been made, and the outcome is in the balance until the last hard move. First ascents, for many who are fortunate enough to have made them, normally make up a small percentage of a mountaineer's ascents in general, but they have an extra quality added by the manner of their genesis. The excitement of heading up into the unknown, of finding the best line, making original decisions and physically overcoming hitherto unknown difficulties, all lend an air which outstrips repeating a climb. Ironically, Thomson was initially biased against the production of guidebooks to specific areas –

> He believed, in a spirit new to his time, that the relationship between mountain and mountaineer was a purely personal one. For years he fought against the idea of producing detailed guides to specific areas, and it was only the continuing popularization of the sport which eventually induced him to believe, against his better judgment, that the publication of such information was the lesser of two evils.[15]

This philosophy was not unique to one person, though perhaps Thomson was the first to vocalise it. Collie was renowned for not recording routes he made, with perhaps more than a touch of the prankster in his actions. Decades later this philosophy would lead the SMC into a well-meaning but ultimately self-defeating corner, when for some years they imposed a moratorium, a unilateral halt to the publication of new climbs in the Northern Highlands. The hope here was that this would provide for future climbers a greater opportunity to experience wildness and the sense of exploration which was becoming increasingly more difficult to find elsewhere. There was perhaps also a pragmatic issue underpinning this hope, as guidebook authors struggled to keep abreast of developments in the far-flung north-west areas. In the end, it proved impossible to suppress all climbers from spreading information. It did lead to a period of confusion, and ultimately was a failed experiment.

The early pioneers, as stated here several times, were very aware of their lack of protection, and, despite some bold climbing, nonetheless took safety as a high priority. Inevitably there were some accidents, but these to date had no fatalities, at least in Scotland. There had been a few close calls with avalanches and the odd slip here and there, while minor events most likely went unreported. Now and then however, private correspondence or diaries gave a few details otherwise not seen in the journals. One such source was the diaries of Willie Ling, who often climbed with Raeburn both in the Scotland and in the Alps. In one of his diaries, as revealed in Chapter 14, he records a serious accident involving Raeburn. It was one in which the absence of a safe belay led to a potentially fatal accident through no fault of the leader.

❄ ❄ ❄

In May 1909, George Glover and Willie Ling had enjoyed three good days at Poolewe, and had seen rocky buttresses in the distance, at the far end of the Fionn Loch. At Easter 1910, they made an ascent of Beinn Airidh Charr, seeing again rocky buttresses. They were slightly disappointed as they had been looking in vain for towers such as might be found '*...on the celebrated Scottish mountain, the Distincthorn, non-Munro though it be.*' In his article describing their third visit to this glorious area in June 1911, Glover warned potential visitors that –'*...the places hereinafter mentioned are all in the heart of strictly preserved forest, and that permission is absolutely necessary to enter and should not be asked between 1st July and the end of the year.*'[16]

The area Glover refers to, between Loch Maree and Little Loch Broom, consisted largely of the Fisherfield and Letterewe Forests, here not meaning here covered in forest *per se*, but being mostly moor where red deer roamed and were hunted. This area in fact continued to be ruled by 'difficult' landowners until fairly recently, but the access conditions endured by Glover and contemporaries were particularly draconian, and partly explain the slow climbing development of some areas in Scotland, especially in the large sporting estates of the North West Highlands.

The summer of 1911 was a good one, though Glover and Ling, motoring into the area on 21st June, struck one of the few poor patches of weather. They drove up to Dundonnell, and 'finding it full', decided to continue on foot that night to Larachantivore, where they had permission to stay. They also noted the influx of cars, which somewhat spoiled the earlier sense of remoteness. They were soon walking up the track in Gleann Chaorachain through sheets of rain, to ford the Abhainn Srath na Sealga, about six hours before it was in spate and not fordable. Their hosts, Mr and Mrs Angus, were surprised to see them, but they were soon listening to the rain under their tin roof.

Thursday 22nd June saw thick mist, heavy rain, and raging burns painting the hillsides white. Undeterred, they set off up Gleann na Muice Beag, on an improving path. The weather also improved somewhat at the pass, but worsened again as they approached Lochan Fèith Mhic'-illean, a '*weary-looking*' place on such a misty day. They retreated where the path turns westwards, and where they would normally have enjoyed a grand view of the Dubh and Fionn Lochs, backed by Beinn Lair. Back at Larachantivore at 2.20pm, they found that Fionn Loch had received the worst of the storm, so after tea and a change of clothing Ling decided on Beinn Dearg Mor, towering above their hut. Ling and Glover had made one ascent already in this corrie, on 20th May 1907, climbing the central gully by ledges, scree, and snow. Their ascent in 1911 turned into a circuit, with some scrambling on the way on the north-east horn of Coire nan Clach, where it is almost a shock to find no lochan. They scanned the countryside to the west, seeing little appreciable rock potential, except perhaps on the south bank of Loch Toll a' Mhadaidh (in fact only one route has been recorded here, and the guide suggests it only worth the long approach should solitude be sought). Back down to their hut, gained at 8.15pm –

> ...after some pleasant scrambling down the chimneys and slabs directly facing the farm, whose inmates, unknown to us at the time, watched us and criticised our form on rocks, having like most Highlanders, up to now considered such a route as this descent on their familiar hill impossible.

Glover and Ling commented that with this hill, the scenery will always be better than the climbing. The rock is steep on the final summit towers, there was a great lack of hand holds at the top of each pitch, and there were many awkwardly sloping grass traverses and ledges. This was in summer of course, in winter Coire nan Clach was to provide worthwhile winter routes in the future. Morrison and Ling had climbed on the left side of this corrie in 1899, finding an entertaining scramble.

The next day dawned fine, and the pair set off up the Gleann na Muice Beag path again, finally gaining the col above the Dubh Loch, with its wonderful view across to Beinn Lair and the Torridon giants beyond. Beinn Lair, Glover wrote, will always be a disappointment, as his experience with Ling found the rock slabby, sloping the wrong way, and often unsound. But they had come to find their *'Torr na h' Iolaire'*, or Eagle's Tower, and they were not disappointed when the next turn of the path saw them confronted with a grand sweep of crag, some 800ft high. Glover wrote of the colouring of land and water here, and the general *stimmung* or atmosphere of the place, as they sat there having lunch in brilliant June sunshine.

> How different the place must be just now on a stormy evening in December—as I write— when the wind is shrieking around it; as old Angus told us when we returned that day, "Carnmore (the farm below this crag) is a terrible and lonely place in winter, with Beinn Lair opposite and the crags around one sheet of black ice for weeks."

On Torr na h' Iolaire, after a false start which led to an overhang, the pair began a route starting up a prominent rib about south-west of the summit, at a height of 1500ft. Their description includes several rock pitches, broken by some grass and heather. At one point they were looking straight down on the roof of Carnmore farm below, where, in an adjoining field, some workers occasionally glanced up at the two climbers. Their route was described as being about 500ft in length, but does not appear in the current guide. It was described in the 1932 SMC District Guide to the Northern Highlands, with Willie Ling the author.

Glover and Ling had thus made the first ascent of Torr na h' Iolaire, finding rock as good and firm as any they had come across in the Northern Highlands. Glover remarked that any climb here was in no sense to the summit of a hill, but rather to the edge of a big plateau, in which case there was '*...a lack of mountaineering éclat.*' On their last day, Saturday 24th, they headed up the Abhuinn Gleann na Muice, eventually gaining the col between Beinn Tarsuinn and A' Mhaighdean. There they investigated the cliff of Stac a' Chaorruinn, which they thought would provide a climb, but by now the mist was descending and they wished to examine the rocks of A' Mhaighdean.

Sadly, the higher they climbed the thicker became the mist. They found its summit easily enough, but never saw further than 50 yards continuously; now and again the sight of a perfect ridge to the south-west would appear, then disappear. They eventually gave up waiting and continued on, heading for Ruadh Stac Mor and the sharply-defined col between Fuar Loch Mor and the western arm of Gleann na Muice. At about 2100ft they emerged from the mist to find they were a little west of the col, but seeing a good path below they headed for that. It would have been hard to have found a more desolate scene than that of Fuar Loch Mor. They finally headed for the col above Loch Beinn Dearg and hence by the zigzags into Gleann na Muice Beag and their bothy, reached at 3.10pm.

They left after tea, and reached Dundonnell Glen, which looked lovely (no doubt due to the woods, as a marked contrast to the rocky wilderness they had left), and waited for the car which took them back to Garve Inn, just missing a night of rain. The next day the train took them south to their respective homes. In Glover's case, he found that the previous day had delivered 3.25 inches of rain in 24 hours, probably he wrote no unusual occurrence in wild North-West Ross-shire – '*...but in Northumberland sufficient to take Nature by surprise and decimate the birds in the best partridge ground of that county.*'

❄ ❄ ❄

On 28th September 1911 Raeburn and Arthur Russell were on Ben Nevis. They had been attempting the hardest of the numbered gullies, Number Two Gully in Coire na Ciste, without the aid of snow. To date they were aware of one prior ascent, and that under snow conditions. However, on this occasion, the rocks were in a very wet and poor condition, and on one pitch near the top a large amount of wet snow had avalanched onto the leader. Without axes, they decided to abandon ship. In summer, Number Two Gully was not climbed until 1942, at 'Scottish VS', is described as '*fierce*', and is best avoided. Back at the foot of the gully, level with the foot of The Comb, they were loath to lose the height gained, yet were even less inclined to risk avalanches on any steep rock.

Their solution gave rise to what is now called *Raeburn's Easy Route* (300m Easy), which takes a line of zig-zags on ledges below the steep wall which stretches rightwards from Glover's Chimney. It therefore finishes easily on the plateau, left of Number Two Gully and offers the easiest route out of Coire na Ciste other than Number Four Gully. It is perhaps worth mentioning that in icy conditions, the slabby wall right of the usual start can provide harder variation starts. It was first climbed in winter in April 1920 by an SMC party who did not record their names.[17]

Raeburn ended his description of this route with the following advice, almost certainly having in mind the epic which Goodeve's party had endured on the steep buttress above –

> It might be worth noting that any party climbing the Tower Ridge as far as the Tower, and finding the upper rocks of Nevis in too icy condition, might make a safe descent to Coire na Ciste by this route. Crossing the Tower Gap Chimney about half-way of its height, the upper ledge would be gained. Thence the upper snowfield above the "Garadh" is easily reached.—H. Raeburn.[18]

At the AGM of the SMC on 1st December 1911, the Treasurer reported the donation of £100 from the Gaiter Club towards the cost of the new guide book. For this purpose Scotland had been split into six areas and a sub-editor assigned to each. The sub-editors and their areas were: North (Willie Ling), North-west (HC Boyd), West (Harry MacRobert), East (George Duncan), South (John J Waugh) and Islands (Willie Naismith). Like many a publishing timetable, plans would drift, but there had been a steady series of sections published in the club journal, so that in many cases minor updates and some editing would see a finished section.

By 1912, there were signs that the golden age of Scottish Mountaineering had passed. It was nothing dramatic other than a slowing of first ascents, a number of club meets becoming larger but often with little of note done (usually due, it must be said, to poor weather), and a growing background, unvoiced in the club journals but affecting everyone, of social and political changes. By 1913 the middle class made up about 20% of Britain's population. One definition of this group included employing at least one servant. In 1911, one out of every seven employed persons was a domestic servant. The professional class still dominated mountaineering clubs, able to enjoy climbing holidays in the Alps and stay in hotels for club meets, to which they travelled ever increasingly by train or cars. The last luxury was of course out of reach for the working class. William Inglis Clark, early car owner, may well have paid today's equivalent of over £40K for his Arrol-Johnstone 'dog-cart', which would equate to his economic worth being today's equivalent of a salary of circa £250K. Not only could he afford a car, he could afford two fine homes.

The New Year Meet of the SMC for 1912 was held at Tarbet on Loch Lomond. Weather was poor, though a record number were present: some 32 members and 13 guests, including a member of the Canadian Alpine Club. The only ascent of a route listed was the McLaren-Shadbolt Gully on Creag Tharsuinn, now known as *McLaren's Chimney* (60m Very Difficult). It was described in the meet report as the wettest and most difficult climb of the Meet. It remains a route to avoid in summer. On 27th February 1912, a special dinner was held in Edinburgh, with 28 SMC members present, to celebrate the temporary return of the club's first Journal Editor, Joe Stott. Godfrey Solly, the SMC President, was in the chair, with no less than four ex-Presidents present. Stott had left for New Zealand some 20 years earlier, and as far as we know, this would be the only occasion he returned.

On 9th March, William MacAlister was lucky not to be killed by an avalanche on the Crianlarich Ben More.[19] A Glasgow solicitor, MacAlister joined the SMC in 1904 with an impressive record of walks and climbs and with the yet more impressive name of Norman Collie as his proposer. Starting out with three others, the party climbed Stobinian, then MacAlister and James Young climbed Ben More. Descending by the hanging corrie facing Crianlarich, they found 18 inches of new snow over frozen old snow. It was unsuitable for a glissade, either sitting or standing, so MacAlister began kicking his way down. A loud crack above and the whole field of snow parted transversely above him and swept him down. The axe was torn from his grasp as he was thrown off his feet and carried down, more often buried than not.

He finally shot out of the avalanche near its edge, below some cliffs over which he must have been carried. The snow had packed hard and he was buried up to his waist, unable to struggle free. A pocket knife made slow progress at digging himself out, and it was only quarter of an hour later that his shouts were answered by Young, who, after a further 15 minutes, appeared out of the mist, himself unhurt. Young had not liked the snow conditions, and had traversed out of the corrie. The avalanche was possibly of the slab type, and had carried him down about 850ft vertically. Apparently, this corrie had made earlier attempts on others, with Maylard in February 1902, and McLaren in 1910. Major MacAlister, sadly, was destined for another fate, and was killed on the Somme in 1916.

Increasing social unrest in Britain saw a National Coal Strike being mounted. As the strike period included Easter, which in 1912 began on

Friday, 5th April, those hoping to use the train for travel that weekend, including those attending the SMC Easter Meet, faced many cancellations. The setting was Glen Coe and as the Meet Report indicated, Ballachulish had the largest hotel and attracted the Sybarite section of the club, while the Clachaig and Kingshouse contained the Spartan. On the week of the Meet, trains for Ballachulish became available only on Wednesday or Saturday. Those worst affected were from Aberdeen, Dundee and England, while others made their chosen hotel by '*forced marches*'.[20] Two members, for example, walked from Corrour Station over Sgurr Eilde Mor to Kinlochleven, thence by steamer to Ballachulish.

In the event, it mattered little, as the weather was so bad, with a severe gale, that no climbs were done. Raeburn was absent, while Herbert Boyd, who had been on the first ascent of Church Door Buttress, emigrated to Canada, possibly influenced by the Scottish climate. Or perhaps by the fact that he had been earmarked to sub-edit the north-west section of the new guide.

There were crises in the Balkans in 1912 and 1913. The growing instability in that region would as yet have little impression on those enjoying the mountains of Scotland and the Alps; there would be a few more climbs to be found before the nightmare that would be the Great War encompassed Europe and changed the old order.

Glen Coe had been somewhat neglected since Raeburn's Central Buttress Original Route of 1909, at least as far as significant new climbs were concerned. On 16th July 1912, John Hirst (1884–1970) and Robert Ernest Workman enjoyed a fine day on Stob Coire nam Beith, the sprawling, pyramidal mountain which looks down on Loch Achtriochtan. The pair attempted a gully at first, but abandoned this on seeing the rock above them on the second pitch. A steep, awkward slab led to a '*...great overhanging cave topped with a titanic jammed block with no apparent way up...*'[21] The use of the word *titanic* by Workman was probably no accident, as that great but ill-fated liner had been sunk by a collision with an iceberg three months earlier, on April 15th.

The pair then turned their attention to a conspicuous chimney on the left, running parallel to the gully and starting about 80ft up the face. This gave them an enjoyable ascent, with Hirst leading the difficult sections. The chimney section Hirst found difficult and strenuous, due to its awkward right slant. He had to make a 70-ft runout, as the climbers did not wish to stop short of the anchorage they could see above. This must have been a stressful lead, as he very likely had no protection. *Crack Climb* (120m Difficult) , is a good Grade III in winter. As for the gully they looked at initially, it would be climbed in 1936 and named *Deep-Cut Chimney* (150m Very Difficult). It is best kept for a winter ascent at Grade III, first climbed in 1939 by Bill Mackenzie and Bill Murray.

❄ ❄ ❄

In late August 1912, two young English rock climbers, Herford and Laycock, arrived on Skye, having sailed there from Mallaig. Siegfried Wedgwood Herford (1891–1916) was born in Wales of a German mother. He made his name with the first ascent of Central Buttress on Scafell on 24th April 1914, climbing with Sansom, Holland and Gibson. Until then, this route had been regarded as being unclimbable. Inevitably, he became a member of Winthrop Young's entourage in Pen-y-Pass, where he also climbed with George Mallory.

John Laycock (1887–1960) was a gritstone expert, publishing a guide to gritstone in 1913.[22] It included several crags of other rock types, including limestone and sandstone, and was the first ever published rock climbing guidebook for the Peak District National Park, with some 116 pages. The Rucksack Club was opposed to its publication, as some of the crags were on private property; Laycock resigned in protest at this. The Yorkshire Ramblers in a review in 1913,[23] described it in mixed fashion, including the comment that –

> It must have required considerable nerve to adventure a volume which was assuredly liable to be dismissed by a percentage of mountaineers as a Baby Book on Toy Climbs. Nevertheless, it is to be regretted that Mr. Laycock should have commented on the hindrance and discouragement he received. A book should be its own vindication, and it may fairly be said that this volume fulfils this condition.

This attitude contrasts poorly with that of some of the leading Scottish climbers such as Naismith and others, who were well acquainted with enjoying a few hours' tussle on small local outcrops. The reviewer, initials CEB, was probably Claude E Benson.

Reaching Skye, the two climbers chose to pitch their tent, unusually, '*...about 3 or 4 miles south-west of Glen Brittle, in the middle of a bog.*'[24] It is possible that Laycock meant south or south-southeast on the Loch na h-Airde peninsula, but in any case he wrote in the Manchester University Magazine that '*...we spent the wettest, hardest and, I think, the happiest fortnight of my life. Each day we trudged miles, climbed something – anything.*'[25] They may have been happy days, but Laycock was brutally direct about what he thought of climbing on Skye. Their first route was Cioch Direct, which started out with rain and developed into a cloud-burst –

> I should consider this climb entitled to a similar place in a graduated list as the Intermediate Gully, Doe Crags. It is a good and pleasant climb, but we were fresh from the Crowberry Ridge, which is emphatically superfine, and we were a little disappointed.
>
> We were amused to note in this land of high mountains and long climbs that all the severe climbs are, if anything, shorter than Cumberland standards (I

except the Waterpipe Gully, of course), as well as less difficult and inferior in general interest. The plain fact is that the hills themselves, and not the individual climbs, constitute the real attraction of Skye.

They climbed Slanting Gully –

This, and particularly its lower half, is a pleasant climb, but to call it the finest gully climb in Great Britain is simply preposterous. In comparison with the Great Gully on Craig-yr-Ysfa it contains much less climbing ; it is not continuous ; the rock is decidedly inferior in parts, and the climbing is not of the same degree of difficulty at all.… To compare this gully to Walker's Gully would be an indignity to that noble cleft.[26]

It was of course Ashley Abraham who had described Slanting Gully as the finest gully climb in Britain, following the first ascent in 1907. Elsewhere on the island Herford and Laycock had spotted what appeared to be two chimneys while sailing past the southern end of Skye, in Coire nan Laogh. The two chimneys on approach turned out to be three gullies, imaginatively named A, B and C. A was a mere walk, C was a pleasant Difficult, while B, which Herford led, was Severe and was described by Laycock as a remarkable place providing a very worthy climb, almost unique in Laycock's experience.[27]

These climbs in Coire nan Laogh were described in the 1923 SMC guide by Steeple and Barlow as three gullies, West, Central, and East. In that guide and up until the current guide, the routes have been wrongly described. However, as a recent SMCJ article by Noel Williams explains, Laycock was correct in his original observation saying that there were two gullies.[28] These are now known to be *Central Gully* (150m Severe, the left-hand one, B above), and *East Gully* (150m Difficult, the right-hand one, C above). For any climber looking for a remote, solitude-filled corrie, descriptions plus a diagram will be found in the same Journal.[29]

Herford would be killed by a German rifle grenade at Ypres in January 1916. He was in his 23rd year and was recognised as being the leading climber of his generation, as much regarded as Mallory. Those wishing to dig deeper can be directed to the biography by Keith Treacher.[30] As for Laycock, he went to Singapore in 1920 where he entered politics. He died in 1960, aged 73.

In the summer of 1912, two Irishmen sailed to Skye on the ketch *Kelpie*. They were regular guests at Winthrop Young's Pen-y-Pass parties. Edward Conor Marshal O'Brien (1880–1952), a republican gunrunner and original member of Sinn Féin, was a proficient sailor, and owner of the ketch. In a later ketch *Saoirse* he circumnavigated the globe in 1923-25.He invariably climbed in bare feet, claiming that as a sailor he could force his toes further into the crevices than any boot would go. Educated at Trinity College, Dublin, and Oxford, he was a member of the Royal Society of

Antiquities. He served in the Royal Navy Reserve in World War I and was the god-father of Conor Cruise O'Brien, the author, politician, historian and academic. A genuine eccentric, the skull and crossbones flag would not have been amiss on his boat.

O'Brien's companion was Ernest Lawrence Julian. A native of Dublin, he was a barrister and Reid Professor of Law at Trinity College, Dublin. A Lieutenant in the Royal Dublin Fusiliers, he was wounded in the Dardanelles after leading his men during the assault on Chocolate Hill on 7th August 1915. He died of his injuries the next day on a hospital ship, aged 36, and was buried at sea.

A week after reaching Skye, the duo sailed down the coast and moored in Loch Scavaig, a spot which has everything except safety from a sou'westerly gale. From this renowned anchorage, in early August they made two first ascents, both in Coireachan Ruadh. On 8th August they climbed the Coire Ruadh face of Sgurr Dearg, on what they described as an exceedingly steep climb largely on basalt. This provided climbing on small holds, and was dangerously slippery in places. *O'Brien and Julian's Climb* (150m Severe) has some complex route finding.

Three days later, on 11th August, they found themselves at the foot of the Coire Ruadh face of Sgurr Mhic Choinnich, below a conspicuous gully. The lower part was easy, and led to an overhanging flake, climbed by a sensational traverse on its top edge. Just above, a pull up on to a small, steeply sloping shelf with minute fingerholds, usually wet and greasy, was necessary. Faced with such a serious move, 10ft above a good stance, they protected the leader by throwing a bight of the rope over a rock some 10ft higher. The pair considered that from a spectacular point of view, this was perhaps the finest gully in the Cuillin. *North-East Gully* (120m Very Severe) as it was named, comes with the warning that the gully has not been climbed by anyone who has provided information for guidebook authors, and is likely to be considerably harder.

Given the awkward approach to this corrie, and its shaded outlook, it is no surprise that these routes suffered a period of neglect. Indeed they were not repeated until a climber from Leeds, Christopher Mike Dixon (1931–2004) along with Dan Stewart, succeeded on both repeats on 7th September 1951. Mike Dixon, a member of the Climbers' Club, was still at school when he first visited Skye in 1949. He began climbing in 1948, but with intensive climbing, often solo, on gritstone crags near Leeds he soon gained a good level. With Neville Drasdo he climbed the Crack of Doom, then the hardest route in their pre-World War II guide. [31] His eye for a good line soon picked on the Coireachean Ruadh face of Sgurr MhicChoinnich, and he would eventually help pioneer routes in this area, some 10 in all, climbing with Brooker, Patey and others.

In his appropriately named article in a 1952 SMCJ,[32] Dixon described his early visits to this face, the first in 1950 with Bill Brooker (1931–2011), the Aberdeen climber he met by chance in Glenbrittle. Brooker was then a member of the Cairngorm Club, joining the SMC in 1957. The pair climbed *North East Buttress* (120m Very Difficult) on their first visit on 24th July, as time was short. This was originally graded Difficult by the pair, and lies on the minor buttress right of the main buttress of MhicChoinnich, separated from it by North-East Gully. Brooker had attempted a line on the main buttress in 1949, but had been defeated. The explorations of Dixon with Brooker and others will be covered in a later volume, but on 7th September 1951, while on a second visit to Skye, Dixon finally made an ascent of North-East Gully. With Brooker he had made a serious attempt to climb the gully on 14th August, but had been defeated by wet weather. Brooker then had to depart, and Dixon teamed up with Dan Stewart, a member of the JMCS.

With Stewart leading, they succeeded in climbing the gully. Both agreed that it was at least Hard Severe, and they doubted it had been climbed since its first ascent in 1912. That they had followed the original line Dixon was certain, as he had since seen O'Brien's account of the first ascent. O'Brien considered that North-East Gully was the hardest route in Skye at the time, and Dixon agreed. He finished his 1952 article with a general description of the ambience of this area –

> And the finish of each climb gave great delight, for we would pull up, steep rock and space below, and suddenly, surprisingly, burst out into the sun, with the view of Coire Lagan and Glenbrittle, the sea and the Western Isles poised like gems upon the haze. What cliff could give more completely the spirit of the Cuillin than this crag rising from the Coireachan Ruadha, the forgotten cliff of Sgùrr Mhic-Coinnich?

Steeple and Guy Barlow, along with Doughty, were back on Skye in late August/early September 1912. Some five new climbs were recorded, four of which have received their hard-earned stars in the current SMC guide. They began with an ascent of *West Gully* (105m Very Difficult), the first route to be found on the Coire a' Ghrunnda or south face of Sgurr Alasdair, the highest peak in the Cuillin. This is a magnificent face of steep rock, some 100m high. The narrow gully gives good climbing on steep, clean rock. All three were on the first ascent, and their description in the Climbers' Book at Sligachan concluded with the observation that – *'The climb is very attractive owing to its remarkable steepness.'*[33] This was further amplified in an article Steeple wrote for the CCJ –

> This little gully is remarkable for its extreme steepness – a stone tossed a foot or so outwards from the top pitch fell on the scree below, quite clear of the cairn at its foot – and also for a number of short pitches of nearly equal height, divided

> only by small stances, suggesting the quaint idea that a gully of respectable length has been telescoped by some convulsion of nature. It is also noteworthy as an instance of the comparatively rare occurrence of sound rock on a face having a south aspect.[34]

In winter it also provides a good climb at Grade V,6. Next, they found two routes on the Eastern Buttress of Sron na Ciche, *Direct Route* (180m Severe), and *Chimney Route* (180m Difficult). Eastern Buttress lies to the left of the Cioch, and is bounded on the left by the Sgumain Stone Shoot, and on the right by Eastern Gully, with Direct Route the obvious nose in the middle giving two distinct faces to the buttress. The guide introduces Direct Route as the classic low grade route, climbing from the toe of the buttress to the top. In the Sligachan book, Steeple wrote that – *'Although containing no section of exceptional severity, it would probably be difficult to find a route in the Coolin which would afford finer situations or grander rock scenery.'* All three were on this route, with Steeple commenting in the CCJ article that –

> The route is one of absorbing interest, as few of the pitches can be seen from those which precede them, and there is a constant feeling of glorious uncertainty as to the nature of the difficulties ahead. The superlative quality of the rock and the many fine situations lend a charm to the climb, which is only tempered by regret that the buttress is not as high as its more westerly neighbour.'[35]

Direct Route was still being praised decades after its first ascent, including by WH Murray, who wrote in 1951 describing an ascent with Kenneth Dunn, Angus Smith and George Marskell in June 1937 –

> Our delight was intense on finding ourselves launched upon the most charming route in Skye. None of us knows a better. The standard is difficult, but not by such standards should one judge the excellence of any rock-climb. The route goes on brown gabbro, in great clean-cut steps over steep and exposed rocks, round exhilarating corners, up an endless variety of slabs, cracks, chimneys, and edges…The crux of the route came just where it should – at the penultimate pitch. The last two pitches were crack climbs on a steep wall. The first of them was very hard – decidedly harder than the route's official classification, although not exposed enough to be called severe. I cannot remember enjoying a Cuillin climb more than this one.[36]

Chimney Route, on the Eastern Gully side of Eastern Buttress, gave a much easier route, climbing chimneys and corners. It was climbed by Steeple and Barlow. In contrast to Direct Route, Steeple noted that it follows a very definite line, which rarely allows variation. It has a striking situation he also noted, on the outer edge of the great left wall of Eastern Gully.

It should be pointed out that this burst of exploration did not enjoy ideal weather. During their stay at Glen Brittle, the wind blew with great vigour from all points of the compass, accompanied by rain from every quarter – *'Barlow, Doughty and I assaulted this magnificent buttress during one of the temporary lulls in the August Cyclone.'*[37] They had another major line in their wish list, but had left it until the last week of their planned holiday. The weather was bad, but they were so keen on climbing it that they decided to stay for a few extra days, in the hope that the gale would exhaust itself.

> High wind was our chief trouble. One gets accustomed to wet and greasy rocks; but when, in addition, the rocks are cold and the fingers lose all sensation, and a 100 mile-an-hour wind is sweeping across the cliff, with the thermometer somewhere below 40, exposed traverses are not altogether desirable.
>
> The tempestuous weather continued for five days and nights without cessation. On the sixth day, however, the wind dropped, and we made a dash for the traverse. It was accomplished in steady rain – I believe more than half an inch fell during the expedition – but the rocks were comparatively warm.[38]

The traverse referred to was no less than *The Girdle Traverse of Sron na Ciche* (900m Very Difficult), commencing on the Sgumain Stone Shoot at the first obvious break in Eastern Buttress, which is traversed round to the top of the chockstone of the second pitch of Eastern Gully. The Cioch Slab and Buttress are then traversed to the Amphitheatre of the central gully and a line continued to a point in the western gully at the same altitude as the starting point. The trio took 5hrs 30 minutes, plus a brief lunch break. This is the longest climb in the Cuillin, is on well-marked and sound rock, and as the current guide notes – *'Descent pitches can appear terrifying and are abseiled by some parties. It is a major challenge of route finding, rope trickery and bold confident climbing. "The leader and last man should be expert climbers."'* All this on a Very Difficult!

The Girdle was obviously a fairly early example of its type, and may well have been prompted by girdles which appeared on gritstone crags. Herford climbed a well-known one the previous year for example, on Castle Naze in Derbyshire, and doubtless there were other, less well known traverses made for fun or while training on local outcrops. Naismith and Thomson traversed the Cartland Crags near Lanark some time before 1892, while in search of suitable training afternoons. (See Chapter 5.) Many of the major cliffs and buttresses in the UK have a girdle traverse, though their popularity has probably declined. Steeple and Barlow's time of 5hrs 30 minutes indicates steady climbing, especially taking into account the necessary exploration required on the pitches. In their favour regarding time, there would be no messing about putting in runners!

In their notes on the routes in the SMCJ, Steeple mentions that the hardest problems encountered were on the traverse into the eastern gully from the buttress on the left.[39] In 1912, Steeple and Barlow found one more new climb, the modest *East Corner* (150m Difficult) on the South Buttress of Sgurr Dearg. This also the last time they recorded routes in the Sligachan Climbers' Book. Subsequently, they would stay at Mary Campbell's Cuillin Cottage in Glen Brittle, or camp high in the corries.

Steeple and Barlow returned in late July 1913, staying at Cuillin Cottage and with Arnold Doughty, their last visit before war broke out. They enjoyed a holiday with excellent weather for a change, though from the point of view of high quality climbs it was not as productive as 1912. For some reason they seemed to have concentrated on gullies, with five new ascents. August saw ascents of *An Dorus Gully* (Moderate), the notch on the ridge south of An Dorus, and the lowest point on the ridge between Mhadaidh and Ghreadaidh.

On 1st August, the trio climbed *Gully A* (130m Difficult) on the Stone Shoot Face of Sgurr Thearlaich, upper Coire Lagain. This face is more popular in winter (Grade III) due to its altitude. Perhaps their best route from 1913 was *Second-Third Gully* (150m Very Difficult) on Sgurr a' Mhadaidh. This has fine lower pitches but the gully morphs into scree at about half-height when most parties will then traverse over to finish up the upper part of *First-Second Gully* (150m Difficult) first climbed by Steeple and Barlow. In the first week of September, Steeple and Barlow attempted to make a complete ascent of Eastern Gully. They succeeded in climbing the upper second pitch. It was not until 1938 that a complete ascent of the gully was made. Their explorations and good recordings of routes climbed would later prompt the SMC to invite them to author the Island of Skye District Guide Book, first published in 1923.

❄ ❄ ❄

In the Cairngorms, Lochnagar saw the last new climb recorded before war broke out, when Mabel Inglis Clark, Mrs W Hunter and Henry Alexander climbed the chimney which cuts into the right-hand wall of the Black Spout's Left-Hand Branch. This was on 21st December 1913 and the only real difficulty found was at the finishing cornice. In the 1928 guide to the Cairngorms, written by Henry Alexander, he modestly records the route with the two ladies' names and a 'friend', the latter being none other than Alexander himself. The party presumably did not provide any name for their route, as it was not until 1926 that following a summer ascent it was named *Crumbling Cranny*. In winter it is a 60m Grade I, though the cornice can still present an impressive challenge. It was the first recorded female first ascent in the Cairngorms.

This volume began listing the first true mountaineering routes in Scotland as being on the Cuillin of Skye; it seems appropriate to finish with what would be the last climb to be recorded before the onset of the First

World War, also on the Island of Mist. On their second visit to Skye in June 1914 were two Liverpool climbers, James Bowen Burrell of the FRCC, and C Norman Cross, who stayed at Mary Campbell's Cuillin Cottage. On 15th June they made a seven-hour ascent on the Western Buttress of Sron na Ciche. Their route, *Trap Face Route* (260m Very Severe), is exposed and steep, but has suffered from somewhat confusing descriptions and several later variations. Aberdonians Bill Brooker and Mike Dixon climbed it in 1951, and left their own description, including a new finish. They considered it a fine route, with the continuous severity of the crux pitch adding much character to the route.[40]

The first ascenders also left a description, in the Sligachan Climbers' Book, including a sketch of the buttress indicating the line.[41] The description was duplicated in the SMCJ,[42] and highlights the crux pitch –

> From here an almost perpendicular chimney rises, up which there are few holds except small, smooth, wrongly-sloping foot-ledges. It was necessary to push hard with the hands against one wall of this shallow chimney in order to keep in at all, as one could not wedge and nowhere was it possible to stand upright on this stretch of 80 feet. This is the most awkward part of the climb and is exceedingly difficult.

The route name comes from the intrusions of basalt which the route partly follows, known as trap rock. Brooker and Dixon considered the route a really hard Severe in boots, probably just Very Severe, and certainly Very Severe in wet conditions. The two in fact climbed it in light rain.

❄ ❄ ❄

From 1890-1914 some 292 first ascents are on record in the current guidebooks covering Scotland (excluding outcrops). Of these routes, 124, or 42% were climbed in the five years 1894-98. These figures exclude Skye before 1890, which has 52 routes on record, many of which are peaks. Comparing the main climbing regions, the figures for 1890 to 1914 indicate that the number of first ascents were: Arran and Southern Highlands 25, Ben Nevis 48, Skye 106, Glen Coe 30, Cairngorms 23, Northern Highlands 18.

The initial surge in exploration on Skye is well indicated, eased early on by relative ease of access by boat. Next are Arran and the Southern Highlands, close to the centres of population in the Scottish Midland Valley, and with easy access. The train network explains the high number of routes on Ben Nevis, the line opening there in August 1894. Glen Coe access was usually by poor roads, the Cairngorms had few local climbers and long approaches on foot, while the Northern Highlands was a long way off for short trips and generally was the last of the major areas to be accessed by the rail network.

On 28th June 1914, the assassination of the Archduke Franz Ferdinand, heir to the Austro-Hungarian Empire, became the trigger which plunged the world into the Great War. Its effects would reverberate for decades, not only during its four-year martial period, but in the social upheavals it would promulgate, with the downfall of empires, and the rise of socialism. The first page of the SMCJ for October 1914 was devoted to the war, and has the following opening paragraph –

> The great war now being waged has cast a shadow over the whole nation: many of us have taken no holiday, and even those who took a curtailed one felt that all zest had departed from it. Very little shooting was done on the "Twelfth," and the hills have been quite open to climbers, but there were no climbers.[43]

Let us finish this book with a reminder that despite the learning curve of this new game, the often difficult and potentially dangerous conditions in which climbing took place, and the almost total lack of any form of real protection while on a climb, not one fatality was recorded in Scotland to any mountaineer during these early years. This is surely an outstanding feat, and one for which the pioneers should be rightly respected.

References

1. J.R.Y. [James Reid Young]. *Forty-sixth Meet of the Club, New Year 1911 – Loch Awe.* In: Proceedings of the Club. SMCJ 11, 64, Feb. 1911, 224-229.
2. Parker, James A. *The Black Pinnacle of Coire Brochain, Braeriach.* SMCJ 12, 68, June 1912, 84-89.
3. *Ling's Diary*, Book 9, p.40. Alpine Club Archives.
4. Campbell, Robin N. *100 Years Ago: The Club in 1911.* In: Miscellaneous Notes, SMCJ 41, 202, 2011, 532.
5. Shadbolt, L.G. *Early Days in Skye.* Climbers' Club Journal.1956, Vol XI, 2, 81, 190-196.
6. Shadbolt, L.G. *The First Traverse.* Letter to SMC. In: Miscellaneous Notes. SMCJ 30, 163, May 1972, 87.
7. Drasdo, Harold. *The Ordinary Route.* (Glasgow: Ernest Press, 1997.)
8. Clark, Ronald W. and Pyatt, Edward C. *Mountaineering in Britain.* (London: Phoenix House, 1957), p.103.
9. Geoffrey Winthrop Young, Geoffrey Sutton and Wilfrid Noyce. *Snowdon Biography* (London: J.M. Dent & Sons, 1957), p.52.
10. Reynolds, Ernest Septimus. *An Account of the Epidemic Outbreak of Arsenical Poisoning occurring in Beer Drinkers in the North of England and the Midland Counties in 1900.* Medico-Chirurgical Transactions. 1901; 84: 409-452.
11. Thomson, J.M. Archer. *A Week's Exploration on the Coolin.* (Alpine Journal, Vol. XXVI, 17, 1912, page 17 et seq.)
12. Thomson, J.M. Archer. *New Climbs in the Isle of Skye.* SMCJ 12, 68, May 1912, 31-40, 37.
13. Ibid.

14. Shadbolt, L.G. *Early Days in Skye*. Climbers' Club Journal, XI, 1956, 2, 81, 190-196.
15. Clark, Ronald W. and Pyatt, Edward C. *Mountaineering in Britain*. (London: 1957, Phoenix House), p.86.
16. Glover, Geo. T. *Fisherfield and Letterewe*. SMCJ 12, 67, Feb. 1912, 21-30.
17. F.S.G. [FS Goggs]. *Easter Meet at Fort William and Spean Bridge, 1920*. In: Proceedings of the Club, SMCJ 15, 90, October 1920, 327-333.
18. Raeburn, H. *Ben Nevis – Coire na Ciste – An Easy Way Out*. In: Excursions and Notes. SMCJ 12, 67, Feb. 1912, 54.
19. MacAlister, W.G. *Avalanche on Ben More*. In: Excursions and Notes. SMCJ 12, 68, June 1912, 124-126.
20. Rennie, J., Ling, W.N. & Buchanan, J.H. *Forty-Ninth Meet of the Club – Easter 1912 – Glencoe*. In: Proceedings of the Club. SMCJ 12, 68, June 1912, 112-119.
21. R. Ernest Workman. *Stob Coire nam Beith*. In: Excursions and Notes. SMCJ 12, 69, October 1912, 185-186.
22. Laycock, John. *Some Gritstone Climbs*. (Manchester: Refuge Printing Department, 1913.)
23. C.E.B. [Claude Benson] *Review of Some Gritstone Climbs*. In: Reviews, Yorkshire Ramblers Journal, Vol.4, 13, 196-201.
24. Laycock, J. *Impressions of Skye*. FRCC Journal, Vol.3, 2, 61-64.
25. J.L. *In Memoriam, S.W.H.* The Manchester University Magazine, Vol. 12, 6, 9th May, 1916, 82-83.
26. Laycock, J. *Impressions of Skye*. FRCC Journal, Vol.3, 2, p.62.
27. Ibid. 63-64.
28. Williams, Noel. *No one said it would be easy. Part 1 – Coire nan Laogh*. SMCJ 42, 203, 2012, 102-109.
29. *New Climbs. Coire nan Laogh*. SMCJ 42, 203, 2012, 160.
30. Treacher, Keith. *Siegfried Herford: An Edwardian Rock-Climber*. (Glasgow: Ernest Press, 2000.)
31. Drasdo, Neville. *Christopher Michael Dixon – Obituary*. CCJ, 2008-2010, 123, 132-133.
32. Dixon, C.M. *The Forgotten Corrie*. SMCJ 25, 143, 1952, 2-13.
33. Steeple. *Sligachan Climbers' Book*, 101A-102.
34. Steeple, E.W. *New Expeditions in the Coolin*. CCJ, 2, Feb., 1913.New Series, 26-31.
35. Ibid.
36. Murray, W.H. *Undiscovered Scotland*. (London: J.M. Dent & Sons, 1951, 117-118.)
37. Steeple, E.W. *New Expeditions in the Coolin*. CCJ, 2, Feb., 1913.New Series, 22-26.
38. Ibid. 26-31.
39. *Sgurr Alasdair and Sron na Ciche, Skye*. In: Excursions and Notes, SMCJ 12, 69, October 1912, 187-188.
40. *Entry in Log Book at Glen Brittle House*. Saturday, 11th August, 1951.
41. Sligachan Climbers' Book, 15th June, 1914, p.102A.
42. Burrell, Jas. B., Cross, C.N. *Sron na Ciche – Trap Face Climb*. In: Excursions and Notes, SMCJ 13, 75, October 1914, p.176.
43. *The War*. SMCJ 13, 75, October 1914, p.123.

Index

Note: to avoid confusion between routes with the same name, most have been indexed under their respective mountains, with the route name italicised. A few notable routes have their own index entry.